Wide-ranging in scope, rigorous in analysis, and exceptionally up to date with developments in social media and societal responses to it. This book not only offers us a systematic synthesis of research on criminal justice and social media but also helps to develop a conceptual vocabulary and theoretical framework with which trends can be better grasped and explained. A book that will be of genuine value to students, scholars, criminal justice practitioners, and policymakers alike.

Majid Yar, *Professor Emeritus of Criminology, Lancaster University, U.K.*

Reflecting controversies regarding *Google*, *Facebook*, X (aka *Twitter*), and *TikTok*, Xiaochen Hu and Nicholas P. Lovrich have written *Social Media and Criminal Justice*; a work that delivers the disciplines of criminology and criminal justice a much-needed service. As social media devices have become smaller and keyboardless, crime and justice have haphazardly evolved alongside the technology and communication capabilities. Contemporary society and the justice system today must deal with social media-driven cyber, copycat, and performance crime while simultaneously incorporating social media's positive potentials into their operations. In practice, however, the fields of criminology and criminal justice have been slow catching and keeping up with changes induced by social media. Hu and Lovrich address this gap. Their book answers the questions of how social media has evolved, what it means for crime and justice, and where it is likely going. In doing so, *Social Media and Criminal Justice* provides a well-grounded overview of the history, current state, and likely future of the intersection of social media, criminality, and criminal justice. This book is strongly recommended for readers wishing to gain a sense of the past, present, and future of the powerful shift in communication and society occurring from the rise of social media.

Ray Surette, *University of Central Florida, U.S.*

Social media and the criminal justice system are two major pillars of social life. Comprehensive scholarship addressing the extensive interplay between these two pillars is rather limited. Filling a void in the research, this important, ambitious, and necessary book offers a thorough understanding of the scope and impact of social media on multiple facets of the criminal justice system, including police, courts, and corrections. Not only do Hu and Lovrich provide valuable insights, but they also offer some justice-related matters to consider as social media evolves. This timely book will be of interest to criminal justice practitioners, scholars, students, and anyone with a general curiosity in contemporary issues in criminal justice.

Christopher J. Schneider, *Brandon University, Canada*

Hu and Lovrich's *Social Media and Criminal Justice* is an especially timely book as the world navigates issues and problems posed by social media and the acceptance of "alternative facts." This book will find an audience from criminal justice researchers, students and practitioners, and anyone seeking more insight into the intersection of social media and criminal justice.

Mitchel Roth, *Professor of Criminal Justice and Criminology, Sam Houston State University, U.S.*

Xiaochen Hu and Nicholas P. Lovrich's book *Social Media and Criminal Justice* provides a cogent and timely overview of the multiple intersections between criminal justice and social media. While written from a largely policy- and practical-based perspective, the book also offers multiple theoretical insights and is backed up by original research. As an introduction to this field, or a broad overview, or to engage more specific research questions, this book will provide a well-organized and valuable addition to the quickly evolving and changing relationship between social media and criminal justice practice. Criminal justice is now enmeshed in social media – for better and worse. *Social Media and Criminal Justice* helps us make sense of it.

Murray Lee, *Professor of Criminology, University of Sydney Law School, Australia*

SOCIAL MEDIA AND CRIMINAL JUSTICE

Discussing social media-related scholarship found in criminology, legal studies, policing, courts, corrections, victimization, and crime prevention, this book presents the current state of our knowledge on the impact of social media and the major sociological frameworks employed to study the U.S. justice system.

Building a theoretical framework for the study of social media and criminal justice in each chapter, the chapters provide a systematic reflection of extant research on social media in cybercrime, operations of courts, administration of institutional and community corrections, law enforcement, and crime prevention. The book fills the gap between the contemporary state of knowledge regarding social media and criminal justice with respect to both empirical evidence and types of sociological frameworks being employed to explore and identify the societal costs and benefits of our growing dependence upon social media. In addition to providing an up-to-date overview of our current state of knowledge, this book highlights important areas of future research, wherein the benefits of social media can be expanded and the negative aspects of its broadening use can be minimized.

Social Media and Criminal Justice will be of interest to students, scholars and practitioners in the areas of judicial administration, corrections management, law enforcement, and criminal justice-engaged community-based nonprofit organizations involved in court-referred treatment and/or active collaboration with local law enforcement agencies.

Xiaochen Hu is Associate Professor in the Department of Criminal Justice at Fayetteville State University (FSU) in Fayetteville, NC, U.S. He conducts both quantitative and qualitative studies related to police decision-making, police culture, police and the law, community-oriented policing, gangs, victimology, and criminal justice and mass media. He has co-authored *Electronic Community-Oriented Policing: Theories, Contemporary Efforts, and Future Directions* (2020). His scholarship has been published in multiple refereed journals.

Nicholas P. Lovrich is Regents Professor Emeritus and a Claudius O. and Mary W. Johnson Distinguished Professor of Political Science in the School of Politics, Philosophy and Public Affairs at Washington State University. Moreover, he is an Affiliate Researcher in the Department of Criminal Justice and Criminology at WSU. He remains highly active in scholarship. In 2023, he was the recipient of the Legacy of Excellence Award at WSU in recognition of "a professor emeritus who, in retirement, continues to make outstanding contributions to academia, the University, and the community."

Routledge Studies in Crime, Culture and Media

Routledge Studies in Crime, Culture and Media offers the very best in research that seeks to understand crime through the context of culture, cultural processes and media.

The series welcomes monographs and edited volumes from across the globe, and across a variety of disciplines. Books will offer fresh insights on a range of topics, including news reporting of crime; moral panics and trial by media; media and the police; crime in film; crime in fiction; crime in TV; crime and music; 'reality' crime shows; the impact of new media including mobile, Internet and digital technologies, and social networking sites; the ways media portrayals of crime influence government policy and lawmaking; the theoretical, conceptual and methodological underpinnings of cultural criminology.

Books in the series will be essential reading for those researching and studying criminology, media studies, cultural studies and sociology.

Social Media and Law Enforcement Practice in Poland
Insights into Practice Outside Anglophone Countries
Edited by Paweł Waszkiewicz

True Crime and Women
Writers, Readers, and Representations
Edited by Lili Pâquet and Rose Williamson

Social Media and Criminal Justice
Xiaochen Hu and Nicholas P. Lovrich

For more information about this series, please visit: www.routledge.com

SOCIAL MEDIA AND CRIMINAL JUSTICE

Xiaochen Hu and Nicholas P. Lovrich

Routledge
Taylor & Francis Group
LONDON AND NEW YORK

Designed cover image: gettyimages.com

First published 2025
by Routledge
4 Park Square, Milton Park, Abingdon, Oxon OX14 4RN

and by Routledge
605 Third Avenue, New York, NY 10158

Routledge is an imprint of the Taylor & Francis Group, an informa business

British Library Cataloguing-in-Publication Data
A catalogue record for this book is available from the British Library

Library of Congress Cataloging-in-Publication Data
Names: Hu, Xiaochen, author. | Lovrich, Nicholas P., 1944– author.
Title: Social media and criminal justice / Xiaochen Hu and Nicholas P. Lovrich.
Description: Abingdon, Oxon ; New York, NY : Routledge, [2025] | Series: Routledge studies in crime, culture and media | Includes bibliographical references and index.
Identifiers: LCCN 2024026443 (print) | LCCN 2024026444 (ebook) | ISBN 9781032418490 (hardback) | ISBN 9781032418506 (paperback) | ISBN 9781003360049 (ebook)
Subjects: LCSH: Criminal justice, Administration of—United States. | Social media—United States.
Classification: LCC HV9950 .H89 2025 (print) | LCC HV9950 (ebook) | DDC 364.973—dc23/eng/20240621
LC record available at https://lccn.loc.gov/2024026443
LC ebook record available at https://lccn.loc.gov/2024026444

ISBN: 978-1-032-41849-0 (hbk)
ISBN: 978-1-032-41850-6 (pbk)
ISBN: 978-1-003-36004-9 (ebk)

DOI: 10.4324/9781003360049

Typeset in Sabon
by Apex CoVantage, LLC

I dedicate this book to my mother Ping, my wife Danting, and my daughter Abigail. Most importantly, it is dedicated to my father Jun Hu (1956–2023), a police officer who devoted his life to the people he was sworn to protect and serve.
Xiaochen "Gibbs" Hu

I dedicate this book to the memory of Nichole R. Lovrich, JD. She was a public defender of the highest order, whose noble efforts to promote justice continue to serve to inspire young lawyers working in public interest law positions in the Pacific Northwest.
Nicholas P. Lovrich

CONTENTS

FIGURES

TABLES

FOREWORD

Social media – in some form – is everywhere. As a member of Generation X who grew up as a kid in the 1980s, I had the privilege of coming of age without it. Yes, we all thought we had it pretty good back then. We had great music, weird clothes, and very little in the way of parental supervision (everyone my age knows what it meant when the streetlights came on). Of course, it wasn't all good – we also had widened income inequality, the disappearance of the middle class, and the beginning of a half-century of massive national debt, but we were too young to know or care too much about any of that stuff at the time. So even in spite of all of that, we can now look back from our perch at middle age and take comfort in the fact that when we were young – unlike the youth of today for whom social media is ever present – our mistakes were not nearly as well documented (or public), the evidence of such mistakes could be easily destroyed (throwing the Polaroid picture away is a lot easier than scrubbing the Internet of one's misdeeds), and we could eat our breakfast without feeling compelled to share a picture of it with the rest of the world.

Yet those of us in the older generations now have a complex relationship with social media. On the one hand, we like it. We can find videos of baby goats, we have seen the revival of 1970s rock music among the younger generation (Fleetwood Mac in particular), there are guitar tutorials and videos on how to fix a motorcycle clutch, and all manner of cooking videos that I personally like to watch while I'm eating. But, on the other hand, it has become fashionable among anyone over the age of 40 to attribute the full spectrum of social and cultural horrors to social media. Indeed, considerable research on public opinion shows that older adults are convinced that social media has played a fundamental role in everything from the rise in school shootings and other forms of deadly mass violence, to health problems among young people (recall the hysteria over kids eating laundry detergent pods), to elevated rates of depression and social isolation among young people.

It is important to note that these kinds of moral panics aren't new. The last century alone is littered with them: communism (or socialism) was going to destroy America in the 1950s, Elvis Presley and the Beatles were the "Devil's music" that was going to corrupt an entire generation of kids (particularly girls), the "social" game of Dungeons and Dragons was going to turn kids in the 1980s into a bunch of Satanists, and video games that contain an element of violence were going to cause kids who play them to become violent themselves. None of that happened despite the pearl clutching of those in the older generations. At the same time, we need to be cognizant of the well-documented fact that every time we get a new form of technology, new opportunities for crime and victimization come along with it. For example, when television sets got smaller – and therefore easier for one person to carry (they used to a piece of furniture, sometimes weighing hundreds of pounds) – it prompted an increase in residential burglaries by people who wanted to steal them. When technology gave us laptop computers and cellular phones, they became the targets of thefts and interpersonal violent crimes like robbery. And the internet gave us all manner of new and innovative ways to defraud others and for offenders to harass and stalk their victims.

The same can be said for social media. To be sure, a large body of research shows that social media contributes in important ways to multiple forms of crime and victimization. Social media use has been found to be an important vehicle for bullying among young people – sometimes even to the point of suicide for the victims of such harassment. Studies also demonstrate how gang members use social media to coordinate illegal activities with one another. And social media has certainly been linked to social-developmental problems in young people, particularly when the bulk of time spent on social media is done so on smartphones, where clicking away with thumbs and staring at a small screen have taken the place of direct human contact, conversation, and socialization for many among our youths.

And that is why this book is so timely and important and should prompt those across a wide range of social science disciplines – from criminology to education to developmental psychology – to bring this area of study into the mainstream. While the effects of social media have been a core focus of the media and politics for a long time, they have largely been on the periphery of social science research for far too long. To be sure, if *YouTube* and *Facebook* were people, they would almost be old enough to legally drink; *Twitter* (or *X* as it is officially known but nobody cares) became the preferred method of communication for a U.S. President; *Instagram* has the capability to make people "internet famous"; and *TikTok* has become so popular that conservatives in Congress want to ban its use in the U.S.

So in an effort to call attention to this important area of social behavior, Hu and Lovrich's *Social Media and Criminal Justice* has done a masterful job of putting together a comprehensive book on the relationship between social media, crime, victimization, and the criminal justice system. What Hu and Lovrich have done spans a wide range of substantive areas: the relationship of social media to policing, courts, corrections, and even crime prevention. It is heavily rooted in empirical literature – particularly when it comes to not just the fact that people may be on social media but what they are actually doing when they're on it (an important distinction that much of the literature fails to make). And it also carries considerable theoretical weight, trading a "siloed" approach that would be easily confined to criminology for a much more nuanced and interdisciplinary approach that is not wedded to one set of perspectives. It instead cuts across multiple ways of thinking (including micro- and macro-level perspectives) in an integrated way that treats this area with the complexity it deserves.

In the end, what Hu and Lovrich show here is that social media isn't the sole cause of problems related to crime and criminal justice, but neither is it blameless. They have taken a carefully balanced and comprehensive approach – one that turns the volume down on ideology and fear and cranks it up with clarity and evidence. Students and scholars alike should take notice and heed their call to bring greater attention to how social media has found its way into the study of crime and its consequences.

Travis C. Pratt
University of Cincinnati, 2024

INTRODUCTION

At this writing, information technology, the Internet, and social media have come to generate a monumental amount of digital data worldwide. It is estimated that by 2010 the volume of digital data created, captured, copied, and consumed in the world was in the range of two zettabytes (Statista, 2023a). One zettabyte of data would require about one billion 1TB hard drives (typically installed in a personal computer) to store. By 2020, the number was 64 zettabytes. Moreover, this figure is projected to be 180 zettabytes by 2025 (Statista, 2023a). Clearly, there is no historical precedent for such an ongoing and ever-increasing flood of digital data, requiring societies' major governmental and civil society institutions to adapt as best they can.

Social media has become an important part of daily life for most people, especially the youth. Many people now choose to read the news, gain new general knowledge, secure post-secondary education, enjoy entertainment, seek gainful employment, and socialize via social media. Social media has become an important aspect of modern culture that influences its ever-growing number of users, *both* positively and negatively. Certainly, social media impacts criminology and the criminal justice system as much as it does other aspects of our private and public lives. While much of clear value has been written about social media and the criminal justice system in recent years, no major published work has been produced, as of yet, bringing together our current knowledge to formulate a broad picture of the phenomenon of social media permeation of the criminal justice societal space. This book gathers much of the extant scholarship and public commentary on social media and criminal justice from both the empirical research and philosophical perspectives. It summarizes and discusses social media-related work found within the multiple literatures of criminology, legal studies, policing, courts, corrections,

DOI: 10.4324/9781003360049-1

victimization, and crime prevention. The book characterizes the contemporary state of knowledge regarding social media and criminal justice with respect to both empirical evidence and the major types of sociological frameworks being employed to explore and identify the societal costs and benefits of our growing dependence upon social media.

The book serves as a systematic reflection upon research on social media in criminology and in criminal justice. Over the course of the past decade, social media has become a major topic of research in the social sciences generally and in computer science. In the criminal justice discipline, social media studies are becoming quite numerous, but as an area of serious study the extant literature remains highly fragmented. The existing research features work in the areas of criminology, crime victimization, the policing of cybercrime, the operations of courts, the administration of institutional and community corrections, law enforcement, and crime prevention. Books that summarize empirical research in these areas often focus on a single topic. For example, Salter's book *Crime, Justice and Social Media* published in 2016 focused on online abuse. Schneider's (2016a) *Policing and Social Media: Social Control in an Era of New Media* details how some Canadian police departments have made use of Facebook, Twitter, and YouTube to engage with the public online. Hu and Lovrich's (2020) book titled *Electronic Community-Oriented Policing: Theories, Contemporary Efforts, and Future Directions* focuses exclusively on police use of social media within community-oriented policing contexts Hoffmeister's (2014). *Social Media in the Courtrooms: A New Era for Criminal Justice* discusses how social media affects the judicial process and the major players in the criminal justice system. Other books may include one or several chapters discussing the use of social media in the criminal justice system and in criminology. For instance, Lee and McGovern's (2014) *Policing and Media: Public Relations, Simulations, and Communications* has several sections discussing police use of social media and policing social media. Surette's (2015a) *Media, Crime, and Criminal Justice: Images, Realities, and Policies* has one chapter that discusses new media, crime, and justice. There is, however, no scholarship that pulls together all these disparate contributions to our knowledge base to gain a comprehensive picture of criminal justice and social media. This current book attempts to fill this serious void in the literature.

In addition to providing an up-to-date overview of the state of current knowledge, this book identifies some areas of future fruitful research, wherein the benefits of social media can be expanded and the negative aspects of its broadening use be minimized. One fascinating feature of social media is that it is ever-evolving. At this writing, *Facebook*, *Twitter*, and *YouTube* remain the most widely used social media platforms, globally speaking. Perhaps, ten years from now *TikTok* will be the most widely used platform. This is the precise reason that we want to build a theoretical framework of social media and criminal justice in each chapter; experience teaches us that theoretical frameworks typically persist longer than physical forms. Also, we select social media platforms based on the number of research studies conducted on them. *Facebook* and *Twitter* have been studied for over a decade, and we want to assemble and critique the current knowledge base to get a comprehensive understanding of social media impacts on the criminal justice system.

We think this book will be of major interest to both educators and practitioners who are interested in knowing more about the findings of contemporary research on criminal justice and social media. Criminal justice scholars, particularly those who are interested in doing social media research and guiding their undergraduate and graduate students toward these topics, will find this book useful because it provides cutting-edge information on this topic. Furthermore, criminal justice system professionals and practitioners will be able to establish and adapt their policies with insights derived from the empirical evidence (employing evidence-based practices) and informed speculation provided by the proposed book. In addition, both undergraduate and graduate college students who are interested in this topic will find it a useful resource in their education. Instructors can also use this book as reading material in criminal justice courses, such as policing, media and crime, victimology, juvenile justice, corrections, and media and criminal justice. Moreover, making ample use of social media within the criminal justice process is now a genuinely global phenomenon, and much of the global criminal justice epistemic community conducts its research and presents its findings from whatever country in the English language. We trust this volume will lead other scholars elsewhere in the world to conduct systematic research and publish findings to be reported in the next edition of this book.

1

SOCIAL MEDIA, CRIMINOLOGY, THE CRIMINAL JUSTICE SYSTEM, AND HUMAN BEHAVIOR

Opening Story: When single parent Camila walked into Judge Frank Caprio's courtroom to address the matter of four overnight parking tickets issued at the same location, she did not anticipate that she would walk away from the courtroom with a $50 award from the judge. After a warm greeting, Judge Caprio began to process the tickets and asked Camila to explain. Camila told the judge that she could not get a permit sticker because her car first needed to be registered. The parking area where she lived was full, so she had to park along on the street nearby. Moreover, she asked the judge if she could pay the $200 fine later in October when she started a new job. Upon learning of her situation, Judge Caprio took her circumstances into consideration and fined her for only one of the four tickets, a fine of $20. Also, he said, "I'm gonna give you all the time you need to pay it" (Haynes, 2023). Then, the judge inquired about her family and financial situations. Camila replied that she lived with her ten-month-old daughter and was currently broke. "We have to take the baby into consideration," said the judge, who offered to help (Haynes, 2023). Judge Caprio used a donation from a Florida man to pay the parking fine and gave her an extra $50 to take care of her baby. "There are a lot of generous people in this country and we are on social media and we are on television," said the judge. He noted further that "they send in contributions voluntarily and asked me to give them to people who I think are worthy – and you certainly are" (Haynes, 2023). Finally, Judge Caprio added, "Take care of that little baby, and help somebody else out when you get the chance" (Haynes, 2023).

DOI: 10.4324/9781003360049-2

Social Media and Traditional Forms of Mass Media

The mass media play an important role in our society (Kingshott, 2011). The mass media allow individuals to learn about what has happened in the past, what is happening at the moment, and what will happen in the future without leaving their own homes (Hu & Lovrich, 2020). The traditional mass media like to cover topics related to crime and criminal justice systems given citizens' persistent interest in crime and public safety (e.g., Chadee & Ditton, 2005; Hu & Dittmann, 2019). However, the topics typically covered do not faithfully portray daily life. For example, mass media tend to cover crime-related topics such as homicides and serial killers, relatively rare events. Court-related TV dramas portray nearly every case as going on to trial, which likewise is not the case in actual practice. Researchers have studied the relationship between such a biased portrait of crimes and the criminal justice system characterized by the mass media and individual perspectives toward crime and the criminal justice system quite thoroughly, but the findings are far from consistent. Some studies find a significant relationship (e.g., Boda & Szabo, 2011; Callanan, 2012; Chiricos et al., 1997; Hasher et al., 1977; Kupchik & Bracy, 2009; Romer et al., 2003) while others do not (e.g., Dowler, 2003; Chadee & Ditton, 2005). These findings from extensive research suggest that the relationship between the mass media and public perceptions of crime and the criminal justice system is more complicated than we are inclined to believe (Hu & Lovrich, 2020).

The occurrence and prevalence of social media make the relationship even more complex. In the past, most individuals passively received information gathered, organized, and disseminated by the mass media through newspapers, magazines, TV programs, books, and movies. The content disseminated could be rather effectively controlled to a considerable extent. For example, if police misconduct is discovered locally, the local police department could often keep unfavorable information from spreading through delicate negotiations with local crime reporters and newspaper editors and publishers. Today, due to the presence of the Internet and social media, most individuals can actively and rapidly search for almost any information in which they are interested.

Additionally, some individuals can gain the expertise to be an information/knowledge producer. With social media, they can even be an influential producer of "news" worldwide. Think for a moment about all the police brutality videos which have surfaced on social media in recent years (e.g., Eric Garner, Levar Jones, Michael Brown, and George Floyd). People worldwide can watch these videos if they have Internet access (Hu & Lovrich, 2020). But, at the same time, social media help magnify the good side of the criminal justice system and its professionals. Think for a moment about Judge Caprio in our opening story and about an Arkansas police officer, Tommy Norman, who has received international recognition (more than 1.3 million followers on Instagram as of December 2023) for his acts of kindness to the people in his local community.

In 2022, about 4.6 billion individuals were using social media (Statista, 2023b). On average, they spent roughly two-and-a-half hours daily on social media (Statista, 2023c). While social media is a relatively new form of interpersonal communication compared to mail, telephone, and even texting, it is still fundamentally a communication tool. Thus, it carries much of power that a traditional form of communication carries. For example, both can be used to distribute information to a large audience with relatively little cost. Compared to traditional mass media, however, social media possesses several distinctive features. These features will help us understand why social media plays such an important role in today's criminal justice system. The following section discusses these features.

Distinctive and Noteworthy Aspects of Social Media

First, as noted earlier, one significant difference between traditional mass media and social media is that the public is the audience in mass media, while the public can be both creator/producer and audience in social media. For example, social media facilitates self-disclosure (Hoffmeister, 2014). Studies have shown that teenagers are more likely than adults to make routine use of social media, to adopt new social media platforms, and to share personal information on social media (Hu & Lovrich, 2020). Meanwhile, people may be more likely to share extreme feelings and opinions on social media, whether they are positive or negative (Conway, 2020). Justice agencies can certainly utilize social media to bypass traditional mass media and have a direct dialogue with the public. Doing so may help them gain legitimacy and earn public trust (Grimmelikhuijsen & Meijer, 2015). For example, several studies have shown that many police agencies make productive use of social media to build a positive relationship with the citizens they serve (e.g., Bain et al., 2014; Hu & Lovrich, 2020).

The "you-can-post-almost-anything-on-social-media" characteristic of social media leads to the second distinctive feature. When many social media users use it for personal use, they may post something related to their work; this results in a blurring of boundaries between their personal life and their professional life. In some situations, their occupation may still be impacted even if users do not post any work-relevant information on social media. One widely known example is the Plain View Project (PVP) (https://www.plainviewproject.org/), which examines "public Facebook posts and comments made by current and former police officers from several jurisdictions across the U.S." It was astonishing to learn of thousands of racist and derogatory postings made within just two years in only a few jurisdictions (Epstein,

2019). These findings raised the question of whether individual officers should be disciplined based on their social media posts. In a case reported in the mass media, a 23-year veteran police officer was fired because his social media posts were considered a hindrance to building trust between the police and the public. The officer, however, had never once been disciplined for misconduct and had never behaved in the way he had described in the social media posts (Palmer & Roebuck, 2023). Eventually, the officer's dismissal was overturned and reduced to a 30-day suspension (Palmer & Roebuck, 2023).

Third, social media not only discovers truth (e.g., racist police officers illustrated in PVP) but also often creates and spreads false information. Although traditional mass media also creates and spreads biased and false information, the volume of false information created by traditional mass media does not compare to that created for dissemination by social media. Moreover, the spreading of false information on social media can occur much more rapidly than is the case with traditional mass media (Hoffmeister, 2014). Once again, anyone can post almost anything on social media. Social media platforms struggle to fight false information. One report notes that, in 2019, the top 100 fake news posts on Facebook were viewed over 150 million times (Gilbert, 2019). The top two fake news posts were "Trump's father was a member of the KKK" and "Nancy Pelosi used Social Security money for the impeachment inquiry" (Gilbert, 2019). It should be noted that the data was gathered on Facebook alone and focused on only the top 100 fake news posts. Cox and colleagues (2013) describe a similar negative impact on the police as follows: "Tweets, blogs, and videos sent over the Internet depicting police action or inaction from differing political perspectives may lead to public dissatisfaction, protests, and violence" (p. 22).

Fourth, Hu and Lovrich (2020) point out that junk messages and fake news are virtually everywhere on the Internet and social media. It is difficult, and perhaps impossible, for most people to distinguish genuine information from fictional information. Thus, the burden of screening and filtering such information lies on the shoulders of social media platforms. However, social media companies may not be able (even if willing) to carry out systematic filtering. On the one hand, there are technical issues. For example, algorithms cannot always identify false information correctly. On the other hand, the revenue model of social media companies actually discourages aggressive filtering efforts. Social media companies' enormous revenue is derived from sending ads to their users (Muha, 2022). Accordingly, they want users to spend as much time as possible on their sites to maximize the likelihood of viewing these ads (Muha, 2022). From this perspective, fake news can bring more attention and views to social media platforms. Another important consideration is that social media companies need not worry much about fake news destroying their reputations. Traditional mass media companies must be concerned with the dissemination of fake news because they are, legally speaking, the sources of producing fake news and can be held liable. However, *users*, not the social media companies, are responsible for creating fake news on social media platforms. Thus, even if social media companies are criticized for fake news, they can divert the criticism and legal liability to their users (Mahdi et al., 2022; Tompros et al., 2017).

Fifth, notwithstanding the questionable validity of information, social media affords individuals the best way to conduct social interaction (Hoffmeister, 2014). With the development of modern technology, social media interaction is getting closer to face-to-face interaction. Some early social media platforms, such as *blogs* and *Craigslist*, involved narratives and pictures. Later, the world's most popular social media platforms, such as *Facebook*, *Twitter*, *YouTube*, *Instagram*, and *TikTok*, allowed narratives, pictures, and videos. The newest social media function focuses on live streaming. The most popular live-streaming platform may be *Twitch*. Meanwhile, live-streaming functions have been embedded in some traditional social media platforms (e.g., *Facebook*, *YouTube*, *Instagram*, and *TikTok*). Because of this "new" type of online social interaction, social media redefines "friend" in a rather fundamental way (Hoffmeister, 2014). Although social media users tend to friend other users they know in real life, many users will friend individuals with whom they never physically interact. Accordingly, many criminological concepts may need to be redefined as a consequence. For example, the label "stranger crime" is usually critical in victimology research (Hu et al., 2020). In the past, a stranger meant someone with whom a person was not acquainted. The question remains whether online interaction leads to "acquaintance" in the legal sense. Moreover, social media allows users who have the same interests to become connected to each other. In other words, it provides something akin to social gatherings in the online environment (Hu & Lovrich, 2020).

Last, the rapid evolution of social media brings both challenges and opportunities to criminology and the criminal justice system. Social media has evolved from just narratives and pictures (e.g., computer bulletin boards or BBS, see Webb, 1997) in the early days to integrating narratives, pictures, and videos today. In recent years, live-streaming social media, such as *Facebook Live*, *Instagram Live*, *YouTube Live*, and *Twitch*, have gained in popularity (Zimmer et al., 2018). Devices that carry social media platforms have become more affordable, smaller, and transportable nearly anywhere. Moreover, the COVID-19 pandemic has led us to appreciate the potential value of social media in addressing public health challenges (Hu & Lovrich, 2023). It taught us lessons about how our criminal justice system needed to adopt new communication technologies and how to continue performing criminal justice policing, corrections, and judicial duties under severe duress (Hu & Lovrich, 2023). Meanwhile, social media brings about "new" crimes (e.g., online abuse) and refashion old crimes such as drug selling (Salter, 2016). Moreover, it questions whether some online behaviors violate the law, such as self-posting nude pictures on social media platforms (e.g., *OnlyFans*), sexting, and live-stream sex chat rooms.

A Brief Introduction to Criminology and the Criminal Justice System

This section aims to provide readers with a brief introduction to what criminology and the criminal justice system look like today. While in some respects criminology and criminal justice are two distinct concepts, we adopt a broad and inclusive understanding of criminal justice in this book. We argue that the contemporary criminal justice discipline conducts research on both criminology and the operations of the criminal justice system. There are at least four reasons for taking the inclusive perspective we do. First, the two concepts (i.e., criminology and the criminal justice system) must be understood mutually. The criminal justice system needs criminology to understand why individuals commit crimes to better respond to crimes (e.g., prevention and effective forms of punishment/treatment). Criminology also needs the criminal justice system to define crimes and study specific criminological topics such as recidivism and crime prevention. Second, many introduction-to-criminal-justice textbooks have one or two chapters at the beginning to briefly discuss crime and criminology in historical perspective and in contemporary understanding (e.g., Siegel & Worrall, 2016). Third, no matter whether academic degrees or college academic units are labeled "criminology," "criminal justice," "criminology and criminal justice," or "justice studies" in U.S. universities, the curriculum of studies universally includes courses on criminology and criminal justice systems in core institutions such as police, courts, and corrections. Fourth, many leading academic journals, such as *Criminology*, *Justice Quarterly*, and the *Journal of Criminal Justice*, accept and publish manuscripts from both criminology and criminal justice scholars. These considerations led us to simplify our book title to *Social Media and Criminal Justice*.

Criminology

Criminology, in general, is a discipline that gathers and analyzes data on criminals, juvenile delinquents, and criminal behavior to understand why these individuals commit crimes (Walsh & Jorgensen, 2020). A few examples of questions that criminology tries to answer are the following: Why do crime rates change over time? Why are some people more likely to commit crimes than others? How can we prevent crimes? (Walsh & Jorgensen, 2020). The foundation of criminology is its canon of criminological theories tested and supported by confirmatory evidence drawn from various datasets assembled from empirical research and some qualitative research studies. There are various criminological theories. Some theories study crimes at an individual level, such as rational choice theory (Cornish & Clarke, 2014), deterrence theory (Paternoster, 1987), and developmental life-course perspectives (Loeber & Le Blanc, 1990). Some theories research crimes from a social perspective, such as social learning theory (Akers & Jennings, 2016), social disorganization theory (Shaw & McKay, 1942), social bond theory (Hirschi, 1969), and general strain theory (Agnew, 1992). Some theories focus on geographics and opportunities, such as routine activity theory (Cohen & Felson, 1979) and broken windows theory (Kelling & Wilson, 1982). In recent years, biosocial theories have become more prevalent, which argue that besides individual and social factors, human brain science, genes, and hormones should also be considered in the study of crime and deviance (Walsh & Jorgensen, 2020).

Criminology also deals with a fundamental moral question about crime: What is crime? Why are some harmful behaviors considered to be crimes and not others? Walsh and Jorgensen (2020) modify Tappan's (1947) definition of crime and define it as "an act in violation of a criminal law for which a punishment is prescribed" (p. 2). To determine whether a person is a criminal, the person must have an intent to violate the law (guilty mind) AND the person must have done so (guilty act) (Walsh & Jorgensen, 2020). To better understand this definition, we must first bring criminal justice agencies into the discussion. There are three branches. The legislative branch (i.e., the legislature) decides what behavior is prohibited (the law) and what punishments will be if someone violates the law (Siegel & Worrall, 2016). The judicial branch (i.e., judiciary) interprets the law and oversees if laws or policies enacted violate the federal or state constitutions (Siegel & Worrall, 2016). The executive branch is responsible for the operation of criminal justice agencies under the law (Siegel & Worrall, 2016). Thus, whether a behavior is considered to be a crime is decided by legislative and judicial authorities. There is a consensus that some acts must be viewed as crimes in most cultures, countries, and religions, such as murder and rape. However, the criminality of many acts can vary from time to time, such as homosexual behavior, abortion, and recreational use of marijuana.

The Criminal Justice System

The contemporary criminal justice system has three main components: (1) police, (2) courts, and (3) corrections (Siegel & Worrall, 2016). Among those three, the police have the most direct contact with citizens. The contemporary police have four major tasks: law enforcement, order maintenance, service delivery, and crime prevention (Hu & Lovrich, 2020). For law enforcement, the police are primarily responsible for investigating crimes and arresting suspects. The police are also responsible for maintaining order. For example, they keep vehicular traffic on highways and streets moving freely if a traffic accident happens (Siegel & Worrall, 2016). Additionally, the police provide services to the people they protect and serve, such as emergency rescue, medical first-aid, and mental health first-aid. The police also work closely with local community agencies such as schools and civic groups with crime prevention initiatives, like the Gang Resistance Education and Training (G.R.E.A.T.) Program (Wu et al., 2022). The police force is usually the largest workforce in the criminal justice system both in the U.S. and in many other countries. For example, in the U.S. there are approximately 18,000 police agencies (including about 12,300 local police agencies, about 3,000 sheriff's offices, about 1,700 special jurisdiction agencies, 73 federal agencies, and 50 state police agencies), hiring more than one million sworn officers and civilian employees (Walker & Katz, 2022). Each year, the cost of police service in the U.S. is about $110 billion; on average, this is about $340 per U.S. resident (Walker & Katz, 2022).

Courts are the places where trials occur. Ideally, defendants who are found guilty get convicted and sentenced, and defendants who are deemed innocent are released without any burden (Siegel & Worrall, 2016). While judges and other courtroom staff are formally hired by courts, there are numerous courtroom players such as prosecutors, defense attorneys, victims, witnesses, and jurors. Although the public believes that the court should be a place where truth is sought and justice is obtained (Siegel & Worrall, 2016), the reality can only guarantee a certain degree of fairness. For instance, although the adversary system in the U.S. has prosecutors and defense attorneys pictured as opponents, the "courtroom workgroup" phenomenon is often in clear view (Neubauer & Fradella, 2014). The courtroom workgroup – made up of a judge, a prosecutor, a defense attorney, and other court personnel – must collectively provide for a streamlined flow of court cases. This is done by expediting trial alternatives such as plea bargaining (Siegel & Worrall, 2016). In 2015, more than 97% of U.S. federal and 94% of state convictions were made via negotiated guilty pleas (Wilford et al., 2019). Other countries have also adopted plea bargaining processes in their criminal courts. China had a plea rate of 83% in 2013, and Russia had a plea rate of 64% in 2014 (Wilford et al., 2019). The high rate of plea bargaining primarily comes from a crushing courtroom caseload, despite the large size of the court workforce. In the U.S., there are nearly 17,000 courts and more than 8,000 prosecutorial agencies (Siegel & Worrall, 2016).

Corrections (or correctional agencies) take a variety of forms, such as prisons, jails, mandated treatment facilities, and detention centers. Corrections are primarily responsible for convicted offenders' punishments, mandated treatment, rehabilitation, and parole (Siegel & Worrall, 2016). Correctional facilities vary widely regarding their level of security. For example, community probation often features minimum supervision while maximum-security prisons may have a 23-hour lockdown (Siegel & Worrall, 2016). In the U.S., there are 1,566 state prisons, 98 federal prisons, 3,116 local jails, and 1,323 juvenile correctional facilities (Sawyer & Wagner, 2023). Other correctional agencies also include Native American reservation jails, military brigs, and psychiatric hospitals (Sawyer & Wagner, 2023). Altogether, these facilities house about two million individuals (Sawyer & Wagner, 2023). In addition, the U.S. also has over 3,500 probation and parole departments (Siegel & Worrall, 2016).

The previous section briefly introduces criminology and the criminal justice system. While we will discuss them in detail in each chapter, we trust this brief introduction provides readers with a broad picture of what public agencies we try to connect with social media in this book. The relatively short span of the occurrence of social media and its prevalence have brought enormous challenges to criminology and the criminal justice system. For example, can our traditional mainstream criminological theories still be efficacious in analyzing juvenile delinquency? Can the legislative branch keep up with the rapid development of new forms of social media? Will social media bring new ethical and occupational issues to justice agencies and related professionals? Of course, when we review empirical evidence and propose our analytical models in each chapter, we also need to rely on established theories to organize our findings and construct our models.

Theories, Social Media, and Criminal Justice

The current book covers empirical evidence on the use of social media at both individual and organizational levels. For example, at the individual level, we study how criminals, police officers, prosecutors, defense attorneys, and judges use social media through individual behavior theories, social behavior theories, and mass communication theories. At the organizational level, we study how police agencies, courts, and correctional facilities use social media (Figure 1.1). Here, *theory* is defined as "a logically interrelated set of propositions about empirical reality" (Bachman & Schutt, 2013, p. 31). Theory helps us (1) understand and explain observed phenomena; (2) make reasonable predictions; (3) organize research findings; (4) guide future research; and (5) propose useful public policies (Bachman & Schutt, 2013; also see Hu & Lovrich, 2020). The text on each theory we introduce will feature two sections: (1) a brief introduction to the theory and (2) how the theory may be used to interpret individuals' and organizations' social media behavior. It should be noted, of course, that dozens of individual and organizational theories can be drawn upon to interpret individual and organizational social media behavior. We do not have the space here to explain all of them and show how they inform our understanding of social media effects. We have selected those theories we believe are the most useful for our readers to

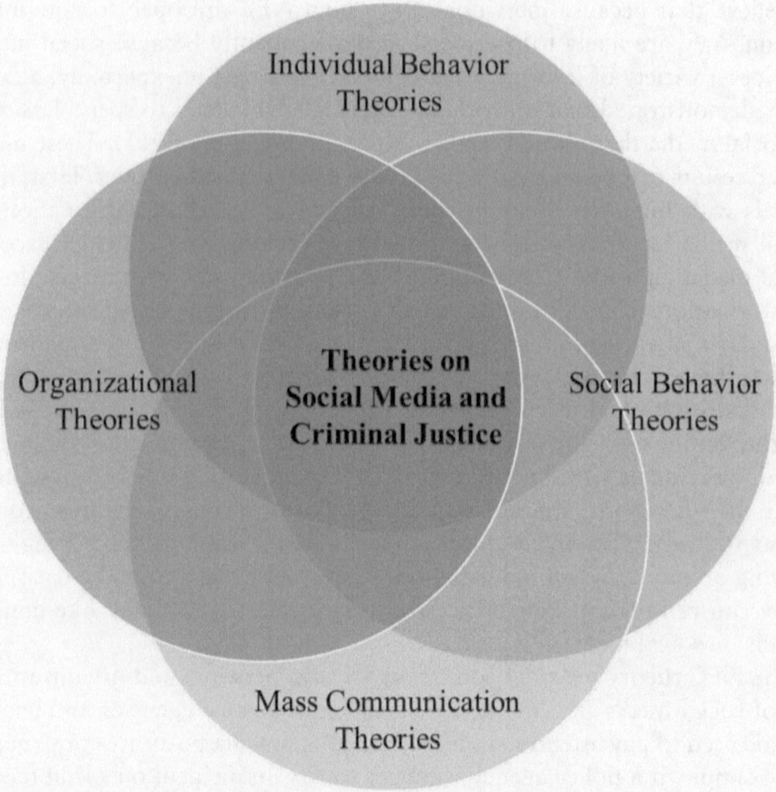

FIGURE 1.1 Theories on social media and criminal justice.

Source: Modified from Hu and Lovrich (2020, p. 30)

understand and appreciate their usefulness in seeing how social media effects are at play in the contemporary criminal justice system.

The Need for Cognition Theory

The need for cognition theory (NFC) argues that "the tendency for an individual to engage in and enjoy thinking" varies among individuals (Cacioppo & Petty, 1982). Individuals with high NFC tend to process new information on a daily basis (Petty & Cacioppo, 1986). They are likely to be open to new ideas, follow ongoing debates, and engage in problem-solving. Most importantly, they are likely to engage in new information seeking when making important decisions (Verplanken, 1993). In contrast, individuals with low NFC tend to be highly influenced by others' opinions and tend to avoid engagement with complicated issues (Zhong et al., 2011). It is reasonable to believe that because individuals with high NFC are open to new information, they are likely to use social media frequently because social media provides a variety of informational content. However, unexpectedly, a 2011 study demonstrated that individuals with high NFC tend to spend less time on social media than those with low NFC (Zhong et al., 2011). These unexpected results can be understood from three distinct perspectives. First, individuals with high NFC may be more efficient in searching information on social media, so they spend less time on it (Zhong et al., 2011). Second, social media algorithms typically do NOT provide users with diverse forms of information. The algorithms deciding what postings you will receive on a given day make use of a user's prior likes and shares; social media platforms wish to have their users stay on the platforms as long as possible. Many individuals with high NFC have taken due note of this fact, so they switch to other online tools for searching information (e.g., Google and Wikipedia). Third, individuals with low NFC tend to rely on trusted others' opinions to make their decisions (Zhong et al., 2011). Social media algorithms provide an environment wherein users will primarily see information supporting their existing opinions. When individuals with low NFC need to make decisions, many can rationalize their choices by taking cues from many like-minded friends on social media.

The NFC theory provides some insights into personal and organizational use of social media in criminal justice systems. Justice agencies and professionals need to pay attention to how their social media posts are constructed. For example, if a police agency wants to clarify an incident on social media, a simple "yes or no" answer is sufficient for individuals with low NFC (Hu & Lovrich, 2020). However, individuals with high NFC will not be satisfied with a simple answer. They often hunger for more contextual information (Hu & Lovrich, 2020).

The Big Five Theory

As one of the most widely researched psychological theories, the Big Five theory proposes the existence of five core personality traits: (1) extraversion (e.g., being active and talkative); (2) agreeableness (e.g., being appreciative and kind); (3) conscientious (e.g., being organized and reliable); (4) neuroticism (e.g., being anxious and tense); and (5) openness (e.g., being curious and insightful) (McCrae & John, 1992). Researchers have used the Big Five theory to study social media usage (Hu & Lovrich, 2020). For example, extraversion and openness are found to be positively related to social media usage, and neuroticism is negatively related to social media usage (Correa et al., 2010). Moreover, both extraversion and conscientiousness are positively related to the persistent use of social media (Rosen & Kluemper, 2008). One study has reported that individuals with high extraversion tend to perceive more value from social media use than people who are more introverted (Lu & Hsiao, 2010).

The Big Five theory indicates the types of individuals that criminal justice agencies and professionals may interact with on social media. These individuals tend to be active, productive, organized, curious, and insightful (Hu & Lovrich, 2020). To some extent, justice agencies and professionals should take advantage of the existence of this attentive audience. Because individuals who frequently use social media tend to be open to new information and ideas, they may be persuaded to understand that criminal justice agencies are not only established to punish criminals, which has been portrayed by traditional mass media for a long time (Surette, 2015a), but also deeply interested in providing timely services. For instance, social media allows law enforcement agencies to bypass traditional mass media and directly deliver their information and messages to the public (Hu et al., 2018). Agencies can show that they are not only crime-fighters but also compassionate problem solvers (Hu & Lovrich, 2020). The police can humanize themselves and their agencies by posting informal social media posts, such as greetings and funny stories connoting a caring agency culture (Hu & Lovrich, 2020).

The Technology Acceptance Model

The technology acceptance model (TAM) holds that different individuals have different levels of acceptance of new technologies (Hu & Lovrich, 2020). Such acceptance levels are principally determined by two factors: (1) perceived usefulness of the new technology and (2) perceived ease of use (Davis, 1989). Studies on blogs (one of the earliest social media formats) have shown that the assessment of the potential utility of blogs and the perception of the ease of use largely determine the level of actual use (Hsu & Lin, 2008; Steyn et al., 2010). Perceived ease of using social media is decided by not only whether a social media platform is easy to use but also an individual's current level of ability to use communication technology generally. For instance, a study on 436 college students reports that individuals who are more interested in communication technology innovations (e.g., smartphones) and spend more time on the Internet are more likely to make frequent use social media platforms (Zhong et al., 2011). The same consideration would seem to apply to organizations. Hu and Lovrich (2019) report that police agencies with a more developed social media technology use platform (e.g., having an active official website) are more likely to use various types of social media for maintaining social outreach efforts to their service community.

The TAM theory indicates that if justice agencies want more individuals to follow them on social media platforms, they need to make sure that their social media posts are viewed as useful to their attentive public. However, a concern is that usefulness is not universally defined by individuals (Hu &

Lovrich, 2020). For instance, a court may post a judge's opinion on a particular matter on Facebook. Legal professionals, such as prosecutors and attorneys, may think this opinion is useful while others not steeped in the law do not. Thus, the usefulness of a social media post is more subjective than objective. The TAM also indicates that it is not easy for justice agencies, especially small ones, to engage in the use of various social media platforms. There are dozens of social media platforms available. In Chapter 2, we will discuss the ten most widely used social media platforms (as of 2023). While the public may be able to use all of them, justice agencies cannot. Many agencies started using social media more than a decade ago, yet most are still just using "traditional" social media platforms such as Facebook and Twitter. As of yet, relatively few criminal justice agencies use innovative platforms such as TikTok, which was released worldwide in 2018.

The Theory of Reasoned Action

The theory of reasoned action (TRA) argues that individuals' behaviors and attitudes are strongly related (Ajzen & Fishbein, 1980). An individual's attitudes and subjective norms toward a specific behavior can predict whether he or she will engage in the behavior (Doswell et al., 2011). In other words, if individuals value the behavior and think the behavior will benefit them (i.e., attitudes toward a behavior) AND their important others (e.g., family members and best friends) think they should do it (i.e., subjective norms), they are more likely to engage in the behavior. For example, if a person believes the use of social media can help him or her stay connected with family and friends, and his or her family and friends are currently using social media, then the person is more likely to start using social media.

TRA provides two valuable insights. First, people are more likely to follow justice agencies' social media pages if they hold a positive attitude toward them. For example, if a person likes police officers generally, he or she is more likely to follow their local police department's social media (Hu & Lovrich, 2020). If following a local court's Twitter can benefit a journalist who often reports on local court decisions, then the journalist is more likely to do so. This brings us to the second insight: Justice agencies perhaps need to provide more useful information (based on the public perspective instead of the agencies' perspective) on social media if they want their social media strategy to work to maximum benefit.

The Expectancy Violations Theory

As a communication theory, the expectancy violations theory (EVT) holds that communication can be conceptualized as an exchange of behaviors among individuals (Burgoon, 1978). EVT focuses on what will happen if the exchange violates the expectations of individuals. Individuals will review the violations and react either positively or negatively upon reflection (Burgoon & Hale, 1988). The violation does not always lead to a negative reflection. To have a positive reflection, we must ensure that the direction of violation is what we desire. For example, in the Lieberman et al. (2013) study on police use of Facebook, a picture of an NYPD officer who purchased a pair of shoes for a homeless man received over 600,000 likes. From the EVT perspective, the public traditionally views the police as crime-fighters. The story of a police officer purchasing shoes for a homeless person violates public expectations. As a direct consequence, the picture dramatically drew public attention – causing engagement of both those persons who are inclined to like police and those who typically do not. Meanwhile, the picture shows a positive direction of this violation by showing how humanistic the police could be. That posting received a great number of positive reflections in the form of "likes" on Facebook.

The EVT can be used to reconstruct and restore public belief in criminal justice systems. Hu and Lovrich (2021) report that a relatively small police agency received a great deal of social media attention because its chief wrote departmental *Facebook* posts in an interestingly different way (also see Oliver, 2013). The Brimfield OH police department's Facebook posts that were written in a folksy vernacular featuring slang terms and relating humorous stories dramatically contradicted the solemn public image of the police (Hu & Lovrich, 2021). The theory can also help explain the popularity of Judge Caprio, as he is not seen as the traditional image of a sober, aloof, go-by-the-book judge.

Social Influence Theory

Social influence theory argues that an individual's behavior is influenced by others via how this individual perceives himself or herself in relation to others (Hu & Lovrich, 2020). There are different types of social influence. For example, Kelman (1958) proposes three types of social influence: (1) compliance (i.e., people are influenced by others because they wish to appear to agree with others; (2) identification (i.e., people are influenced by others who are highly regarded and respected; and (3) internalization (i.e., people are influenced by a group norm because they value it). Social influence theory has been applied widely to study online behavior. For example, college students' intention to use Facebook has been shown to be affected by both social identification and subject norms (Cheung & Lee, 2010).

Social influence theory is considered powerful in explaining individual social media behavior (Hu & Lovrich, 2020). For example, a person will start using a new social media platform if his or her family and friends use it. Social influence theory may also be useful to guide criminal justice agencies' social media posts. For instance, if an agency wants more followers on social media, simply putting "follow us on *Instagram*" seems to be an insufficient action. Instead, the agency can have a celebrity spokesperson. Justice agencies (especially police agencies) are now viewed as service providers, and the public is viewed as consumers (Walker & Katz, 2018). From a commercial advertising perspective, having a *celebrity spokesperson* to advertise an agency's mission and services is now quite common. The "celebrity" in question need not be a favorably regarded person. For example, local sports teams can serve as agency spokespersons. Many police agencies post their active support for local sports teams (e.g., MLB, NBA, NHL, NFL, NCAA), and those teams reciprocate (Hu & Lovrich, 2020). Agencies may even create their own virtual celebrity spokesperson. For example, the Tokyo Metropolitan Police Department (Japan) has used the fictional Pipo-kun (i.e., yuru-kyara) since 1987 to carry out its public relations mission and structure its youth outreach (Todd, 2017), just like McGruff, the crime-fighting dog, is used in many U.S. agencies.

Social Capital Theory

Social capital is defined as "the goodwill available to individuals or groups" and "its source lies in the structure and content of the actor's social relations" (Adler & Kwon, 2002, p. 23). Among the various dimensions of social capital, social trust may be the most critical to interpreting online information-sharing behavior (Hu & Lovrich, 2020; Ngai et al., 2015). A study on online gamers' knowledge-sharing behavior suggests that social trust and shared goals are two significant predictors of knowledge-sharing behavior (Hau & Kim, 2011). Another study on blogs suggests a similar pattern obtains. Trust in bloggers and trust in blog providers are positively related to bloggers' knowledge sharing (Chai & Kim, 2010).

The importance of social trust in social capital theory suggests that building mutual trust is essential to a good relationship between the public and justice agencies. The police now encourage the public to report crimes via social media (Henderson, 2017). Individuals can remain anonymous when reporting crimes on social media, which helps build trust between crime reporters and the police (Hu & Lovrich, 2020). Additionally, for example, some judges now allow social media to be present in their courtrooms, which is believed to enhance public access to justice (Bosland & Townend, 2018; Small & Puddister, 2020).

Social Loafing Theory

Social loafing theory argues that individuals tend to expend fewer individual efforts into performing tasks if they are in a group than when they are working alone (Latané et al., 1979). In an online environment, the social loafing phenomenon can be a significant problem. For example, social loafing is negatively related to individual contributions to online communities (Shiue et al., 2010). Considering social loafing theory and NFC theory together, individuals could spend less effort on exploring a topic by themselves and rely on the opinion of others to make decisions (Hu & Lovrich, 2020). Such a passive information-receiving habit may lead to extreme viewpoints; political polarization is a good example. The Pew Research Center reports that fewer and fewer Americans now hold a mix of conservative and liberal views. Instead, Americans have become predominately liberal or conservative where once the "moderate middle" predominated (Kiley, 2017). Scholars have argued that social media has made a significant contribution to this polarization phenomenon (e.g., Kozinets, 2017).

This polarization today applies to the police. Many citizens have come to hold extreme attitudes toward criminal justice systems and the professionals working in them. An example is views on police brutality. Individuals who are frequently exposed to looped information showing police shootings of innocent people on social media tend to believe that all the police will shoot innocent people, a belief which is clearly not true (Hu & Lovrich, 2020). Although part of the reason is that social media users are not always critical thinkers, it is clearly the case that social media algorithms promote polarization. For example, if you search "police shoot innocent people" on YouTube just to watch one or two clips, the algorithm on that platform will keep feeding you similar content long after you have lost interest in this topic.

Social Power Theory

In the context of social media, social power refers to "the capacity to influence as many audiences as possible" (Wei, 2009). The vast distributional features of social media make it an efficient tool for disseminating information far and wide (Hu & Lovrich, 2020). Movie stars, popular vocal artists, professional athletes, corporations, visual artists, scientists, and even U.S. Presidents make use of social media to influence as many targeted audiences as possible. The question arises, what helps to amass social power on social media? Knowledge is perhaps a crucial asset for social power, and control of knowledge is "central to development and maintenance of power" (Donohue et al., 1973, p. 652). Another element of social power may be information that can rouse emotional reactions, whether the emotion is positive or negative. For example, "#Icantbreathe" rouses individuals' anger against police brutality, and "#metoo" triggers individuals' awareness of sexual abuse and harassment.

On social media, social power is reflected by many indicators. One of the most obvious indicators is the number of followers/subscribers. There appears to be a long journey ahead for justice agencies to gain social power on social media. For instance, as one of the most popular police agencies on

Facebook, the New York City Police Department's *Facebook* page has about 950,000 followers as of December 26, 2023. As a revealing point of contrast, Taylor Swift's *Facebook* page had about 80,000,000 followers on the same day. One of the most popular courtroom *YouTube* channels, which features the widely admired Judge Frank Caprio, had about 2.6 million subscribers as of December 26, 2023.

Cultivation Theory

Cultivation theory holds that the level of media acquisition influences the audience's structure of beliefs (Gerbner et al., 1994). Individuals who spend more time watching television are more likely to believe that "reality" is the same as it is depicted on their TV screen (Gerbner et al., 1994). Television, as well as other types of broadcasts, typically does not present the reality of the criminal justice system (Shrum, 2009). A good example is seen in the research done on "the CSI effect." After watching many episodes of CSI and other crime-related dramas featuring forensic evidence, many jurors believe they know how a crime can be solved and tend to overemphasize the role of forensic analysis in the trial process (Robbers, 2008). In reality, most crimes are solved by a combination of confessions and the courtroom testimony and depositions taken from victims and witnesses. Moreover, most offenders are convicted after plea bargaining negotiations. Cultivation theory, of course, can be used to study social media influence on a broad scale (Morgan & Shanahan, 2010). For example, social media can be employed strategically to cultivate politicians' reputations and build their relationships with the public (Shami & Ashfaq, 2018).

Cultivation theory highlights the importance of criminal justice agencies using social media to communicate directly with the public. Agencies cannot solely rely on traditional mass media to cultivate public trust and respect for public safety officers and agencies (Hu & Lovrich, 2020). For example, mass media typically describe the police as "crime fighters" and courts as "revenge factories" (Revier, 2021). In fact, the police are doing far more than fighting crimes (Hu et al., 2018), and courts are used not only to convict offenders but also to find the best form of intervention for most of the people who come before them. The so-called problem-solving courts (now numbering in the 1,000s) engage in "therapeutic jurisprudence" for DWI offenses and domestic violence, veterans' courts seek out avenues for treatment as alternatives to incarceration, and family courts typically facilitate the connection of families in distress to social services and targeted treatment and/or educational services. Social media allows justice agencies involved in such therapeutic jurisprudence to have some degree of control over what the public record says about their contributions to public safety beyond the dispensation of sanctions and punishments (Hu & Lovrich, 2020).

Uses and Gratifications Theory

The uses and gratifications theory argues that individuals will choose specific media to meet their specific needs (West & Turner, 2013). The U&G theory is particularly useful when researchers try to answer the question: How do individuals select the social media platforms to which they attend? If individuals want to share short messages, they may choose *Twitter*. If individuals want to share videos, they may choose *YouTube*. If individuals want to share pictures, they may choose *Instagram*. If they want to make a comprehensive post, they may choose *Facebook*. In recent years, the various major social media platforms have been *homogenizing* – they now tend to assemble all social media functions (narratives, pictures, long videos, short videos, live streams) into a single product. Social media companies hope to attract more users by doing so. However, a recent study report suggests that because of an increasing number of ads and sponsored posts appearing on the established social media platforms, these platforms have become less "social" – a fact which pushes some users to move to smaller social networks where overt advertising and sponsored posts are not commonplace (Chen, 2023).

The original purpose behind social media is to help users connect with family and friends who are geographically apart. Users select social media platforms because they desire such a connection. After almost two decades of use of social media, individuals now use it for many purposes beyond interpersonal connection, such as acquiring news, making new online friends, sharing their ideas, shopping, earning money, and even committing crimes (Hu & Lovrich, 2020). From the uses and gratifications theory perspective, justice agencies need to determine what kinds of things the public wants most from their social media posts.

Information-Processing Theory

The proponents of information-processing theory suggest that everyone has his or her own information-handling strategies that can be used to locate useful information and screen out useless/unwanted information (Baran & Davis, 2015). There are many sub-theories within information-processing theory. A classic such sub-theory is schema theory, which argues that individuals often use prior experiences to build cognitive schemas. These schemas can be used to filter out unwanted information and analyze new information deemed worth processing (Baran & Davis, 2015). For example, Nobel Prize Laureate Paul Romer thought the notification calls being sent from Sweden were spam calls, and he let the calls go to his voicemail twice before realizing he was a *bona fide awardee* (Phorn, 2018). A report done on the incident notes that Romer was of the widely mistaken belief that only telemarketing calls arrive in the early morning – a belief arising from the fact that he had received a great many such spam calls in recent years (Phorn, 2018). Here, Professor Romer used numerous spam calls to build his schema of spam calls and used it to assess the calls coming from Sweden.

Information-processing theory may help explain many commonplace criminal behaviors and victimizations. For instance, identity thieves will use various approaches to lure victims to click the links and provide their personal information (Hu et al., 2023). Some approaches, which individuals have seen before, may get filtered immediately. Other approaches may get through. These approaches often belong to the "social engineering" genre, which entails the manipulation of people into disclosing sensitive and personal information (Salahdine & Kaabouch, 2019). Such social engineering scams have become one of the biggest challenges of the upcoming decade (Guitton, 2020). In 2016, the cost of social engineering attacks in the U.S. was estimated to be about $120 billion (Salahdine & Kaabouch, 2019).

Contingency Theory

The previous theories we introduced focus on individual and social perspectives. In other words, these theories can be used to explain social media behavior among individuals, such as common people, criminals, crime victims, police officers, judges, probation officers, and other criminal justice professionals. Starting with this section, we will introduce the four most widely used theories employed to explain *organizational behavior*. Contingency theory argues that organizations are created to achieve specific goals (Hu & Lovrich, 2019). Goals can be changed, so organizations must change to adapt to the changes occasioned by value shifts (Walker & Katz, 2022). For example, the emergence of community-oriented policing is partially due to the failure to control crimes by the police themselves using long-standing methods of law enforcement (Hu & Lovrich, 2020). The emergence of police body cameras is partially due to the greater emphasis being placed on police accountability and legitimacy (Nowacki & Willits, 2018). The emergence of domestic violence courts is partially due to the need to expedite the processing of domestic violence cases (Hemmens et al., 2017). Based on contingency theory, criminal justice agencies should become increasingly nibble in adopting social media to help achieve some new goals reflective of changing societal values. For example, the police can use social media to collect criminal intelligence more effectively. Likewise, the courts can be more flexible in admitting some forms of social media evidence to convict some offenders. Truly, all types of justice agencies can make more effective use of social media to get and stay more closely connected to the public they serve.

Resource Dependency Theory

Resource dependency theory argues that organizations must obtain resources (e.g., funding, capable workforce, even public support) to achieve their organizational goals (Hu & Lovrich, 2019). Take law enforcement agencies, for example. Studies on community-oriented policing indicate that there was a remarkable increase in the adoption of community-oriented policing in the period 1993 to 1996 because of the ample availability of state and federal funding (e.g., Oliver, 2008; Zhao et al., 1999). Another study on police gang units documented that police agencies which received external funding for anti-gang purposes were nearly five times more likely to create a gang unit than those which do not receive such funding (Katz et al., 2002). Research on police body cameras indicates that police agencies with larger operating budgets are more likely to adopt body cameras (Nowacki & Willits, 2018). To some extent, the broader adoption and routinization of social media use among justice agencies may not require extra funding because (1) many justice agencies already have public information officers (PIOs) who can manage social media accounts and (2) mainstream social media platforms are now mature products so PIOs can just go and use them directly without the extra cost of specialized training (Hu & Lovrich, 2020). However, it should be noted that while using social media seems relatively effortless, it will nevertheless be somewhat costly and time-consuming if agencies want their social media pages to be of high quality to attract the attention of public.

Institutional Theory

Institutional theory argues that organizations are social institutions, so their operations must be understood within a social context (Walker & Katz, 2018). Criminal justice agencies are shaped to a substantial degree by the ideas held by powerful environmental actors who are impacted by the police and the policies and practices they establish (Hu & Lovrich, 2020). For example, the use of community-oriented policing typically meets the needs of the people in the communities adopting this type of policing (Crank, 1994). While the fundamental purposes of the criminal justice system have not changed greatly (i.e., retribution, incapacitation, rehabilitation, deterrence, and restoration), both the public and justice agencies place more emphasize on procedures than outcomes – viewing transparency, legitimacy, and accountability are essential elements of good policing. These goals can be advanced by establishing an open, civil, and direct dialogue between the public and the justice agencies serving them. Social media, of course, provides a great opportunity to promote such a dialogue. Therefore, justice agencies may use social media as a powerful tool in their bridge-building endeavors to connect to their community-based stakeholders. In many cases, these public stakeholders demand this new channel of interaction (Hu & Lovrich, 2020).

Diffusion of Innovations Theory

Justice agencies are not like ordinary people who can freely try out different social media platforms as they develop over time. Any new technology

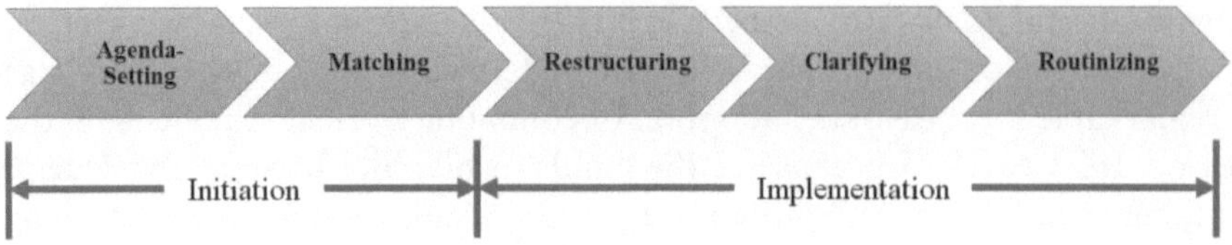

FIGURE 1.2 Five stages of diffusion of innovations theory.

Source: Proposed by Rogers (2003, pp. 420–430); also see Hu and Lovrich (2020, pp. 44–45)

will have to go through a series of evaluative processes before it is finally accepted/routinized by justice agencies. Rogers (2003) proposes the theory of diffusion of innovations, one which can be used to explain why technological innovations generally require quite a bit of time before they achieve widespread adoption. Rogers (2003) describes a five-stage process that an organization typically goes through regarding the adoption of a technological innovation (Figure 1.2).

The first two stages (i.e., agenda-setting and matching) relate to innovation initiation (Rogers, 2003). The following three stages (i.e., restructuring, clarifying, and routinizing) relate to implementation (Rogers, 2003). During agenda-setting, an issue arises causing the organization to believe that a noteworthy innovation is required to manage the issue at hand (Rogers, 2003). Then, during the matching process, the organization selects an innovation developed in another organization and uses it to try to manage the issue being addressed (Rogers, 2003). Typically, the innovation often does not solve the issue entirely. Accordingly, the organization will often modify the innovation somewhat during the restructuring stage (Rogers, 2003). Sometimes, the organization may even change its structure in a major way (e.g., gang unit in the police). The relationship between the innovation and the organization is becoming more apparent during the clarifying stage (Rogers, 2003). At last, the organization routinizes the innovation and makes it part of the organization's standard operating procedures (Rogers, 2003). Rogers's (2003) diffusion of innovations theory can be used to interpret many criminal justice agencies' adoptions of innovations. For example, it has been used to study technology innovations in police organizations (e.g., Burruss & Giblin, 2014; Gayadeen & Phillips, 2014; Hu & Lovrich, 2019; Skogan & Hartnett, 2005). It certainly can be used to understand justice agencies' adoption of social media, together with the previous three organizational theories.

Conclusion

In this chapter, we began with a broad discussion of the difference between social media and traditional mass media, focusing on the most distinctive features of social media. Then, we briefly introduced the core elements of contemporary criminology and the U.S. criminal justice system to illustrate what principal topics we will cover in the book. We selected several individual behavioral theories, social behavior theories, mass communication theories, and organizational theories, all of which we believe to be theoretically and practically essential to understanding social media, criminology, and the criminal justice system as they function in contemporary society. We use these concepts and theoretical frameworks to guide our thinking on the positive and negative consequences of the ever-expanding permeation of societal life by social media. We show how criminology and the criminal justice system are affected in both positive and negative ways by the ever-broader impact of social media on our daily lives.

2

SOCIAL MEDIA AND CONTEMPORARY MAINSTREAM SOCIAL MEDIA PLATFORMS

Opening Story: On October 5, 2017, the *New York Times* reported a series of sexual abuse allegations against Harvey Weinstein, a well-known Hollywood producer (Kantor & Twohey, 2017). Ten days later, on October 15, 2017, actress Alyssa Milano posted the following on Twitter, "If you've been sexually harassed or assaulted write 'me too' as a reply to this tweet." Within the tweet, there was a picture stating "If all women who have been sexually harassed or assaulted wrote 'Me too' as a status, we might give people a sense of the magnitude of the problem." Shortly thereafter, the *MeToo Movement* and the hashtag "#metoo" went viral on a global scale on social media. Within a month, more than 2.3 million tweets with #metoo were posted. More than 24 million people on *Facebook* participated in the #metoo conversation (Fox & Diehm, 2017). Within one year, more than 19 million #metoo messages were used on *Twitter* (Anderson & Toor, 2018). Although the term "me too" was originally created by Tarana Burke in 2006 on a social media called *MySpace* to promote awareness of sexual abuse happening to women of color (Tippett, 2018), it has also now been used on a variety of themes, including domestic violence and gender bias (Kantor & Twohey, 2022).

Defining Social Media

The #Metoo movement has made many individuals more fully aware of how often sexual harassment and sexual offenses occur near them to people they care about. Even if we cannot say with certainty that social media played a decisive role in spreading this awareness, we can safely aver that social media played an important role. Rhode (2019) argues that besides President

DOI: 10.4324/9781003360049-3

Trump's broadly disseminated derogative comments about women and the formal accusation of criminal behavior by Harvey Weinstein, journalists' persistent coverage of Weinstein's case and Trump's anti-feminism over social media platforms are indisputably important in encouraging many women to share their personal stories. It is technically easy to post #metoo stories on social media, but it is emotionally and psychologically very difficult for most victims to speak out due to a combination of shame, fear of retaliation, and lack of support from family, friends, and acquaintances. Social media helps deal with these concerns to some extent, as it reinforces the key concept of "you are not alone." Also, it helps create a so-called institutional memory – once it is online, it is online forever (Rhode, 2019).

The #metoo movement is just one of the many examples of the massive impacts social media can have on social movements and public policy members. Social media has been broadly recognized as a powerful tool for online activism – particularly in the areas of environmental advocacy, women's rights, LGBTQ+ rights, and police reform (e.g., see Cammaerts, 2015; Chon & Park, 2020; Steinberg, 2016). Criminal justice agencies also use it to investigate crimes and improve communication with citizens (e.g., Hoffmeister, 2014; Hu & Lovrich, 2020). Vice versa, members of the public also use social media to oversee criminal justice agencies.

To fully understand social media's impact on criminal justice and criminology, the very first matter we must address is that of the proper definition of the term social media. When we say social media, people usually think about *Facebook* and *Twitter*. However, the concept social media must take into consideration an individual's age. In social media research, researchers use "digital immigrants" to represent individuals who were born before the 1980s and grew up in a time when digital technology was virtually unknown (Kesharwani, 2020). The term "digital natives" refers to individuals who were born after the 1980s and started using phone-based digital technology at an early age (Kesharwani, 2020). Digital immigrants and digital natives tend to have quite different patterns of use of digital technology. For example, digital immigrants often are the users of online content while digital natives often are the creators of such content. Digital immigrants tend to use digital technology for functional purposes, while digital natives tend to use it for networking and personal interaction (Kesharwani, 2020). Digital immigrants may remember social media as *Six Degrees* (1997–2000) and *MySpace* while digital natives are more familiar with *Facebook* and *Twitter*.

Moreover, if we understand that digital immigrants and natives alike can be self-selected into social media, Generation Z, born between 1995 and 2009, have little choice since they grew up with social media and a virtually ubiquitous Internet. Multiple studies have shown that Generation Z typically spends hours on social media every day (Briggs, 2022). Vițelar (2019) and others have concluded that Generation Z as whole is creative, adaptive, and has a "digital mindset." To them, social media is seen to be constantly evolving. Compared to "old-fashioned" social media such as *Facebook* and *Twitter*, Generation Z tends to favor newer platforms such as *Snapchat*, *Instagram*, and more recently *TikTok* (Viţelar, 2019). Additionally, Generation Alpha, born between 2010 and 2024, is deeply and irrevocably embedded within the social media scene.

At least two factors contribute to this deep connection to social media. First, Generation Alpha's parents are either digital natives or Generation Z, people who already display a certain level of use of and familiarity with social media. Second, the evolution of smartphones makes it possible to access social media virtually anywhere, at any time. For example, *Facebook* was founded in 2004, and early users had to use it on their desktops/laptops. The iPhone app of *Facebook* was not launched until 2007, and the Android app was launched in 2010. As of 2023, all mainstream social media platforms have their mobile apps in wide use. More importantly, a Pew study reported in 2022 that about 95% of U.S. teens have smartphones while only 90% have desktops/laptops (Vogels et al., 2022). In a study conducted in 2014–2015, about 71% of teens reported use of *Facebook*, followed by *Instagram* (52%), *Snapchat* (41%), and *Twitter* (33%). In a study conducted in 2022, however, about 95% of teens reported use of *YouTube*, followed by *TikTok* (67%), *Instagram* (62%), *Snapchat* (59%), *Facebook* (32%), and *Twitter* (23%) (Vogels et al., 2022). The significant drop in *Facebook* usage among U.S. teens suggests that *Facebook* is an "old-fashioned" social media platform from teens' perspective, even though it still commands the largest number of monthly users. Thus, if you ask a teen to name a favored social media platform (as of 2023), *TikTok* may be the most frequently mentioned.

Such a rapid evolution of social media makes the term difficult to define; the manifestations of social media are broad, and the applications of social media are quite diverse (Aichner et al., 2021). Scholars seeking to provide a definition such as Aichner and colleagues (2021) note the existence of 21 major definitions of social media advanced over the period 1994 to 2019. An early definition of social media refers to computer-supported social networks (Wellman et al., 1996). Later, definitions of social media focus on a virtual community that brings people with common interests together (e.g., Hagel, 1999; Ridings et al., 2002). Recent definitions emphasize "user-generated" and "user-driven" aspects of social media (e.g., Carr & Hayes, 2015; Kapoor et al., 2018). Aichner and colleagues (2021) note that among the 21 definitions investigated, the most frequently used word is "social," followed by "people," "virtual," "network," and "content." They conclude that there is no commonly accepted definition of social media. However, keywords such as social, user, and content should be included in any definition proffered.

In criminal justice and criminology research, social media is also not well defined. Some scholars divide contemporary mass media into traditional media (e.g., newspapers, films, radio, and television) and new media characterized as *digital interactive media*. Surette (2015a) defines new media as those communication modes which "are made up of devices and capabilities encompassing digital and Internet technology that are characterized by interactive social media and multimedia content" (p. 14). Hoffmeister (2014) points out that any definition of social media must be broad enough to cover past, current, and future social media platforms. His research on defining social media focuses on three overarching themes: (1) technology; (2) user creation; and (3) community (Hoffmeister, 2014). These themes, and Aichner et al.'s (2021) work, will lay a firm foundation for defining social media.

Besides the three broad themes, another important aspect to be considered in advancing a definition of social media is the inclusion of as many types of social media as possible. Although these platforms are all referred to as social media, most have their own targeted population and specialized functions. These special functions, however, do not mean that only one platform has them and they cannot be incorporated into other platforms. For example, all the social media platforms allow users to send both text messages and pictures to other platform users. Text and pictures sent by *Snapchat*, however, are available only for a short time, and then they will self-destruct. It is generally recognized that *YouTube* is the most suitable platform for circulating videos, *TikTok* is typically used for sharing short-form videos, and *Instagram* is used for sharing pictures/photos. However, both *YouTube* and *Instagram* have recently made available their own short-form video functions (i.e., "Shorts" for *YouTube* and "Reels" for *Instagram*).

In this book, we hereby propose our definition of social media to read as follows:

> Social media is made up of Internet-based platforms that run on multiple devices with the purpose of creating and exchanging user-generated multimedia content within users' digital social networks.

We believe that this definition captures most, if not all, of the key features of social media platforms. First, social media platforms are all Internet-based. A high-speed Internet connection is the foundation of exchanging multimedia content such as pictures and videos. Meanwhile, a high-speed Internet connection is crucial to live streaming, which has become one of the most widely used social media interaction formats in current use. Second, users must be able to use social media platforms on multiple devices. Early on, social media platforms ran only on desktops/laptops. Now, very nearly every mainstream social media platform can be accessed by personal computers, smartphones, and tablets alike. These devices are not, and will not be, the only devices that run social media platforms. Wearable devices, such as smart glasses and VR headsets, can be considered the next generation of social media carriers.

Third, user-generated multimedia content is the key to each social media platform. No matter if a user is a leader of a country, an employee of a government agency, a representative of a large corporation, a pop music singer, or a common person, they are all able to produce and share multimedia content (e.g., pictures and videos) over social media. Take the case of contemporary policing as an example. Hu and Lovrich (2020) point out that the police had never been so intensively monitored by the public until the rapid development of social media. In the past, an event which might constitute police brutality could become widely known about only if (1) a victim contacts a journalist or a journalist discovers the event; (2) the journalist writes about the event, and it gets broadcast; and (3) the audience knows about the event via traditional mass media such as TV news and newspapers. All three steps must be accomplished; otherwise, the event just gets buried. For example, the victim cannot find any interested journalists. A journalist contacted does not wish to follow up after hearing the story of the police encounter. The editor refuses to publish the journalist's story. The story is reported by newspapers with only a small circulation. Social media can overcome *all* these obstacles to dissemination. The victim can simply upload the event (whether in the format of videos, pictures, or mere narratives) to social media platforms and use #policebrutality. The victim can also upload their account of the event to multiple social media platforms simultaneously to acquire the largest possibility of being viewed and shared. Of course, social media does not guarantee that the event will be massively noticed and handled in an appropriate manner. In sum, everyone can become a "reporter" at any time with the assistance of social media.

Fourth, social media is used for information exchange among users. When social media platforms were originally created, the principal purpose was to facilitate online interactions (staying in touch) among people who might know each other somewhat but cannot see each other due to geographic separation. Today, social media is much more than just about social connection maintenance. Users can learn new skills and even take formal courses over social media. They can follow celebrities and attend to their updates without subscribing to magazines. They can "friend" other people they may never be able to see face to face via social media. Moreover, most social media platforms now allow merchandise links to be inserted in posts so that users can buy goods from social media platforms. Many users now use social media as an alternative Internet-based television. They watch posts (e.g., pictures and videos) quite often, although most people seldom view their own posts. In fact, some critics argue that the future of social media is less social because it has become "corporatized" with abundant professionally prepared content from influence peddlers and commercial marketers (Chen, 2023). Such widespread promotion of products and services over traditional social media platforms may have caused many one-time users to move off some platforms, and the future of social media may be one of a plethora of special interests posting highly focused content (Bajarin, 2023).

Finally, we wish to highlight the point that in our definition of social media, a user's digital social network can be either broad or narrow, depending on the platforms' privacy settings and user privacy settings. While social media does eliminate physical locational boundaries, its privacy settings create digital boundaries among users. For example, many *Instagram* users use it to share photos and videos with known family members, relatives, and friends. Their privacy settings may be set up to "private account," meaning only the followers they approve of being able to view their posts. Otherwise, their accounts will be treated as "public accounts," and any person can view their posts even if they do not have an *Instagram* account. On *YouTube*, most videos are open to the public. However, *YouTube* also has privacy settings that allow video uploaders to decide who can watch their videos. Thus, a user's digital social network can be as extensive as all Internet users worldwide or as small as a few people he or she selects to share content.

Introduction to Contemporary Mainstream Social Media

As we write this book in 2024, a few social media platforms have undoubtedly become massive with respect to both their number of users and the breadth of their content. We select ten of the most widely used (worldwide) social media platforms based on the estimated number of monthly active users as of January 2023, according to Statista.com. *Facebook* ranks number one with almost three billion monthly active users, followed by *YouTube* (2.5 billion), *WhatsApp* (2 billion), *Instagram* (2 billion), *TikTok* (1 billion), *Messenger* (900 million), *Telegram* (700 million), *Snapchat* (600 million), *Twitter* (550 million), and *Pinterest* (450 million) (Statista, 2023d). We describe each of these social media platforms, report how many people use them, and what users are able do with them. Also, we also point out some criminal Justice and criminology research results pertaining to these popular platforms. More detailed discussions on these studies will be provided in later chapters.

Facebook

Facebook was founded in 2004, and it is the largest social networking site in the world. It ranks third among the most visited websites worldwide as of August 2023 (Similarweb, 2023). *Facebook* allows visitors to view some aspects of the public information it has on its users. Visitors need to register before they can fully access other users' public information, featuring such information as demographics, photos, videos, and posted narratives. Its privacy settings also allow users to "friend" other users before seeing each other's private information and posts. *Facebook* can be accessed from personal computers (desktops and laptops), smartphones, and tablets equipped with Internet connections. Besides traditional social media posts composed of narratives, photos, and videos, *Facebook* now may have the most diverse and complicated set of features such as a news feed (what happened to your friends recently), timeline (multimedia information arranged chronologically), reaction buttons ("likes," "haha," "love" to posts and comments), groups (collaboration among users who have the same interests), events (announcements of what, when, and where an event is going to happen), marketplace (buying and selling things via *Facebook*), places (marked places a user has visited), and videos (a *Facebook* version of *TikTok*).

Facebook has almost three billion monthly active users as of January 2023 (Statista, 2023d). In January 2021, *Facebook* was the social media platform that U.S. users spent the most time on daily (about 33 minutes) (Statista, 2023e). Roughly, 60% of the U.S. users are aged between 18 years and 44 years (18% are aged between 18 and 24 years) as of August 2023 (Statista, 2023f). Since *Facebook* is one of the "oldest" social media platforms, its use and users have been studied by researchers in criminal justice and criminology (CJC) quite often in the areas of policing (e.g., Hu et al., 2020; Lieberman et al., 2013), offenders (e.g., Moule et al., 2013; Napier et al., 2021), victimology (e.g., Kokkinos & Saripanidis, 2017; Scarduzio et al., 2019), corrections (e.g., Hitz, 2014), and research methods (e.g., Lipnicky et al., 2020).

YouTube

Founded in 2005, *YouTube* is the largest video-sharing platform in the world. *YouTube* allows users (known as "YouTubers") to create and share videos. *YouTube* can be accessed from personal computers, smartphones, and tablets with Internet connections. Initially, *YouTube* was designed to share user-generated videos exclusively. Today, its content includes video clips, music videos, news (in collaboration with traditional television news), shorts (short videos), films, motive trailers, and live streams. Most videos on *YouTube* can be watched without registering on the platform. Once a user registers, he or she has additional options such as subscribing to a YouTuber service to get new video notifications, simple editing and uploading his or her videos, clicking "like" or "dislike" on videos, saving videos for later re-play, and sharing videos. Its sharing has an embedding function that allows users to select when to start and share videos in other software (e.g., MS Word and PowerPoint) and on other social media platforms such as *Facebook*, *Twitter*, and *Pinterest*. Conference presenters often use this

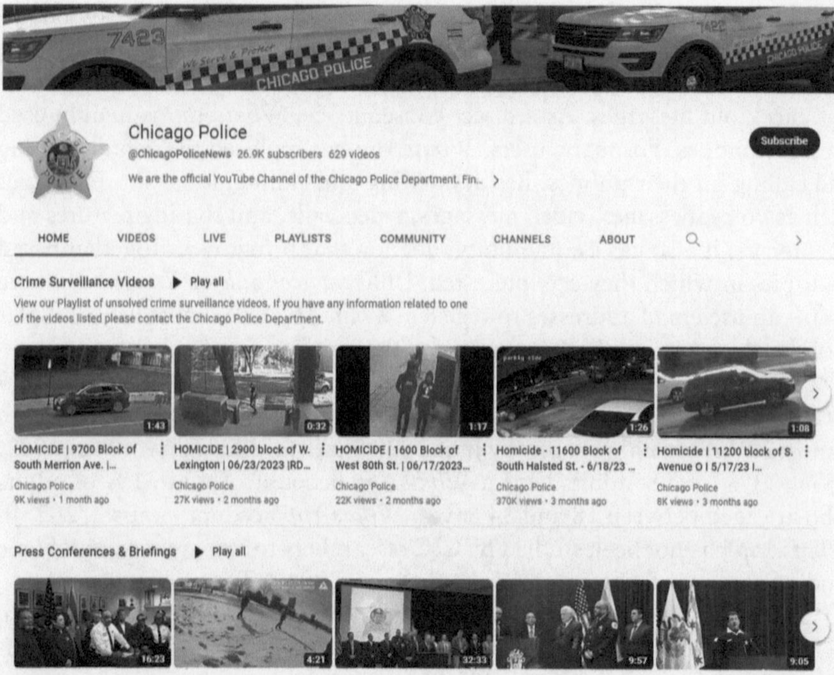

FIGURE 2.1 Chicago Police Department's YouTube channel (accessed on September 27, 2023).

function so that they can play videos in PowerPoint without redirecting to the *YouTube* website.

As of January 2023, *YouTube* had about 2.5 billion monthly active users (Statista, 2023d). In April 2022, about 500 hours of videos were uploaded to *YouTube per minute* (Statista, 2023g), compared to 300 hours in 2019 (Hu & Lovrich, 2020). In November 2022, most traffic on *YouTube* was accomplished on mobile devices (about 72 billion visits) while only eight billion visits came from desktops/laptops (Statista, 2023h). Compared to *Facebook*, *YouTube* has been less often studied in CJC. Some existing studies involve the areas of offenders (e.g., Johnson & Schell-Busey, 2016; Revier, 2021), policing (e.g., Brown, 2016; Schneider, 2018; also see Figure 2.1 for an example), victimization (e.g., Halder & Jaishankar, 2014; Harrington 2019), and crime prevention (e.g., Manning, 2013; Stickle et al., 2020).

WhatsApp

WhatsApp was founded in 2009. Unlike *Facebook* or *YouTube*, which were initially built as a self-standing website, *WhatsApp* was created as a phone app (application). Users could not use *WhatsApp* in a web browser or a desktop/laptop until 2015, but they still needed their phones to log in. As of 2023, the web version of *WhatsApp* still has a major limitation – that is, users cannot check old messages. As a direct consequence, *WhatsApp* is mainly used on smartphones. For many users, *WhatsApp* has replaced the default texting and calling on their phones. Besides texting and calling, it has more features such as voice messages, video messages, video calls, and sharing pictures and documents. It also has a community function that brings users together based on topics in which they are interested. Unlike *Facebook* or *YouTube*, where users can use email addresses to register, *WhatsApp* users must use a cellular mobile telephone number to sign up for the service.

WhatsApp has about two billion monthly active users as of January 2023 (Statista, 2023d). It is the world's most popular mobile messenger app, with almost 2.8 billion unique users by June 2023 (Statista, 2023i). As of May 2022, about 23% of U.S. adults have a *WhatsApp* account. About 31% of adults who are aged between 18 and 34 have a *WhatsApp* account (Statista, 2023j). *WhatsApp* has not been studied by CJC researchers to any great extent. Some studied areas are forensic science (e.g., Anwar, 2019; Trisnasenjaya & Riadi, 2019), crime prevention (Mols & Pridmore, 2019; Van Steden & Mehlbaum, 2022), victimology (e.g., Aizenkot & Kashy-Rosenbaum, 2021), and criminology (e.g., Ghazali & Ghani, 2018).

Instagram

Founded in 2010, *Instagram* was originally designed to share photos publicly or with users' followers. Like *WhatsApp*, *Instagram* was designed for smartphones. Since 2012, *Instagram* can be accessed via its website with limited functionality. One important feature of *Instagram* is that it has an internal photo/video editing function that allows users to upload, record, and edit photos and videos. The function does not require a user to be a professional and is rather easy to use, making *Instagram* popular among teenagers. *Instagram* allows photos and videos to feature geographical tagging. It also has a function called "stories." A user can post content chronologically, and his or her followers can access the content posted within 24 hours. The function is so popular that in 2019 it was already being used by 500 million users daily (Hutchinson, 2019).

Instagram has about two billion monthly active users as of January 2023 (Statista, 2023d). Roughly two-thirds of its users are teenagers and young adults. About 31% are aged between 18 and 24, and 30% are aged between 25 and 34. Some 8% of its users are aged between 13 and 17 (Statista, 2023k). CJC research on Instagram has focused on criminology (e.g., Bakken & Harder, 2023; Bekkers et al., 2022), policing (e.g., Prabowo & Rusfian, 2019; Walby & Wilkinson, 2023), crime prevention (e.g., Peters & Ojedokun, 2019), and victimology (e.g., Vitis & Gilmour, 2017).

TikTok

In September 2016, the Chinese company ByteDance released a short-form video-sharing app named "Douyin." It soon became one of the most popular social media platforms in China. It attracted 100 million users within a year and had more than one billion video views daily (Graziani, 2018). In September 2017, ByteDance launched *TikTok*, which is Douyin's international version. *TikTok*'s major features include the recording and editing of videos, adding music to the videos, and live streaming. Unlike *YouTube*, *TikTok* focuses on the market of short-form videos, whose length is from three seconds to ten minutes. *TikTok* allows one user to invite another to create a video together using the "duets" function. Starting in 2019, *TikTok* also allowed its users to embed merchandise sale links into their posts.

As of January 2023, *TikTok* has roughly one billion monthly active users (Statista, 2023d), which makes it the most popular short-form video-sharing app worldwide. Due to concerns over data security, more than half of U.S. states and the federal government have banned *TikTok* in government-issued devices (Richmond, 2023). Meanwhile, many U.S. universities such as the University of Wisconsin System and the University of Texas at Austin have blocked *TikTok* from campus Wi-Fi, although students can simply use their cellular phones to get on the platform (Maheshwari & Holpuch, 2023). Ironically, the U.S. has the largest *TikTok* audience as of July 2023, with almost 122 million users (Statista, 2023l). *TikTok's* users are relatively younger than those in other mainstream social media. In a 2022 survey, two-thirds of respondents aged between 18 and 19 use *TikTok*, followed by respondents aged between 20 and 29 (56%) and respondents aged between 30 and 39 (45%) (Statista, 2022). Moreover, just like other social media, a person can be a creator, a viewer, or both on *TikTok*. As of September 2022, the majority of *TikTok* content creators are aged between 18 and 25. Moreover, about 7% of creators are under 13 years old (Statista, 2023m). Since *TikTok* is a relatively new social media platform, it has not been studied by CJC researchers to any great extent. The existing scant research available focuses on criminology (e.g., Shejuti, 2023), hate crime (e.g., Weimann & Masri, 2023), and prisoners (e.g., McMann et al., 2022).

Messenger

Messenger was originally developed as a chat function on *Facebook* in 2008. In 2011, it was separated from *Facebook* and started having its own app on smartphones. Because it was rooted in *Facebook*, users of *Messenger* were required to be friends on *Facebook* before they could send messages to each other. Starting in 2013, that requirement has been lifted, and *Messenger* allows users to send direct messages to other users if they have their phone numbers. Today, the functions of *Messenger* are like those of *WhatsApp*.

Messenger users can make phone calls and video calls and even hold up to 50-person video calls. They can text each other and send money to each other. They can also share their locations. Because it is still more or less connected to *Facebook*, users can also see content on their *Facebook* feeds through *Messenger*, such as "stories," and the app does remind users of their *Facebook* updates.

Messenger has about 900 million monthly active users as of January 2023 (Statista, 2023d). In the U.S., there are about 188 million users. As of August 2023, most *Messenger* users are aged between 25 and 34 (23.4%), followed by users aged between 35 and 44 (20.8%) and users aged between 45 and 53 (16.7%) (Statista, 2023n). About 10% of its users are young adults, and about 1% are aged between 13 and 17 (Statista, 2023n). The existing CJC and *Messenger* studies focus on online sexual harassment (e.g., Sultana et al., 2021), pornographic content distribution (e.g., Sunardi & Ardiningtias, 2022), and threat message distribution (e.g., Razalan, 2022).

Telegram

Telegram is a multi-platform messaging service that can be accessed via personal computers, smartphones, and tablets. It was first launched in 2013 on smartphones. Like *WhatsApp* and *Messenger*, *Telegram* allows users to send text and voice messages, make voice calls and video calls, and share multimedia documents such as pictures and text files. It also allows users to join different channels based on their interests. Some features make *Telegram* different from either *WhatsApp* or *Messenger*. For example, *Telegram* is a cloud-based mobile and desktop messaging app, meaning that users can access their messages and files on all devices at any location. Meanwhile, there is a high limit on the size of the files sent via *Telegram* (up to 2GB). *Telegram* allows users to send messages in a massive group with up to 200,000 members, compared to *WhatsApp* with up to 1,024 members (Davies, 2023). It has a "secret chats" feature, which users are not able to forward or screenshot messages, and messages can be self-destructed (Gordon & Fernandez, 2023). Moreover, *WhatsApp* and *Messenger* usually require users to use phone numbers to add new friends. *Telegram* allows users to use usernames or even a one-time QR code to add new friends, so the new friends will never know who they really are (Gordon & Fernandez, 2023). Additionally, *Telegram* claims that the company's business model does not include data collection and sharing (Gordon & Fernandez, 2023). Meanwhile, *Telegram*'s API (application programming interface) is public and free, meaning that developers, besides the *Telegram* company itself, can create clients (Gordon & Fernandez, 2023). Thus, *Telegram*'s focus on privacy and flexibility makes it different from other messaging apps, making it quite popular.

As of January 2023, *Telegram* has roughly 700 million monthly active users (Statista, 2023d). According to a research blog studying Android messaging apps from 100 countries, *WhatsApp* ranks first in 63 out of the 100 countries, *Messenger* ranks first in 16 out of the 100 countries, and *Telegram* ranks first in 10 out of the 100 countries (March, 2023). According to a 2023 survey, about 85% of *Telegram* users follow news channels, 62% follow entertainment channels, 58% follow educational channels, 50% follow political channels, and 45% follow personal channels of friends (Statista, 2023o). *Telegram* has not been studied by CJC researchers to any great extent. The existing scant research focuses on extremism (e.g., Walther & McCoy, 2021), criminal marketplaces (e.g., Blankers et al., 2021; Lummen, 2023), drug intervention (e.g., Rolando et al., 2023), and surveillance (e.g., Akbari & Gabdulhakov, 2019).

Snapchat

Snapchat is a multimedia messaging app that allows users to send text messages, pictures, and videos (called snaps). When launched in 2011, the platform was designed to share photos person-to-person. For a long time, *Snapchat* has only smartphone apps. Now, it has a desktop app, and users can also use *Snapchat* on the web via browsers. The principal feature of *Snapchat* is that messages, pictures, and videos are available only for a short time to their recipients, ranging from 1 to 10 seconds. *Snapchat* does not block screenshots, but it will send a message to the sender if a screenshot has been taken. Starting in 2017, senders can set up snaps to be viewed with unlimited time until recipients choose to close them. Such a feature automatically leads to criticism that *Snapchat* will be abused to send sensitive content such as sexual content. However, a 2014 study found that only about 1.6% of respondents use *Snapchat* for sexting, and about 14% of respondents have at least sent sexual content once (Roesner et al., 2014). Many respondents (about 75%) are not in favor of sexting (Roesner et al., 2014). Moreover, most respondents (about 60%) primarily use *Snapchat* to share funny things (Roesner et al., 2014). Nevertheless, its high prevalence among teenagers leads to many parents' concerns. In 2022, *Snapchat's* feature "Family Center" allows parents to monitor their kids' activities on *Snapchat*.

Snapchat had about 600 million monthly active users as of January 2023 (Statista, 2023d). *Snapchat* seems to be more popular among the youth (see Figure 2.2 for an example). Based on a survey of Generation Z social media users in the U.S., 60% used *Snapchat* weekly in 2019, 54% in 2020, and 54% again in 2021 (Statista, 2023p). As of January 2023, about 20% of its worldwide users are aged between 13 and 17 (Statista, 2023q). *Snapchat* has not been studied by CJC researchers often. A 2023 review opines that crime on *Snapchat* is extremely under-researched (Huie et al., 2023). The

FIGURE 2.2 The National Police (France) on Snapchat. As one of few police agencies on Snapchat, the National Police (France) also actively involves in other social media platforms such as Facebook, Twitter, Instagram, LinkedIn, YouTube, and TikTok as of October 2023.

review reports a few types of crime being committed using *Snapchat*, including blackmail, solicitation of minors, cyberstalking, cyber threatening, hate crime, identity theft, and hacking (Huie et al., 2023). Data collection may be one of the biggest difficulties researchers must overcome because messages on *Snapchat* are often not public and exist only for a short time. Almost all studies must rely on self-reported data collected through surveys.

Twitter (X)

Known as X after July 2023, *Twitter* was founded in 2006. It allows users to send short messages known as "tweets" up to 280 characters (was up to 140 characters before 2017). The latest change is that if a user has subscribed to *Twitter* monthly (called X Premium), then he or she can post a tweet of up to 4,000 characters (Fingas, 2023). The limit makes *Twitter* different from other social media platforms, and it is recognized as a good tool for sending real-time short updates (Heverin & Zach, 2010). Although *Twitter* has length limits, it allows users to send text, images, videos, and links. Users can also like, retweet (repost), comment, and quote tweets. The hashtag (#) and mentioning (@) are also Twitter's early features. Today, users can also go live stream on *Twitter* by using its live video function. With Internet connections, *Twitter* can be accessed from personal computers (desktops and laptops), smartphones, and tablets.

As of January 2023, *Twitter* has roughly 550 million monthly active users (Statista, 2023d). The U.S. has the largest number of *Twitter* users (95 million), followed by Japan (67 million), India (27 million), and Brazil (24 million) (Statista, 2023r). In the second quarter of 2022, there are about 41 million monetizable daily active *Twitter* users in the U.S. and almost 240 million users worldwide (Statista, 2023s, 2023t). On average, *Twitter* users spend about 35 minutes per day on *Twitter*, compared to *Facebook* users who spend about 30 minutes per day on that platform (Smith, 2023). As one of the "traditional" social media platforms, *Twitter* has been studied more often than new social media platforms in the areas of criminology (e.g., Gerber, 2014; Vomfell et al., 2018), victimology (e.g., Aurrekoetxea-Casaus, 2020; Moody-Ramirez & Cole, 2018), policing (e.g., Crump, 2011; Procter et al., 2013), courts (e.g., Small & Puddister, 2020), and public attitudes toward CJC topics (e.g., Hosterman et al., 2018; Tillery, 2019).

Pinterest

Founded in 2009, *Pinterest* is noted for letting users share their ideas (called "pins") with the world. Typically, these ideas include, but are not limited to, cooking recipes, home decor ideas, and new-look clothing outfits. *Pinterest* allows users to share their ideas using narratives, pictures, and videos. Like other social media platforms, other users can comment upon and share these ideas. *Pinterest* can be accessed from personal computers (desktops and laptops), smartphones, and tablets with Internet connections. On computers, users are not required to log in to the platform to see "recipes."

As of January 2023, *Pinterest* has about 450 million monthly active users (Statista, 2023d). The proportion of female users is significantly higher than that of male users. About 76% of *Pinterest* users are female while only 17% are male (Statista, 2023u). While *Pinterest* is considered as an "old" social media platform, the youth embrace it even more fully than *Twitter*. About 21 million of Generation Z in the U.S. use *Pinterest*, while only about 17 million use *Twitter* in 2022 (Statista, 2023v). Unlike *Facebook* or *Twitter*, CJC research on *Pinterest* is limited. Some existing research involves the area of drugs (e.g., Laestadius et al., 2019), policing (e.g., McVey, 2022), and intimate partner violence (e.g., Carlyle et al., 2021).

What New Forms of Social Media Can We Expect?

In the previous section, we introduced ten of the most widely used social media platforms worldwide. Certainly, the current social media platforms are not going to end the evolution of social media. Innovative social media platforms are ever on the way, and traditional social media platforms will keep incorporating new functions. As students of the criminal justice system and individuals within the criminal justice system, we will need to be ready for these new platforms and prepare to face the challenges they may present.

To predict new forms and functions of social media likely to appear in the near future, we first go back to our definition of social media. Our first topic of focus on is the Internet. Of course, the Internet will continue to be a must-to-make use of social media platforms. However, the speed of the Internet dictates what we can do with social media platforms. By the late 2000s, most wireless connectivity was 3G (third generation). The 3G's maximum speed is about 2 Mbps. At present, the most widely used connectivity is 4G (fourth generation, also known as Long Term Evolution or LTE). The 4G's maximum speed is about 20 Mbps. Recently, 5G (fifth generation) has been widely adopted in some locations, such as municipal areas. The maximum speed of 5G can go from 400 Mbps to 1 Gbps (Pegoraro, 2022). With a higher speed of the Internet, devices can perform more functions. For example, live streaming, a function that many social media platforms support, depends mightily on high-speed Internet. With 5G, VR (virtual reality) and AR (augmented reality) will be advanced in their dissemination. *Meta* (formerly known as *Facebook*) is working on the so-called metaverse which will "help individuals connect with people when they are not physically in the same place and get them even closer to that feeling of being together in person" (Meta, 2023).

Meanwhile, the high-speed Internet makes it possible to connect to more devices. For example, in the past, individuals accessed social media platforms (e.g., *Facebook* and *Twitter*) via their personal computers. Today, 4G and smartphones make it more convenient for individuals to access social media platforms on their smartphones. Consequently, the majority of social media users now use smartphones for online social media use. With 5G, social media platforms will soon be running on additional wearable devices, such as smart watches, VR headsets, and smart glasses. At the same time, the high-speed Internet makes it possible for non-latency or low-latency cloud services, which could make AI (artificial intelligence) "smarter" on personal wearable devices. The direct benefit of a smarter AI is a more precise voice control that allows users to use voice to handle social media content so devices can be made much smaller without an actual keyboard.

User-generated content will continue to be the critical feature of any social media platform. A user, however, does not always mean a person. It can be a company or any other organization. We have seen this trend in today's social media posts. In the past, social media platforms were mainly used by people (human beings). New feeds on social media were mainly about texts, images, and videos posted by friends and family members. Today, a high proportion of new feeds come from *influencers* on social media. The presence of influencers on social media alerts us to the need to redefine what is *social* in the digital era. Social media is supposed to help individuals interact with each other online because they cannot be physically present in the same place, which represents a two-way channel of communication. Although some influencers occasionally interact with their audience on social media, following influencers or watching advertisements is typically a one-way communication. Imagine if a person uses a social media platform only to read posts and watch and listen to imbedded video materials. Can we still hold to the view that he or she is using that social media platform for social interaction, or are they simply making use of a customized online television?

Clearly, influencers on social media indeed make social media platforms less social. Researchers call this phenomenon the "influencer paradox." On the one hand, influencers do keep social media platforms vivid because they bring new users in and keep old users engaged. On the other hand, influencers slowly kill the social function of social media platforms as more and more people start focusing increasingly on influencers rather than friends or family members on social media. Influencers have become a major part of social media. And social media platforms rely on influencers to generate their revenue. Influencers help keep users on social media, and social media platforms profit because they disseminate advertisements to their users (Muha, 2022). People today see ever more new feeds on their social media coming from advertisements made by corporations marketing their products. People who realize this may decide to choose more special interest-focused social media platforms in the future, moving away from the massive traditional social media platforms (Bajarin, 2023).

Besides profit-motivated influencers, *algorithms* are also helping social media platforms derive profits. AI-assisted social media algorithms aim at maximizing engagement by users to keep them online. It has been broadly recognized that these algorithms cause issues, particularly among youth where social media addiction has become a recognized disorder (e.g., Allahverdi, 2022; Cheng et al., 2021; Dogan et al., 2019; Masoed et al., 2021). One of the main issues in this area is that social media gives rise to online extremism and fragmentation, especially from a political perspective (Muha, 2022). In his book *#Republic: Divided Democracy in the Age of Social Media*, Sunstein (2017) describes how social media algorithms sort users into groups of the like-minded and amplify their views, creating polarization and even political extremism. Such an effect may be stronger on teenagers as their range of experience is limited and their intellectual maturation is not fully developed. In 2022, the most popular social media platform among Generation Z in the U.S. is *Snapchat* (44.5 million users), followed by *Instagram* (37.3 million users), *TikTok* (41.4 million users), *Facebook* (31.8 million users), *Pinterest* (20.9 million users), and *Twitter* (16.7 million users) (Statista, 2023v). Scholars, policymakers, educators, child psychologists, and concerned parents have taken note the often-maladaptive consequences of excessive use of social media by teens (e.g., Adorjan & Ricciardelli, 2021; Soh et al., 2018; White-Gosselin & Poulin, 2024; Yayman & Bilgin, 2020).

In fact, nearly all social media platforms' pages on Wikipedia feature a section listing criticisms against it, including but not limited to creating addiction and low self-esteem, spreading fake news and conspiracy theories, contributing to extremism, facilitating human manipulation, and frequent compromises of user privacy. The following is typical of such listings of concerns on Instagram's Wikipedia page (https://en.wikipedia.org/wiki/Instagram). All reported scientific research findings have a citation or multiple citations.

Depression, anxiety, and stress: Khodarahimi and Fathi found evidence that *Instagram* users displayed higher levels of depressive and anxious symptoms compared to non-users . . . Multiple studies have found that increasing time spent on *Instagram* increases social anxiety and anxiety related to personal traits, physical appearance, and high-stress body areas in particular . . .

Body image: *Instagram* users report higher body surveillance (the habitual monitoring of one's body shape and size), appearance-related pressure, eating-disorder-related-pathology, and lower body satisfaction than non-users . . .

Instagram addiction: A study showed that users who feel that they spend too much time on Instagram report higher levels of "addiction" to Instagram, which in turn was related to higher self-reported levels of stress induced by the app . . .

Under great social and political pressure from the U.S. Congress, social media companies have taken some actions to self-regulate and will likely take more actions in the future, particularly in controlling teenagers' access to social media. Under Section 230 of the Communications Decency Act of 1996, social media companies are not responsible for what their users say. The U.S. Department of Justice and many interested parties – including some actors within the social media community – are interested in strengthening protests against illicit content and the dissemination of misinformation by adding teeth to the "good faith effort" at self-regulation provided for by the blanket protection of Section 230. We should expect to see renewed interest in greater governmental regulation of social media as AI-assisted algorithms compound the problems associated with a weakly regulated industry.

Conclusion

Compared to other mass media, social media is relatively new and features ongoing changes and expansion of societal impact. Accordingly, this chapter offers a definition of social media and describes the major contemporary mainstream social media platforms in broad use. We discuss the most prominent platforms such as *Facebook*, *X* (known as *Twitter*, and we will use "*Twitter*" in this book), *YouTube*, *Instagram*, and *TikTok*. The chapter provides readers who are unfamiliar with social media platforms some up-to-date general information about what they are, how widespread their use is, and what users are enabled to do with them. We provide a brief overview of some criminal justice and criminology academic research on these now-ubiquitous social media platforms. An informed view on the most likely new developments to take place in social media in the future is provided in a concluding section of the chapter. The pressures to revise Section 230 provisions of the *Communications Decency Act of 1996* are mounting in good measure due to the criminal activity and civil misconduct made possible by social media.

The most likely area of change will be to bolster the requirement for "good faith self-regulation" engaged in by social media platforms by way of new federal regulations, with the criminal justice and criminology research literature providing important guidance for well-informed and evidence-based regulation in the public interest.

3

SOCIAL MEDIA AND CRIMINOLOGY

Opening Story: John was a successful real estate developer who owned a real estate company in Houston. He had a large house located beyond the suburbs of Houston. John loved art, so the house displayed some priceless works of art. John often showed off some of his newly acquired artwork on social media. His teenage children loved to post pictures of the family's overseas vacations on social media. One day, after returning from a vacation, John found that his house had been invaded. Cash, jewelry, and some valuable paintings were taken. John was perplexed and could not figure out how the burglars had found his house since it was "in the middle of nowhere." John is a fictional character. However, the story might not be. It was reported that a group of seven individuals were arrested by the Houston Police Department in 2019 for burglary (Almasy, 2019). This burglary ring's *modus operandi* was to search social media posts for wealthy homeowners on vacation or at work (Almasy, 2019). The HPD detective on the case noted that these criminals would research the homes of owners who bragged about their possessions (Almasy, 2019). Besides jewelry, computers, and guns, the criminals also took away artwork and learned how to sell on an active artworks black market (Almasy, 2019). Another report revealed that some burglars used social media posts to select the houses they planned to break into (Meek, 2022). They often used geo-tagging, check-ins, holiday posts, and posts bragging about expensive goods to "plan the best way of making a move" (Meek, 2022).

Defining Crime

Using social media posts to select suitable targets is just one criminal application of social media. In fact, we must openly admit that social media makes

DOI: 10.4324/9781003360049-4

some types of crimes far easier to perform than in the past. For example, cyberstalkers can easily use social media to threaten, frighten, and harass others without physical contact but bring the same, or even worse, physical and/or emotional damage to their victims. Social media also makes some types of crimes less detectable. For instance, offenders can easily commit identity theft on social media without being detected if social media users are not aware of how to secure their privacy on social media platforms. Meanwhile, the low visibility of some types of crimes conducted via social media makes it more difficult for the police to investigate them. Moreover, investigating such crimes often requires advanced technology and knowledgeable investigators. Social media provides motivated offenders with criminal minds, means of crime, and even criminal companions with more powerful tools to bring harm to victims.

However, not all "weird" behaviors on social media can be considered crimes. For instance, repeatedly visiting a person's social media page is generally not considered to be cyberstalking. Cyberstalking, by definition, refers to the "use of the Internet, computers, and related technology to repeatedly threaten, harass, or frighten another individual" (Maras, 2017, p. 232). If a person just repeatedly views open content of another person's social media page (e.g., pictures, videos, blogs), this is not considered cyberstalking. However, if the person uses the information, such as geographic information and contact information connected to social media content, to stalk the victim, then it becomes a punishable crime. It becomes a crime if the person hacks the victim's social media accounts and spreads inappropriate information. However, many topics remain to be discussed regarding social media postings and behaviors associated with them. For example, what constitutes a genuine *threat*, which often is at the core of cyberstalking cases, in social media posts? In *Elonis v. United States* (2015), the U.S. Supreme Court ruled that the "reasonable person standard" inference of intent is not sufficient grounds for enforcement action in criminal cases. A social media post must include evidence of *subjective* intent to threaten to be identified as a *bona fide* threat post. In other words, it must be proven that the person who wrote the post must intend the post to be interpreted as a threat. The situation where reasonable people interpret the post as a threat only constitutes *objective* intent, which cannot be used to criminalize the threatening person's action.

In the beginning of this book, we argued that to understand criminological theories and how the criminal justice system works, we must first have a clear understanding of crime. Criminal justice textbooks often define crime as "an act in violation of a criminal law for which a punishment is prescribed" (e.g., Walsh & Jorgensen, 2020, p. 2). Two elements are worthy noting in this definition. The first is the commission of an "act." A criminal mind cannot solely determine a crime if the mind's thought does not become an observable action. For example, say a person gets into a dispute with his neighbor. He was so angry that he wanted to exact revenge on the neighbor by spreading untrue rumors on social media. The thought – spreading untrue facts about this neighbor on social media – is not considered a crime unless he acts accordingly. On the contrary, an act can be considered a crime even without a criminal thought having been formed. For example, a person who had left an unattended infant in a car on a hot summer day would likely face a charge of criminal neglect in the U.S. If the infant dies because of it, the person may be charged with negligent homicide in some states. According to noheatstroke.org (2024), between 1998 and 2023 about 960 children died because of Pediatric Vehicular Heatstroke (PVH). It is difficult to indicate that these parents (or infant caregivers) had an intent to cause the death of these innocent children. However, at least some of these parents (or caregivers) did face serious criminal charges.

The second element is "criminal law." The legislative branch of the government (i.e., the legislature) often decides what behavior is prohibited (the law) and what punishments will be meted out if someone violates the law (Siegel & Worrall, 2016). Criminal law comes from a variety of sources, such as constitutions, statutes, ordinances, administrative regulations, and common law (Walsh & Hemmens, 2020). Scholars, practitioners, legislators, and the public may differ in their opinions on what acts should be included as criminal offenses. However, there are a few things on which there is virtual agreement. First, what constitutes a crime is constantly changing. For example, sodomy was illegal in many states in the U.S. until 2003, and burning American flags was illegal until 1989 (Walsh & Jorgensen, 2020). Cyberstalking was not illegal conduct until 1999, when California made it a criminal offense – believed to be the first cyberstalking law in the U.S. (Dean, 2000). Second, a criminal act must be a harmful action, and most often the harm in question must be a social harm (Walsh, 2012). For example, it is not against the law in most countries for a person to smoke (an act harmful to the person) at his or her home. However, most countries forbid smoking in public places, especially if a crowd of people is there and the smoker is doing harm to others. Additionally, the harm can be indirect. For example, debate on the legalization of prostitution typically focuses on whether prostitution is a form of sexual liberation or a form of violence against women (Swanson, 2016). At first blush, prostitution is simply a trade – exchange of money for sex. However, numerous studies have shown that prostitution is materially related to exploitation of women by pimps and even human trafficking (e.g., Charnley & Nkhoma, 2020; Cho et al., 2013; Farley, 2009; Hughes, 2000).

Without question, crime in the digital age has become much more complicated. The main issue is how to balance privacy rights and accountability for criminal conduct. Social media helps increase privacy by reducing face-to-face contact. A person can acquire all manner of information, whether legal or illegal, without leaving the confines of their room. But it also breaches privacy by promoting self-disclosure of personal information. For example, should someone be punished for posting "threatening look" posts on social media just after he or she just had a really bad day? If so, what is the difference between posting on social media and writing it down in a diary? Additionally, what if the person truly intends to do some awful thing he or she writes on social media?

Social Media and Crime

This section provides a broad understanding of the relationship between social media and crime. We divide this section into two major parts. The first part of the section discusses, from a mass media perspective, how social media may impact crimes in ways traditional mass media did not. The second part of the section discusses in considerable detail how the ubiquity of social media impacts "old-fashion" crimes and enables "new-fashion" crimes, today broadly known as cybercrimes.

Traditional Mass Media: Biased and Criminogenic?

Academia has long recognized that criminals and criminality portrayed by the mass media are typically out of sync with the realities of crime and justice. Criminals are generally portrayed as white, mature, and middle or upper class in the entertainment and news media, whereas most arrestees are minority, young, and underprivileged (Surette, 2015a). Crimes covered by the mass media are nearly always extremely violent (e.g., murder), business-related (e.g., white-collar crime), or bureaucratic (e.g., treason) while street crimes (e.g., theft, drug-related, and robbery) make up most of the official crime data (Surette, 2015a). Meanwhile, media-portrayed criminals are often animalistic, deeply evil, irrational, and significantly different from law-abiding people, whereas most actual offenders are much more like ordinary people in actual reality (Surette, 2015a).

Surette (2015a) uses "criminogenic media" to indicate that media content may constitute a direct cause of crime. For example, violent media content, such as violent video games, have historically been believed to have a direct connection with individuals' aggressiveness. However, consensus is lacking on the relationship between violent video games and aggression. Some studies have concluded that violent video games do increase aggression (e.g., Anderson et al., 2008; Burkhardt & Lenhard, 2022; Bushman & Gibson, 2011; Greitemeyer, 2018; Konijn et al., 2007; Möller & Krahé, 2009). Greitemeyer (2018) reports, however, that in the comparison of aggressive and nonaggressive offenders matched into similar pairs vis-à-vis background traits, there was no difference in their violence video use.

In addition, numerous studies have examined offline violent video gameplaying, a format for video gameplaying that has become quite popular today. A study on online violent video gameplaying found that playing online violent video games increases aggression (Hollingdale & Greitemeyer, 2014). Some studies, however, find no evidence of a material correlation between playing violent video games and aggression (e.g., Adachi & Willoughby, 2011; Dowsett & Jackson, 2019; Ferguson et al., 2008; Griffiths, 1999; Kühn et al., 2019). Many studies that report a significant correlation suffer from methodical problems, such as focusing on only short-term aggression (Griffiths, 1999) and measuring competitiveness instead of aggression (Adachi & Willoughby, 2011). Thus, the most solid conclusion to be drawn from the extant research at this time is that for some children under some conditions playing violent video games will increase their level of aggression. For most children under most conditions, there is no correlation between violent video game playing and aggression (Surette, 2015a). The conditions mentioned here by Surette (2015a) refer to risk factors. We will discuss these risk factors in the developmental theories section of this chapter. The more risk factors a child has, the more likely he or she will be influenced by violent video games (Surette, 2015a). Also, we must realize that aggression is not the same as crime. A person with a high level of aggression seldom becomes a criminal. All things considered, the statement "violent video games cause crime" is highly questionable.

The second example of "criminogenic media" is copycat crime – that is, when some individuals will mimic media-portrayed criminal acts (Surette, 2015a). Social learning theory (see criminological theories in the next section), particularly imitation from role models' behaviors, can provide a decent explanation of copycat crimes (Surette, 2015a). However, it does not necessarily mean that if a person watches too much crime-related media content, he or she will commit crimes. Surette (2015a) summarizes what variables may push an individual to commit copycat crimes. Immersion in crime-related content seems to be very important, as well as personal traits, psychological traits, criminal history, history of punishment, family and community ties, and cultural environment (Surette, 2015a). In fact, copycat crime is not well defined or measured because of its complexity (Surette, 2016). Surette (2015a) argues that "for a crime to be a copycat crime, it must have been inspired by an earlier, media-publicized or generator crime – that is, there must be a pair of crimes linked through the media" (p. 84). The research on media impacts on copycat crimes is quite limited. However, based on what existing empirical research we have, a few conclusions about copycat crimes can be safely made. First, crime-related media content does impact an ordinary individual's criminal motivation (*mens rea*) or behavior (*modus operandi*) (Helfgott, 2015). Second, such impacts appear significantly more in criminals than in ordinary people, and more in some types of crimes than in other types of crimes. Copycat criminals who have been apprehended tend to be career criminals involved in property crimes rather than first-time criminals involved in violent crimes (Surette, 2015a). Third, instead of "triggering" crimes, crime-related media should be viewed as a "rudder" that provides instructional models to motivated offenders (Rios & Ferguson, 2020; Surette, 2013). Finally, as social media, communication technology, and the digital culture continue to advance and enrich our lives in many ways, it is crucial to incorporate media (especially social media) into studying copycat crimes and crime prevention (Helfgott, 2023).

While much research has been conducted on mass media and crime in recent decades, no solid general conclusion has been reached among scholars and researchers that mass media are highly biased and often criminogenic. A safe summary would be that some types of mass media (e.g., entertainment media, TV shows, and movies) may be biased, and other types of mass media (e.g., news media) may be relatively objective (e.g., Hu & Dittmann, 2016, 2019). Likewise, mass media is not criminogenic viewed on a large scale (Surette, 2013). Instead, mass media may well serve as a "crime enhancer" among motivated offenders. However, we should not eliminate the possibility that a normally law-abiding person suddenly starts committing crimes after watching a misrepresentative TV show. Should that occur, the person's criminal behavior must be understood within broad individual and societal contexts.

Social Media: A Replication of Traditional Mass Media?

What do crimes and criminals look like on social media? A substantial number of researchers have started using social media posts to collect and analyze big data related to crime and fear of crime (e.g., Malleson & Andresen, 2015; Prieto Curiel et al., 2020). Most of their research involves the analysis of tweets (e.g., Bendler et al., 2014; Cvetojevic & Hochmair, 2018; Williams et al., 2017). Their studies have shown that, like traditional mass media, social media may generate negative biases toward criminals and persons accused of crime commission. For example, social media news consumption (reading news on social media) is positively related to the holding of criminal stereotypes, misconceptions suggesting that violent crimes, property crimes, and drug crimes are disproportionately committed by African Americans (Intravia & Pickett, 2019). Social media may generate violent crimes by failing to arrest the spread of extreme viewpoints on right-wing social media posts (Müller & Schwarz, 2021). Social media discrimination on the basis of race, ethnicity, and national origin is significantly related to the number of hate crimes committed (Relia et al., 2019).

These reported findings in the research literature do not necessarily mean that social media is "criminogenic media." Under certain circumstances, social media may bring benefits. For instance, engaging in crime-related news on social media (e.g., making comments and actively sharing posts) is behavior negatively related to the holding of criminal stereotypes (Intravia &

Pickett, 2019). It is hypothesized that individuals who engage more often in crime-related news on social media are more likely to challenge criminal stereotypes. Additionally, social media may help us better understand crime patterns. For example, when using the volume of social media messages (social media message density) instead of the residential population, crime hot spots tend to shift spatially (Malleson & Andresen, 2015). Another study on crimes in New York City suggests that combining traditional crime data and social media data can significantly improve crime hotspot prediction accuracy (Yang et al., 2018). Both examples indicate that we may need to consider social media data when allocating crime control resources. Social media can be used to predict offline crimes, such as robbery, burglary, aggravated assaults, stalking, gambling, and hit-and-run crimes (e.g., Gerber, 2014; Wang et al., 2012). Besides, social media can be effectively used to predict cybercrimes such as cyberstalking, hacking, cyberharassment, phishing scams, cyberbullying, and data breaches (e.g., Abbass et al., 2020; Hao & Dai, 2016). Interestingly, criminologists now have used social media to engage in public criminology (Wood et al., 2019).

Despite these potential benefits, it is still debatable if we can use social media posts to collect and analyze crimes on a large scale, as is done with the FBI's annual Uniform Crime Report (UCR) and the Bureau of Justice Statistics' annual National Crime Victimization Survey (NCVS). There are a few reasons for this. First, as is the case with traditional mass media, social media displays a strong bias toward sexual and violent crimes (Prieto Curiel et al., 2020). Crimes that spread the most quickly on social media and generate the most reactions (e.g., homicide) actually occur only rarely in reality. Other biases include the propensity to tweet about crime issues (not everyone posts or discusses victimization experiences on social media) and the propensity to geolocate posts (not everyone includes geolocation in their social media posts) (Williams et al., 2017). Accordingly, social media may not be of great help in detecting crimes (Prieto Curiel et al., 2020).

Second, the notion that "anyone can post anything on social media" means that some posts on social media do not accurately reflect what happens. Misinformation on social media is fairly common, and the dissemination of falsehoods is listed by the World Economic Forum (WEF) as one of the main threats to human society (Del Vicario et al., 2016). Misinformation can be completely fictional or made up by drawing upon inaccurate information, and it can spread to a very large number of social media users in a very short time (Amoruso et al., 2020). Besides, crime-related posts take up only a very small proportion of all types of social media posts. Crime-related social media posts are usually mentioned by news agencies and only by a few users (Prieto Curiel et al., 2020). Third, not every crime-related social media post instantly gets attention after the crime occurs. It frequently happens when a crime gets public attention on social media after it occurs months later

(Kounadi et al., 2015). Variables related to the likelihood of discussing general or specific crimes on social media include homicide, crime with a knife, and crime involving young victims (Kounadi et al., 2015).

Compared to using social media posts to analyze general crime patterns, it may be much more beneficial to help understand public reaction to individual crime incidents of public interest (e.g., Cvetojevic & Hochmair, 2018; Powell et al., 2018). For instance, an analysis of tweets after the 2015 Paris terrorist attack shows that both the public and professional journalists used *Twitter* to spread information, and tweets with pictures were widely circulated (Cvetojevic & Hochmair, 2018). Social media can also be useful in detecting and measuring fear of crime (Prieto Curiel et al., 2020). Studies show that social media consumption of crime-related content is significantly related to fear of crime (e.g., Intravia et al., 2017; Näsi et al., 2021). In this regard, a study on a sample of college students revealed that, compared to crime-related content in traditional mass media, social media has a much greater impact on college students' fear of crimes (Intravia et al., 2017). This result is not in the least surprising because social media is prevalent among the younger generations, and their attention to mass media is very limited (see Chapter 2).

Based on the distinctive noteworthy aspects of social media we discussed in Chapter 1 (e.g., the public as a content producer, the prevalence of false information, and social media algorithms) and some empirical studies we have discussed earlier, it is safe to conclude that social media is not simply a more effective replication of traditional mass media. It introduces a new set of societal effects on its own. Accordingly, its impacts on crime must be continuously examined and documented. Because of these distinctive and additive features of social media, research around social media and crime will yield far different from those which typify earlier studies of mass media effects on crime. For example, social media allows users to be information providers. If social media users can contribute reliable, timely information during a crime event, social media can help in the fight against crime.

For instance, the Vancouver Police Department used videos and pictures posted on *Facebook* to investigate a 2011 riot in their city and made hundreds of arrests accordingly (Schneider & Trottier, 2012). However, if social media users in such contexts contribute and spread misinformation consciously or unconsciously, they can be regarded as accomplices to crimes being committed. For example, in January of 2024 nude images of Taylor Swift created by AI tools went viral on *Twitter*. These fake images were viewed more than 27 million times with over 260,000 likes within 19 hours before being removed (Burke, 2024). It is reported that the fake images disseminated could be traced back to *4chan*, an online imageboard website widely known for its controversial content (Gibson, 2024).

The technology, often called "deepfake," is the creation or manipulation of facial and bodily appearance in pictures and videos (Juefei-Xu et al.,

2022). While there is a long history of misuse of doctored pictures and videos which were once quite easily detectable, AI makes detection far more difficult. A 2020 study on a sample of 2,005 participants found that only 50.8% of them were not deceived by a deepfake product (Vaccari & Chadwick, 2020). The rate is almost equal to simple guessing. Creating and spreading fake news, pictures, and videos constitutes only a small portion of what criminals can do to cause harm on social media. In the following two sections, we discuss how social media has impacted "old-fashion" crimes and enables "new-fashion" crimes known as cybercrimes.

Enhancing Traditional Crime With Social Media

When criminal justice and criminology textbooks discuss crime rates in the U.S., two major national crime statistics are often relied upon: the annual Uniform Crime Reports (UCR) and the annual National Crime Victimization Survey (NCVS). The UCR is traditionally viewed as the official source of crime statistics in the U.S. It is compiled by the Federal Bureau of Investigation (FBI) regarding crimes known to police agencies (Walsh & Jorgensen, 2020). At least three reasons make the UCR an incomplete compilation of crimes occurring in the U.S. The first is that the UCR does not include federal crimes committed before 2014 (Walsh & Jorgensen, 2020). The second reason is that U.S. police agencies' participation in the UCR program is voluntary; although most agencies have chosen to contribute to the effort, some have not taken active part; and among those participating, often their compliance with reporting requirements is haphazard (Walsh & Jorgensen, 2020). The third reason is that the UCR only captures crimes that receive police attention. Crimes that have not been reported to the police are captured by the UCR. Despite these noteworthy limitations, the UCR can still be viewed as a highly valuable official record of crime rates.

The UCR features two groupings of crimes. The first group, "Part I offenses" (also known as "index crimes"), includes the most severe crimes (Walsh & Jorgensen, 2020). The index crimes include four violent crimes (i.e., murder, forcible rape, robbery, and aggravated assault) and four property crimes (i.e., larceny-theft, burglary, motor vehicle theft, and arson). Crime rates (per 100,000 population) of these eight index crimes from 2013 to 2019 are shown in Figure 3.1. Forcible rape and aggravated assault increased over this time-period. Robbery, burglary, larceny-theft, and arson decreased. Murder and motor vehicle theft remained largely the same over the period 2013 to 2019. The second UCR grouping, "Part II offenses," includes crimes commonly viewed as less severe (Walsh & Jorgensen, 2020). Some examples are vandalism, fraud, embezzlement, prostitution, gambling, DWI, public drunkenness, and drug offenses. To be noted, the UCR does *not* include every type of crime, even some crimes which have many victims and broad

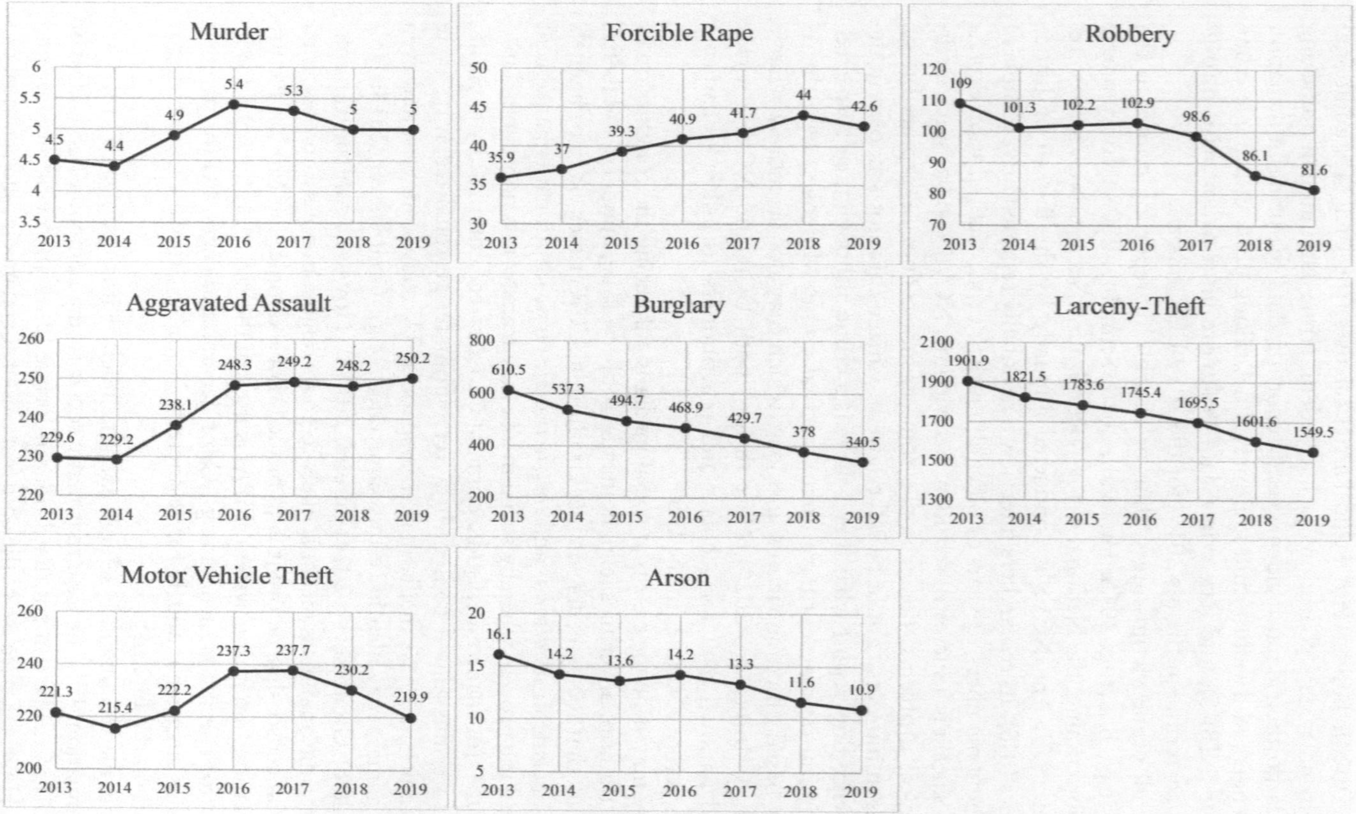

FIGURE 3.1 Crime rates (per 100,000 inhabitants) of eight index crimes in Uniform Crime Reports from 2013 to 2019.

Source: FBI: UCR, Crime in the U.S. (available at https://ucr.fbi.gov/crime-in-the-u.s)

societal impacts, such as identity theft (Hu et al., 2021a, 2023; Randa & Reyns, 2020). Besides Part I and Part II offenses, the UCR has additional supplementary data collections such as federal crime data, human trafficking data, cargo theft data, incident-based reporting data featuring information on offenders and victims and multiple crimes taking place in a single crime incident (NIBRS), and hate crime data (for more information, visit https://ucr.fbi.gov/crime-in-the-u.s/2019/ for the 2019 UCR report).

Not all crime victims are willing or capable of reporting crimes to the police (e.g., Boateng, 2018; Hu et al., 2020; Schnebly, 2008). To overcome this shortcoming, the National Crime Victimization Survey (NCVS) was created in 1973. The NCVS is conducted annually by the Bureau of Justice Statistics (BJS). Its researchers interview a nationally representative sample of household members 12 years or older about their crime victimization experiences. Since it is a survey of self-identified victims, NCVS also has some methodological problems. For example, some crimes cannot be captured (e.g., victims in murders cannot be interviewed). Citizens are not schooled in the law; hence they report what they believe is a crime although their suspected victimization may not have been an actual crime. Moreover, reporting is largely based on crime victims' memory, which may not be entirely reliable (Walsh & Jorgensen, 2020). Nevertheless, both UCR and NCVS provide fruitful national data for scholars and practitioners to utilize to gather a broad picture of crimes in the U.S.

How may it be the case that social media is enhancing the commission of these "traditional" crimes (e.g., homicide, robbery, rape, burglary, and theft)? We think that social media enhances traditional UCR crimes via two channels of enhancement: *ideational* and *instructional*. First, ideational enhancement refers to the process whereby social media may transform a noncriminal into a criminal (or make an episodic criminal into a career criminal) by exposing them to crime-related content in a very intimate, personalized way. Note that traditional mass media (e.g., newspapers, TV shows, movies, and even video games) may also have this same effect (e.g., Greitemeyer, 2018; Hollingdale & Greitemeyer, 2014; Surette, 2015a). However, content transmitted in traditional mass media is likely to go through a process of professional editorial censorship before it is published. For example, the Motion Picture Association film rating system (MPA) is used in the U.S. to rate content suitability for specific audiences (e.g., G for general audiences, PG for parental guidance suggested, and R for restricted). Nothing akin to such filtering is present on the Internet.

Social media content is seldom examined before it is "published" for mass dissemination. It is the case that many social media companies do endeavor mightily to delete content that is inappropriate (often involving violence and hate). However, because of the core features of social media, such content can be widely viewed even if it gets deleted with dispatch. For example, several reporters have reported on a case wherein a deranged offender beheaded his own father and displayed his severed head in a *YouTube* video (Winter et al., 2024 from NBC; Hadero & Swenson, 2024 from AP; Goldman, 2024 from CNN). According to these reporters, the video was circulated for hours before it was removed (Goldman, 2024). It should be noted that there is a certain period between uploading videos to *YouTube* and having it viewed by the public, a time gap which leaves *YouTube* a short period to review video content. Even with this "safety window review period," *YouTube* failed to filter this horrific violent content. Of course, we should not expect social media companies to be able to filter all inappropriate content for us; the volume of postings is such that this is an unreasonable expectation at this time. It goes without saying that it is even more difficult to filter inappropriate content in live streams and private groups on social media (e.g., *Telegram* and *Messenger*).

It is easy for troubled persons to become immersed in violent and hateful content on social media. In a 2016 study, the authors collected and analyzed about 512 million tweets made in one year and identified roughly 20,000 hate speech tweets (Silva et al., 2016). More than 37% of these tweets target black people (Silva et al., 2016). Other hate targets include white people, gay people, rich people, Chinese people, Indian people, religious people, Jewish people, and overweight people (Silva et al., 2016). We hasten to point out that some hate targets, such as overweight people, are generally not included in official hate crimes counts (e.g., UCR hate crime data); these acts of hate speech can be deeply harmful to the people attacked (Silva et al., 2016). Moreover, even though hate speech takes up only a relatively small proportion of social media posts, social media platform algorithms may *reinforce* hate-filled minds by circulating hate-inspiring content (Hu & Lovrich, 2020). There is no doubt that individuals' minds will be impacted by social media content. Many possible explanations for such harmful effects can be found within the theories of individual and organizational social media behavior discussed in Chapter 1 and criminological theories which will be discussed later in this chapter.

Besides ideational enhancement, which impacts the minds of criminals, instructional enhancement can likewise impact criminal behavior. The crime described in the opening story is a good example of using social media as an instrument for committing crimes. Social media can be used to identify potential targets, acquire and improve criminal skills, develop counter-investigation capabilities, and contact criminal associates. In 2016, celebrity Kim Kardashian was robbed of $10 million worth of jewelry in Paris (France & Verdier, 2016). As one of the most popular stars in social media circles, Kardashian had 84 million followers (364 million as of February 2024) on *Instagram* and frequently posted pictures of herself on that social media platform. These posts, according to the police, led her to be robbed in Paris (France &

Verdier, 2016). Meanwhile, social media may impact crime via promoting "performance crime" – "[individuals] performing acts of crime and deviance in order to record them, share them, and upload them to the Internet" (Yar, 2012, p. 246). The previously noted beheading case is a good example. Performance crime can vary from minor crimes such as open drug use and petty theft to serious crimes such as homicide and terrorism (Surette, 2015b). Surette (2015b) argues convincingly that although performance crime has existed for a long time, the advent of social media has made performance crime much more prevalent.

One study on homicide provides a good example of how social media can enhance homicide both ideationally and instructionally. In a study on 48 homicides, Yardley and Wilson (2015) identified six different ways in which social media was implicated in the homicides committed by perpetrators. The first involves social media posts spurring homicidal actions. Some perpetrators committed homicides because they were deeply offended on social media, and they were moved to attack their victims offline (Yardley & Wilson, 2015). The second involves the use of social media to conduct performance crimes (Surette, 2015b; Yar, 2012), where perpetrators used social media to broadcast their intentions to kill and then commit homicide (Yardley & Wilson, 2015). The third involves hostile exchanges on social media which get escalated and lead to offline killings (Yardley & Wilson, 2015). The fourth is that some perpetrators use social media to fashion a fantasy and then fulfill that fantasy (Yardley & Wilson, 2015). The fifth involves that social media is used to lure victims into a trap (Yardley & Wilson, 2015). And the sixth one is to use social media to hinder investigations by making postings from their victims' social media accounts making it seem that the victims are still alive (Yardley & Wilson, 2015). Although the public likely think it is a rare occurrence, social media homicide confessions are not uncommon (Yardley, 2017).

Enhancing Cybercrime With Social Media

Cybercrime has been receiving increasing attention in recent years. Crime reports and victim surveys, which often measure conventional crimes, have started collecting data on cybercrime (e.g., UCR and NCVS). A broad meaning of cybercrime is used as crimes committed by criminals who "attack, offend, threaten, humiliate, harass, steal from, and otherwise harm victims and exploit and damage computers and other technological devices" (Maras, 2017, p. 4). There are a few noteworthy features of cybercrimes. First, cybercrime is not restricted by geographical locations (Maras, 2017). Hackers, for instance, can commit (or try to commit) hacking from anywhere in the world. This feature also makes investigating cybercrime and arresting cybercriminals difficult in the absence of international collaboration. Second, a few types of cybercrime do not only exist exclusively in the cyber world. For example, stalking often occurs in a face-to-face situation, and cyberstalking is one of the most common cybercrimes. Cybercrime involves using the Internet, computers, and other digital devices (Maras, 2017), while conventional crime often involves person-on-person physical force.

It is difficult for victims to detect some types of cybercrime in a timely manner (e.g., identity theft). Despite the difficulty of detection, cybervictims, just like conventional victims, suffer emotional distress, physical distress, and financial loss (e.g., Golladay, 2017; Randa & Reyns, 2020). Some types of cybercrime are committed on a large scale. For example, in a data breach incident regarding *Capital One*, over 100 million customers' personal information were stolen (Chapple, 2019). In another data breach regarding the *Equifax* credit bureau, 147 million individuals were impacted (Cowley, 2019).

In her book *Cybercriminology*, Maras (2017) divides cybercrime into six categories. The first category is cybertrespass and cybervandalism. Cybertrespass refers to unauthorized access to digital systems and devices (Maras, 2017). The most common cybertrespass is hacking. After illegally getting access to digital systems and devices, criminals can commit other types of cybercrime, such as cybertheft and cybervandalism. Social media provides hackers with a useful platform for recruiting, sharing knowledge and tools, and performing coordination (Babko-Malaya et al., 2017). Meanwhile, social media has become a great tool for conducting social engineering – a psychological manipulation of individuals so they divulge confidential information (Uebelacker & Quiel, 2014). The most common performance of social engineering is phishing. Offenders often use fake emails and messages, forged online banks and payment sites, and false emergencies to collect personal information, such as usernames, passwords, credit card information, home addresses, social security numbers, and medical records (Aleroud & Zhou, 2017). For example, you may receive an email from the Internal Revenue Service (IRS), or at least looks like it is from the IRS, asking you to help solve an urgent issue related to your tax returns. The email contains a link and asks you to click the link to reset your bank account information. If you do that, your bank account information, personal information, and money will be taken. In fact, to combat phishing, the IRS created an email account (phishing@irs.gov) to collect phishing scams related to the IRS.

This example is the most common and accessible form of social engineering. There are other forms of social engineering (Salahdine & Kaabouch, 2019). For example, offenders may pretend to develop a romantic relationship with victims on social media. After establishing trust, they execute exploitation and then disappear (Salahdine & Kaabouch, 2019). Successful phishing may create a chain effect. Once offenders access victims' emails and social media accounts, they can perform a secondary phishing strategy by using these real emails and social media accounts to send false information to

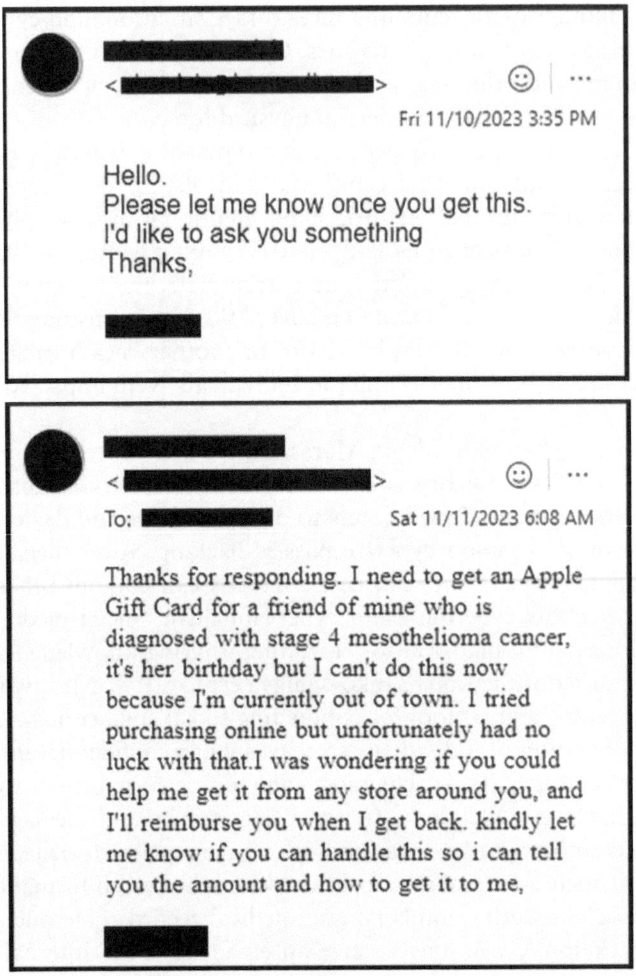

[redacted]
<[redacted]>
Fri 11/10/2023 3:35 PM

Hello.
Please let me know once you get this.
I'd like to ask you something
Thanks,

[redacted]

[redacted]
<[redacted]>
To: [redacted] Sat 11/11/2023 6:08 AM

Thanks for responding. I need to get an Apple Gift Card for a friend of mine who is diagnosed with stage 4 mesothelioma cancer, it's her birthday but I can't do this now because I'm currently out of town. I tried purchasing online but unfortunately had no luck with that.I was wondering if you could help me get it from any store around you, and I'll reimburse you when I get back. kindly let me know if you can handle this so i can tell you the amount and how to get it to me,

[redacted]

FIGURE 3.2 An example of social engineering via phishing.

additional potential victims. One of the current book authors once received an email from his friend (Figure 3.2 top). He double-checked and verified the email address and the signature. He replied and got another email (Figure 3.2 bottom). Eventually, he checked with his friend through the phone and confirmed that the friend's email was hacked. Cybertrespass, hacking, and social engineering are often the starting points of other types of cybercrime, such as cyber vandalism. Cyber vandalism refers to defacing websites. In 2015, two *Twitter* and *YouTube* accounts belonging to the U.S. Army were taken over by ISIS supporters for close to an hour (ABC News, 2015). The ISIS supporters replaced the account logo of the U.S. Central Command with the message "I love you isis" (ABC News, 2015).

The second category is cybertheft. The target of cybertheft can be either money or personal information (e.g., medical records, financial records, home addresses, and bank accounts). The most common cybertheft is identity theft. Unlike in the past when identity thieves stole personal mails, tampered with ATMs, or went through trash cans, nowadays identity thieves are more prone to steal personal information via the Internet (Hu et al., 2021a). What is most troublesome, a person can be an identity theft victim even if he or she does not engage in high-risk behavior (Hu et al., 2023). Data breaches on a large scale are not uncommon (e.g., Chapple, 2019; Cowley, 2019). Researchers have highlighted the growing importance of studying social media and identity theft as more and more people conduct much of their business on the Internet (e.g., Irshad & Soomro, 2018; Patel et al., 2017; Reznik, 2012). As we noted in the discussion in social engineering and phishing, social media is a powerful tool for offenders to gather information on victims and "customize" their strategies. Offenders can steal others' profile pictures, create fake profiles, pretend to be victims' acquaintances, and conduct social engineering (Shahria et al., 2020).

The third category is interpersonal cybercrime, which often includes cyberbullying, cyberharassment, and cyberstalking (Maras, 2017). Cyberbullying often occurs among youths, and it has significantly negative impacts on their well-being (Garett et al., 2016; Giumetti & Kowalski, 2022). Studies have shown that the use of social media is one of the common approaches employed to conduct interpersonal cybercrime. In a 2015 study, the venues reported by victims who are being bullied are texting (56.8%), followed by *Twitter* (45.5%), *Facebook* (38.6%), *Instagram* (13.7%), and *YouTube* (11.4%) (Whittaker & Kowalski, 2015). Similar to cyberbullying, social media can be a tool for conducting cyberharassment and cyberstalking (e.g., Burke Winkelman et al., 2015; Kaur et al., 2021; Kircaburun et al., 2018; Stevens et al., 2021; Van Laer, 2014). For example, the non-consensual dissemination of intimate images, recognized as image-based sexual abuse, often occurs on social media such as *Twitter* and *Telegram* (McGlynn & Rackley, 2017; Semenzin & Bainotti, 2020; Uhl et al., 2018). Sometimes, these images (and videos) are fake (e.g., Juefei-Xu et al., 2022; Vaccari & Chadwick, 2020). Cyberbullying, cyberharassment, and cyberstalking can occur on social media 24/7. Offenders can be completely anonymous. Content on social media can persist for a long time (Maras, 2017).

The fourth category is cyberdeviance, which involves cybercrime related to a violation of social norms and expectations (Maras, 2017). Such violation is not always illegal. Maras (2017) offers an example of online paraphilias, where paraphilia can be either legal (e.g., foot fetish) or illegal (e.g., biastophilia). The legality of some types of cyberdeviance is determined by local jurisdictions. For instance, online gambling or sports betting is legal in some countries and illegal in other countries (Maras, 2017). Besides the fact that social media can directly provide such information (e.g., *OnlyFans*), it also provides an efficient way of disseminating and marketing deviant content (Kaakinen et al., 2020). For example, studies on online gambling find that social media users may actively share gambling promotions with other social media users or other gamblers (e.g., Gainsbury et al., 2015, 2016). At this point, it seems that social media is effective in accelerating the spread of non-criminal deviant content (e.g., foot fetish pictures and videos, gambling in some jurisdictions where online gambling is legal).

The fifth is organized cybercrime. Like organized crime, it involves different types of cybercrime (often conventional) and is run by an organized crime group (Maras, 2017). Common illicit activities are hacking, identity theft, online fraud, selling drugs and firearms online, online prostitution, and online trafficking. In a study on *Craigslist*'s impact on prostitution trends, Chan and colleagues (2019) demonstrated that *Craigslist* led to a 17.58% increase in prostitution across 1,796 U.S. counties. Additionally, they find that most prostitution activity on *Craigslist* is controlled by organized vice groups; only a small proportion involves voluntary participation (Chan et al., 2019). It is worth noting that Chan et al.'s study used data from 1999 to 2008 when *Craigslist* was one of the most popular classified advertisements websites. Nowadays, social media seems to be the primary advertising platform for online prostitution (Juditha et al., 2022).

The last category is political cybercrime. The methods of committing political cybercrime can vary, such as hacking and cybervandalism, but political cybercrime aims to reach a political goal (Maras, 2017). An example is that Russian hackers cyberattacked the homepage of the Ukrainian president and pro-Chechen websites (Maras, 2017). In another example, Maras (2017) describes a retaliation for the Ku Klux Klan (KKK) by *Anonymous*, one of the world's most famous hacker groups. The KKK posted radical tweets after the grand jury decided not to charge former officer Darren Wilson who had killed Michael Brown, an unarmed African American. *Anonymous* hacked the KKK's *Twitter* account and revealed the identity of its members (Maras, 2017). Although *Anonymous*'s hacktivism is political cybercrime, the public indeed supported its action against the KKK (Maras, 2017). This brings us to an ongoing debate on whether socially acceptable but legally unacceptable behavior constitutes a crime.

Social Media and Criminological Theories

Criminological theories endeavor to explain why individuals commit crimes and informs the criminal justice system on how to deal with these offenders. There are various criminological theories to be considered, not all of which are affected by social media. In this section, we select several of the most popular criminological theories and connect them to the use of social media. For each theory, we first introduce the theory and discuss its theoretical framework. Then, we cite and summarize a few related studies to illustrate how contemporary criminologists have used the theory to structure their research. At the end, we incorporate social media into each theory and discuss how social media may impact factors related to each theory. We believe that the criminological theories presented in this chapter, together with social media behavior theories presented in Chapter 1, provide a most useful interpretation of the relationship between social media and crime.

Crime and Personality

Personality is defined as "the enduring configuration of characteristics and behaviors that comprise an individual's unique adjustment to life" (American Psychological Association, 2018). There are many components of personality, such as self-concept, values held, and emotional patterns displayed (APA, 2018). Criminologists call these components *personality traits* (Walsh & Jorgensen, 2020). A notable thing about such traits is that every individual has all the traits, but they are each expressed at different levels. For example, we all are capable of aggression. Some people express more aggression than others. Personality traits, and all the other factors proposed by different criminological theories to be discussed later, affect the likelihood of committing crimes. Some factors increase the likelihood of criminal conduct while others decrease it.

Some personality traits have been shown to be associated with criminal behavior. For example, impulsiveness refers to the tendency to act without thinking too much about the consequences (Eysenck, 1981). Sensation seeking refers to the tendency to actively look for risky sensations (Zuckerman, 1990). Both impulsiveness and sensation seeking are strong predictors of substance use, and substance use is strongly associated with adult crime and delinquent behavior (Delcea & Enache, 2021). Besides substance use, other types of addiction (e.g., alcohol and gambling) are also related to crime and delinquency (Jennings et al., 2015; Lind et al., 2015). Negative emotionality refers to the tendency to view many situations as negative and react negatively to them (Tipples, 2008). Empathy refers to the ability to understand the feelings of others (Walsh, 2012). Weak empathy has been shown to be associated with the development of antisocial and criminal behavior (Jolliffe & Farrington, 2004; Trivedi-Bateman & Crook, 2022). Agreeableness refers to the tendency to be friendly and helpful and willing to work with others (Walsh, 2012). Conscientiousness refers to an organized, disciplined, and responsible trait (Roberts et al., 2014). Both low agreeableness and low conscientiousness are related to offending (Walters, 2018).

Some personality theories have been developed to explain why particular personality traits predispose some individuals to crime. For example, arousal theory argues that people differ in their arousal patterns in the autonomic nervous system (ANS) and reticular activating system (RAS) (Kochanska & Aksan, 2004; Walsh, 2012). Individuals with low arousable ANS and/or RAS tend to have difficulty in socialization, experience no fear, and feel no guilt or remorse after wrongdoing (Walsh, 2012). Lifestyle theory argues that crime occurs because of "thinking errors" that criminals make due to biological and/or environmental conditions (Walters, 1990). For instance, living in a poor neighborhood with a high unemployment rate and high gang activities can lead to criminals coming to believe that joining a gang is the only way they can survive their circumstances. A personality type that is often depicted by the media is that of the profoundly antisocial personality. We usually call these people psychopaths or sociopaths, criminals lacking sense of guilt, empathy for others, and moral shame (Walsh, 2012).

Studies have reported that social media and personality are likely mutually influenced. Some studies suggest that certain personality traits (e.g., conscientiousness and openness) are significantly related to the frequency of social media use (e.g., Özgüven & Mucan, 2013) and how social media is used (e.g., Seidman, 2013). In return, social media posts can be used to predict the personality traits of users (e.g., Azucar et al., 2018; Golbeck et al., 2011). In a 2016 study, researchers were able to predict personality traits using social media profile pictures (Liu et al., 2016). In another study, researchers found evidence that high frequency of social media use can increase neuroticism and reduce honesty (Andrews et al., 2020). Given these types of evidence, it can be safely assumed that the pattern of use of social media may impact crime and delinquency via its advert impact on personality for some social users.

Rational Choice Theory

Rational choice theory assumes that individuals, including criminals, make decisions based on a combination of personal and situational factors (Cornish & Clarke, 2014). These decisions are made by evaluating possible pleasures (benefits) they will gain and possible pains (costs) they will suffer. Individuals will choose crime if the perceived pleasures are significantly more than the perceived gains in a criminal act (Walsh & Jorgensen, 2020). Individuals' rationality is bounded, however, we all try to make the best life decisions based on our available knowledge and innate cognitive abilities. As Clarke and Cornish (2001) point out, "Offenders are generally doing the best they can within the limits of time, resources, and information available to them" (p. 25).

To further investigate the benefits and costs of a criminal act, scholars argue that costs considered can be formal costs (e.g., being arrested by the police) and informal social costs (e.g., disappointing others), and benefits can be intrinsic (e.g., the thrill of violating social norms), monetary, and social (e.g., status in a gang) (Matsueda et al., 2006; Pratt, 2008; Thomas et al., 2022). Benefits and costs are often subjective in nature, with some individuals highly valuing formal costs while others highly valuing informal social costs. The same applies to the personal calculation of benefits. The subjective variance among people is due to both individual factors (Loughran et al., 2016) and environmental factors (Thomas et al., 2022). In a 2022 study, Thomas and colleagues (2022) reported that neighborhood disadvantages are associated with individuals' lower perception of the social costs of crime and being arrested by the police and their higher perception of social rewards. Meanwhile, individuals' perceived neighborhood disadvantages were positively related to their tolerance of the risks and costs associated with crime (Thomas et al., 2022).

We argue that it is likely for social media to affect people's rational choice calculations regarding the commission of crime and delinquency. The argument is based on a fundamental fact – social media provides individuals with much more *objective* information, whether the information is about benefits or costs of crime. The burglary in the opening story is a good example of how social media provides information on more benefits (valuable assets) and fewer costs (less likely to be caught). Meanwhile, social media provides individuals with more *subjective* information. For example, regarding cyberbullying, many victims choose to bully back (Whittaker & Kowalski, 2015). They have seen other teenagers doing the same thing without being punished. Accordingly, they feel that they will be less likely to be punished for cyberbullying as well.

Deterrence Theory

While many criminological theories seek to explain why individuals commit crimes, deterrence theory tries to answer the question of why individuals do not commit crimes. Deterrence is the prevention of crimes by using or threatening the use of punishment (Walsh & Jorgensen, 2020). Scholars often discuss two types of deterrence: general deterrence and specific deterrence. General deterrence aims to impact the general population by publicly punishing one individual and using this individual as an example to others, including potential criminals (Lab, 2016). For example, even in the course of the most vehement disagreements we do not murder our neighbors in part because we know that the punishment for murder is severe. Specific deterrence aims to keep criminals from committing crimes in the future (Lab, 2016). For instance, an ex-offender tries to stay law-abiding after being released from prison because he or she does not want to reincarcerated. Two aspects of punishment are also essential to make both general deterrence and specific deterrence work as intended. The *certainty* of punishment refers to the likelihood of being caught and punished for a criminal activity (Paternoster, 1987). The *severity* of punishment refers to the pains (costs) meted out for a criminal offense (Paternoster, 1987). It is reasonable to assume that both high certainty and severity of punishment lead to a deterrence effect. However, this does not mean that the severity of punishment should always be set at the maximum, such as life in prison for a petty theft. Proportionality between crimes and punishments is a key feature of a just legal system.

While rational choice theory sets a foundation for deterrence theory in its assumption that offenders and potential offenders are rational and fear punishment for crime commission, empirical evidence suggests that only "a marginal deterrent effect for legal sanctions" typically obtains (Paternoster, 2010, p. 765). Most available evidence suggests that legal punishments (e.g., mandatory minimum sentences) and punishment threats (e.g., intensive supervision probation) have a rather minimal effect on crime deterrence (Nagin, 2013; Pratt et al., 2017). This disconnect may be primarily due to the typically long-delayed imposition of punishment by the criminal justice system (Paternoster, 2010). For example, in the U.S. a significant number of offenders never get arrested. Based on the 2019 UCR Index Crimes, among the violent crimes, tracked murder has the highest clearance rate (61.4%), followed by aggravated assault (52.3%), rape (32.9%), and robbery (30.5%). Among property crimes, arson has the highest clearance rate (23.8%), followed by larceny-theft (18.4%), burglary (14.1%), and motor vehicle theft (13.8%). To be noted, UCR Index Crimes report only four types of violent crimes (i.e., murder and nonnegligent manslaughter, rape, robbery, and aggravated assault) and four types of property crimes (i.e., burglary, larceny-theft, motor vehicle theft, and arson). Selected as the most severe violent and property crimes, these eight types of crime enjoy more police resources than other types of crime. Even so, the clearance rates are low. Moreover, the UCR features only those crimes reported to the police. It follows that the actual clearance rate of crimes may be much lower than what we report here.

Besides legal punishment, non-legal punishment factors may deter crimes more effectively (Paternoster, 2010). For example, researchers have found that focused deterrence approaches adopted by the police have achieved noteworthy crime reductions (e.g., Braga & Weisburd, 2012). Focused deterrence, often referred to as "pulling-levers policing," often sends direct messages to offenders that immediate and intense police response will come their way if they trigger something unwanted by the police (e.g., gang violence) (Braga & Weisburd, 2012). In the example of the Boston Operation Ceasefire program, gang members are told by the police that the Ceasefire Working Group will come after them intensively if gangs engage in violent behavior (Braga & Weisburd, 2012). Studies also find that, in many situations, the social costs of criminal behavior (e.g., shame and loss of respect) produce a better deterrent effect than severe legal punishments (Lee, 2017; Pratt et al., 2017). A meta-analysis of deterrent theory-inspired research studies suggests that the certainty of punishment (Paternoster, 1987) tends to deter white-collar crimes rather effectively (Pratt et al., 2017). Considering all the foregoing, deterrence theory may still be considered valuable in explaining why some individuals do not commit some types of crimes.

Similar to our argument on social media's impact on rational choice, social media may provide potential offenders with enough information on the severity of punishment to deter them from committing crime or engaging in delinquency. Specifically, social media shame may play a significant role. For example, Hu and Lovrich (2020) argue that the ubiquity of camera phones has greatly affected police use of force actions. Law enforcement leaders and the police understand full well that they are now being watched 24/7 by many members of the public; any serious misconduct is now highly likely to be recorded and rapidly disseminated on social media channels reaching audiences both near and far (Hu & Lovrich, 2020). An in-depth discussion on how social media can be used to deter crime is featured in Chapter 7.

Self-Control Theory

Self-control theory argues that individuals with lower self-control are more likely to commit crimes. The definition of self-control is "the extent to which people are vulnerable to the temptations of the moment" (Gottfredson & Hirschi, 1990, p. 87). Individuals with low self-control may have the following traits: (1) they are oriented to the present more than the future; (2) they are drawn to risk-taking; (3) they lack persistence, patience, and diligence; and (4) they are self-absorbed and feel little guilt after committing crimes (Walsh & Jorgensen, 2020; also see Gottfredson & Hirschi, 1990, pp. 89–90). Low self-control primarily comes from poor parenting and a lack of adequate socialization in early childhood (Tehrani & Yamini, 2020; Walsh & Jorgensen, 2020). It tends to persist over the long term and negatively impacts important life experiences such as employment, school commitment, and marriage (Gottfredson & Hirschi, 1990). Gottfredson and Hirschi (1990) argue that criminal opportunity is another reason why low self-control individuals tend to commit crimes disproportionately. Studies on morality and self-control indicate that a strong sense of morality uprightness can diminish, even sometimes eliminate, the effect of low self-control (Antonaccio & Tittle, 2008; Schoepfer & Piquero, 2006; Wikström & Svensson, 2010; Wikström & Treiber, 2007).

The relationship between low self-control and crime and delinquency has been well established by many empirical studies (e.g., Hay & Meldrum, 2015; Wright et al., 1999). Cross-sectional, longitudinal, and meta-analysis studies have amassed substantial empirical support for this relationship (Baron, 2003; Burt & Simons, 2013; Tehrani & Yamini, 2020; Vazsonyi et al., 2017). The relationship appears to remain strong throughout life (Gottfredson, 2017). Since the connection between low self-control and crime is empirically solid, many crime prevention programs focus on improving children's self-control through the parenting process (Gottfredson, 2017). For instance, a meta-analysis on early self-control improvement programs suggests that these programs are highly effective in reducing delinquency (Piquero et al., 2016). Sadly, low self-control individuals also have a higher likelihood of being victims of both personal and property crimes (Pratt et al., 2014; Schreck, 1999). Moreover, low self-control seems to be a strong predictor of online victimization, where risk-taking can produce many unfavorable results (Pratt et al., 2014).

When low self-control is coupled with social media addiction (e.g., Du et al., 2018), it is likely that social media is compounding self-control problems. Meanwhile, an indirect relationship between social media and self-control may be assumed. Low self-control comes from incompetent parenting and inadequate socialization in early childhood (Walsh & Jorgensen, 2020). We may be able to predict that a child who grows up in a family where both parents are addicted to social media and neglect the child's needs may develop a low self-control trait.

Labeling Theory

Labeling theory argues that individuals' behavior is impacted by the label attached to them (Besemer et al., 2017). For example, a child who has been called the "son of criminals" is more likely to be delinquent than a child not so labeled. Two major perspectives may explain how labeling works. First, individuals who have been labeled are more likely to associate with delinquent peers, as they feel that they are "one of them" (Paternoster & Iovanni, 1989). Second, individuals who have been labeled are more likely to be pushed into a criminal lifestyle because their noncriminal pathways (e.g., jobs and education) are blocked (Bernburg & Krohn, 2003; Besemer et al., 2017; Kirk & Sampson, 2013). An interesting part of labeling theory is that it argues that no act is a crime by its nature; instead, a criminal act is defined by how it is judged by others (Walsh & Jorgensen, 2020). For example, homosexual behavior was considered as crime in many states in the U.S. It was not until 2003 that all laws against homosexual behavior were invalidated by the U.S. Supreme Court in *Lawrence v. Texas*. Thus, labeling theory shifts the focus from criminals (why they commit crimes) to the criminal justice system (why some acts are crimes) (Walsh & Jorgensen, 2020).

Scholars of labeling theory argue that the criminal justice system amplifies, not reduces, offending behavior (e.g., Besemer et al., 2017; Mingus & Burchfield, 2012). This statement has received overwhelming support from empirical studies (Bernburg, 2019). For example, in a study on 677 juveniles, researchers found that formal criminal justice intervention (measured by arrest) increases juveniles' delinquent self-identity and association with delinquent peers and decreases their prosocial expectations (Restivo & Lanier, 2015). In a longitudinal study on 870 adolescents, researchers found that formal juvenile justice system involvement (e.g., probation, community service, detention, and appearance before the court) increased their involvement in deviant groups (e.g., gangs) and engagement in serious delinquency (Bernburg et al., 2006). In another longitudinal study across 16 years, Lopes and colleagues (2012) observed that individuals who are arrested or contacted by the police at age 14–18 are more likely to be involved in crimes and arrested at age 21–23. They are also more likely to be unemployed at age 29 and use drugs at age 29–31 (Lopes et al., 2012). Therefore, it is very likely that being labeled by the criminal justice system has an adverse impact on individuals' behavior (criminal and non-criminal) throughout their life course. It seems, however, that some factors can overcome criminal labeling. For example, a qualitative study on 23 juvenile offenders found that their desire to change and move to new neighborhoods can help them desist from committing more crimes (Abrah, 2019).

It is not difficult to imagine that social media makes criminal labeling worse. The reentry of ex-offenders into society becomes more difficult when criminal information spreads on social media. Meanwhile, criminal labeling may lead ex-offenders to have no choice but to hang out with other ex-offenders (and offenders) on social media.

Social Learning Theory

Social learning theory holds that individuals commit crimes because they learn how to do so from others. Moreover, embedded in operant psychology, social learning theory explains why individuals commit crimes and why they continue or desist from them (Walsh & Jorgensen, 2020). Operant psychology asserts that human behavior is governed by its consequences through a reinforcement or punishment process (Skinner, 1965). There are four types of reinforcement and punishment (Skinner, 1965). *Positive reinforcement* (i.e., rewards received) and *negative reinforcement* (i.e., punishments received) will reinforce behavior and make it more likely to persist (Skinner, 1965). For example, if we want a teenager to desist from a local gang, we can use extra pocket money (positive reinforcement) and not be grounded (not given punishments) for not participating in gang activities. We can also use being grounded (given punishments) and make the teenager lose his street gang reputation (not given rewards) for participating in gang activities. Social learning theory places a major emphasis upon the concept of *differential association* (Sutherland et al., 1992) – "the interactions that persons have with others in their peer group such as neighbors, churches, schoolteachers, the law, and authority figures, as well as "virtual groups" such as those established through the mass media, the internet, etc." (Akers & Jennings, 2016, p. 232). Social learning theory holds that differential association will impact an individual's attitudes and values toward crime, deviant behavior, and conforming behavior, which further affects his or her nonconforming or conforming behavior (Akers & Jennings, 2016).

Empirical research provides "greater empirical support for social learning theory than for any other major social psychological theory of crime and deviance" (Akers & Jensen, 2017, p. 37). Social learning theory has been proven to help explain engagement in many types of crimes, such as sexual crimes (e.g., Felson & Lane, 2009), intimate partner violence (e.g., Cochran et al., 2017), violent crimes (e.g., Koon-Magnin et al., 2016), theft (e.g., Brauer, 2009), stalking (e.g., Fox et al., 2011), gangs (e.g., Smith et al., 2019), terrorism (Akers & Silverman, 2014), juvenile delinquency (e.g., Watt et al., 2004), and even police shootings of unarmed suspects (e.g., Maskaly & Donner, 2015). For example, offenders who are sexually abused as a child are more likely to commit sexual offenses, and offenders who are physically abused as a child are more likely to commit violent offenses (Felson & Lane, 2009). In a 2010 meta-analysis of 133 empirical studies related to social learning theory, Pratt et al. (2010) found that *differential associations* (parents' behaviors and attitudes, peers' behaviors and attitudes, and others' behaviors and attitudes) and *definition* (individuals' criminal beliefs) are consistently the strong predictors of crime and deviance. Also, they found that differential reinforcement (parental reactions, peer reactions, others' reactions) and imitation (role models' behavior) are somewhat weaker but nonetheless significant predictors of crime and deviance (Pratt et al., 2010).

There is no doubt that social media plays an important role in social learning. Individuals nowadays can learn about many different things via distance learning. For example, they can learn violent norms from violent social media posts. They can learn criminal skills from other criminals active on social media. Most studies on the relationship between social learning and crimes involve face-to-face peers. Virtual peers, however, have been found to be just as important as face-to-face peers in explaining digital deviance (e.g., illegally downloading software, music, or videos) and traditional deviance (e.g., theft and assault) (Miller & Morris, 2016).

Social Bond Theory

Social bond theory emphasizes the importance of social control in explaining and predicting criminal behavior. Hirschi (1969) identifies four elements of social bonds: attachment, commitment, involvement, and belief. Attachment refers to the emotional bonds between individuals and their immediate others, such as family, school mates, and friends (Hirschi, 1969). Family and friendship bonds make us feel valued and respected (Walsh & Jorgensen,

2020). Commitment refers to the dedication that individuals invest in achieving personal goals (Hirschi, 1969). For example, if an individual spends much time and effort on their work, they are less likely to be committing crimes. Involvement is a consequence of commitment (Walsh & Jorgensen, 2020). If a person is dedicated to conventional activities such as school work, sports, or a job, he or she will have scant opportunity for exposure to criminal activities (Walsh & Jorgensen, 2020). The concept of belief refers to adherence to mainstream social norms (Hirschi, 1969). Individuals who subscribe to these social norms are less likely to commit crimes than those who do not attempt to live by such norms.

Social bond theory has received overwhelming evidence, especially in juvenile delinquency studies. Research has strongly suggested that persons who have stronger attachment, deeper commitment, greater involvement, and firmer belief are less likely to commit crimes and engage in deviance (e.g., Basto-Pereira & Farrington, 2022; Durkin et al., 1999; Hoeve et al., 2012; Hoffmann & Dufur, 2018; Krohn & Massey, 1980). Moreover, having strong social bonds helps offenders and delinquents desist from further crime and delinquency (e.g., Abeling-Judge, 2021; Rocque et al., 2013). Additionally, weak social bonds are associated with a higher likelihood of being victimized (e.g., Popp & Peguero, 2012). Social bond theory is also often tested along with self-control theory. Low self-control is associated with weak social bonds, resulting in a high likelihood of crime and delinquency (e.g., Back et al., 2018; Intravia et al., 2012; Longshore et al., 2004; Manzoni & Schwarzenegger, 2019).

Social media certainly can be used to enhance social bonds regarding all four aspects of bonding. For example, social media can help maintain emotional bonds between persons and their family and friends. It can help set personal goals in which an individual can invest their energy. Social media distance learning can be used to acquire job skills, helping an individual remain gainfully employed. Social media is also used often to broadcast mainstream social norms and provide living examples of noble conduct. However, all these functional uses of social media can turn on their head. For example, social media addiction may diminish an individual's bonds with family and friends. Social media may give an individual an unrealistic goal that is impossible to achieve by established conventional approaches to self-betterment. Access to criminal activities is facilitated by social media, and criminal subcultures are ubiquitous on the Internet. This fact provides a good segue to the next topic – dealing with how goal setting and emulation of success can often lead to criminal engagement.

General Strain Theory

As a principal tenet of general strain theory, strain theory holds that a major pathway to committing crimes comes from the adoption of challenging goals and expectations. First, society puts pressure on its members to achieve goals valued by that society (e.g., the American dream and wealth accumulation in the U.S.) (Merton, 1938). Second, many individuals lack legitimate means to the achievement of these goals (Merton, 1938). Given this situation, people must adapt by either rejecting these goals or using illegitimate means to attain those goals (Merton, 1938). Derived from strain theory, general strain theory expands the sources of strain to include three major types: (1) actual or anticipated failure to achieve positively valued goals; (2) actual or anticipated removal of positively valued stimuli; and (3) actual or anticipated presentation of negatively valued stimuli (Agnew, 1992, p. 47). The first type is similar to the strain proposed by Merton (1938): individuals cannot reach their goals (called traditional strain; see Lilly et al., 2018). The second type means that individuals lose things they value, and the third type means that individuals are treated negatively (Lilly et al., 2018).

In general, the more strains an individual experiences the more likely they are to engage in crimes via criminal adaptation. There are objective strains (conditions disliked by society) and subjective strains (conditions disliked by an individual) (Agnew, 2013). Compared to objective strains, subjective strains are more likely to impact crime and delinquency (Agnew, 2013). Meanwhile, some strains are more likely to result in crime and delinquency than others. Agnew (2017, p. 319) summarizes four features of those strains which are the most salient for criminal engagement: (1) strains perceived as unjust; (2) strains perceived as high in magnitude; (3) strains related to low self-control; and (4) strains related to incentives to committing crime and delinquency.

For example, accidents, illnesses, or serious injuries are all strains, but they are not directly related to crime or delinquency (Agnew, 2017). Individuals who experience such strains will differ markedly in how they weather such inevitable life's storms. Many people will learn valuable lessons from adversity and move on; others will be seriously derailed into deviance. General strain theory proposes several factors that materially diminish the likelihood of a criminal adaptation after a life shock. The factors of major significance are a strong sense of self-efficacy, demonstrated coping ability (resilience), presence of social support from family and friends, the fear of punishment for wrongdoing, and lack of access to illegal means (Agnew, 1992). General strain theory views strain as a direct consequence of negative (self-harming) emotions caused by troubled relationships with others important in one's life (Walsh & Jorgensen, 2020).

Like social bond theory, general strain theory has received much empirical support. All three types of strain (i.e., failure to achieve valuable goals, paucity of valued objects, and introduction of negative stimuli) are positively associated with crime and delinquency (e.g., Agnew & White, 1992; Broidy, 2001; Broidy & Agnew, 1997; Moon et al., 2009; Pérez et al., 2008; Piquero & Sealock, 2010). Some studies also show that these types of strain can also lead to weakened social bonds which, according to social bond theory, result in a high likelihood of criminal engagement and delinquency (e.g., Agnew, 2013; Paternoster & Mazerolle, 1994).

Research in this area has found that social media can create new strains, such as approval anxiety and misinformation (Wolfers & Utz, 2022). For example, seeing many stories of noteworthy accomplishments and happy people celebrating their successes on social media may trigger self-doubt, envy, and resentment (i.e., anticipated failure to achieve positively valued goals). However, social media can also serve as a resource for self-help (Wolfers & Utz, 2022). For example, social media may help individuals under stress to build and sustain social capital (Domahidi, 2018). Social media may also be used as a coping tool (Wolfers & Utz, 2022). Individuals experiencing stress may find social support on social media (e.g., victims on social media, see Chapter 5), and they can use social media as a healthy distraction from ongoing strains (De Wit et al., 2020).

Social Disorganization Theory

Social disorganization theory was originally built upon a 20-year epidemiological study of 21 U.S. cities. Based on longitudinal analyses, researchers were moved to observe that neighborhood ecological characteristics greatly impact individuals' criminal behavior (Shaw & McKay, 1942). Persons living in areas afflicted with high rates of crime, persistent poverty, inadequate housing, and high population turnover are substantially more likely to commit crimes than people residing in more favorable neighborhoods (Shaw & McKay, 1942). Social disorganization, a term reflecting such conditions in some urban neighborhoods, is argued to negatively impact crime presence in two major ways: (1) the lack of informal social control and (2) the lack of prosocial values (Walsh & Jorgensen, 2020). Originally, prosocial values were believed to be formed by a group of individuals of the same race, culture, or ethnicity in a community. When individuals from other races, cultures, or ethnicities move to this community, they also bring different values and social norms that conflict with the existing ones (Shaw & McKay, 1942). Hence, the community starts losing its sense of community, and it becomes disorganized (Walsh & Jorgensen, 2020). Crimes and delinquency occur. The original notion of prosocial values was limited to racial or ethnical factors. Contemporary criminology prefers the concept of *collective efficacy*, which refers to the extent to which community members are able to get together to improve their community (Sampson, 2004). This capacity for effective collective action can be achieved by having shared goals, shared norms, and shared expectations (Walsh & Jorgensen, 2020). Social cohesion is another term applied to this same notion of ability for a local community to come together for community improvement (Hirschfield & Bowers, 1997).

Research has shown that low level of collective efficacy, lack of informal social control, lack of social support, lack of opportunity, high ethnic heterogeneity, high residential instability, weak local friendship networks, and lack of financial resources in the neighborhood are predictive of neighborhood high crime and delinquency rates (e.g., Errol et al., 2021; Kingston et al., 2009; Markowitz et al., 2001; Sampson & Groves, 1989; Steenbeek & Hipp, 2011). Although social disorganization theory plays a critical role in explaining neighborhood crime and delinquency (Bellair, 2017), a number of scholars have called for the incorporation of additional variables of interest. Factors such as urban economic and political contexts, presence of formal social control in the neighborhood, networks of cultural and social interaction, and reciprocal effects of crime on community have all been proposed as additional areas of likely relevance (e.g., Charis & Ronald, 2017; Lynch & Boggess, 2016; Warner, 2003).

From a crime prevention perspective (see Chapter 7), building strong collective efficacy and informal social control in a community can reduce crime and delinquency. Social media may have two opposite effects on collective efficacy and formation of social control. In some communities, residents are willing to join community social media groups (e.g., *Facebook* groups) and contribute to managing their communities together with their neighbors. In other communities, social media may contribute to community disorganization. For example, gang members who join two rival gangs may expand their reach via social media and add to the divisiveness present. There is good reason to believe that social media can have adverse impacts on physical disorganization (e.g., abandoned houses and graffiti). Narratives, pictures, and videos of physical disorganization on social media may attract more offenders to come to this neighborhood, as well as push law-abiding residents to move out.

Broken Windows Theory

Broken windows theory observes that if a window in a building is broken and no one fixes it, other windows will be broken in due course. The unfixed window sends out a message to the surroundings that no one is taking care of the building, there is no cost to breaking more windows, and breaking windows is always fun (Kelling & Wilson, 1982). Broken windows theory argues that signs of deviant behavior (e.g., vandalism), physical disorders (e.g., graffiti), social disorders (e.g., prostitution), and crimes (e.g., gang) will create an environment that encourages more crimes to occur committed by persons sensing that few guardians are on duty, and few people care if crime is taking place (Kelling & Wilson, 1982). Moreover, it argues that minor disorders and crimes, if left unaddressed, will lead to more serious disorders and crimes (Kelling & Wilson, 1982). Therefore, from a broken windows perspective, if we want to prevent serious crimes, we need to address visible minor crimes by active intervention and public display of enforcement actions to communicate that disorder crimes are not tolerated (Kelling & Coles, 1997).

Studies on broken windows theory provide somewhat equivocal empirical evidence of the efficacy of the theory. Some studies have shown that disorder has strong effects on crimes and residents' quality of life (e.g., Chappell et al., 2011; Kelling & Coles, 1997; Konkel et al., 2019; Xu et al., 2005). Some studies have reported that disorder indirectly impacts crime and crime prevention efforts through its direct impact on fear of crime and collective efficacy (e.g., Gau et al., 2014; Ren et al., 2019). Other studies find minimal or no effects (e.g., Cerdá et al., 2009; Harcourt & Ludwig, 2006; O'Brien et al., 2019; Rowan, 2017).

Broken windows theory is often used to justify policing strategies focusing on order maintenance, disorder reduction, and misdemeanor enforcement. For example, the police can make more misdemeanor arrests and work with municipal agencies to address street lighting and disorder issues such as condemned properties maintenance. Results are also mixed regarding the advisability of such efforts. Some studies suggest that these kinds of policing strategies can reduce actual crime rates and improve residents' perceptions of crime rates in the neighborhood (e.g., Berk & MacDonald, 2010; Braga et al., 2015; Messner et al., 2007; Rosenfeld et al., 2007) while others do not (e.g., Taylor, 2018; Weisburd et al., 2011). Moreover, aggressive broken windows policing (e.g., many arrests for minor crimes) may lead to unwanted consequences that can become criminogenic (e.g., Collins, 2007; Howell, 2009). Based on the mixed results observed, some scholars have called attention to efforts to address "broken windows" through such activities as proactive problem-solving partnerships with local communities and reducing the presence of signs of physical disorders (e.g., removing graffiti and improving street lighting) (Welsh et al., 2015). While empirical findings are mixed in this area, the deeply experienced scholar Wesley Skogan (2008) points out that we must take signs of disorder seriously because "disorder undermines the capacity of neighborhoods to defend themselves; those who can do so move away, many of those remaining withdraw from community public life, and everyday uses of public space wither" (Skogan, 2008, p. 196).

Broken windows theory has several connections to social media. Besides, we argue that social media can be effectively utilized as an important tool to use to address "broken windows" (disorders), especially for the police engaged in open collaboration with a crime-ridden neighborhood. The police can make use of social media in various ways to improve police-public relations, facilitate problem-solving with people in the community, and enhance intelligence collection for addressing social and physical disorders (Hu & Lovrich, 2020). We elaborate on this theme in some detail in our next chapter.

Routine Activity Theory

Routine activity theory (RAT) views crimes as being in major part the consequence of the simultaneous presence of motivated offenders, suitable targets, and the absence of effective guardianship (Cohen & Felson, 1979). A motivated offender refers to a criminal or a potential criminal who is willing and able to commit crimes (Felson & Cohen, 1980). A suitable target refers to a person or property that the offender wishes to victimize (Lilly et al., 2018). A capable guardian can be a person (e.g., family, friends, security personnel, the police, and the owner of the suitable target) and/or security devices such as CCTV cameras and security alarm systems (Lilly et al., 2018). Routine activity theory also emphasizes crime opportunity – the three elements must converge in time and space (Lilly et al., 2018). A crime is less likely to occur if any one of these three elements is missing.

Research has shown that three elements of routine activity theory can be used effectively to explain many street crimes and victimization, such as robbery, shoplifting, drug use, vandalism, and sexual offense (e.g., Culatta et al., 2020; Drawve et al., 2014; Groff, 2007; Miller, 2013; Pusch & Holtfreter, 2021). Routine activity theory can also be applied to the understanding of online crime and victimization, including, but not limited to, virus attacks (e.g., Choi, 2008), hacking (e.g., Leukfeldt & Yar, 2016), online harassment (e.g., Holt & Bossler, 2008; Marcum et al., 2010), Internet fraud (e.g., Pratt et al., 2010), online threatening (e.g., Van Wilsem, 2011), malware (e.g., Bossler & Holt, 2009), phishing (e.g., Hutchings & Hayes, 2009; Leukfeldt, 2014), identity theft (e.g., Hu et al., 2023; Williams, 2016), and cyberstalking (e.g., Reyns et al., 2011). Not all the studies conducted in this area have found significant relationships between RAT variables and online crime/victimization (e.g., Bossler & Holt, 2009; Leukfeldt, 2014). However, some RAT variables have been shown to be negatively associated with online crime/victimization, such as using anti-virus software/programs, spending less time on social media, doing less online shopping, doing less Internet banking, adding few online strangers to one's friends list, doing less downloading, and engaging in less online communication (Choi, 2008; Hu et al., 2021a; Leukfeldt & Yar, 2016; Marcum et al., 2010; Pratt et al., 2010; van Wilsem, 2011).

There is no doubt that routine activity theory can be used to understand the relationship between social media activities and crime, particularly cybercrime. A few studies have explored this topic in considerable detail (e.g., Al Boni & Gerber, 2016; Arntfield, 2015; Kumar et al., 2021; Vakhitova et al., 2019; Zhang et al., 2022). For example, exposure to offenders (e.g., social media activities and social media friends) is significantly related to cyberharassment victimization (Näsi et al., 2017). In another study, it was shown that individuals who use more types of social media platforms, update social media more often, have more photos on social media, add strangers as friends on social media, believe some online friends are deviant, and personally involve in online deviance are more likely to become cyberstalking victims (Reyns et al., 2011). In general, more risky social media activities (i.e., suitable targets) and use of fewer cybersecurity management approaches (i.e., lack of guardianship) lead to more cybercrime victimization (Choi & Lee, 2017).

Developmental Theories

Developmental theories argue that the causes of crimes change across the lifespan, along with biological, psychological, and social conditions of living (Walsh & Jorgensen, 2020). Developmental theories focus on exploring risk factors – variables that may increase the likelihood of committing crimes during the lifespan. For example, personality risk factors are having an attention-deficit/hyperactivity disorder (ADHD) condition, high aggression expression, antisocial behavior inclination, drug abuse, recklessness (high risk taking), and dishonesty. Family risk factors are criminal parents, poor parenting, victim of child abuse, broken home (family disarray), and weak child–parent relationships. School risk factors are low school performance, poor attitude toward school, and being a victim of school bullying. Peer risk factors are having antisocial friends, delinquent peers, and friends who are in a gang. Community risk factors are high crime rates in the neighborhood, unstable population, and physical disorganization (for a complete list, see Walsh, 2012, p. 151). Using these risk factors, developmental theories try to explain "the onset, acceleration, and deceleration of offending, and finally desisting altogether" (Walsh, 2012, p. 148).

There are three development theories worth noting. In *super traits theory*, Agnew (2005) identifies five life domains related to crimes: (1) personality (e.g., low self-control and low empathy), (2) family (e.g., poor parenting and child abuse), (3) school (e.g., negative school experiences and school bullying), (4) peers (e.g., delinquent peers and gang friends), and (5) work (e.g., unemployment and low-paying job). In *integrated cognitive antisocial potential* (ICAP) *theory*, Farrington (2003) focuses on the development of antisocial potential (AP) in individuals. When they have opportunities, individuals with higher AP are more likely to demonstrate deviant behavior (Farrington, 2003). There are long-term AP and short-term AP variants. Individuals with short-term AP may temporarily increase AP to respond to a situation (Farrington, 2003). This is usually not a matter of major consequence. However, individuals with long-term AP tend to come from low-income families and are poorly socialized, and they tend to offend across the entire life course (Farrington, 2003). Meanwhile, short-term AP may become long-term AP through the reinforcement of offending (Farrington, 2003).

The previous two theories explain how risk factors can send individuals to a criminal trajectory from early childhood to later adulthood. The *age-graded theory* emphasizes human agency and environmental circumstances and argues that individuals are not "locked" by risk factors to a criminal trajectory (Walsh & Jorgensen, 2020). Sampson and Laub (2017) argue that life consists of a series of major transitions and that there are numerous turning points that can change one's life's trajectory. These turning points – such as marriage, taking a new job, going off to military service, going away to college – will bring offenders back to prosocial life and facilitate crime desistance (Sampson & Laub, 2017). Laub and Sampson (2006) explain that these turning points can lead to the creation of strong social bonds and increase informal controls. Meanwhile, these turning points alter offenders' routine activities from unstructured to structured and fill them with prosocial responsibility (Lilly et al., 2018).

Social media may be used to understand risk factors related to personal, family, school, peer, and community. It appears to be that at least some real-life risk factors can be transferred to some risk factors on social media. For example, aggression in reality may be transferred to aggression on social media (e.g., Eraslan & Kukuoglu, 2019; Mishna et al., 2018). Hanging out with deviant friends may be transferred to associating with deviant friends on social media (e.g., Reyns et al., 2011). Offenders and victims of school bullying are more likely to be offenders and victims of cyberbullying (e.g., Sobkin & Fedotova, 2021). Meanwhile, risk factors on social media and in reality are mutually influenced (e.g., Andrews et al., 2020; Azucar et al., 2018).

Biosocial Criminology

In recent years, biosocial criminology has become a more prevalent feature of criminological research. Advocates of biosocial criminology argue that besides individual and social factors, one's brain patterns, one's genes, and one's hormones should also be considered in the study of engagement in crime (Walsh & Jorgensen, 2020). Some well-studied biological and genetic factors studied by scholars are discussed in the following paragraph.

Serotonin is believed to have a positive relationship with self-control – a factor that impacts criminal behavior (Gottfredson & Hirschi, 1990). A low level of serotonin is related to low self-control (Crockett et al., 2010). Another hormone, testosterone, is believed to have a positive relationship with violent behavior and impulsiveness (Armstrong et al., 2022). Cortisol is believed to have a negative relationship with social aggression (Terburg et al., 2009). Resting heart rate is believed to have a negative relationship with antisocial behaviors (Boisvert et al., 2020). Regarding genes, the MAOA gene and its relationship with aggression was discovered by a group of genetic researchers in the Netherlands (Brunner et al., 1993). In a short version, a low activity level of MAOA is associated with a poor regulation of aggression in humans, which in turn leads to use of violence in adults and delinquency among children (Brunner et al., 1993; Cooke et al., 2018). Regarding brain functions and structures, reward dominance theory argues that the imbalance of behavioral activating system (BAS) and behavioral inhibiting system (BIS) may lead individuals to be addicted to pleasures such as gambling, alcohol, drugs, and some forms of crime (Day & Carelli, 2007; Walsh, 2012). BAS is impacted by dopamine and pleasure areas in the brain, and BIS is impacted by serotonin and memory areas in the brain (Walsh, 2012). Prefrontal dysfunction theory argues that individuals who have a dysfunctional frontal lobe (an area in the brain) are less likely to keep themselves from hurting others (Walsh, 2012). To be noted, biosocial criminology does not argue that there is a "criminal gene," "criminal hormone," or "criminal area in the brain" of a criminal. Biosocial criminology emphasizes the interaction between biological/genetic factors and environmental factors (Barnes et al., 2016). Therefore, although social media does not affect an individual's biological or genetic traits, it may amplify the effects of these traits on an individual's behavior via interacting with environmental factors, such as family, school, and peers, as we discussed in the previous sections.

Social Media and Criminology: An Integrated Model

Our review on social media, crime, and criminological theories highlights four major points. First, crime is evolving along with the development of technology. New technology produces new crimes and new methods for the commission of "old" crimes. Appropriate legislation is always delayed with respect to these new crimes and new criminal methods (e.g., cyberstalking and cyberbullying). Thank goodness, researchers can swiftly investigate these topics and provide empirical evidence for appropriate legislation. Second, criminology is moving forward into new areas of research to keep up with technological change which is truly relentless. Researchers will continue developing new theories, revising contemporary theories, and empirically testing these theories to understand new crimes and new criminal methods facilitated by social media. For example, the ubiquity and many variations of cybercrime may require the development of a major subfield of *cybercriminology*. Third, it is unlikely that a single criminological theory will be able to explain all types of crimes and juvenile delinquency. Accordingly, when we test a criminological theory, we can benefit from the incorporation of selected variables from other theories. For instance, self-control is now often included in testing social bond theory and general strain theory, particularly with respect to cybercrime offending. Fourth, social media can impact many factors that have been empirically shown to have a relation to the commission of crime and engagement in juvenile delinquency. Because of the prevalence of use of social media in contemporary society, we argue with deep conviction that researchers should include variables related to social media when they empirically test criminological theories. Accordingly, we propose here an integrated model of social media and criminology (Figure 3.3) to advance our argument.

The core element of the model reflects the belief that the widespread use of social media in contemporary society will influence the five essential elements of an individual's decision-making with respect to engaging in criminal behavior. The first element is related to personal factors. For example, social media use has an association with self-control (Du et al., 2018), aggression (Eraslan & Kukuoglu, 2019), and neuroticism (Andrews et al., 2020). Social media may also provide individuals with coping skills to fight against stress (Wolfers & Utz, 2022) and enhance social capital (Domahidi, 2018). The second element is family. For instance, parents' addiction to social media may lead to poor parenting. Social media also provides individuals with a convenient form of communication so they may stay close to their family. The third element is related to peer associations. Clearly, social media can be used to communicate with delinquent peers and groups of youth engaged in deviant conduct (Miller & Morris, 2016), but it can also be used to remain closely connected with positive role models and gain emotional support from supportive friends. We argue here that connection to positive role models and supportive law-abiding friends on social media do not require exclusively face-to-face friendships. Social media influencers are quite popular today, especially among teenagers and young adults. Unfortunately, research on social media influencers currently clusters heavily in business and marketing with only scant presence of criminal justice topics (e.g., Kay et al., 2020; Ki & Kim, 2019).

The fourth element is related to social factors. Social media can be used with major impact to disseminate social norms and build collective efficacy in a community (e.g., *Facebook* group for neighborhood watch). At the same time, social media may also promote the spread of social disorders (e.g., online prostitution and rumor mongering). The last element is related directly to the criminal justice system. For example, social media may change a person's belief toward the justice system, and social media often polarizes opposing beliefs because of how its algorithms are designed to attract and sustain the attention of platform users (see Chapter 1). Meanwhile, social media provides individuals the opportunity to interact with criminal justice system actors without being in the system (e.g., being arrested or serving as a juror). We cover these topics in considerable depth in the following chapters.

A final point needs to be made concerns how we might best measure social media use in studying its connections to crime commission and engagement in delinquency. We think items designed to measure an individual's social media use should meet both breadth and depth requirements. The breadth

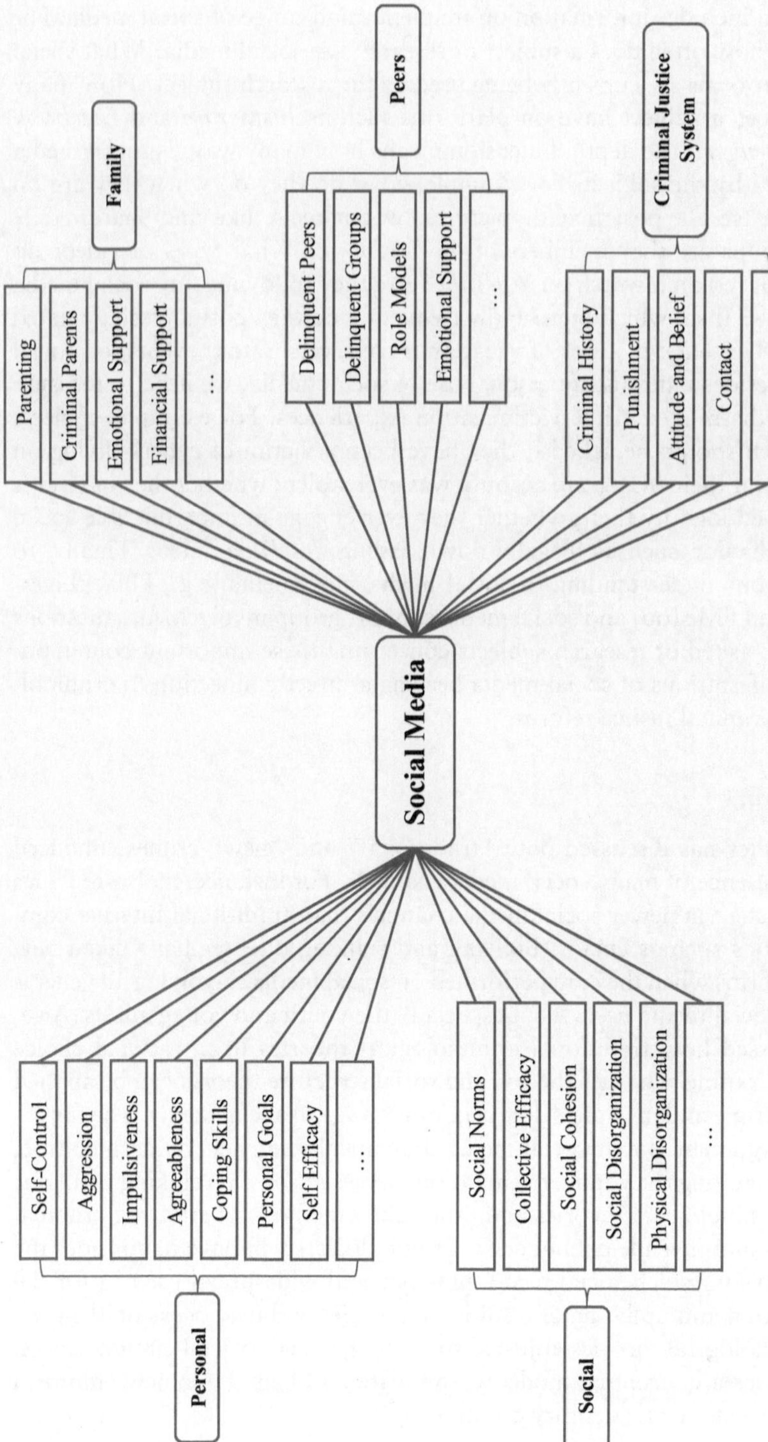

FIGURE 3.3 An integrated model of social media and criminology. To be noticed, these variables are not exhaustive. They are sample variables in each category.

dimension includes information on frequency and range of social media. For example, how often does a subject of research use social media? What social media platforms are currently being used by the research subject? How many friends does a subject have on platforms such as *Instagram* and *Facebook* and *Messenger*? The depth dimension means how many ways is social media being used by the subject. For example, what do they do when they are on *Facebook* (scroll, post text or pictures, watch reels, like and share, etc.)? What groups are they members of on *Facebook*? What types of videos do subjects of research watch on *YouTube*? Are they following any social media influencers? If so, which ones? How frequently do they post anything related to themselves (e.g., pictures of vacation travels, celebratory events) on social media? Besides patterns of personal use of social media, we need to measure social media-related crime victimization experiences. For example, subjects of research should be asked if they have been a victim of cyberbullying on *Facebook*; if their *Instagram* account was ever stolen; whether they have ever experienced identity theft; whether they ever engage in impermissible social media behavior, such as illegally downloading *YouTube* videos. Finally, to promote our understanding of social media movements (e.g., #BlackLivesMatter and #MeToo) and social media support group involvement, questions should be asked of research subjects concerning these important contemporary manifestations of social media bearing a direct connection to criminology and criminal justice reform.

Conclusion

This chapter has discussed both "traditional" and "new" crimes enhanced by the presence of many social media channels. For instance, malware issues spread faster via newer social media channels than traditional Internet communications such as emails. Bullying and stalking offenses have taken new horrific forms when they are performed on social media, involving all generations of social media users – but especially the youth and young adults. Also, we discussed how traditional criminological theories (e.g., rational choice theories, routine activities theory, and social structure theory) can be applied to adult crime and juvenile delinquency in the age of social media. The fundamental argument is that social media dramatically impacts modern culture, especially among the younger generation, necessitating a rethinking of all our major criminological theories and established methods of studying criminal offending and juvenile delinquency. Criminologists will have to consider the many ways in which social media presence and widespread use call for the modification and updating of traditional theories and may occasion the need for criminological theories adjusted to contemporary societal circumstances. We advance a conceptual model to stimulate and help guide new empirical research work in 21st-century criminology.

4

SOCIAL MEDIA AND THE POLICE

Opening Story: How did a small police department chief become a social media superstar within a year? Chief Oliver was the chief of the Brimfield Ohio Police Department. He was also the person who maintained the department's *Facebook* page. The department had fewer than 20 sworn officers and served a town with a population of approximately 10,000. However, the department had over 160,000 "likes" on *Facebook*, which made it second place among all police agencies in the U.S. on *Facebook* as of October 1, 2014 (The first one is the New York Police Department with over 280,000 "likes.") (Hu & Lovrich, 2020). Chief Oliver wrote most of the *Facebook* posts in an informal tone and used a great deal of humor, making the department's page very entertaining to the public. Meanwhile, he used a lot of self-made slang. For example, "crazy cousin" refers to the department's followers on *Facebook*. The term "bed and breakfast" refers to the county jail. And the term "mope" refers to an offender (Hu & Lovrich, 2020). According to his book, "*No Mopes Allowed*," people from all 50 states and 29 foreign countries regularly visited the department's *Facebook* page (Oliver, 2013). However, the department's fame did not last for very long. No *Facebook* posts were made between December 23, 2014 and August 14, 2015 (Hu & Lovrich, 2020). Local newspapers reported that Chief Oliver was accused of sexual harassment by one of his female officers (Jones, 2016). Later, Chief Oliver pleaded *no contest* to four misdemeanor charges (Jones, 2016). People can still buy Chief Oliver's book on Amazon. One posted comment observed, "I didn't see the twist coming at the end where he turns out to be a criminal too."

DOI: 10.4324/9781003360049-5

How Do the Police End Up Using Social Media?

Chief Oliver's successful use of social media to engage with the public occurred almost ten years ago. Imagine what would happen if he were posting today with various social media platforms newly available (e.g., *TikTok*) and an unimaginable number of social media users (almost five billion worldwide as of October 2023; see Statista, 2023w). Meanwhile, we should carefully analyze and evaluate Chief Oliver's social media strategy to avoid falling into the undesirable "leader branding" trap (Hu & Lovrich, 2021). In this section, we discuss why the police *have little choice but to* make effective use of social media, focusing on police adoption of new transportation and communication technologies historically and the development of policing strategies in recent decades. Also, we discuss why the police *need to endeavor to* use social media to prevent and fight crimes more effectively and to maintain a strong, interactive police-public relationship.

Technology and the Evolution of Policing Strategies

Advances in technology have revolutionized police practices repeatedly in the past (Chan, 2001). From call boxes, two-way radios, police vehicles, to DNA identification and body cameras, technology has played a pivotal role in the evolution of policing (Hu & Lovrich, 2020). A very brief and admittedly oversimplified history of American policing illustrates why and how the police have ended up using social media today. American policing practice is rooted in England, with British settlers bringing the *night watch system* to American shores prior to independence (Walker & Katz, 2018). By the 1800s, Sir Robert Peel, the father of modern policing, established the London Metropolitan Police based on military organizational command rank principles and a strong connection of civil society institutions (Cox et al., 2013). By the middle of the 19th century, some major American cities had replaced the old night watch system with centralized and government-supported police agencies focusing on fighting crime, crime prevention, and some aspects of public service delivery (Walker & Katz, 2018). These functions later developed into four major police tasks deemed appropriate in a democratic society: (1) law enforcement; (2) order maintenance; (3) service delivery; and (4) crime prevention (Hu & Lovrich, 2020). If we combine the latter three tasks, the police have two *core missions*: (1) crime-fighting and (2) the provision of ongoing proactive public service (Pollock, 2019).

These two core missions have evolved along with the maturation of the American political system. The first era (1830s to early 1900s) in American policing is often described as the *political era* (Anderson & Newman, 1998). Police officers developed a strong tie to the major political parties which came into prominence over time, and one of their major tasks was to help local politicians gain voter loyalty to the dominant political party in their community (Langworthy & Travis, 2002). Police officers were selected based less on high standards of conduct and ability and more on the basis of their partisan loyalty (Walker & Katz, 2018). They received very limited training and tended to use excessive force in enforcing laws. Americans generally viewed their local police agencies as corrupt and notoriously partisan (Cox et al., 2013). The second era (the early 1900s to 1970s) started with the recognition of police professionalism proposed by August Vollmer, known as the father of American policing and police professionalism. To achieve police professionalism and separate the police from the realm of political affairs, Vollmer and his colleagues adopted five approaches: (1) providing police officers with higher education and ongoing in-service training; (2) centralizing police administration and holding police officers and agencies accountable for misconduct; (3) avoiding political influence; (4) establishing specialized police units; and (5) incorporating modern technology into police work (Langworthy & Travis, 2002). Because of persistently high crime rates, particularly drug-related crimes, in the 1960s and 1970s, the police focused primary attention on crime-fighting and crime control through the progressive militarization of police practice (Hu & Lovrich, 2020).

Seeking a decisive victory in the war on crime, the police used an aggressive arrest approach, an approach which led in time to mass incarceration and patently undesirable consequences vis-à-vis racial and ethnic disparities (Hu & Lovrich, 2020). The public started losing faith in the police, particularly people of color. Police officers were isolated from the public they were sworn to protect and serve (Cox et al., 2013). They became resistant to the help offered by the public because they did not think the public knew how to fight crime and deal with offenders (Sparrow et al., 1992). In the early 1980s, police administrators and scholars came to the recognition that the police acting on their own could neither control crime nor maintain a good police-public relationship (Cox et al., 2013). The ideas of problem-oriented policing (POP) and community-oriented policing (COP) were proposed as citizen engagement-based alternatives to progressive militarization and aggressive arrest, and American policing entered its third era (1980s to present).

A further examination of the POP and COP era conducted by Oliver (2000, 2008) divides the period into three "generations." The period of 1979 through 1986 was seen as the "innovation generation" phase, as two major publications attracted major attention among both scholars and public decision-makers. One publication introduced POP (Goldstein, 1979), and another introduced broken windows theory (Wilson & Kelling, 1982). Oliver (2008) argues that these two publications laid the foundation for the emergence of COP. COP practices started to appear in policing in a few large municipal police agencies such as Baltimore and Houston (Hu & Lovrich, 2020). The period of 1987 through 1994 was seen as the "diffusion generation" when COP became widely known and broadly adopted in many large police agencies. COP programs and units were established using state and federal funding (Oliver, 2008). However, during this period, smaller police agencies were slow to adopt COP in part due to a chronic paucity of resources (Oliver, 2008).

The period from 1995 to current times was seen as the "institutionalization generation." With substantial local, state, and federal funding, medium- and small-sized police agencies could develop their own COP programs – or at least include COP in their policing strategies (Oliver, 2008; Zhao et al., 1999). Oliver (2008) concludes that "the institutionalization of community-oriented policing has improved policing in the United States" (p. 19). Today, POP and COP have become the major policing strategies in almost every police agency. COP has also been widely adopted in Europe, Australia, and New Zealand (Hu & Lovrich, 2020). The President's Task Force on Twenty-First Century Policing (2015) represents the ultimate flowering of the COP perspective. The task force proposed six "pillars" supporting democratic policing: (1) building trust and legitimacy; (2) policy and oversight; (3) technology and social media; (4) community policing and crime reduction; (5) officer training and education; and (6) officer safety and wellness (The President's Task Force, 2015; see also Hu & Lovrich, 2020, p. 51). The six pillars reinforce our expectation in contemporary policing that the police should not only succeed in fighting crime but also provide services to the public and build favorable police-public relations while promoting legitimacy, transparency, and accountability (Mayes, 2021).

Reasons for Police Adoption of Social Media

The high standard of modern policing requires the police to adapt to the context of their external social environment (Walker & Katz, 2018). The existing, and perhaps future as well, social environment is one in which both criminals and the public are using social media on a broad scale. Police administrators, and their stakeholders, increasingly emphasize evaluating both what the police do and how they do their jobs as police accountability measures proliferate in the wake of documented cases of police brutality and the advent of the Black Lives Matter movement (e.g., Schenwar et al., 2016). Accordingly, we believe that police agencies – along with the other elements of the criminal justice system – must make effective use of social media in the digital age to develop and publicize the use of evidence-based practices in the performance of their mission to serve and protect.

First, social media can help the police fight crime. Entering the 21st century, cybercrime and crime via social media have become commonplace, as we have discussed in Chapter 3. The rapid development of cybercrime and social media crime has forced the police to respond. For example, some police agencies have used social media-monitoring software to mine crime-related posts (Parascandola, 2011). It usually does not require a warrant to search public social media posts (Murphy & Fontecilla, 2012). Additionally, social media can be a good information-gathering tool (Mergel, 2012), especially in an era of homeland security (Oliver, 2008). Before social media appeared, the police had used their official websites to post wanted-suspect profiles. However, the public seldom pays attention to police websites. Social media provides a solution to distribute in a timely manner wanted-suspects profiles to a large audience at low cost (Hu & Lovrich, 2020). Many studies have provided empirical evidence suggesting that wanted-suspects posts constitute a substantial proportion of police social media posts on social media platforms such as *Facebook* (e.g., Dai et al., 2017; Hu et al., 2018) and *Twitter* (e.g., Crump, 2011; Heverin & Zach, 2010; Jungblut & Jungblut, 2022). Additionally, social media can help the police gather information on non-crime-related cases of particular public safety interest, such as missing persons and runaway youth (Jeanis, 2020).

Second, social media helps the police establish and maintain strong police-public relations (Hu & Lovrich, 2020). A number of studies have shown that police-public relation posts often constitute a major proportion, if not the greatest proportion, of police social media postings on social media platforms such as *Facebook* (e.g., Hu et al., 2018; Livingstone, 2022), *Twitter* (e.g., Kudla & Parnaby, 2018; O'Connor, 2017), and *Instagram* (e.g., Walby & Wilkinson, 2023). This phenomenon can be understood as an effective use of the new communication channel which social media provides. The police have historically relied upon traditional mass media (e.g., newspapers, radio, and TV) to broadcast their information and to display their preferred public image (Surette, 2015a). Often, that image portrays the police as consummate crime-fighters. With the Internet and official websites, the police can sculpt a more complete and nuanced police image to the public they serve. With social media, the police can bypass the traditional mass media and have more power to portray who they are and what they do for the public than ever before (Hu & Lovrich, 2020; O'Connor & Zaidi, 2021). Grygiel and Lysak (2021) argue that police use of social media reduces the gatekeeping role of journalists once quite important to how the police were perceived in the local communities they served. On the public side, community residents would seem to favor the police's use of social media. A survey study conducted in the U.K. reported that over 90% of respondents had seen *Facebook* postings made by their local police agencies, and about 70% of them even actively follow their local agencies' *Facebook* pages (Cartwright & Shaw, 2020).

Of course, even a very favorable police social media image skillfully sculptured by the police does not mean the public will fully buy it. After all, the public has many channels to receive police-related information, and they can

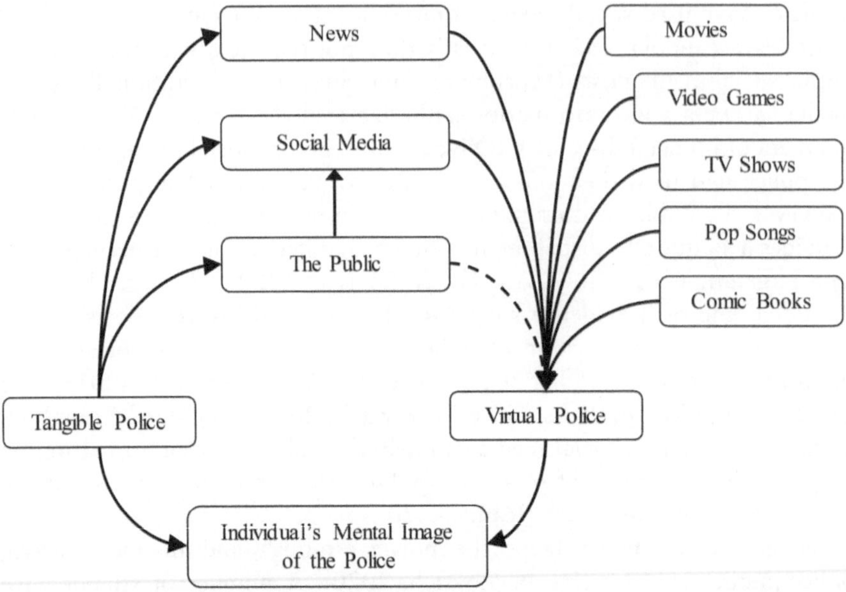

FIGURE 4.1 The construction of an individual's mental image of the police.
Source: Adopted from Hu and Lovrich (2020, p. 20)

use the information gathered to build their mental image of the police. The image will be partially impacted by access to police misconduct news (Lee et al., 2023), negative social media posts toward the police (Oglesby-Neal et al., 2019), and questionable police conduct reported upon globally (e.g., the George Floyd murder at the hands of the police) (O'Connor & Zaidi, 2021). Figure 4.1 shows Hu and Lovrich's (2020) model of how the public mental image of the police is likely created from diverse sources.

In general, the public receives police-related information from both direct (personal) and indirect (vicarious) experiences. The concept of *tangible police* refers to the police officers an individual sees and interacts with in person (Hu & Lovrich, 2020). Numerous studies have documented the importance of police-public direct encounters and their deep impacts on public attitudes toward the police (e.g., Dai et al., 2020; Dai & Hu, 2021; Hinds, 2009; Li et al., 2016; Murphy, 2009). The concept of *virtual police* refers to the police that an individual sees and interacts with in the virtual world – such as in movies, on TV shows, in video games, and on the Internet (Hu & Lovrich, 2020). To maximize their influence over the public mental image of the police, the contemporary police "must exercise a positive influence on both the tangible police and virtual police images acquired by the people they serve" (Hu & Lovrich, 2020, p. 21). The tangible police seem a little easier to manage as long as police officers continue conducting procedural justice, community-oriented policing, and many other strategies designed to enhance police professionalism. It only requires the police to perform better on their side. To manage the virtual police, however, the police must "compete" with traditional mass media and overcome the often-distorted myths created by it.

For the police, it is not easy to win in such a competition among diverse images of the police broadly in circulation. Historically, in their public "watchdog" role, mass media journalists typically critically question the police about their transparency and seek to promote police accountability. Accordingly, a good deal of the content about the police appearing in the mass media tends toward the negative (Hu & Lovrich, 2020). In fact, mass media generally describe the police as being more aggressive than is the case in reality (Oliver, 1994; Scharrer, 2012). The current effort to expand the use of body-worn cameras reflects this interest of the mass media in access to video evidence on police conduct (National Policing Institute, 2020). With the adroit use of social media, the police are now able to build legitimacy by increasing their transparency and demonstrating their accountability with timely postings and commentaries from trusted sources (Bullock, 2018; Grimmelikhuijsen & Meijer, 2015).

Numerous studies have shown that performing procedural justice in police work is an excellent way to improve police legitimacy in tangible police contacts (e.g., Dai & Hu, 2021; Gau, 2015; Jonathan-Zamir et al., 2015; Mazerolle et al., 2013). Scholars have identified four core aspects of police procedural justice: (1) participation (individuals are given an opportunity to speak out; (2) neutrality (police decisions are made in an unbiased manner); (3) dignity and respect (the police treat individuals with politeness, dignity, and respect their rights); and (4) trust in the motives of the police (individuals believe the police truly care about them and their quality of life) (see Jonathan-Zamir et al., 2015, pp. 847–848). In the past, performing procedural justice during an encounter may be known only between the police officer(s) and the citizen(s). Now, with body-worn cameras and social media platforms the public can view actual footage of police encounters and make an informed judgment. In actuality, most direct police-citizen contacts are carried out in accordance with the core elements of procedural justice. Most police agencies would like to post videos presenting a positive image of their officers, and some are even willing to post videos on "bad apples" no longer employed. In a sample of police *Facebook* posts from 15 police agencies in the U.S. between October 1, 2013, and October 1, 2014, Hu and Lovrich (2020) found that the Chicago Police Department (IL), Dallas Police Department (TX), and Philadelphia Police Department (PA) each had posted *Facebook* postings related to officers who had engaged in misconduct and committed crimes. These posts showed that these agencies did not cover up for their problematic officers but rather were proactive in their prosecution for crimes committed while on duty.

Additionally, the police can utilize social media to contact populations that are traditionally difficult to reach (Hu & Lovrich, 2020). The most typical population in this regard is that of teenagers. There are at least three reasons why the police should try their best to connect with teenagers on social media. First, as a bell-shaped curve, the age–crime curve discovered in developmental criminology (also see Chapter 3) suggests that criminal behavior peaks in adolescence (aged from 14 to 18) and then decreases in adulthood (Le Blanc, 2020; Shulman et al., 2013). Thus, the population with whom the police most often interact during a law enforcement situation is teenagers. Second, studies have shown that compared to older populations, younger populations – especially teenagers – tend to have a negative attitude toward the police (Hu et al., 2020). This is mainly due to the high frequency of negative police-teenage contact. Meanwhile, teenagers' attitudes toward the police are important for overall public attitudes toward the police because today's teenagers will be the primary consumers of police services in the future (Bain et al., 2014). Third, although police agencies now have some programs that bring the police and teenagers together, such as the Gang Resistance Education and Training (G.R.E.A.T.) program and the Drug Abuse Resistance Education (D.A.R.E.) program (Hu & Dittmann, 2016; Wu et al., 2022), these programs often focus on teenagers engaged in their respective schools and cannot target a large number of school-disaffected teenagers.

In their survey on social media, Ruddell and Jones (2013) reported that younger survey respondents tend to express favorable attitudes toward police use of social media. Another 2013 study reported that college students in general support police use of social media (Spizman & Miller, 2013). A 2014 study of adults similarly reported that police use of social media is positively viewed and seen as a good way to stimulate favorable public perceptions of the police (Bain et al., 2014). All these studies suggest that police agencies can benefit from putting efforts into selecting social media platforms and content based on teenagers' and college students' interests, knowing that they, unlike adults, are not frequent users of newspapers and other forms of mass media for the acquisition of public affairs information.

Moreover, the police must adopt social media to directly counter "fake news" or "untrue stories" posted on social media platforms. Social media allows almost anyone to post almost anything. Favorable and true stories about the police are to be found on social media. Likewise, however, there are a lot more negative and often fictionalized stories about the police on social media. Some scholars are worried about social media's negative impacts on the police given the proliferation of fake and/or misleading postings. For example, Cox and colleagues (2013, p. 22) observe in this regard, "Tweets, blogs, and videos sent over the Internet depicting police action or inaction from differing political perspectives may lead to public dissatisfaction, protests, and violence."

These worries indeed have a theoretical foundation. Negative bias theory suggests that "bad is stronger than good," meaning that the negative police-public contacts are likely to have a stronger influence on public attitudes toward the police than positive contacts, overriding beneficial factors such as positive police-public contacts, supportive neighborhood contexts, and citizen demographics (Li et al., 2016). Negative bias theory has been supported in both face-to-face environments (e.g., Dai et al., 2019; Li et al., 2016) and online environments (e.g., Brainard & Derrick-Mills, 2011). It follows, therefore, that the police should endeavor to make appropriate use of social media channels to speak out about misinformation. At this point, social media provides a variety of channels for them to do so.

Clearly, stories unfavorable to the police on social media are often well-based. The police understand fully that they are increasingly being supervised by citizens equipped with mobile electronic devices who enjoy ready access to social media (Ellis, 2023; O'Connor & Zaidi, 2021; Walsh & O'Connor, 2019). The days of "I'm gonna kick your ass and get away with it" may be long gone for many police departments with the advent of social media. Watching over the police in action and holding them accountable is necessary in any democratic society (Hu & Lovrich, 2020). That said, excessive oversight may well lead to unwanted results. For example, the "Ferguson effect" refers to the idea that

> officers are conscious of the negative publicity surrounding their profession, understand that their actions could be recorded by the public at any given time, and become less willing to do their job as a way to avoid being accused of racial profiling or excessive force.
>
> *(Wolfe & Nix, 2016, p. 1)*

The Ferguson effect may lead the police to reduce proactive investigatory activities, and crime rates may increase as a direct consequence (e.g., MacDonald, 2015; Sutton, 2015; Rosenfeld, 2015; Wolfe & Nix, 2016). In the digital age, the "no comments" strategy to a public posting of questionable police conduct seems to be a bad strategy for handling a public trust crisis in the police (Fowler, 2017).

Finally, compared to other police strategies, social media entails somewhat lower costs (Hu & Lovrich, 2020). It may be true that using social media to fight crimes (e.g., monitoring social media posts) may require extra staffing, new equipment, and periodic software upgrades. However, using social media as a police-public communication tool is undoubtedly cheaper than simply adding more officers to the beat. Most popular social media platforms, such as *Facebook*, *Twitter*, *YouTube*, and *Instagram*, are free to use. Public information officers (PIOs) and civilian employees can use these platforms to stay connected to the public without a great deal of extra cost (Hu & Lovrich,

2020). Creating pictures and videos may necessitate extra manpower and skills. However, nearly all digital media materials can be shared across platforms. For example, one police agency may make an appealing advertisement video. That video can be used on its *Facebook*, *Twitter*, *YouTube*, *Instagram*, *Snapchat*, and other mainstream social media platforms. Additionally, the low cost of using social media is very important to small communities and rural police agencies which lack staff and funding for conducting frequent face-to-face community engagement events (Bullock et al., 2023).

What Are the Police Currently Doing on Social Media?

Many studies have been conducted to explore what the police are doing on social media. In this section, we divide the extant literature on this topic into two broad categories based on their primary goals being sought. The first goal is to use social media to fight crime. The second is to use social media as a police-public communication tool. It appears from existing research that police officers generally support the use of social media for both crime-fighting and fostering favorable police-public relationships (e.g., Beshears, 2017).

Use of Social Media as a Crime-Fighting Tool

The police began using the Internet to fight crime quite a while back. Early in 2011, the New York City Police Department (NYPD) announced that it would form a special social media unit to mine posts on a variety of social media platforms, looking for criminal activities and producing evidence which could be used in prosecuting crimes (Parascandola, 2011). Usually, a search warrant is not required to gather public social media posts (Murphy & Fontecilla, 2012). If suspects use private settings to block non-friend views of their posts, the police can (and often do) create a fake profile to friend them or contact suspects' cooperating friends (Murphy & Fontecilla, 2012). It has been reported that *Facebook* is the platform most often used by the police to conduct such crime-fighting activities, followed by *Twitter* and *YouTube* (Fortin et al., 2023).

First off, social media is an excellent tool for collecting criminal intelligence given its time-stamped quality. One way in which police gather criminal intelligence is directly from suspects or offenders' social media pages. An ethnographic study on U.S. police officers' perspective toward the use of social media found that officers in general consider social media to be a powerful tool for conducting criminal investigations (Fallik et al., 2020). In a study on 177 Canadian police officers, Fortin and colleagues (2023) found that officers viewed social media as an important investigatory tool for fighting both online and offline crimes, such as witnessed in organized crime and street gang investigations. Schneider and Trottier (2012) documented the use of social media by the Vancouver Police Department; the department used pictures and videos uploaded on *Facebook* to identify rioters engaging in a 2011 riot which led to hundreds of arrests. A second way the police gather criminal intelligence is by posting BOLOs (i.e., be on the lookout) on social media, asking the public to provide information. We consider this use to be a police-public communication and elaborate on this use in the "social media as communication tool" section to follow.

Second, social media can be used to conduct proactive surveillance of social media users for threat assessment (Fallik et al., 2020). Most often, suspected criminal users are not aware that the police are monitoring them (Fallik et al., 2020). The police observe suspects interacting publicly with friends without being physically present (Fortin et al., 2023). The police are interested in posts featuring gang signs, graffiti, tattoos, and most importantly firearms (Fallik et al., 2020). Conducting social media surveillance can help police detectives and investigators build a criminal profile by analyzing posted photos, stated interests, lifestyle habits, and places frequently visited (Fortin et al., 2023).

Third, during informal interviews and/or formal interrogations, social media posts can be used as a baseline-check tool for the validity of victims', suspects', and witnesses' statements rendered to the police (Fallik et al., 2020). In these circumstances, social media posts often become legal evidence (Uncel, 2011), admissible in courts (Kessler, 2011). Police must be careful about collecting, preserving, and utilizing social media evidence and avoid entrapment. Hoffmeister (2014) identifies five specific legal grounds for making use of social media evidence in a court proceeding (i.e., relevance, authentication, hearsay, best evidence rule, and character evidence). We discuss each of these in detail in Chapter 5.

When it comes to fighting crime, police can also use social media to broadcast crime-prevention tips (Fortin et al., 2023). Hu and Lovrich (2020) apportion police crime prevention tips posted on *Facebook* into four groups based on purposes sought: (1) to teach the public how to conduct crime prevention activities; (2) to teach the public what to do if they are victimized; (3) to deter potential offenders with severe consequences of committing a crime; and (4) to broaden public awareness of police crime prevention activities (e.g., DWI checkpoints). The police may also participate in crime prevention activities on social media by getting involved in online crime prevention groups that are not initiated by the police, such as WhatsApp Neighborhood Crime Prevention groups (Pridmore et al., 2019; Van Steden & Mehlbaum, 2022). We discuss these police crime prevention efforts in some detail in Chapter 7.

It is worth noting that besides the fact that social media can be a powerful tool for fighting crimes, it also can create some barriers for the police while they are attempting to fight crime. In Chapter 3 we gave some examples of how offenders sometimes use social media as both a communication tool and a direct means of crime, in both personal crimes and property crimes. For example, motorists can drive by a police DWI checkpoint and share the location with others on social media so that other motorists ("confederates") can avoid it. In a study on 890 motorists who use drugs (e.g., marijuana and methamphetamine), 94 motorists use organized social media police location groups to avoid roadside drug testing (Mills et al., 2022). Compared to another 125 motorists who do not use information shared in social media police location groups, these 94 users tend to have a higher level of drug use and intention to offend, and they view local police location postings more frequently (Mills et al., 2022). The "anticipatory benefit" (Smith et al., 2002) associated with motorists stopping the use of drugs before driving because of the risk of encountering a police checkpoint is likely blunted by this type of use of social media. The Mills et al. (2022) study indicates that, sadly enough, the anticipatory benefit is less likely to occur among frequent drug users, the prime target of such motorists (Mills et al., 2022).

Use of Social Media as a Communication Tool

Social media has been used more and more as an important communication tool between the public and governmental agencies (Bertot et al., 2012). Perhaps, how the police use social media to connect and communicate with the public has been among the most frequently probed areas in recent police research. After all, effective police-public communication is truly essential to law enforcement management in a democratic society in the 21st century (Hu & Lovrich, 2023), and social media happens to be a communication tool of vast potential for beneficial use.

Studies on police use of *Facebook* reveal that there are a variety of themes being covered by the police on this platform. Three highly cited studies (Dai et al., 2017; Hu et al., 2018; Lieberman et al., 2013) on a wide number of police agencies' *Facebook* accounts generally divide police posts into five major categories (see Table 4.1 for examples). The first category is that of crime-related postings. In this area, the police often post local crime statistics, information on wanted suspects, information on persons of interest, and performance data on solved and unsolved crime incidents (Lieberman et al., 2013). Clearly, police departments post such information because they are law enforcers and want to demonstrate to the public that they are doing their job with vigor and having noteworthy success (Hu et al., 2018). The police, however, need to be somewhat cautious about posting crime-related posts. One study analyzed nearly 100,000 police *Facebook* posts that reported the race of suspects and arrestees and compared them to local and aggregate police arrest statistics (Grunwald et al., 2022). The study showed that police *Facebook* posts featured an overexposure of Black suspects across crime types and geographic regions, raising the risk of reinforcing negative racial stereotypes about crime and criminals (Grunwald et al., 2022). A similar finding was reported in a 2021 study on images of criminals featured on police *Facebook* pages (Sever et al., 2021).

TABLE 4.1 Examples of police *Facebook* posts based on primary themes

Major Themes	*Content*	*Agency*	*Source**
Crime-Related	Units are on the scene of a shooting in the [street name omitted]. Victim shot in the stomach.	Baltimore PD	Lieberman et al., 2013
	In 2013, Brimfield officers handled 14,118 calls for service, which is up about 8% from last year. Officers traffic stopped 5,046 vehicles and gave warnings to 4,417 of those drivers. The rest were either ticketed or arrested for criminal or driving offenses. 647 citations (tickets) were issued, for a percentage of about 12.5% of vehicles stopped.	Brimfield PD	Hu & Lovrich, 2020**
Tip-Related	Keep your purse close to your body. Avoid talking on cell phones as you walk through malls, parking lots. Phone conversations are a distraction that makes you vulnerable to robbers. Don't resist if someone tries to take any of your belongings. Don't chase someone who robs you, they may have a weapon. Instead, call 911.	Dallas PD	Hu & Lovrich, 2020
	The HPD reminds you not to drink and drink this holiday weekend. Additional officers will be deployed at high-risk locations around the Houston area to conduct DWI enforcement efforts during times that alcohol-related crashes are most frequent.	Houston PD	Hu & Lovrich, 2020
Police-Public Relations	Another successful National Night Out in Omaha! We hope you enjoyed your party and got to meet your firefighters and police officers. . . . Partnering with your public safety officials is one of the best ways to make your neighborhood safe!	Omaha PD	Lieberman et al., 2013
	Good morning HPD Facebook fans. Looks like we might get some sun today!	Houston PD	Lieberman et al., 2013
	Tomorrow morning at 08:00, we will be taking nearly 100 kids from [school name omitted] to [shopping center's name omitted]. Each child will be buying brand new clothing, including pants, shirts, socks, and shoes, for the return to school.	Brimfield PD	Hu & Lovrich, 2020

(*Continued*)

TABLE 4.1 (Continued)

Major Themes	*Content*	*Agency*	*Source**
	Can you tell us when the NYPD Mounted Unit was created?	New York City PD	Hu & Lovrich, 2020
	LVMPD wants to hear from you! How well are doing? Specifically, what could we be doing better? What are your thoughts on crime and the community in general? This brief survey will take approximately five minutes to complete.	Las Vegas Metropolitan PD	Hu & Lovrich, 2020
	Happy Mother's Day to all mothers out there! If you live your life with the goal of making your mother proud – you'll never go wrong!	Philadelphia PD	Hu & Lovrich, 2020
Police Personnel	This morning [four officers' names omitted] were promoted to Sergeant of Police and [officer's name omitted] was promoted to Lieutenant of Police. Everyone here at HPD congratulates you and wishes you the best in your new assignments.	Houston PD	Hu & Lovrich, 2020
	Detective [name omitted] was accompanied by his family earlier today as he was released from [hospital's name omitted]. He was there for two days after being shot on Monday while he and two U.S. marshals were attempting to apprehend a man wanted on a warrant.	New York City PD	Hu & Lovrich, 2020
	On Friday, June 13, 2014, K-9 [name omitted] was shot and killed, and her handler wounded, after responding to a home in the [address omitted] to search for a rape suspect. The subject opened fire inside the home, killing [name omitted] and wounding her handler in the neck, before being taken into custody. [name omitted] had only served with the Walker County Sheriff's Office for eight weeks.	Walker County Sheriff's Office	Hu & Lovrich, 2020
Services and Contacts	Text 911 is not a smart application, because in an emergency situation, voice tone and specific information are critical for sending the appropriate assistance.	Richmond PD	Lieberman et al., 2013

(Continued)

TABLE 4.1 (Continued)

Major Themes	*Content*	*Agency*	*Source**
	New JSO Audio Traffic App has been launched! The Jacksonville Sheriff's Audio Traffic app gives residents of the entire metro-Jacksonville, Florida area up-to-the-minute traffic reports they can hear right from their smartphone . . . And the JSO Audio Traffic app also gives Jacksonville residents access to information bulletins from the Jacksonville Sheriff's Office with information on everything from criminal activity to missing children and endangered adults.	Jacksonville Sheriff's Office	Hu & Lovrich, 2020

* Dai et al.'s (2017) article does not provide examples. However, it has identified 16 categories: crime information, law enforcement, asking for tips, crime prevention, safety advice, community interaction, community events, traffic updates, agency-related information, recruitment, government services, information sharing, holiday greetings, non-police related advertising, and road conditions.

** Categories were discussed in Hu et al.'s (2018) article, and detailed posts were presented in Hu and Lovrich's (2020) book.

The second category of police postings is that of crime tip-related posts. Within this category, both crime-related tips and non-crime-related tips are featured (Hu et al., 2018). Crime-related tips often focus on crime prevention regarding both personal crimes and property crimes. Crime-related tips often focus on frequently occurring crimes out of the limelight seldom covered by traditional mass media, such as white-collar crime, identity theft, DWI, and theft (Hu & Lovrich, 2020). Non-crime-related tips often refer to safety tips, such as winter driving safety and summer safety tips relating to the danger of drowning. Meanwhile, this category often includes traffic updates, road conditions, road construction projects, and timely weather updates (Dai et al., 2017). After all, crime prevention and order maintenance are among the major police tasks in modern policing (Walker & Katz, 2018).

The third category is about police-public relations. This is a broad category with the primary purpose of conducting community-oriented policing on social media (Thomas et al., 2022; Walkington et al., 2018). Posts within this category often portray the police as reliable friends and good neighbors and representing an integral part of a healthy and safe community (Hu & Lovrich, 2020). Topics covered by this category include newsletters (with a focus on police-public activities), online events (e.g., Q&A sessions), greetings (e.g., good morning greetings and good weekend greetings), thank you notes (e.g., during COVID-19), and many forms of non-police-related public interest information (Hu & Lovrich, 2023; Hu et al., 2018; Lieberman et al., 2013). Specifically, many police agencies post non-police-related information such as local sporting events, hotel and restaurant locations, and local park and recreation facilities. Hu and Lovrich (2020) explain police involvement in this activity by noting that the police want to build an image of general helpfulness with the hope that the public will view them as a principal trusted informational source for their community.

The fourth category is related to police personnel, including sworn officers, civilian employees, four-legged officers (i.e., K-9 and patrol horses), and law enforcement recruitment (Dai et al., 2017; Hu et al., 2018). Many police agencies introduce their new police officers on social media and share promotions, retirements, and awards receptions for their officers and their families (Hu et al., 2018). Likewise, they often report on officers who are ill, injured, or killed in the line of duty (Lieberman et al., 2013). Most often, such posts get a great deal of attention on *Facebook* (Hu et al., 2020). Posts related to police personnel are most likely to be positive in valence vis-à-vis the police. The police, of course, want to display their best social image to the public. However, some police agencies do post items on "bad apple officers" who have seriously misbehaved (e.g., see Hu & Lovrich, 2020, p. 97).

The last category is about police agencies' services, contact information, and postings on other social media platforms (Dai et al., 2017). Some police agencies occasionally advertise their open positions on other social media accounts (e.g., *Twitter*, *Instagram*, and *YouTube*) in addition to posting on their *Facebook* pages (Lieberman et al., 2013). Meanwhile, with more and more police agencies starting to own their phone apps, they also often introduce these apps on *Facebook* and ask the public to install them on their cell phones (Hu & Lovrich, 2020). Other studies on police *Facebook* content (e.g., Bullock et al., 2023; Jeanis et al., 2021; Livingstone, 2022) reveal that the above five categories cover nearly all police *Facebook* content. The content areas on police *Facebook* pages have become quite common, although the proportions of different kinds of content vary rather widely across police agencies.

A few studies have examined public reactions to police *Facebook* posts (e.g., Cartwright & Shaw, 2020; Huang et al., 2016; Jeanis et al., 2021; Livingstone, 2022). For example, in a study of 7,116 posts gathered from the 14 most popular police *Facebook* accounts in the U.S., Hu and colleagues (2020) reported that the public favors postings with police-public relations and police personnel, and the public particularly favors posts featuring pictures. The public seems to have somewhat less interest in crime-related posts (Hu et al., 2020). Another study on a large sheriff's department's *Facebook* page found a similar pattern – that is, the public is more likely to engage with police *Facebook* pages related to missing persons and traffic updates than other areas (Jeanis et al., 2021). Crime-related posts, such as wanted suspects and apprehension of offenders, are either negatively related to public engagement or not related to public engagement at all (Jeanis et al., 2021).

A study on *Facebook* "likes" received by police agencies finds that postings related to community interaction and agency-related information tend to receive many "likes" (Dai et al., 2017). Further, a study focusing on public *Facebook* reactions (i.e., like, love, haha, wow, sad, and angry) to police *Facebook* posts also finds that the public tends to react most favorably to postings related to police-public relations (Livingstone, 2022). A U.K. study on 294 participants reports that more than 90% of respondents have seen their local police agencies' *Facebook* posts, and about 70% actively follow their local agencies' *Facebook* pages (Cartwright & Shaw, 2020). The follower participants were likely to indicate that they wished to see more *Facebook* posts related to updates on incidents, missing persons, and police helping members of their communities (Cartwright & Shaw, 2020).

Studies done on police use of *Twitter* show similar results. Topics covered by the police on this platform include, but are not limited to, police activities, public announcements, tips, events, missing persons, wanted suspects, officer success stories, solved crimes, and police-community interactions (Ceccato et al., 2021; Cheng, 2021; Crump, 2011; Dai et al., 2017; Heverin & Zach, 2010). Pictures and videos are also used in many police *Twitter* postings (Cheng, 2021). Hyperlinks to police agencies' official websites are frequently provided in those postings (Cheng, 2021). Since *Twitter* allows only a certain number of characters in each tweet, police tweets are mostly short, often providing links to other websites (e.g., official websites) and other social media platforms (e.g., *Facebook*). If *Twitter* users just want to skim police tweets, they do not need to click those links. However, if they are interested in having more details, the links provided allow them to secure that information easily.

Some studies have tested the effects of police *Twitter* use. For example, Dai and colleagues (2017) found that "information-sharing" tweets receive relatively more favorites, retweets, and comments than any other categories. This finding strengthens the argument that *Twitter* is an excellent information-sharing tool. Ferguson and Soave (2021) analyzed the use of *Twitter* in locating missing persons. They observed that images and hashtags can significantly increase public engagement with these police tweets (Ferguson & Soave, 2021). Walby and Gumieny (2020) explored how the police frame philanthropic and charitable work on their *Twitter* accounts. They found that the police tend to focus on community, youth, diversity, and crime prevention themes to enhance perceptions of police legitimacy and benevolence (Walby & Gumieny, 2020).

Stickle and colleagues (2022) argue that the police should use *Twitter* to engage more often with the public about the problem of human trafficking. Police tweets that use informal communication are particularly likely to be forwarded by *Twitter* users (Van de Velde et al., 2015). Moreover, a study on the NYPD's *Twitter* content indicates that the platform can be used to tweet about all the principles (e.g., enforcement, prevention, community interaction, and timely information) and themes (e.g., strategic and tactical approaches) associated with community-oriented policing (Thomas et al., 2022). Some studies focus on individual police officers' use of *Twitter*. Officers often use their formal identity on *Twitter* and use the platform to communicate both externally (outside police agencies) and internally (among officers who share mutual interests) (Meijer & Torenvlied, 2016). One study focused on police officers' use of *Twitter* while off duty. Its author found that "official off-duty use of *Twitter* delineates the individual officer from the policing institution but does so in an official capacity, a presentational strategy that diminishes the appearance of authoritarian relations traditionally associated with police" (Schneider, 2016b, p. 129).

Studies on police use of *YouTube* are far less common than is the case with *Facebook* and *Twitter*. Walby and Joshua (2021b) analyzed 64 police *YouTube* recruitment videos posted in Canada and found that more than half of the videos are women-centric (53%), followed by men-centric (30%) and equal representation (14%). At first glance, this may seem to be a good sign because police agencies are always trying to hire more female officers. However, these videos do not reveal what policewomen too often experience in what remains a hypermasculine work environment in law enforcement (Walby & Joshua, 2021b). From a feminist perspective, the authors conclude that "diversity is portrayed in ways that contradict and distract from the continuing history of sexism, sexual harassment and racism in public policing" (Walby & Joshua, 2021b, p. 151).

In a study examining the top ten U.S. municipal police departments and their use of *Facebook*, *Twitter*, and *YouTube*, the *YouTube* platform is the least frequently used social media platform for police-public online interaction (Brainard & Edlins, 2015). Even though the public seems to be interested in interacting with their police agencies on *YouTube*, agencies may view the platform as a primary tool for disseminating information rather than a tool for active dialogue (Brainard & Edlins, 2015). However, the police may wish to make greater use of *YouTube* because several studies have found that camera phones and *YouTube* significantly increase the public's exposure to good police conduct and misconduct alike (e.g., Antony & Thomas, 2010; Brown, 2016; Schneider, 2018). Moreover, members of the public often make comments on alleged police misconduct videos posted on *YouTube* to either defend the officer(s) or condemn them, depending on what segments of the original body-worn camera footage are released to the public (Canevez et al., 2022). The police may need to share more body-worn camera video footage on *YouTube* to effectively present their counterclaims to the public when they come under fire for alleged misconduct (Schneider, 2017).

Studies on police use of *Instagram* remain relatively rare. *Instagram* focuses on pictures and videos shared by short notes (captions) explaining them. Users can sort their posts using either text-based hashtags (#) or geolocation hashtags. The police use *Instagram* primarily to create positive relations with their communities and enhance police legitimacy (Walby & Wilkinson, 2023). In a study on five Canadian police agencies' use of this social media platform, Walby and Wilkinson (2023) categorize police *Instagram* images into four groups. The first group includes pictures of how the police demonstrate their ongoing connections to the local community (Walby & Wilkinson, 2023). Images posted often feature a "feel good" story about how the police actively get involved in community activities and help community members. A second group includes images highlighting diversity in policing (Walby & Wilkinson, 2023). Women and people of color often appear in pictures of police personnel and recruitment events. The third group includes specific pictures of police demonstrating support for LGBTQ persons. Finally, the fourth group focuses on pictures of police connections with Indigenous people and communities (Walby & Wilkinson, 2023).

In a study on public perceptions of and attitudes toward police *Instagram* communication in Sweden, Sjöberg and colleagues (2023) report that police *Instagram* posts on safety tend to bring participants a sense of protection, proximity, and approachability. After seeing the pictures posted, most study participants opined that the police are broadly present in the community and endeavor to protect them (Sjöberg et al., 2023). By being exposed to some details of police work and police personnel, most study participants came to a "humanized" view of police work and felt closer to their police (Sjöberg et al., 2023). Also worthy of note, some study participants pointed out the need for the police to better explain the meaning of their *Instagram* images because some images were vague or seemed out of place to lay members of the community (Sjöberg et al., 2023).

Besides the "regular" police social media posts discussed earlier, there is also another type of police social media posting that merits mentioning. Several studies have shown that social media can be an especially effective tool for timely communication with the public following a police-public relations crisis (e.g., Cheng, 2021; Fowler, 2017; Steele & Blau, 2023). The police generally view the traditional mass media as anti-police (Nix et al., 2018). In fact, the police may have to engage in proactive communication because social media posts are often blamed for escalating police-public crises (Procter et al., 2013). The police can sometimes help to de-escalate conflicts by publicizing relevant information unfiltered by traditional mass media (Cheng, 2021).

For example, Steele and Blau (2023) analyzed six police agencies' *Facebook* and *Twitter* posts after the killing of George Floyd while under police custody in open view by bystanders. They found that these police agencies used social media to convey empathy, to signal their own self-efficacy, and to issue commitments and assurances to stakeholders (Steele & Blau, 2023). Postings showed that the police empathized with the victim and condemned the misconduct (Steele & Blau, 2023). Most importantly, the police emphasized that they valued BLM protestors and minority communities, would keep commitments made to citizens protesting the misconduct, and promised to change policies and practices giving rise to the incident (Steele & Blau, 2023).

Another study on 115 large U.S. police agencies' *Twitter* postings before and after the killing of George Floyd found that these agencies tweeted substantially more often after the killing, with an increased number of civil unrest-related tweets being posted (Dong & Wu, 2022). Meanwhile, the public also increased their engagement with the police on *Twitter* after the killing of George Floyd (Dong & Wu, 2022). The police deal with different types of police-public crises in varying ways on social media. In community-related crises (e.g., mass shootings, dangerous felon at large), the police tend to provide information in a unidirectional manner. In contrast, in organizational-level crises (e.g., misconduct by police), the police tend to provide information designed to reduce reputational damage (Jungblut et al., 2022). It has been reported that those law enforcement officers who maintain agencies' social media accounts believe that *Twitter* is generally their first choice for trying to handle crises, followed by *Facebook* (Jungblut et al., 2022).

Besides earlier studies on *Facebook*, *Twitter*, *YouTube*, and *Instagram*, there are a few studies on police use of newer social media platforms, such as *WhatsApp*, *Telegram*, *Snapchat*, *TikTok*, *Messenger*, and *Pinterest* (see top ten most popular social media platforms worldwide in Chapter 2). *WhatsApp* has been studied regarding how the police get involved in neighborhood crime prevention groups (e.g., Mols & Pridmore, 2019; Pridmore et al., 2019; Van Steden & Mehlbaum, 2022). *Telegram* and *Snapchat* have been studied regarding police surveillance (e.g., Akbari & Gabdulhakov, 2019; Matthews et al., 2021). Gathering data on police use of these platforms is difficult since their use by police remains quite limited. Nevertheless, studies (e.g., the current book; Hu & Lovrich, 2020) have called for more research on police use of social media on platforms old and new alike.

A Theoretical Framework of Police-Public Communication on Social Media

The literature review on police use of social media presented here highlights a few critical points. First, the police must be quite careful about using social media as an investigative tool. There should be ethical and legal limitations to it with respect to honoring privacy rights, especially when the police use social media to conduct surveillance (Fallik et al., 2020) and then make use of social media posts as evidence (Kessler, 2011; Uncel, 2011). The elements of probable cause for the surveillance need to pass strict scrutiny standards. The American people rightfully expect a certain degree of privacy in the use of their social media accounts, even though most of their posts are open to the public. They certainly do not want their local police agencies to be actively monitoring them online.

In contrast, unlike conducting surveillance on social media, the police often use social media to post BOLO (i.e., be on the lookout). Tolerance for this use of social media is quite high because it differs little from posting wanted persons/vehicles on police agencies' websites and in other public venues. Police agencies' social media accounts certainly cannot post all manner of content like the owners of individual accounts can do, but a variety of topics are clearly of some interest to different segments of the communities being protected and served by their local police. Posts related to police personnel and favorable police-public interactions are particularly favored (see Hu et al., 2020). Likewise, posts written in an informal tone (non-legalistic) are welcomed by the public (Hu & Lovrich, 2021). These observations from prior research lead us to a reasonable inference that the police should become adroit in the use social media to build and sustain police-public relations, a conclusion which leads us in turn to a discussion of the proper scope of community-oriented policing in the digital age.

Electronic Community-Oriented Policing (E-COP)

In the previous section, we discussed how community-oriented policing has become the most prominent policing strategies in the 21st century. The development of modern information and Internet technologies makes conducting community-oriented policing *virtually* a distinct possibility (Mayes, 2022; Walkington et al., 2018). We discuss this topic at some length here, given its great importance to the future of policing practice. Governmental agencies of any kind generally employ four strategies in their use of social media: (1) *push strategy*, which refers to broadcasting information to the public; (2) *pull strategy*, which refers to gathering information from the public; (3) *networking strategy*, which refers to interacting with the public online; and (4) *transaction strategy*, which refers to delivering government services to the public via the Internet (Mergel, 2012). Enlightened by Mergel's (2012) classifications, we argue here that as a part of governmental agencies' activities, police agencies should employ social media to achieve three major purposes: push, pull, and interaction. We believe all three purposes are important for the effective implementation of community-oriented policing online.

The idea of conducting community-oriented policing (E-COP) online is not an entirely new one. In the late 1990s, Webb (1997) argued that computer bulletin boards could be used to perform community-oriented policing tasks. The concept of E-COP was originally proposed by Cordner and Perkins (2013) in a U.S. Department of Justice report. In *Electronic Community-Oriented Policing: Theories, Contemporary Efforts, and Future Directions*, Hu and Lovrich (2020, p. 71) set forth a definition of E-COP as follows (see also Hu, 2016, p. 43):

> A systematic approach to policing that applies established theories of individual behavior, social behavior, and mass communication in policing practice. It makes use of push strategies, pull strategies, and networking strategies to conduct community-oriented policing online without reference to specific geographical locations. Its implementations and goals include broadcasting information to the public, gathering information from the public, and interacting with the public through the Internet to improve the public–police relationships and enhance the quality of life of citizens.

The general structure of E-COP is shown in Figure 4.2. The push strategy allows police agencies to broadcast timely information (Hu & Lovrich, 2020). Police agencies can achieve this goal by using departmental websites, social media platforms (e.g., *Facebook*, *Twitter*, and *YouTube*), and social media mobile apps (e.g., *Messenger* and *WhatsApp*). Pertinent information may include crime statistics, major criminal cases, crime prevention tips, greetings, agency newsletters, introductions of new police officers and civilian employees, and recruitment advertisements (e.g., see Dai et al., 2017; Hu & Lovrich, 2020; Lieberman et al., 2013). The general purpose of the

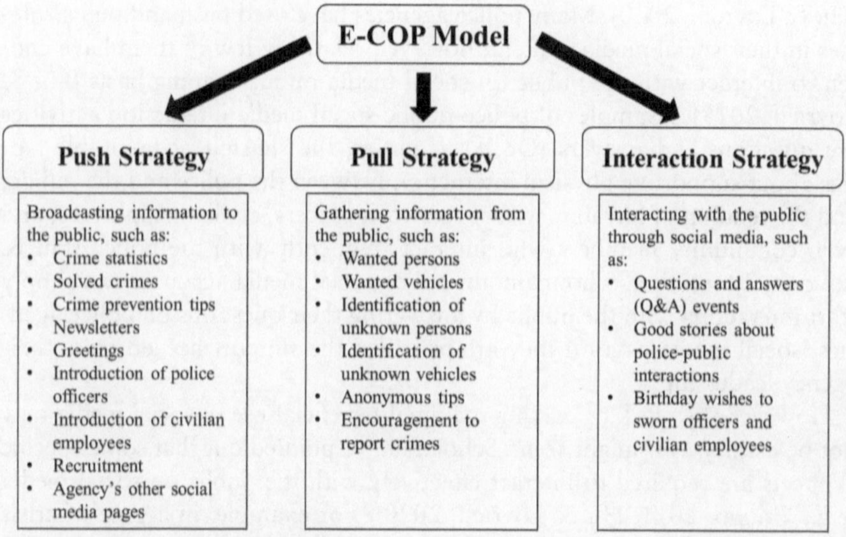

FIGURE 4.2 The model of E-COP.

Source: Created based on Hu and Lovrich (2020)

push strategy is to inform the public about what the police are doing, what they can do, and also permit the public to view them not only as "crime fighters" but also as trusted members of the local community who are connected to the youth, schools, social services, sports, and quality of life elements of the community's civil society.

The pull strategy allows the police to gather valuable information from the public (Mergel, 2012). There should be at least two types of information the police desire to gather: (1) intelligence of crimes that have happened, are happening, and will happen; and (2) surveys on public perceptions of and attitudes toward the police that can be used to improve police service. The police have undertaken these tasks in traditional community-oriented policing by holding police-public meetings and conducting citizen surveys. Community participants taking part in these meetings let the police know how they are doing and what they might do to improve their service and often pass on possible clues as to crime issues. In these meetings, the police typically inform the public that calling 911 or walking into police agencies are not the only ways to report crimes or articulate concerns. Texting, emails, and using "@" in social media posts can all be the new ways of contacting the police (Hu & Lovrich, 2020). For example, Crump (2011) describes *Twitter* as "undoubtedly useful as a means of collecting information" (p. 22).

The interaction strategy (or networking strategy in Mergel, 2012) requires the police to interact with the public on social media on an ongoing basis

(Hu & Lovrich, 2020). Many police agencies have used push and pull strategies in their social media content; however, relatively few of them have chosen to interact with the public on social media on an ongoing basis (Hu & Lovrich, 2018). Examples of police-public social media interaction activities are questions-and-answers (Q&A) activities, the sharing of favorable stories about supportive physical interaction between the police and the public, and the sending of birthday wishes to sworn officers, civilian employees, and even community members who interact frequently with the police (Hu & Lovrich, 2018). Staff who maintain police social media accounts can simply start interacting with the public by answering their questions on police agencies' social media pages if they are provided the support needed from their agency leadership.

However, the work of making maximal beneficial use of social media may not be as easy as it might seem. Scholars have pointed out that some specific skill sets are required to interact effectively with the public on social media (e.g., Crump, 2011; Hu & Lovrich, 2020). For example, in a time of crisis of public trust in the police, how should the police respond on social media? A news report published in August of 2021 noted that the Wilmington Police Department in North Carolina no longer allowed the public to comment on its *Facebook* page (McAdams, 2021). The report noted, "[Comments] allowed people to post unflattering words about the police department, and divisive comments in general" (McAdams, 2021, p. 1). The WPD's reason for terminating *Comments* was that "people were engaging in adversarial conversations through the *Facebook* platform that could easily lead to violence and the department does not want to enable such communication on its page" (McAdams, 2021, p. 1). We revisited WPD's *Facebook* page in January of 2024. The restriction upon making comments still existed. However, members of the public can still react to posts on the department's website and *Facebook* page by clicking "reactions" (e.g., "like" and "love") and sharing them.

An Advanced Model of E-COP

The definition of E-COP given by Hu and Lovrich (2020) highlights what the police can do regarding police-public communication on social media. The three strategies are useful for categorizing police social media posts (not just for *Facebook* posts but for other social media platforms as well). Meanwhile, the categories help police agencies identify their purposes for using social media and allocate resources accordingly. For example, if a police agency simply wants its *Facebook* page to be another official website for the agency (i.e., emphasizing push strategy), it can just ask staff who maintain the official website to copy and paste content from the official website to the *Facebook* page. However, many social media studies have concluded that *how* social media posts are written (i.e., the tone of writing these posts and avoidance

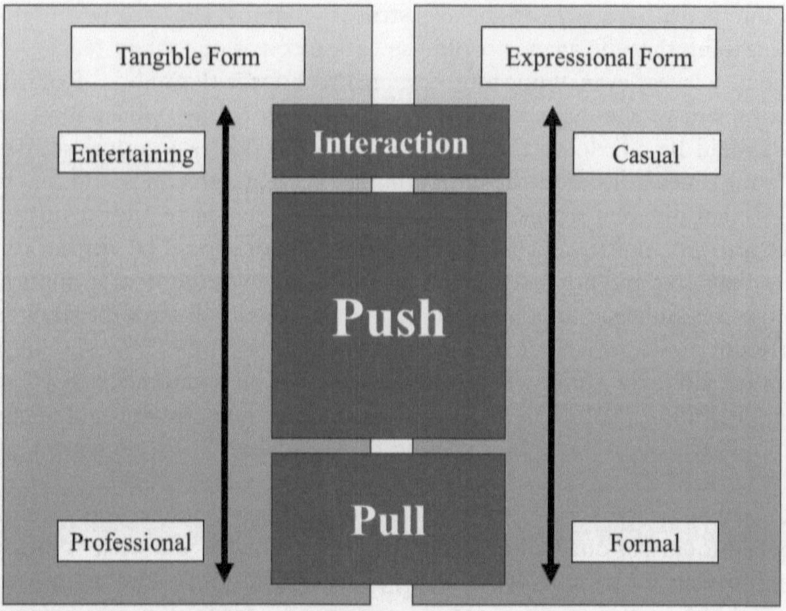

FIGURE 4.3 An expanded model of E-COP.

of law enforcement formalism and legalistic language) can have a significant impact on the audience's responses (e.g., Barcelos et al., 2018; Bode et al., 2020; Denef et al., 2013; Mirbabaie et al., 2020; Oh & Ki, 2019; Zavattaro et al., 2015). Accordingly, we modify Hu and Lovrich's (2020) E-COP model as shown in Figure 4.3.

The enhancement of the prior E-COP model entails adding two concepts relating to forms of communication, namely *tangible form* and *expressional form*. The tangible form refers to the content posted on social media, and the expressional form refers to how the police construct the content (Hu & Lovrich, 2023). The logic underlying this enhancement of the E-COP model is quite simple – individuals are attracted to both the content and the format of social media posts. A previous study on 7,116 police *Facebook* posts revealed that the public is particularly interested in posts related to police personnel and police-public relations and to posts featuring pictures and videos (Hu et al., 2020). Pictures of K-9 units are also highly welcomed on police social media (Hu & Lovrich, 2020). We include an axis indicating that content can be primarily entertaining, primarily professional, or somewhere in-between. Regarding posts related to the act of gathering information from the public (i.e., pull strategy), we believe it is better to be professional, meaning that postings should be written in the way the agency's official website would prescribe. Regarding postings related to police-public online interactions (i.e., interaction strategy), we believe strongly that it is better to be entertaining, meaning that the agency could use various types of content (e.g., Q&A, birthday wishes, even humorous content) to attract the public. Regarding posts related to the dissemination of information to the public, sometimes they should be a little on the police professional side (e.g., crime statistics) and sometimes a little on the entertaining side (e.g., greetings and newsletters) so that different segments of the public can be attracted to the postings.

We also set another axis to indicate how content should be written based on its character and purposes. How the police write the content is important because the audience (i.e., other social media users) will have different feelings about messages written in different tones. Some studies have shown that the police do use a variety of tones when they write social media posts. For example, humor is often used when the police frame narratives and express opinions (Hu & Lovrich, 2021; Wood & McGovern, 2021). A neutral tone is always used if what they post is tragic (Hand & Ching, 2020).

Regarding posts related to the pull strategy, they would best be written in a formal tone. No one wants to see the police making jokes when they are trying to identify criminals. However, posts related to the interaction strategy could be written in a casual tone, even with a sense of humor being evident in some cases (e.g., Wood & McGovern, 2021; see also Chief Oliver's example). After all, the public wants to interact with "a human" instead of a law enforcement institution. Regarding posts related to the push strategy, the tone can depend on the content. For example, crime statistics may be better written in a formal tone, and greetings may be better written in a casual tone.

The expanded model of E-COP also indicates what proportion of the social media communication space each strategy (i.e., push, pull, and interaction) should occupy. Based on Figure 4.3, content related to the push strategy should take the majority of police social media posting space, and content related to the interaction strategy should take the least. We humbly recommend such proportions based on these three reasons. First, modern policing dictates that the police should not be seen as crime-fighters exclusively (The President's Task Force, 2015). They should also play the roles of service providers and community members advancing the quality of life in their respective communities. Accordingly, police social media content should include more than just wanted suspects or crime statistics (Surette, 2015a).

Second, most police agencies' postings involve broadcasting information to citizens, families, friends, and other social media users, with the most reasonable expectation that said information will be passed on to the "friends" of those users on the basis of shared interests and concerns. Third, compared to the push and the pull strategies, the interaction social media strategy will undoubtedly cost significantly more in terms of staffing resources. For example, a police agency seeking to maximize the utility of its social media operation may need to form a working group of agency personnel (supplemented perhaps by college/university interns) to actively monitor its social media posts and reply to any comments posted; this is clearly not a simple task to organize, establish, and sustain (Crump, 2011). For relatively small law enforcement agencies, only one or two members of the workforce may be available to maintain agency social media accounts. In such cases, we would suggest that agency social media postings closely related to police-public online interactions should be rather limited in quantity, but they should be purposefully fully included among police social media strategies to the fullest extent feasible.

An Example of Applying the Advanced Model of E-COP

The advanced model of E-COP is examined here within the context of a very trying time wherein face-to-face police-public communication was greatly limited. Social media has been shown in prior research to have particular value in establishing and maintaining communication with the public during community crises being dealt with by public safety agencies, such as during hurricanes (e.g., Chauhan & Hughes, 2015) and during serious flooding (e.g., Bruns et al., 2012). From late 2019 to early 2023, the COVID-19 pandemic was responsible for the deaths of millions of people worldwide. Besides COVID-19's impact on public health, the pandemic's impact on crime and crime rates has been studied in numerous areas of high concern, such as juvenile delinquency (e.g., Buchanan et al., 2020; Revital & Haviv, 2023), cybercrime (e.g., Buil-Gil et al., 2021; Hawdon et al., 2020), hate crimes (e.g., Gover et al., 2020; Tessler et al., 2020), and domestic violence (e.g., Kourti et al., 2023; Piquero et al., 2020).

As the principal gatekeepers within the criminal justice system, the police were studied closely for how they altered their behavior during the COVID-19 pandemic. They were classified as "essential workers" virtually everywhere, along with all other first responders and medical personnel. They were not allowed to work remotely or take leaves of absence while the virus was spreading. They were in an *all-hands-on deck* situation with only scant medical knowledge available about the new, too often deadly virus. Most local and state police agencies altered their operations substantially in an effort to reduce officer exposure to the disease (Farmer & Copenhaver, 2022). Fewer officers were on the street, and police-public interaction was minimized to the extent possible (Nouri & Kochel, 2022).

Almost every community-oriented policing activity was shut down during the pandemic (Smylie et al., 2023). Community-oriented policing officers reported that traditional community-oriented policing strategies were no longer possible to plan and implement, and public perception of the police was being negatively impacted as stay-at-home directives began to be issued by many businesses and schools (Smylie et al., 2023). At the early stage of the pandemic, officers were concerned about being infected due to the lack of personal protective equipment (PPE) such as masks, disinfectants, and hand sanitizers (Mourtgos & Adams, 2021). Moreover, from late March 2020 to early May 2020, more than 90% of U.S. residents received stay-at-home orders (White & Fradella, 2020); local police were often involved in unpopular actions taken trying to enforce these social distancing orders (Hu et al., 2022; Jones, 2020). In their ongoing effort to maintain police legitimacy, display respect for human dignity in their work, and experience full accountability for their actions, the police needed to find a way to explain to the public why there were fewer officers on patrol when crime rates rose for some offenses and why their officers needed to enforce stay-at-home orders to back up public health officials dealing with local hospitals busting at the seams with COVID-19 patients.

Research done on police use of social media during the COVID-19 pandemic are quite instructive (Carrier et al., 2021; Cartwright & Shaw, 2020; Hu et al., 2022). Hu and colleagues (2022) examined 14 police agencies' *Facebook* pages at the early stage of the COVID-19 outbreak. They concluded that, at least in those police agencies, *Facebook* became a routinized tool in use for maintaining police-public communication during highly stressful times (Hu et al., 2022). Examination on how the public reacted to police use of *Facebook* during the pandemic revealed that posts with COVID-19 content received more attention than posts without COVID-19 content (Hu et al., 2022). In a follow-up study, Hu and Lovrich (2023) applied the advanced E-COP model to theorize how these 14 police agencies made ample use of *Facebook* during the pandemic (Figure 4.4).

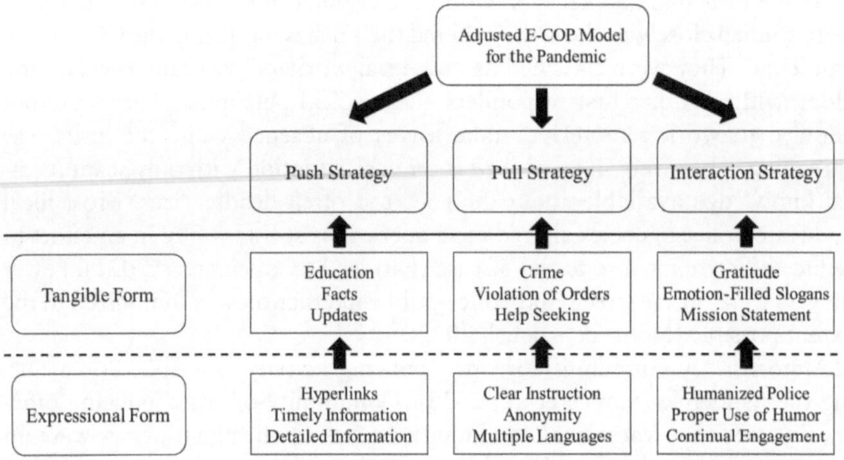

FIGURE 4.4 An advanced model of police-public online communication for the pandemic.

Source: Adopted from Hu et al. (2022, p. 178)

The model clearly shows how tangible and expressional forms of communication differed regarding police social media strategies. During COVID-19, the police used social media to broadcast education on COVID-19 and provide updates on changes in departmental operations (Hu & Lovrich, 2023). These messages were often posted in a timely manner and featured detailed updates along with hyperlinks from public health agencies such as the Centers for Disease Control and Prevention (CDC). When stay-at-home orders were being enforced (Jones, 2020), the police used social media to encourage the public to report individuals who violated the orders and who were engaged in crimes such as online scams, domestic violence, and hate crimes. These posts often provided clear instructions on what the police were on the lookout for and how people could contact them with timely information. They were often written in multiple languages and emphasized that all crime reporting would be strictly anonymous (Hu & Lovrich, 2023).

The police also interacted with the public on social media during the pandemic by sending notes of gratitude and posting emotion-filled slogans and feel-good stories. For example, messages such as these were commonplace: "We are all in this together!" "Love your city and do your part. Spread facts, not fear. Stay safe. Stay home. Stay calm" (Hu & Lovrich, 2023, p. 183). Many individuals would react favorably to these posts, such as "thank you for your service" and "god bless the blue" (Hu & Lovrich, 2023). In a study on police personnel who are responsible for maintaining agencies' social media accounts in England, the authors report similar patterns of activity the police relied upon involving the adroit use of social media to keep engaging with the public during the COVID-19 pandemic (Ralph et al., 2022). The study also reported that the police shifted back to more conventional police-related content when they judged that the public had grown weary of pandemic-related postings (Ralph et al., 2022).

Improving Police Use of Social Media

Compared to other criminal justice agencies, such as courts and corrections, police agencies use social media more often and more routinely. Our review of the literature on police use of social media indicates that the police can use social media to great benefit in their effort to fight crime and to communicate with the public they are sworn to serve. In this section, we propose several organizational and social media content suggestions for police agencies which seek to make effective use of social media and endeavor to maintain social media accounts on *Facebook* and other social media platforms.

Organizational Suggestions

In this chapter, we mainly treat police use of social media as an organizational behavior rather than an individual behavior. Students of policing know quite well that police agencies are widely known to be highly resistant to change (Crank, 2015). However, our previous analyses based on empirical evidence suggest that among three major components of the criminal justice system, the police may be the one component that is under the greatest pressure to utilize social media in its ongoing work. Given this marked sense of urgency, we put forward the following suggestions for police organizations regarding proactive uses of social media.

First, police agencies would be wise to make the effort to determine how the greater use of social media might promote their agency mission. Although we highly recommend including the adroit use of social media into modern policing strategies, some studies have found that a good number of police agencies are not very active on social media even though they have social media accounts (e.g., Lieberman et al., 2013). Investments of organizational resources and staffing are needed in addition to the establishment of an agency social media presence to realize the benefits of online social media communications in service to community-oriented policing (Hu & Lovrich, 2020). In addition, police agencies need to decide what "social media image" they wish to cultivate. Hu and colleagues (2018) studied police use of *Facebook* and identified four types of social media images of police agencies found on *Facebook*. "Crime fighters" publish a large number of crime-related posts and often use *Facebook* as another platform to disseminate BOLO announcements. "Traditional cops" mainly focus on crime-fighting, but at the same time they are inclined to post a few police-public partnership postings. "Public-relations facilitators" primarily focus on using *Facebook* as a tool for building and maintaining a good police-public relationships. And "mixers" post all kinds of things on *Facebook* without a specific focus (Hu et al., 2018). Police agencies should find its own social media *voice*, one that fits its history, traditions, and contemporary realities.

Second, after determining that they need social media and after identifying the purposes for using social media, police agencies need to determine what social media platforms can best meet their needs (Hu & Lovrich, 2020). Relatedly, they need to determine the start-up and maintenance costs associated with establishing an effective social media component in the agency. Here, we do not mean that police agencies must pay for using social media, because most social media platforms are free of charge. However, some platforms are expensive. For example, the best way to connect with teenagers on social media may be *TikTok*, as most *TikTok* users are in the 13–29 age demographic (Statista, 2023m). However, making an appealing *TikTok* video is much more difficult than crafting an appropriate *Facebook* posting. Having a social media presence on *TikTok* may require hiring staff or paying for consultants with special skills in filming and editing, as well as the rental or purchase of special video equipment. The same applies to *YouTube*. Social media platforms should also be selected based on whether they can meet the agencies' needs. For example, *Facebook* is a good social media platform for general use. *Twitter* is better employed as a rapid information dissemination tool. *YouTube* is a great platform for visually portraying police agency assets and police personnel and recruiting applicants for employment (Hu & Lovrich, 2020).

Although we introduced the ten most popular social media platforms in Chapter 2, very few police agencies use *Instagram* or *TikTok*. Besides these commercial social media platforms, some police agencies may find it beneficial to create their own social media *phone apps* (Elphick et al., 2021). For example, the Waynesville Police Department, NC, launched its own mobile application in 2023 (Long, 2023). The phone app features a variety of functions, such as "most wanted," "report human trafficking," "annual report," "meet the WPD," and "active crime prevention," which address both the crime-fighting and the community policing missions of the agency. These considerations of initiation and maintenance costs may be easier for larger police agencies to make use of a variety of social media platforms given their resources (Hu & Lovrich, 2019). This does not mean, however, that smaller police agencies cannot succeed in using social media (Take Chief Oliver's case as an example; see Hu & Lovrich, 2021).

Third, police agencies must determine who will have access to official social media accounts (Dekker et al., 2020). In large police agencies, public information officers (PIOs) are most likely to be responsible for maintaining official social media accounts (Hu & Lovrich, 2020). In small-size police agencies, sworn officers or civilian employees may take on the responsibility. Hu and Lovrich's (2021) study on a small police agency's success on *Facebook* (also shown in the opening story) highlights the importance of placing such a responsibility on a group of people instead of a single person. In their case study, Hu and Lovrich (2021) reported that one reason this relatively small police agency received a great many *Facebook* "likes" was that the agency's *Facebook* account was actually the chief's personal account. As such, the chief could pontificate on his philosophy of policing in a personal way other police agencies would never allow. Such leader branding causes a potential issue: the agency's social media voice is "hijacked" by the leader. Anything that happens to that leader will be attributed to the agency, good or bad. As shown in the opening story, the chief pleaded no contest to four charges of sexual harassment misdemeanors (Jones, 2016). The scandal caused a significant decrease in the agency's *Facebook* "likes," and the agency stopped posting new posts for almost eight months (Hu & Lovrich, 2021). Moreover, once the agency returned to its *Facebook* account, the content of new posts was "boring," and postings were written in a formal/legalistic tone, just like other standard police social media pages. Considering the foregoing, we believe that the content and tone used in police social media accounts should be consistent with the goals being sought and that a group of agency people should always be working together to maintain an agency's social media accounts. Importantly, police agencies need to provide appropriate technical training to those staff members who step forward to maintain departmental social media accounts (Dekker et al., 2020).

Fourth, social media platforms provide potentially valuable opportunities for two-way, real-time communication between the police and members of the public (Brainard & Derrick-Mills, 2011). Social media provide the potential for reaching the kinds of people who are not likely to be attracted to traditional police-public interactions such as community meetings (Hu et al., 2020). However, many studies have shown that while the police would appear to be continuing their use of social media as a broadcasting tool, two-way dialogues between the public and the police do not occur frequently on social media (Hu & Lovrich, 2022; O'Connor & Zaidi, 2021). If the public articulates a desire for more active engagement vis-a-vis social media, then police agencies should try to meet all reasonable needs. Police agencies should also provide a reasoned justification for not meeting some expressed public needs. For example, police agencies should be able to explain why they do not release any dashboard mounted or body-worn camera footage immediately after an incident occurs. It should be noted here that determining public needs is not as difficult as it once was. Police agencies can simply use social media to conduct public surveys. For example, they can pose "How are we doing?" or "What would you suggest to improve the PD?" on *Facebook* and encourage residents to make comments. To be noticed, some studies point out that there may be many individuals simultaneously following police *Facebook*, *Twitter*, and/or other social media platforms (Dai et al., 2017; Hughes et al., 2012). Accordingly, the police should not just simply copy and paste the same content across its different social media platforms.

Fifth, policies on agencies' use of social media should be drafted carefully and then implemented thoroughly. These policies should cover some points we have discussed earlier (e.g., who has access to the agency's social media accounts, what content might be posted, and the tone of the content). Meanwhile, the policies should cover at least four important points. First, clear instructions on how to adopt a new social media platform or abandon an old platform should be assembled. The social media space is evolving very quickly. The police should remain prepared to adjust and refine their use of social media, as continued advancements in digital communication technology are made (Hu & Lovrich, 2020). The police must adopt social media platforms in line with the public with whom they seek to connect. For example, as of now (March 2024), *TikTok* is the most popular social media platform among teenagers. Sadly, few police agencies are present on *TikTok*. If the police truly wish to maintain contact with teenagers on social media, they need to figure out what it would take to make effective use of *TikTok*. Second, privacy and confidentiality standards should be developed, both for the public and for agency personnel. For example, policies should provide guidelines to police officers regarding their private social media usage. In recent years, we have heard enough news about how police officers were investigated and fired after they posted offensive and racist messages on their social media (e.g., Dewan, 2019; Koch & Jackson, 2023; Winton, 2021; also see the Plain View Project mentioned in Chapter 1). The police know they are being "watched" (and possibly video-recorded) both in their face-to-face encounters with citizens and in their online activities. Third, a protocol for situations requiring crisis management should be developed when events of the day may call into question the public standing of the law enforcement agency (Dong & Wu, 2022). Finally, police agencies need to have policies in place to regulate how the police can use social media as a crime-fighting tool, policies setting forth appropriate probable cause criteria to be met before conducting online surveillance and collecting criminal evidence on social media (Fortin et al., 2023).

Police agencies operating in the digital age must be prepared to try out new social media platforms and test the utility of new features on "old" social media platforms. There are a variety of new social media platforms available, and the established platforms keep evolving. *Twitter* (now called X) was often used to send short messages (140-character limit). Now, the platform supports longer messages (280-character limit). An X premium subscriber can post up to 25,000 characters (*Twitter*, 2023). *YouTube* is commonly used to share videos. Of late, the platform has added the feature of sharing short videos (less than 60 seconds) called "shorts." *Instagram* is often used to share pictures. Now, it too has a similar short video feature it calls "reels." Some social media platforms also have a live-streaming function that allows users to engage other users in real-time interchanges (e.g., *Facebook*, *TikTok*, and *Twitch*). Most police agencies now use one or a small number of "traditional" social media platforms for posting conventional police social media posts. Only a few agencies have utilized innovative functions or tried new social media platforms. We argue here that because police agencies need to be resilient and adaptive social institutions (see Chapter 1), they need to adapt to the rapid changes of social contexts within which they carry out policing duties. It is our hope that successful innovations in the adroit use of social media are well-documented and quickly disseminated among reflective practitioners and policy scholars over the course of the next decade.

These organizational suggestions are proffered based on the situation in which the police use social media as a tool for conducting E-COP. Special suggestions should be addressed regarding police use of social media as a crime-fighting tool. For example, some past police monitoring of social media users may have raised constitutional issues regarding privacy rights expectations and warrantless searches (Fallik et al., 2020). Given such a potential for misuse, police investigators have need of special training in properly employing social media as a crime-fighting tool (Fortin et al., 2023). A recent study of detectives' perspectives toward the use of social media in their work revealed that although detectives generally embrace making use of social media, they acknowledge the presence of some serious barriers to social media mining for evidence of criminal misconduct (e.g., time-consuming) (Dewald, 2023). Training should also be given regarding preserving and utilizing social media evidence in courts (Hoffmeister, 2014). Regarding using social media as a BOLO tool (e.g., Hu & Lovrich, 2020), the police must be careful about the content posted to avoid the danger of reinforcing racial stereotypes about crime (e.g., Grunwald et al., 2022; Sever et al., 2021). Regarding using social media as a crime prevention tool, the police can distribute crime prevention tips widely at modest cost on their social media platforms (e.g., Dai et al., 2017; Lieberman et al., 2013). Besides, they can use social media (e.g., *WhatsApp*) to participate in or lead neighborhood crime prevention programs (e.g., Mols & Pridmore, 2019; Pridmore et al., 2019). These crime control and crime prevention goals cannot be achieved without the support coming from police agency leaders providing adequate staffing, training, equipment, and sustained funding.

Social Media Content Suggestions

Besides organizational suggestions, we also would like to propose several social media content suggestions for police practitioners and policymakers. First, the public favors the use of pictures in police social media posts (Hu et al., 2020). Accordingly, a well-considered picture can catch the public's attention far more effectively than a well-crafted bit of prose. For example, pictures of positive interactions between the police and the public are more likely to draw the public's attention than a bullet item in prose (Hu & Lovrich, 2020). Pictures of missing persons will attract more public engagement in locating the persons than a list of traits (e.g., height, weight, color of hair and eyes) (Ferguson & Soave, 2021). Moreover, some information such as wanted suspects and crime-related tips is better placed in a picture than a narrative. For instance, the police can craft eye-catching flyers based on crime prevention tips. Figure 4.5 shows a picture of property crime prevention tips posted on *Facebook* by the Manchester Police Department, CT. The public can simply right-click it and save it to their personal devices for sharing and/or future reference.

Second, while many police agencies employ humor (e.g., memes) on social media to increase public engagement (Wood & McGovern, 2021), humor should be applied with due caution. Studies have shown that the public generally welcomes funny pictures, interesting human-interest stories, and amusing videos featuring the police (Hu & Lovrich, 2020; Wood, 2020). These social media posts remind people that the police are vulnerable human beings

FIGURE 4.5 A picture of property crime prevention tips posted by Manchester Police Department (CT) on January 28, 2021 on *Facebook*.

rather than craven law enforcement machines (Mayes, 2022). Moreover, the public tends to interact more deeply with this type of police social media posting (Wood, 2020). However, humor should not be overused. Overusing humor may cause the public to question if the police are serious in their work of protecting and serving (Hu & Lovrich, 2020). After all, most of the public still thinks that the primary goal of the police is to fight crimes and catch criminals. They would benefit from seeing the other service side of the police. Meanwhile, it is likely that humor's effectiveness in attracting public engagement with the police lies in its novelty, which calls into question its effectiveness over the long term (Wood, 2020). Besides humor, studies have found that police tweets that cause emotional arousal are significantly positively related to public engagement (i.e., comments, likes, and retweets) on police *Twitter* accounts (Leppert et al., 2022). The police may also adopt this emotional arousal strategy to attract more public engagement on their social media channels. But just like humor, emotional arousal should not be overused, lest its impact become dulled.

Additionally, the police should be prepared to provide timely and accurate information when misinformation, which could threaten public safety, is in wide circulation (Hu & Lovrich, 2020). With social media platforms readily at hand, the police can bypass traditional mass media and directly communicate with the public (Mawby, 2010). With that being said, the police do not need to wait for the mass media (e.g., newspapers, radio, and TV) to clear misinformation. They can do it on their own. At this point, social media provides the police with a tool for "correcting the public discourse in a timely manner" (Hu & Lovrich, 2020, p. 152). Of course, there are at least two points particularly worthy of note here. First, it is impossible for the police to address all misinformation on social media. The police should allocate resources into addressing those that are in wide circulation and pose immediate or long-term danger to public safety. Second, the police must be very careful about how they address misinformation. Recall that "whatever occurs on-line, stays on-line" (Hu & Lovrich, 2020). They must respond to harmful misinformation, not avoid it, with the timely provision of accurate information. It takes a great deal of time and much consistently trustworthy behavior to build public trust and confidence in the police, but it only takes a short time to destroy it (Thomas, 1998). In this digital age, a simple screenshot of serious police misconduct on social media will be retrievable on the Internet for a very long time (Hu & Lovrich, 2020). Knowing this, when misinformation about police misconduct is posted on social media the police need to be able to respondent with dispatch.

Police social media posts are best written in a concise and organized way. Many social media users skim social media posts and use limited effort to seek out information important to them. Accordingly, police social media posts should ideally highlight important information in a noticeable place in the posting. For example, when a police agency decides to have a "coffee with cops" event and it announces it on its social media page, important information about this event such as its time and place should be displayed in the title or the first paragraph. While some social media platforms (e.g., *Facebook*) allow users to have various kinds of formats (e.g., narratives, pictures, and videos) embedded in a single post, it does not mean that the police should try to include as much information as possible in a single posting (Hu & Lovrich, 2020). Rather, the police need to clarify the primary purpose of each post and try to use the best format that fits the content. For example, pictures are good for spreading crime prevention tips (Hu & Lovrich, 2020) and locating missing persons (Ferguson & Soave, 2021). Videos may be good for explaining police activities in the neighborhood. Police social media posts should also be written in a way that most individuals can easily understand. Unlike courts (we will cover this topic in Chapter 5), the targeted population of police social media posts is the common citizen. The police should not craft their social media posts with too many technical and academic terms. In addition, police agencies must consider using foreign language postings to disseminate their posts if their jurisdictions include substantial limited English-proficient communities (Ballard & Rodriguez, 2023).

The content of police social media posts can give emphasis to commonly occurring offenses that are not featured in the traditional mass media.

Historically, mass media focus on rare offenses such as homicide (Surette, 2015a). Indeed, much of the public believes that dealing with serious offenses is the preoccupation of local police agencies. Police social media posts can move the focus to common crime types such as cybercrimes and property crimes against vulnerable populations such as young children and elderly persons (Hu & Lovrich, 2020), as well as crimes that need to be broadcast on social media such as human trafficking (Stickle et al., 2022). Moreover, the posting of tips need not pertain to crimes exclusively. Some agencies also post non-crime-related tips, such as winter and summer safety travel tips and driving safety tips for seniors (Hu et al., 2018).

The police can use social media to communicate with the public based on the topics that they believe are important. At the same time, it is also prudent to include content favored by the public (Cartwright & Shaw, 2020). Many topics of public interest may have little to do with traditional police work; however, they do help connect the police to the public. For example, empirical evidence suggests that the public loves to see police social media posts with K-9 units, horse-mounted patrols, seasonal greetings, and stories of how the police interact with youth (e.g., Hu et al., 2018, 2020; Lieberman et al., 2013). The police can now collect public feedback on their social media postings quite conveniently. They can encourage the public to provide feedback by making comments on their social media posts and then make use of these comments in refining their posts (Hu & Lovrich, 2020; Walkington et al., 2019).

Of course, not all comments the police receive will be positive. To maintain a positive social image, it is understandable if police agencies delete derogatory comments appearing on their social media platforms. We recommend that police agencies keep a record of the negative comments before deleting them (Hu & Lovrich, 2020). Some such comments may convey quite important information requiring agency action. For instance, the statement, "You guys ain't do shit in my neighborhood" may be a timely signal that a severe crime issue is present in this user's neighborhood, and the police are either unaware or unresponsive. Additionally, during a police-public crisis, such as a police use of excessive force incident, the public wants to hear the police version of events (Dong & Wu, 2022). The police can use social media to convey their empathy and ongoing commitment to public safety (Steele & Blau, 2023).

Finally, based on the E-COP model, we recommend that police agencies maintain a reasonable level of interaction with the public over social media. Online interaction encourages participation among individuals who do not want to physically interact with the police (Hu & Lovrich, 2020). Additionally, sometimes individuals will report their concerns on social media (e.g., via sending direct messages, using @ or # to call out local police agencies, and leaving comments under police social media posts) and expect the police to respond online or offline (Sachdeva & Kumaraguru, 2017). Sadly, studies have found that the police do not interact with the public on social media with any great frequency (Kudla & Parnaby, 2018). For example, Hu and colleagues (2018) found that fewer than 3% of police *Facebook* posts involve direct online interaction. Clearly, the potential for social media to facilitate police-public interactions remains largely untapped (Brainard & Derrick-Mills, 2011; Mawby, 2010). We believe that the concept of online police-public interaction should not be limited to instant online message exchanges but could be expanded to other forms of online interaction. For example, when a police agency publishes an engaging posting, and community members make comments under the posting, agency staff could register a reply to that comment. That reply could lead to a reply in turn.

Such online interactions could be broader. We think public reactions to police social media postings, such as clicking the "like" button and other reaction buttons (e.g., Livingstone, 2022), sharing posts, and making comments, can be broadly treated as police-public online interaction. We think that police agencies should set attainable goals of getting more public reaction/attention to their postings over the coming years. Even for some of the most popular police social media accounts, public reactions remain few in number. For instance, as of January 2024, the NYPD's *Facebook* page has almost 950,000 followers, but many of its posts have generated only a few hundred reactions. Encouraging the public to discuss controversial topics related to policing may be a way to increase police-public online interaction (Crump, 2011). One bit of favorable news is that many mainstream social media platforms now provide a live-streaming function, a service which provides the police with yet another effective way of conducting virtual police-public activities.

Conclusion

Among all social media and criminal justice topics being explored by scholars and reflective practitioners, the topic of social media and the police has been the most frequently investigated and produced the most empirical research and informed commentary. This chapter first has sought to make the case for police agencies making broad use of social media channels of communication in this digital age. We have shown how the police have been, historically speaking, quite adept at making use of new transportation, distance communication, and information technologies as they have matured as public institutions. We envision the police accomplishing the same creative incorporation of new technologies with respect to social media.

Next, we focused on two primary functions wherein the police can make effective use of social media to advance their agency mission of protecting and serving their communities: (1) a crime-fighting function, such as conducting a criminal investigation and conducting online surveillance; and (2) a communication function, such as promoting the goals of community-oriented policing via social media. We have discussed both functions with frequent reference to empirical studies produced by academic researchers and informed commentaries offered by experienced practitioners. Next, we proposed a model for using social media to conduct e-community-oriented policing. In addition, we summarize suggestions for improving police use of social media in both crime-fighting and public relations promotion. We conclude the chapter arguing that contemporary police reform efforts should include the effort to adopt the effective use of social media in contemporary policing in large and small law enforcement agencies alike.

5

SOCIAL MEDIA AND THE COURTS

Opening Story: When defendant Delvon King walked into Judge Robert Nalley's courtroom for a gun charge filed against him, he did not expect to be shocked with 50,000 volts of electricity (ABC News, 2016). During the hearing, when Judge Nalley talked about the jury selection process, King spoke over him and tried to make what he believed was a legal argument (Castaneda, 2016). Judge Nalley said "Stop, stop!" However, defendant King failed to heed the judge's warning and kept on talking. "Use it," said the judge, "Mr. Sheriff, do it, use it." Within a few seconds, King dropped to the ground wailing in pain after receiving a 50,000-volt shock from a stun-cuff attached to his ankle (Castaneda, 2016). The stun device had been placed on the defendant to prevent King from fleeing. "All right. I'm going to take five and I'll be back" said the judge, "Wait until he calms down and I'll be back." Public videos and prosecutor O'Malley confirmed that King did not raise his voice, yell, or make threats to other people in the courtroom (ABC News, 2016). Later, Judge Nalley pleaded guilty to a misdemeanor civil rights violation, received a one-year probation and $5,000 fine, and was required to take a series of anger management classes (ABC News, 2016). Moreover, the Maryland Court of Appeals also banned Judge Nalley from the bench for life (Castaneda, 2016). Judge Nalley did not apologize to King but acknowledged that he made a serious error in judgment (ABC News, 2016). "I regret that it ended this way," said the convicted Judge.

Open Justice or Guilty Before Trial?

Videos about misbehaving judges are not uncommon on *YouTube*. The video of Judge Nalley's case received over one million views and thousands of

DOI: 10.4324/9781003360049-6

comments across different *YouTube* channels. One comment that received many "likes" opines, "Now we know why cameras have been banned in courtrooms." The pace of widely adopting social media by courts may be slower than that in policing, but they seem to have no choice but to adapt to social media and face the challenges associated with its ubiquitous presence in our society. By 2014–2015, many trial courts had incorporated social media into their communication strategies (Johnston, 2017). In the U.S., based on data compiled by the National Center for State Courts (NCSC), as of January 30, 2023, 28 state courts (55%) have adopted *Facebook*, 42 state courts (82%) have at least one *Twitter* account, 35 state courts (69%) have *YouTube* channels, and 10 state courts (20%) use *Instagram* (NCSC, 2023). Courts can benefit from using social media in several clear ways. Social media allows courts to participate in legal networking so that they can learn from innovations attempted in other courts (Mattan et al., 2020). Social media can be used to improve court-public relations (Keyzer et al., 2013) and educate citizens about the importance of jury duty. Social media can be used to make courts more accessible and responsive to the needs of the public (Blackham & Williams, 2013).

However, such potential benefits of this age of social media have been slow to materialize in U.S. trial courts. An analysis on 53 sentencing short clips on *YouTube* collected from U.S. courtrooms imply a clear tendency of judges to reinforce punitive justice frames (i.e., justice-as-retribution, justice-as-entertainment, and justice-as-victim-advocacy); the videos focus on trials dealing with the most severe crimes such as murder, child abuse, and sexual assault (Revier, 2021). These video clips feature almost no contextual detail on the defender or their background, and, in doing so, they broadly circulate the notion that all criminals are monsters and that the criminal justice system operates as a "gigantic revenge factory" (Revier, 2021, p.450). The actual truth is that courts do more than just dole out punishment to the worst among us. Many judges are effective advocates of the use of courts to promote restorative justice and broad use of rehabilitative resources in dealing with offenders. For example, an 80-year-old judge named Frank Caprio has gone viral on social media because of his compassion, humor, and efforts to restore public faith in government (CBS, 2017). The judge observes, "I don't wear a badge under my robe. I wear a heart under my robe" (CBS, 2017). On *YouTube*, a channel named "Caught in Providence" stores videos of Judge Caprio's courtroom. As of December 2023, there are over 2.5 million subscribers to the channel, and videos on this channel have been watched over 500 million times.

Judge Caprio's success on social media is no less than phenomenal. However, there are relatively few court actors following his lead. Unlike police agencies, courts and the judges in charge of court operations generally are inclined to treat the use of social media with utmost caution. A study on social media platforms (*Facebook*, *Twitter*, and *YouTube*) employed by four state judicial systems and the District of Columbia (New York, Florida, Michigan, and North Carolina) revealed that their primary use is to disseminate information such as dicta and rulings in a unidirectional manner (Ure, 2019). Interactions between the courts and social media users are occasional at best (Ure, 2019). Another study on 1,712 tweets sent by the International Criminal Court (ICC) between 2017 and 2019 also indicates that the ICC uses *Twitter* to distribute information rather than collect feedback or generate two-way dialogue (Banks, 2022). A 2020 study on Canadian courts' use of *Twitter* indicates a similar pattern of "official dissemination" use. Mattan and colleagues (2020) analyzed 2,428 tweets from 20 court jurisdictions and documented that informational tweets dominate heavily in how Canadian courts use *Twitter*. About 76% of the total sampled tweets are purely informational. Four jurisdictions post informational tweets exclusively (Mattan et al., 2020). These tweets are used in general to deliver information to lawyers, journalists, and the interested public. An Australian study also opines that courts in that country will continue to serve as simple content providers on social media making digital court documents more broadly available to parties with business before them (Johnston, 2017).

Even though a general sense of trepidation persists among courts and judges about using social media for a broader range of purposes, courts should be encouraged to continue using social media as is done currently and experiment with broadening that use (Jackson & Shelly, 2015). In fact, the courts that continued to operate during the COVID-19 pandemic have shown us that virtual court proceedings can be both effective and efficient (Duhart & Smith, 2021). In 2020, millions of court proceedings (e.g., hearings, arraignments, and even trials) in U.S. courtrooms were conducted via *Zoom* and other online meeting platforms (Scigliano, 2021). It is quite likely that in the future many courts will conduct at least some of their proceedings and trials on social media platforms (with strict access controls in place).

That said, this expansion of use of social media in courts will not take place until key courtroom actors come to agreement on how to balance publicity/transparency and privacy concerns. Publicity, transparency, and privacy are not only important to having fair trials, but they also offer an element of public supervision over legal professionals. Just as in the case with the police, the public uses social media to supervise judges and other legal professionals involved in the criminal justice system. For example, in 2011 Judge William Adams's daughter posted a *YouTube* video showing him beating his then-teenage daughter with a belt (Browning, 2014). The video brought forth a formal police investigation, a temporary suspension, and a public admonishment of Judge Adams (Browning, 2014). Ironically, Judge Adams presided over *family court* (Browning, 2014). However unbelievable, Judge Adams's case is a real one! While social media can help with the policing of judicial conduct and the removal of malevolent judges, misinformation about courts and legal professionals can also be quickly circulated on social media resulting in harm (Keyzer et al., 2013). The following two sections discuss this important question: "Does social media bring healthy publicity and transparency of courtrooms to the public, or does it compromise impartial trials?"

Publicity, Transparency, and Open Justice

Most of the public learns about the criminal courts through the mass media (Neubauer & Fradella, 2014). Social media bring publicity and transparency in courts to a new and higher-level salience for the public. The importance of publicity and transparency is indisputable in a democratic society (Hausegger et al., 2014). These aspects of democratic oversight have been discussed quite extensively in the policing literature because the police are the criminal justice system actors who have the highest frequency of contact with the public. The truly massive societal investment made in body-worn cameras for the police in recent years reflects this preoccupation with democratic oversight. As with the police, courts certainly could use more publicity and transparency because they are the places where criminal defendants are tried and sentenced. In this regard, Johnston (2018) most appropriately cites Jeremy Bentham's observation that publicity is the "very soul of justice" (p. 525). Using Bentham's theory of open justice as a broad framework, Johnson proposes three phases of publicity regarding U.S. criminal courts after the 19th century. The first phase she labels *press coverage*, featuring oversight on behalf of the public by newspapers and other traditional mass media (Surette, 2015a). The second phase she labels *media liaison*, reflecting a process of oversight which involves a court public information officer (liaison to professional journalists) who ensures the accuracy of the information that mass media disseminate on court proceedings (Johnston, 2018). The third phase she labels *the internet*, where the principal news source is social media portrayal of court proceedings (Johnston, 2018). Social media channels allow courts to bypass traditional media and communicate with the public directly if and when they decide to do so (Mattan et al., 2020). Social media also offers the public more channels of access to the judicial aspect of the criminal justice system.

Access to justice is one of the most essential components of a criminal justice system, particularly in democratic countries. This is particularly true of the U.S. where a very high proportion of U.S. judges and prosecutors are ELECTED OFFICIALS. One element of access to justice is known as "open court" or "open justice" (Barrett, 2011; Findlay, 2015). There are three core open justice principles. First, judicial proceedings must be open to the public. Second, the evidence presented at trial must be open to the public who are present in the courtrooms. And third, what happens in the courtrooms must be open to the public not able to be present in the courtroom (mostly via media) (Bosland & Townend, 2018).

Small and Puddister (2020) summarize at least three tangible benefits of the open courts concept: (1) it helps protect the due process rights of the accused; (2) it checks the power of the government, including states and courts through the facilitation of accountability; and (3) it educates the public on how fair trials proceed, thereby sustaining public confidence in the legal system and its ability to provide for the rule of law. As a matter of practice, although the public always has the right to go to courtrooms and watch trials, it is not very convenient for most people to take advantage of this mandatory openness to court observers. With social media, watching live trials no longer is restricted by geographic and temporal limitations. The televised and recorded trial is not an entirely new concept. It can be traced back to the trial of serial killer Ted Bundy in 1979, believed to be the first national broadcast criminal trial (Murray, 2022). Many Americans are familiar with the cable television channel "Court TV" (also known as TruTV), featuring live courtroom proceedings. Court TV was relaunched in 2019 and is now available on streaming services such as *YouTube*.

In the very broadly reported divorce trial involving actors Johnny Depp and Amber Heard (*Depp v. Heard*) resulting in a $7 million award to Amber Hearst, Court TV's viewership "practically quadrupled" during the trial (Murray, 2022). On *YouTube*, Court TV's live stream on the verdict of the Depp case reached over 420,000 viewers. Court TV's competitor, Law&Crime Network, has over 24 million views on streaming this verdict on its *YouTube* channel. Depp's supporters also used highlights from the trial to create the hashtag #justiceforjohnnydepp, which attracted more than 15 billion views (Fielder, 2023).

The Depp case and many other examples (e.g., #MeToo, #BlackLivesMatter) reflect the fact that social media can be used as a powerful tool for conducting online activism for legal issues. According to Steinberg (2016), this tool "has amplified the voices of marginalized individuals and shifted national conversations on important legal and social issues" (p. 413). The public now has access to public debates in a way that was previously impossible (Meyer, 2014). However, some studies suggest that the level of engagement in activism may vary among individuals who write letters to congressmen and who use hashtags and/or click "like." The former tends to have more personal commitment (Steinberg, 2016). Whatever the case may be, social media provides an opportunity for everyday citizens to participate in controversial legal issues, maximizing the publicity role of courts in our criminal justice system (Blackham & Williams, 2013).

A notable distinction must be drawn between publicity and transparency in courtrooms. The *publicity* function focuses on whether the public has access to different stages of a trial. Of course, not all trials or all stages of trials should be completely open to the public. For example, trials involving juvenile offenders are not public out of a desire to preserve the future for a youth in need of assistance. Similarly, attorneys representing the defendant and the prosecutor's office need to meet *in camera* with judges to negotiate ground rules for the trial as it proceeds. *Transparency* focuses on whether the judicial decision-making process is subject to effective external oversight.

For example, a defendant may have committed five robberies with solid evidence, yet the prosecutor will bring only three charges to the courts. The public – and lawyers who may wish to challenge a siting prosecutor in the next election – are sometimes quite curious about how "prosecutorial discretion" was used to decide which three charges to bring to the attention of the court. Historically, this "backstage area" has not been open to the public on the premise that prosecutors can make use of their discretion to negotiate for guilty pleas and maximize certainty of successful conviction – both done "in service to justice" and to enhance the expediency of court operations. Court observers and commentators on social media typically expect social media actors to break through the wall to the previous hidden backstage area.

The question of exposing up the protected areas of court and prosecutorial processes is not a simple one of expanding transparency at all costs. On the one hand, the use of social media is broadly viewed as informal and highly personalized. On the other hand, posts on social media are publicly available and legally discoverable. Such a hybrid character of social media deters judges and prosecutors from opening up the backstage area to parties outside the courtroom to any great degree (Van den Hoven, 2015). It is currently the case that judges are far from united in their views on whether social media use in courtrooms should be expanded; some judges believe that more extensive use of social media in the courtroom, such as allowing the tweeting of trials, would materially improve the criminal justice system (Hoffmeister, 2014). Most judges, however, believe that such activities in the courtroom detract from the solemnity and dignity of the courtroom.

Guilty Before Trial

Enhanced publicity and transparency brought by the advocates of expanding social media access to courts would be an unqualified good only if gains could be balanced with proper concern for privacy. However, the very nature of social media makes it extremely difficult to achieve this ideal balance. For those who are directly involved in criminal cases (e.g., defendants, victims, witnesses, the police, and even judges), compromises of privacy rights may not be a welcome change in the status quo. It has been noted by scholars of judicial administration that "social media has created intense challenges for the law and judicial administration" (Keyzer et al., 2013, p. 47). The Sixth Amendment in the U.S. constitution guarantees a defendant's right to a public trial without unnecessary delay. Social media provides the opportunity to reach both goals – public openness and timeliness of criminal trials. We discussed public trials in the preceding section, and we think enhanced publicity and transparency brought by social media to the courtrooms can be fairly considered to be a positive impact overall. However, publicity and transparency may also lead to a "speedy" trial that should not be so speedy, as to increase the odds of a faulty final judgment by the court. Social media users are inclined to rush to rash conclusions before considering the entirety of evidence brought into court (Hoffmeister, 2014). They often learn of the defendant's previous criminal record and inappropriately consider him or her guilty by association in the current trial. In addition, the anonymity and/or inability to verify sources that is a core feature of social media (McPeak, 2019) which makes it very difficult to attribute information circulated on social media platforms to a specific source. The use of social media in the courtrooms has led to numerous mistrials in which the rights of defendants have been found to have been compromised (Janoski-Haehlen, 2011). Similarly, the use of social media outside the courtroom can interfere with a fair trial through jury pool contamination. Studies have shown that even modest pretrial publicity can lead potential jurors to become biased against defendants (Neubauer & Fradella, 2014).

One such example is the case of the trial for the murder of Gillian (Jill) Meagher in Australia in 2012. Like the U.S., Australian law guarantees a criminal defendant a fair trial and access to an unbiased jury of one's peers. Tubridy (2020) analyzed over 3,000 comments on the RIP Jill Meagher *Facebook* page. As one of the first Australian crimes that attracted substantial social media attention, *Facebook* users frequently opined that the person accused of the crime was a monster, personified evil, and worthy of little mercy from the court. Interestingly, a substantial portion of comments posted on social media asked other users to stop making derogatory comments about the defendant because doing so would "prejudice the hope for a fair trial" (Tubridy, 2020, p. 143). A more in-depth analysis also revealed that from a fair number of *Facebook* users' misguided perspectives, the right to a fair trial was viewed as an unprincipled approach for an accused to use to avoid punishment (Tubridy, 2020).

Fenn (2022) summarizes four constitutional rights that can come into conflict when conducting public trials: (1) the right of courtroom players to privacy; (2) the right of defendants to public trials; (3) the right to freedom of the press; and (4) the right of all defendants to fair trials. Fenn (2022) correctly observes that these important rights must be *balanced* by presiding judges. Moreover, in the age of social media with live streams and playback options, we need to pay special attention to how to achieve an impartial trial if jurors can relatively easily access live streams, playback, and the accompanying commentary on a trial in which they are serving (Fenn, 2022). Meanwhile, social media and its algorithms allow users to see and hear only what they want to see and hear (Hoffmeister & Watts, 2018). Doing so often leads to polarization of views, where the public becomes divided into two vocal groups – one strongly supportive of the defendant and the other strongly opposed – often even before the trial begins. This causes a great challenge in high-profile trials.

Take the globally witnessed divorce trial *Depp v. Heard* noted earlier as an example. Long before the trial began fans of Johnny Depp and supporters of Amber Heard flooded social media with commentary – some relevant to the impending trial and much irrelevant and potentially defamatory. Social media users appear to have decided their positions ahead of any evidence being presented in the courtroom, and social media algorithms constantly reinforced their predispositions by feeding them with many similar posts. For some cases, particularly high-profile cases, the public has decided whether defendants are guilty before juries deliver verdicts. In other words, defendants have been "social media" tried.

Social media trials are neither ethically nor legally acceptable because criminal and civil process defendants are legally *presumed to be innocent* until proven guilty in a forum wherein adversarial proceedings are presided over by a capable judge. Guilt and culpability are decided by a jury of one's peers who take an oath to be unbiased in their hearing of facts and to follow the dictates of the law as explicated by the judge. Moreover, defendants also enjoy the right to privacy – an implied right which has become a part of judge-made law in the American legal system (Glancy, 1979). The U.S. Supreme Court, beginning as early as 1923 and continuing through its recent decisions, has broadly read the "liberty" guarantee of the Fourteenth Amendment to assure a broad right of privacy that has come to encompass decisions about child rearing, procreation, marriage, and many other aspects of a citizen's life.

Sadly, privacy has been greatly diminished in the age of social media, not by any governmental action but rather by the actions of individuals armed with the powers of social media. Social media miners can dig out defamatory information – even that which gets deleted. If we cannot stop them from getting private information on social media, can we at least prevent the information from spreading? Hews and Suzor (2017) conducted an analysis of *Twitter* posts during the murder trial of Baden-Clay, a case which drew a great deal of social media attention in Australia. They examine if *sub judice contempt*, which prohibits publishing prejudicial materials when defendants are set for and during the trials, can minimize the flow of prejudicial information on social media (Hews & Suzor, 2017). Unsurprisingly, professional journalists' tweets mostly contain objective news reports; in contrast, non-journalists' (i.e., the public) tweets are often opinionated and prejudicial (Hews & Suzor, 2017). The researchers conclude that *sub judice contempt* seems to only work on professional journalists. It is nearly impossible to enforce restraining orders effectively among the public (Keyzer et al., 2013). Since *sub judice contempt* has only little impact on the public, jurors are inundated by prejudicial information on social media, and therefore verdicts may be tainted (Hews & Suzor, 2017). Moreover, understandably, the information suppressed by courts will be more likely to go viral on social media because many among the public are suspicious about what the government might be hiding (Keyzer et al., 2013).

There are other potential pitfalls of restrictions on the use of social media by courts. For example, unlike police agencies, courts need to maintain a certain degree of detachment from the public so they can preserve the authority of the courts (Blackham & Williams, 2013). Courts and judges ideally should not be affected by the public when deciding cases. However, social media dramatically reduces such a detachment and may seriously undermine the integrity of courts (Blackham & Williams, 2013). Improper social media postings posted by courts may harm the reputation of courts (Mattan et al., 2020). Blackham and Williams (2013) also note that even if most of the public is now using social media routinely, there is still a population of individuals who do not have social media or do not use social media frequently. Accordingly, court authorities should not rely solely on social media channels to disseminate important information pertaining to the operation of courts.

Major Players in the Courtroom and Their Use of Social Media

In this section we focus on the major actors in the courtroom and examine their use of social media. We primarily focus on what each actor can do with social media, the benefits of using social media, and the potential harm from their use of social media. Law professionals are generally held to a high standard in the processing of legal matters. They are held to a higher standard than citizens in general regarding online communication, and they must seek balance in their professional representational duties when engaged in the throes of the adversarial process of justice (McPeak, 2019).

Defendants

Defendants are not criminals. In most countries, defendants are legally presumed to be innocent until proven guilty. In the U.S., the public generally believes that most criminal defendants receive trials; in reality, most defendants are convicted via a process of expedited judicial hearings reflective of a plea-bargaining process in which the defense and prosecution present a "deal struck" by the two to the judge. According to a 2023 Pew Research report, in fiscal year 2022, about 90% of federal criminal defendants pleaded guilty, roughly 8% of them had their cases dismissed, and only about 2% of them went to a public trial. Among those defendants who went to trial, about 83% were found guilty, and 17% (less than 0.4% in total) were acquitted (Gramlich, 2023). However, the fact that a small proportion of defendants go to trial does not mean the trial process is not important. In the previous section, we discussed how social media may increase transparency and publicity in the courtrooms. Both are critical to ensure a fair trial for defendants. We also discussed how social media may violate individual privacy (defendants' privacy here) by bringing about a speedy but partial social media trial, an action which is fundamentally unjust to defendants. There are some other ways in which social media can adversely impact defendants.

Defendants must be very careful about what they post on social media before, during, and even after trials. In fact, we all need to be careful about our social media posts because once online, they stay online (Hu & Lovrich, 2020) and can be retrieved by persons trained in forensic data mining. CNN reports that Republican Representative Marjorie Greene removed dozens of *Facebook* posts she posted to promote fallacious conspiracy theories calling for the execution of major Democratic politicians between 2018 and 2019 (Steck & Kaczynski, 2021). When these postings were located and reposted, she was removed from all congressional committee roles within a matter of days. Although the Fifth Amendment does provide protection from self-incrimination in official proceedings and court settings (Tomkovicz, 2011), this protection does not apply to self-generated social media posts. Some defendants have posted quite incriminating information pertaining to their own criminal activities on social media, information which led to their conviction later (Murphy & Fontecilla, 2012). Even though defendants may use "privacy settings" to allow only their social media friends to view their posts, the police often gain access to those putatively "private" posts through fake social media accounts and the cooperation of the defendants' media friends (Murphy & Fontecilla, 2012). Up to now, such action by the police and prosecutors has been deemed constitutional.

Some U.S. states have enacted laws to forbid criminal defendants from using social media (Hoffmeister, 2014). Defense attorneys typically suggest that clients make use of social media *wisely* because social media use provides an opportunity for the public and police to invade their defendants' privacy (Keyzer et al., 2013). The privacy invasion in question has two primary aspects. The first is that the public can use social media to circulate any information related to the defendant they wish. The information may or may not be germane to the trial. Often, this is information about a defendant's education, past and/or current employment history, prior criminal offenses, marriage status and/or family relations, and familial background. For example, lifelong anonymity orders (sealing of juvenile records by the court) are often used to protect adults once convicted as juveniles from the ongoing adverse effects of a troubled youth; such sealing is threatened by social media posting alleging a deviant youth (Gordon, 2019). The public can then use the information disseminated to assemble a negative mental image of the defendants facing trial as an adult. The second is that the public uses social media to retrieve a defendant's past social media posts. The public analyzes these posts, and once again portrays the defendant as a bad person. To be noted, members of the public tend to be hypercritical of these postings – any perceived blemishes in character will be amplified and circulated on social media for broad dissemination.

Not only members of the public are interested in some defendant's social media pages, especially in a high-profile case, but so are legal professionals. Neubauer and Fradella (2014) report a case where a probation officer recommended a jail sentence of less than 12 months, but the judge sentenced the defendant to 64 months in prison. The defendant was involved in a fatal accident. She posted a picture of her wearing a t-shirt with "I love Patron" and drinking with friends after the accident on *MySpace*. Witnessing this posting, the judge in the case considered the defendant to be seriously lacking in remorse and accordingly issued her an unusually harsh sentence (Neubauer & Fradella, 2014). In sentencing insurrectionists who engaged in riots at the U.S. Capital on January 6, 2021, federal judges viewed self-incriminating social media posts as probative evidence in their sentencing decisions. One defendant posted, "Overall, I had fun lol" on *Facebook*. Judge Jackson informed the defendant that the social media post made it extremely difficult for her to show the defendant any leniency in assigning a sentence (Reed, 2021).

Some states have state statutes prohibiting ex-criminals from using social media. This type of prohibition brings up the discussion on whether we should keep punishing ex-criminals if they have already been punished appropriately and served their time. The discussion often involves the First Amendment and perhaps also the Fourteenth Amendment. One of the classic cases in this area is *Doe v. Prosecutor*, Marion County Indiana (2013). Doe was not on parole, probation, or supervised release, but he had registered as required by Indiana law as a sex offender upon his release from prison after having served time for child exploitation. Indiana law prohibited Doe from using social media because it would provide him easy access to minors. The lower court upheld the state law, but the Seventh Circuit Court of Appeals reversed the lower's decision, holding that the law was overly broad and detrimental to the rights of the accused and adjudicated offenders. The Seventh Circuit Court did not prohibit the state from placing reasonable restrictions on ex-criminals' access to social media but opined that the state law must be more narrowly tailored (*Doe v. Prosecutor*, 2013). In Doe's case, it was decided that so long as Doe does not improperly communicate with minors on social media, his right to use social media should be protected. Should he violate that ban on improper communication, his right to use social media could be abrogated.

The observations noted previously should not be taken to signify that social media is completely harmful to criminal defendants; in many ways, it can be very useful. For instance, defendants can work with defense attorneys to seek exculpatory evidence and the impeachment of prosecutorial evidence on social media. However, Murphy and Fontecilla (2012) correctly observe that defendants face more challenges in seeking helpful evidence than do governmental agencies. Defendants and their attorneys typically do not have the forensic digital equipment or ability to scan social media posts to look for exculpatory evidence. It is also often very difficult for them to seek a third-party subpoena (Murphy & Fontecilla, 2012). Nonetheless, defendants can make efforts to utilize social media to sculpt their public images in a proactive effort to build public support and gain sympathy for their fate. Both sides in the Depp and Heard trial noted earlier made major, well-funded, and sustained efforts to build public sympathy for the popular actor and his estranged wife claiming spousal abuse.

Defense Attorneys

Defense attorneys represent the interests of the defendants in criminal and some civil cases (Neubauer & Fradella, 2014). In a book published in 2014, Hoffmeister identified three types of defense attorneys based on their attitudes toward using social media as a tool for doing their job. Some defense attorneys completely ignore social media and do not think it will benefit them. Some attorneys are aware of the benefits of using social media, but they do not know how to do it. And the last group of attorneys know the importance of social media and are willing to use it, but they typically claim that they do not have time to do it on an ongoing basis (Hoffmeister, 2014). The overall conclusion drawn by Hoffmeister was that defense attorney does not make extensive use of social media.

A decade after the publication of Hoffmeister's book, however, social media has become a *regular tool* for defense attorneys both in and outside the courtroom. Outside the courtroom, defense attorneys use social media to investigate their own defendants, crime victims, potential jurors, and even judges before whom they argue their cases (McPeak, 2019). In the courtroom, defense attorneys commonly use social media to provide alibis, discredit witnesses, and provide additional evidence at trial that the police may choose to ignore. The occupational use of social media among defense attorneys seems to be a must-have job skill in the contemporary setting. Researchers and legal professionals alike have made note of the fact that a growing number of trial courts now view the use of social media among attorneys as a new basic professional skill (Hoffmeister, 2014). Failure to mine easily accessed information on social media could even be claimed as evidence of ineffective assistance of counsel in some states (Hoffmeister, 2014). Law schools, likewise, have become aware of the need for their graduates to command a knowledge of social media platforms and understand their potential utility in representing their clients.

Existing literature on how criminal defense attorneys make use of social media to serve their clients primarily focuses on using social media to investigate prospective jurors (e.g., Nance, 2015). Although some courts may still be opposed to it, the American Bar Association (ABA) in general views researching prospective jurors' social media as "fair game" (Nance, 2015). Traditional investigations of prospective jurors often entail the use of private detectives and professional jury consultants (Judge, 2015). They typically use the information they gather from diverse sources to develop a "profile" of prospective jurors and ask questions in *voir dire* designed to expose hidden biases (Neubauer & Fradella, 2014). Typically, the investigation process is slow and rather expensive. With social media, it is possible to conduct a much quicker and far less inexpensive examination of prospective jurors carried out by attorneys and paralegals equipped with appropriate social media research skills (Bartels & Lee, 2013).

Hoffmeister and Watts (2018) argue that there are three benefits of using this method of social media posting analysis. First, attorneys are less likely to exercise peremptory challenges (i.e., deselecting jurors without giving any reason) based on their "hunches" alone (Hoffmeister & Watts, 2018). Second, attorneys can make use of social media information to further examine prospective jurors during *voir dire*, knowing what pattern of postings the person has posted in recent times (Hoffmeister & Watts, 2018). Some studies have indicated that prospective jurors are often more candid in their online communications than they are in *voir dire* (Hoffmeister, 2014; Judge, 2015; Marder, 2014). And third, Hoffmeister and Watts (2018) argue that social media can be used to monitor jurors' behavior to reduce the likelihood of juror misconduct. Defense attorneys now make more frequent use of social media to shape public opinions (Hoffmeister, 2014). Moreover, it must be noted that social media provides an opportunity for marginalized people to share their personal stories and narratives, stories which defense attorneys can use to demonstrate public support for a particular issue important to their client's case in the courtroom (Steinberg, 2016).

In fairness, we must acknowledge that most defense attorneys are not highly proficient in the use of social media. As Hoffmeister (2014) noted over a decade ago, while they may wish to make use of social media to promote a vigorous defense for their clients, they often either do not know how or simply lack the time to do it. Besides technological and digital communication skills being limited, there are ethical issues for defense attorneys to use social media during their work, particularly with invasion of privacy issues being encountered (Nance, 2015). Although most of the content on social media is open to the public, meaning that if a person registers as a user they can view the content (sometimes they do not even need to register), some content posted is viewed as *private*. For example, *Facebook*'s privacy settings allow platform users to set their content as private. Only their "friends" can view the information posted – such as profile information, pictures, videos, and posts – on the social media platform. The American Bar Association guideline for defense attorneys suggests not "friending" witnesses or jurors on social media because this action may violate the prohibition against contacting witnesses and jurors which are a common element of federal and state court rules (Klein & Yamamoto, 2020). Interestingly, the New York City Bar even prohibits attorneys from subscribing or following jurors' tweets unless both parties are aware of this activity (Hoffmeister, 2014).

Besides witnesses and jurors, defense attorneys must be cautious about providing suggestions to their clients regarding social media content. It is generally not a violation of ethics for defense attorneys to tell their clients to stop using social media or to maintain a positive image presence. It may be, however, a violation of professional ethics if they instruct their clients to delete incriminating information on social media because such information may be viewed as evidence essential to the fairness of court proceedings (Hoffmeister, 2014). Moreover, defense attorneys must carefully deal with their own posts on social media because it is difficult to control online information that could damage their (and the clients') reputations (McPeak, 2019). Other instances of ethical misconduct may occur when attorneys make commentary about ongoing cases or post online advertising of their services on social media (Hoffmeister, 2014).

Prosecutors

A prosecutor is a legal representative of the government in a criminal case. In general, prosecutors have similar benefits of using social media to those of defense attorneys. They can use social media to investigate defendants, victims, and witnesses (McPeak, 2019). They can also use social media to investigate prospective jurors. Additionally, regarding the use of social media, prosecutors have similar ethical codes of conduct as defense attorneys. They should be careful about contacting victims and witnesses on social media. They should not contact jurors during trials (Klein & Yamamoto, 2020). Moreover, they should pay attention to their social media posts related to commentary about ongoing cases.

Prosecutors are often considered the most powerful actors in the criminal courts (Neubauer & Fradella, 2014). They have ultimate discretion in initiating, conducting, and terminating criminal prosecutions (Neubauer & Fradella, 2014). In this regard, *charging* decisions may be the most important acts carried out by prosecutors (Neubauer & Fradella, 2014). Neubauer and Fradella (2014) list several factors impacting prosecutors' charging decision-making; these include such factors as the seriousness of the offense, degree of harm done, strength of the evidence, offenders' and victims' demographics, and anticipation of judges' and jurors' decisions should a case be taken to court. Today, prosecutors must also deal with social media posts. For example, it is difficult to tell if a narrative/sentence is a true threat or just a joke on social media posts. In face-to-face interaction, a true threat typically involves not only verbal or physical actions but also facial or emotional expressions of a threatener.

The very first case that the U.S. Supreme Court heard regarding true threats and speeches on social media is *Elonis v. United States* (2015). Elonis was convicted for posting threats to a few people, including his wife, an FBI agent, and a kindergarten class on *Facebook*. The U.S. Supreme Court overturned lower courts' decisions and ruled that the prosecution must prove that there is a subjective intent to threaten. In other words, a person posting threats on social media cannot be convicted of committing threats simply because other people view these posts as threatening. Practitioners have argued that the *Elonis* decision makes it much more difficult for prosecutors to charge perpetrators for making threats on social media (Monagas & Monagas, 2015). A simple screenshot of threatening posts on social media is not sufficient. This, however, does not mean that prosecutors and the police should neglect threatening-like posts on social media. To balance the First Amendment and public safety, the police and prosecutors must do more work to document a perpetrator's *mens rea*.

Jurors

Jurors are people who get summoned to courtrooms to hear evidence and return an impartial verdict regarding a conviction or a penalty. Although a jury trial is rather uncommon today in criminal cases, the trial process remains prominent in the justice system and serves as a key feature of maintaining the legitimacy of court judgments (Diamond & Rose, 2018). The jury system is one of the crucial elements of ensuring a fair trial, but some scholars believe its central role is slowly being seriously eroded by the march of social media (Marder, 2014). Ideally, jurors are instructed not to gain information about the case before them outside of the trial. While in trial, they cannot conduct their own research on the case and cannot be contacted by attorneys except during *voir dire*. Historically, it has always been difficult to control jurors and make certain they do not receive case-related information from outside the courtroom setting. With the widespread (perhaps even ubiquitous) adoption of social media among the public, it is almost impossible to expect the jury to comply with this rule of voluntary self-denial of access to case-relevant information. Even so, citizens have been willing to serve on juries, viewing it still as a "civic duty" to be taken seriously. Sadly, public

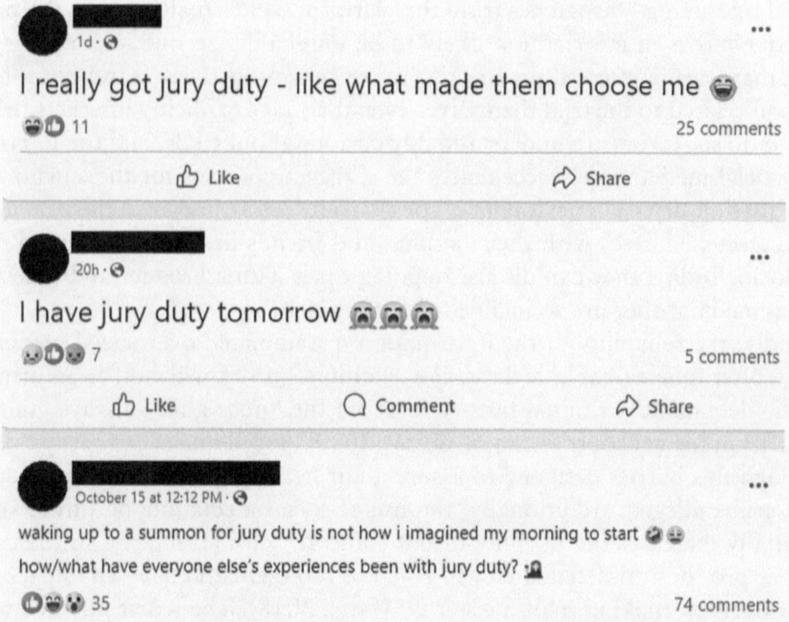

FIGURE 5.1 How people post jury duty-related *Facebook* posts.

reactions to being called for jury duty today are less and less reflective of willingness to serve than was the case in the past. Searching on the term "jury duty" on *Facebook*, one sees dozens of posts related to jury duty each day. Figure 5.1 shows an example of how people posted on their juror experience and how their friends react to those posts. Many postings express outright resistance to the fact that their state government is permitted to compel citizens to "do their duty" as a juror.

There are different guidelines as to how jurors are instructed to make use of social media before, during, and even after a trial (Murphy & Fontecilla, 2012). First, before a person serves on a jury, a *voir dire* will be performed to assess the extent to which the potential juror can be a fair and impartial hearer of facts and adhere to the instructions on the law issued by the judge. It would be ideal for prospective jurors to know nearly nothing about a case at trial. However, if a trial has high visibility in the mass media, a lot of persons will be discussing it on social media. The prospective jurors, or serving jurors, need not actively seek out case-relevant information because such information will be fed to them via social media (Pollack, 2022).

Recall that the algorithms used by social media platforms will keep feeding similar content once a person indicates an interest in a topic (Pollack, 2022). Accordingly, even if a prospective juror accidentally clicks a single post about the trial/defendant, he or she will keep receiving related information. Such "viral marketing" dispatches from the platform will virtually drown the prospective jurors in information likely to be unreliable. Second, if a trial is of high mass media interest, prospective jurors may proactively search for information related to the trial themselves even if a judge explicitly instructs them not to do so. Jurors are understandably curious about trials, and the Internet and social media merely accelerates the searching process for those who are information-driven in personality type (Barrett, 2011). Jurors in the past may have discussed cases with their families and friends despite being asked not to do so. Today, they can discuss ongoing cases with a broader audience via social media if they are so inclined (Marder, 2014).

Sadly, the reliability of the information disseminated over social media is most often questionable at best. For example, jurors will not be informed of the defendant's criminal history to avoid the "once guilty always guilty" mindset in formal court settings (Akhtar, 2020). Social media can easily break through this barrier designed to assure a fair hearing of evidence on the specific crime alleged. Additionally, the use of social media among jurors substantially increases the likelihood that someone with an interest in the case (either pro- or anti-defendant) will reach out to them and have an impact on their decision-making (Hoffmeister & Watts, 2018). The worst possible scenario may be the situation in which jurors express their views and reveal confidential information on social media during or after a trial (Akhtar, 2020). Once discovered, the consequence will most likely be the declaration of a mistrial (Keyzer et al., 2013).

Jurors use social media for a variety of reasons (Bartels & Lee, 2013). Sometimes, even if jurors have a good reason to use social media with no intent to become unbiased, they may fall into the trap called "expert illusion." Expert illusion refers to the situation wherein individuals come to consider themselves an expert of an area after spending just a little time on studying the area on social media; however, they have in fact only been exposed to a fragment of the relevant subject matter needed to understand the area at a higher level of expertise. The CSI effect is one common example of expert illusion.

The CSI effect comes about as a consequence of the popularity of the television program "CSI: Crime Scene Investigation." The CSI effect manifests itself in research findings where it is reported that "juries are holding unrealistic expectations regarding case evidence and these media-generated expectations were altering jury verdicts" (Surette, 2015a, p. 111). After watching many episodes of CSI and other crime-related dramas, jurors often come to believe they now know how to solve a crime and convict a defendant, emphasizing forensic evidence (Robbers, 2008). Although the CSI effect has not been empirically confirmed in additional studies (e.g., Hayes & Levett, 2013; Holmgren & Fordham, 2011; Surette, 2015a), it is likely that many jurors use social media to research their cases and become a victim of "expert illusion." They can use social media to study legal terms, research judges, search the defendant's background, size up attorneys, find background information on witnesses and victims, get familiar with formal trial procedures, and understand the law more fully (Hoffmeister & Watts, 2018; Marder, 2014). These are all good motives per se. However, once again, the reliability of this information is always questionable, and some information, even when reliable, is inadmissible in courtrooms (Simpler, 2012). Additionally, once jurors fall into the "expert illusion" trap, they may be overconfident about the information they acquire from social media and disregard the evidence presented in the courtroom. The term "Google mistrial" was coined to describe a mistrial caused by jurors conducting their own research on Google during a trial (Nuzum, 2019).

Since it is extremely difficult to control the use of social media among jurors, the follow-up question is – how much damage this will bring to a trial? Jurors are asked to only consider the evidence admitted by the court because this evidence is more likely to be vetted and substantiated than the evidence they hear or see on the Internet (Braun, 2017). Both sides (i.e., prosecutor and defendant) are arguing the strengths and weaknesses of the evidence during the cross-examination rather than the facticity of the evidence. Moreover, if all jurors see the same evidence, they can discuss it fairly during deliberations (Marder, 2014). If any juror brings new information outside the trial into deliberations, at least two issues arise: (1) whether the new information itself is reliable and (2) whether the new information can be cross-examined. The answer to the first issue is unknown, but the answer to the second issue is a solid "no." The consequence is often catastrophic since the trial is no longer impartial (Bartels & Lee, 2013). Moreover, jurors cannot avoid comments adverse to the interest of defendants on social media, comments which may alter their opinions. When jurors are found to have accessed social media, mistrials are announced because jury impartiality can be powerfully alleged by defense counsel (Janoski-Haehlen, 2011). Misuse of social media by jurors does not always lead to mistrials. Trial courts and appellate courts may view such behavior as relatively harmless in some cases (Aaronson & Patterson, 2013). The more widely attended to the trial, however, the more likely juror social media misconduct will result in a mistrial.

When social media brings advantages and disadvantages to courtroom players discussed previously (i.e., defendants, prosecutors, and attorneys), we believe that using social media among jurors is almost, if not completely, wrongful. However, what can be done to control jurors' access to social media? Jury sequestration may be a plausible approach, but it seems like an outdated idea with all types of mobile devices being in common use today (Simpler, 2012). While we often cannot lock jurors up and ban Internet use during the trial, we expect that a comprehensive process of juror preparation will minimize the likelihood of harmful use of social media among active jurors.

The preparatory process in question should have at least four components. First, judges must take on the task of providing education to jurors as to all the steps jurors are involved in, such as jury summons response, *voir dire*, trial, and prior to jury deliberations (Robinson, 2011). Jury instructions have been shown to be very important elements of successful trials (Pollack, 2022). Second, punitive measures (e.g., fines and even jail) must be explained and even applied for jurors who violate the typical "no use of social media" policy (Marder, 2014). Third, judges or other court staff should always be ready to answer jurors' questions related to laws, legal terms, and trial procedures so they will not turn to the Internet for answers (Marder, 2014). Finally, reminders should be sent periodically to jurors (Robinson, 2011), and any suggestions made by jurors on how to improve the jury service experience should be promptly attended to (Manhas, 2013). It is difficult to monitor juror misconduct, but *an attempt must be made* to convey the fact that jurors' social media behavior is being watched by the courtroom workgroup actors (Janoski-Haehlen, 2011). An early survey conducted by the Federal Judicial Center revealed that discovering the use of Internet/social media among jurors by judicial staff is very difficult – only 6% of judges reported uncovering internet use by jurors (Hoffmeister & Watts, 2018). Accordingly, we think prevention and self-monitoring is much more important and practical than directing a major effort to document improper use.

The process sketched out here certainly cannot fully eliminate the possibility of social media use among jurors (Janoski-Haehlen, 2011). Although jury sequestration is an extreme option in a small number of cases (Fenn, 2022), which means the complete isolation of jurors from the public until the trial ends, it may be practically impossible and morally wrong to require all jurors to stop using social media outside the courtroom until the trial's end. Since many jurors use social media for daily communication with families and friends (Pollack, 2022), such a restriction would indeed be onerous and further erode the sense of civic duty underlying jury duty service. Courts can ask jurors not to access case-related information on social media, but putting the burden on jurors about what information they should not access, voluntarily or passively, may cause some added resentment toward jury duty (Janoski-Haehlen, 2011). Courts can also order a transfer of venue, which means they move the case to a different location to avoid jury bias (Fenn, 2022). Sadly, one feature of social media is the absence of physical boundaries. Once the "social media trial" starts, all interested social media users will be involved, unless a juror is not a social media user.

Although a jury's use of social media during trials is often considered wrong, social media may positively affect the jury. For example, social media improves how the courts communicate with and educate the public. Helpful information on social media regarding justice and court proceedings may attract the public to serve on jury duty (Hoffmeister & Watts, 2018). As mentioned, social media can also help select an impartial jury during *voir dire* by examining prospective jurors' social media postings. Social media monitoring may also help expose jurors' misbehavior. Bartels and Lee (2013) have provided an example of such monitoring, wherein a selected juror posted "excited for jury duty tomorrow . . . it's gonna be fun to tell the defendants they're GUILTY:P" on *Facebook* (p. 39). The juror, quite properly, was removed from jury duty (Bartels & Lee, 2013).

When the existing empirical research on the use of social media in the courtrooms focuses primarily on jurors (and judges described in the next section), it consistently suggests that we cannot rely entirely on the public's (i.e., jurors and prospective jurors) ability to fully understand how crucial it is to make proper use of social media during trials. The primary burden of maintaining an impartial jury and rendering a just verdict must be placed on judges and other legal professionals; citizens are educable regarding the role of juries in our legal system and will respond to effective judicial instruction. Braun (2017) cites some early studies based on tweets that judges, legal professionals, and jurors posted over the period 2010 to 2013. Braun opines that the level of misuse of social media among jurors was quite low, ranging from 0% to 6%. Another 2014 study suggested that about 8% of jurors are tempted to post information learned from courtrooms on social media (St Eve et al., 2014). Of course, we must note two things about these studies: (1) they both rely primarily on self-report data (bad conduct was quite likely underreported) and (2) the prevalence of social media today is significantly broader than it was ten years ago.

Judges

In criminal trials, a single judge presides in a court of law (Neubauer & Fradella, 2014). Compared to the previous courtroom players discussed up to this point, judges tend to be seen as "old-fashioned" with respect to social media and very strongly inclined to display "judicial temperament" in line with their hallowed robes of office reflecting a tradition of careful judicious thought. They project the image that they are more inclined to follow tradition than embrace the many new things which computers and the digital age have brought into being. Grabowski (2011) writes perceptively about the failure of U.S. Supreme Court Justices to catch up with modern communication methods. In this regard he notes,

> several Justices are embarrassingly ignorant about computing and communication methods that many Americans take for granted . . . it is crucial for our most important decision-makers to keep pace with the times; otherwise, they may make poor legal decisions or avoid hearing important cases because they do not grasp the issues involved.
>
> *(p. 18)*

In the legal system, judges are often held to the highest standard, as their behavior significantly affects the independence of the system (McPeak, 2019). Hoffmeister (2014) argues that judges are the least likely to use social media due to "their age (most are digital immigrants) and the unique role they play in the courtroom" (p. 134). While this might be true at this moment (as of 2023), this lack of facility with modern digital technology will rapidly change as the breadth and scope of social media continue to expand. Contemporary law students and young attorneys who are themselves deeply imbedded in social media will soon be assuming judicial roles in the very near future. Meanwhile, an advanced view of effective judicial social media use can be seen in judicial election campaigning and proactive public outreach (Browning, 2014).

Like everyone else, judges can make use of social media to share their life with social media friends (Meyer, 2014). They must, however, be careful about using social media to communicate judicial matters. Most jurisdictions allow judges to use social media to improve public understanding of the law and for general education purposes (e.g., Ohio and Washington; see Hoffmeister, 2014, pp. 137–138). The question arises, though, as to whether judges are allowed to use social media to conduct their own investigations. For example, can their clerks carry out background checks and monitor the social media behavior of the jurors serving in trials in their own court? Janoski-Haehlen (2011) argues that since both attorneys and jurors may use social media to research their cases in trial, it is understandable for judges to do the same.

The issue of permissible and improper judicial conduct vis-à-vis social media will be resolved by having clear and reasonable professional codes of judicial conduct established by each state bar association and by the Judicial Conference for the federal judiciary. For example, different states in the U.S. have issued varying opinions on whether judges can interact with attorneys appearing before them on social media. Some states favor this interaction, such as Ohio and Kentucky, while others strongly oppose it such as California and Florida (Hoffmeister, 2014). The American Bar Association has provided its advisory opinion on this matter, opining rather vaguely that judges can use social media so long as they follow the applicable judicial conduct rules and do not compromise their duties (Hoffmeister, 2014). To date, the good many issues around proper and improper judicial use of social media use remain open to active debate. The growing consensus is that judges can certainly use social media in their personal life, but they must be extremely careful about what they post, share, and comment upon on social media platforms. Likewise, they must be careful ("judicious") about what they share with their social media "friends" (Fuller, 2022; Janoski-Haehlen, 2011).

In daily life, we may friend (or follow, subscribe to) someone on social media even if we do not personally know the person in question. It is very common among ordinary people to have hundreds of "friends" of this type. Judges, however, must be very cautious about doing this type of friending. Like defendants and jurors, the public may invade the private lives of judges via social media (Keyzer et al., 2013). One obvious issue is whether a defendant can receive an impartial trial if he or she has a "social media relationship" with the judge. Here are two examples where this very issue arose.

Judge Hayden in Pennsylvania refused to recuse himself in a case brought against State Representative Parker, who was one of the judge's many *Facebook* friends (Cooper, 2014). After Judge Hayden suppressed evidence in Parker's case, the state Attorney General appealed the action. The Philadelphia Court of Common Pleas later ruled that the *Facebook* friendship with Parker required the recusal of Judge Hayden (Cooper, 2014). Another Pennsylvania Judge held a preliminary hearing against defendant Horn, but members of the watchdog local press were unhappy about it (Cooper, 2014). Journalists had discovered that Horn was also Judge Placey's *Facebook* friend. Judge Placey recused himself after the case received much social media attention (Cooper, 2014). In the two cases, both judges had hundreds of friends on *Facebook*. It is difficult to conclude if the judges had known the defendants (i.e., true friendship) or if they simply friended each other on social media out of a sense of common courtesy. Clearly, we must rethink if social media friendship carries the same weight as genuine friendship (Browning, 2014). Cooper (2014) argues that, either way, the judges must disclose such a social media connection because (1) disclosure obligations lie in the state's Code of Judicial Conduct and (2) the disclosure maintains public confidence in the judiciary. However, such disclosure may also discourage judges from using social media for other positive purposes such as public education and public outreach.

Besides the personal use of social media, judges are also responsible for regulating the use of social media in their courtrooms and the use of social media by other major players engaged in trials being heard before them. In the courtroom, judges are typically responsible for presiding over criminal trials, maintaining order during court proceedings, and deciding whether evidence is admissible. Judges typically have great discretion in how they organize their courtrooms, with some judges being open to innovation and others staunchly opposed (Hoffmeister, 2014). This, of course, includes how different parties use social media. The major controversial issue is whether individuals can use social media while present in the courtroom. As a matter of open, public courts and maintaining transparency, most courts today allow this behavior. The U.S. Supreme Court has confirmed that the public and media have the right to be present and observe criminal trials (Hoffmeister, 2014). However, the Court has not decided whether the public and media can observe trials remotely on social media. Even in courtrooms with video/audio cameras, judges have the discretion to decide where cameras as positioned and when cameras can be activated (Hoffmeister, 2014). Meanwhile, as stated in the previous section, judges must also decide how parties and jurors can use social media in the courtroom, and even outside the courtrooms in some cases. Special restrictions are often imposed on jurors if the judge decides a case is high-profile to minimize the impact of social media on the trial (Fenn, 2022). Moreover, if jurors misuse social media, it is judges who have a duty to investigate the misuse and decide if prejudice has been introduced (Aaronson & Patterson, 2013).

In conclusion, the use of social media among judges gives rise to a paradox. On the one hand, social media improves judiciary-public relations by providing a great opportunity to connect the judiciary and the public (Mitchell, 2012). On the other hand, misuse of social media among judges can jeopardize a verdict, adversely affect judicial decisions, and even reduce public confidence in the judiciary (Mitchell, 2012).

Victims and Witnesses

Traditionally, victims and witnesses have been largely forgotten in criminal trials (Neubauer & Fradella, 2014). The mass media often focus heavily on defendants, and victims and witnesses are incidental to the stories of defendants. Of course, the lack of attention on victims and witnesses may be due to confidentiality and privacy protection considerations. In the age of social media, victims' statements not only can have an impact in the courtroom but also can prejudice verdicts and sentences. However, some scholars believe that unpolished victim narratives are important to show actual criminal harm (Sheley, 2017). In the past, traditional mass media conveyed victim narratives to the public, and journalists are professionally obligated to ensure that the description of criminal harm is objective. Today, victims can deliver their own narratives to the public without considering if their statements are prejudicial. Sheley (2017) concludes that "if the sentencing process cannot accommodate victim stories, it risks illegitimacy in the eyes of a society" (p. 158).

Social media today is a source of substantial power for victims and witnesses, power which can do serious harm to the process reliant upon the presumption of innocence in criminal proceedings. The so-called social media trial not only causes potential damage to alleged offenders (as we discussed earlier) but also poses a potential threat to victims of crimes. In the past, most victims discussed their victimization only with the police, family members, and close friends. Today, victims have an opportunity to speak out on social media. On the positive side, social media provides crime victims with a way of becoming united in the pursuit of justice for those similarly victimized (Hoffmeister, 2014). The classic example is the #MeToo movement, which is recognized as a social movement against rape, sexual abuse, and sexual harassment (Frye, 2018). On the negative side, social media can also be used as a potent weapon of false accusation. Meanwhile, victims and witnesses often face unimaginable pressure in facilitating criminal investigations and testifying in the courtroom. For instance, they must speak forcefully and avoid being rattled during cross-examination (Neubauer & Fradella, 2014). They must repeatedly recall details of a traumatic incident (Neubauer & Fradella, 2014). They must also be prepared for retaliation from the defendants and their associates and having their privacy invaded on social media.

In this regard, social media often magnifies victim blaming. Take sexual crime as an example. Misconceptions of rape and sexual crime often give rise to misguided beliefs regarding the victims of sexual crimes (Klein & Yamamoto, 2020). For instance, it is argued that women sometimes lie about sexual crimes because they want something from a defendant. Likewise, it is claimed that if a rape does happen, a victim will report it to the police immediately. Similarly, it is claimed that a victim could stop the rape if she/he really wanted to (see Klein & Yamamoto, 2020, pp. 437–438). These types of misguided comments are often seen in social media posts pertaining to sexual crimes. Because of the "like" and "share" functions, people who hold those misconceptions will have them reinforced on social media. Moreover, social media provides an opportunity for the intimidation and bullying of victims and witnesses (Keyzer et al., 2013). However, when used properly, social media may also help protect victims and witnesses from harassment, intimidation, and harm. The harassment and intimidation of victims and witnesses can also be made public. If an intimidator attacks victims and witnesses, he or she has a chance of becoming a public enemy on social media. Harassers and intimidators are often afraid of such negative public opinions.

Regarding witnesses particularly, trial courts often employ the rule of sequestration of witnesses, meaning that a witness is not allowed to sit in the courtroom and listen to other witnesses' testimony. Doing so helps prevent latter witnesses from tailoring their testimony based on former witnesses. However, live tweeting in the courtroom may largely circumvent the sequestration of witnesses because they can read what previous witnesses say online (Flower, 2023; Keyzer et al., 2013). Hoffmeister (2014) reports that this happened in *United States v. W.R. Grace*, a case in which the court discovered that one witness had followed the case online. However, Hoffmeister (2014) also argues that the harm might not be dramatically increased because, except for *Twitter*, witnesses today have a variety of ways of receiving information regarding trials through traditional media (e.g., TV and newspapers) and social media.

Trial Audience

Public access to courtrooms is guaranteed by the First Amendment (Fuller, 2022). Traditionally, even if a trial is a public trial, the audience primarily refers to people who are present in the courtroom. These people are often self-selected (e.g., victims, supportive family members) or mission-oriented (e.g., journalists). Today, very few individuals choose to walk into courtrooms and observe judicial proceedings (Bosland & Townend, 2018). Many individuals who are interested in a trial cannot physically attend court. In the past, they may have had two ways of following a trial: (1) watch televised broadcasts of trial segments or radio commentaries and (2) rely on journalists' reports (Bosland & Townend, 2018). Today, some jurisdictions allow the public to watch trials on live-streaming channels on social media or to tweet what happens in the courtroom for others to read. In Canada, some jurisdictions allow journalists to live-tweet in courtrooms without requiring a judge's prior permission.

Small and Puddister (2020) conducted a content analysis of seven journalists' tweets during two high-profile criminal trials. They found that live tweeting is just like a play-by-play broadcaster calling a sport game. Journalists provide accurate information on what happened during the trials (e.g., who said what and when) but *little else* (Small & Puddister, 2020). Meanwhile, journalists seldom interact with their *Twitter* followers and vice versa, which turns live tweeting into a facsimile of a one-way radio channel (Small & Puddister, 2020). Despite this, Flower (2023) argues that live tweeting and live blogs are important to provide judicial transparency, particularly in jurisdictions where cameras are not allowed in the courtrooms. Additionally, live blogs can improve professional performance because legal professionals are aware of performing to a virtual audience (Flower & Ahlefeldt, 2021). Based on a sample of Swedish and Danish legal professionals, Flower and Ahlefeldt (2021) reported that defense attorneys and prosecutors also use live blogs to cross-examine their notes in the courtroom because they do not always get court records in a timely manner. Accordingly, it seems that social media should continue to be allowed in courtrooms to promote transparency (Krawitz, 2013).

The public is now viewing what is happening in the courtroom more than ever with the advent of social media. The public is using this information to "supervise" legal professionals (Flower, 2023). For example, the public generally expects judges to behave with civility and courtesy in their courtrooms (Goodman, 2013). On *YouTube*, however, there are many videos showing misbehaving judges (like Judge Nalley in the opening story). Scholars have argued that using pictures and videos on social media to publicly shame a judge who loses their temper could bring severe consequences to those judges who are elected officials, consequences which may have a desired deterrent effect. However, "shame from the publicity of wrongdoing can stigmatize the judge, exacerbating his/her anger, hostility, and sense of isolation" (Goodman, 2013, p. 591). Perhaps, there is a balance to be struck between publicity and open justice; too much publicity may harm open justice (Flower, 2023). Some scholars have argued that professional journalists may be the key actors in maintaining such a balance because they usually know what should and should not be reported (e.g., Krawitz, 2013). Sadly, the declining presence of local newspapers and journalists assigned to cover courts means that this important source of potential tempering is growing weaker in most communities.

Members of the public, who do not serve as jurors but develop informed judgments about legal cases based on information posted on social media, have been referred to as "social media jurors" (Grossman & Lev-On, 2023). With the advent of social media, these jurors can do things that legal jurors cannot do. For example, they can participate in group discussions, and these groups can sometimes become very large. They can also bring extra evidence and share it with group members (Grossman & Lev-On, 2023). Of course, not all information being exchanged is reliable and accurate. Two types of such information need to be addressed. The first is misinformation, which refers to false information people share but do not know it is false (Anderson & Duerr, 2022). The second type is disinformation, which refers to false information that people intentionally forge and use to harm (Anderson & Duerr, 2022). Using the formal deliberations of the International Criminal Court as an example, Anderson and Duerr (2022) argue that courts must work more closely with media professionals in the fight against both misinformation and disinformation.

Social Media as Legal Evidence

Today, most people maintain a close connection to social media. In Chapter 3, we discussed how social media can be used as a tool by criminals. In Chapter 4, we discussed how the police can use social media to investigate crimes. All this social media-related behavior generates a fundamental question: Can social media-based evidence be used in a court of law? A short answer to this question is yes. Whether a specific piece of social media evidence can be admissible in a court of law is decided by a judge. Messages and posts on social media platforms can be introduced as evidence under most circumstances (Uncel, 2011). Judges have allowed this type of evidence in the courtroom for more than a decade now on an increasingly routine basis (Kessler, 2011).

In his book, Hoffmeister (2014) identifies five traditional grounds for seeking to admit social media evidence in a court proceeding. The first is relevance. Proving that social media evidence is relevant to court cases is often not difficult. The previous section has noted that prosecutors and defense attorneys can use social media posts as rebuttal evidence. For example, a witness says she saw that the defendant interacted with the victim in the bar last night with confidence, but she posted a picture on Instagram indicating she was drunk. Additionally, as evidence, social media posts need to be interpreted within context, just like text messages (Hlavka & Mulla, 2018). In *State v. Corwin* (2009), the defendant was charged with attempted forcible rape. The defendant and the victim had different stories about the incident. At trial, the defendant attempted to introduce the victim's *Facebook* posts related to drinking and passing out, trying to prove that the victim could not correctly recall the incident that night. Both the trial court and the appellate court held that the victim's previous *Facebook* posts could not be used to challenge her recollections on the attempted rape incident unless the post was posted that same night (*State v. Corwin*, 2009).

The second prerequisite is authentication (Hoffmeister, 2014). Much social media evidence can be collected without a warrant because it is publicly available (Murphy & Fontecilla, 2012). The police in many jurisdictions have started mining social media posts for evidence of criminal activities (Parascandola, 2011). To use social media evidence in the court, social media evidence must be authenticated (Kessler, 2011). The Federal Rules of Evidence (FRE) 901 sets rules for authenticating or identifying evidence. Historically, it is not necessary to authenticate writing so it can be used in the courtroom if a judge finds that there is a sufficient foundation to believe the writing is genuine (Hoffmeister, 2014). However, social media makes it very easy to forge profiles and posts. Judges have taken proper note of this. Studies have found that judges with less technical awareness take more caution when handling social media evidence than their more technically aware peers (Kessler, 2011). Under some circumstances, even when social media evidence is not forged, the real problem lies in how to determine who has posted the information. It is usually very difficult to ascertain ownership of the information posted on social media (Keyzer et al., 2013). Uncel (2011) points out at least two issues arise regarding identifying the author of social media content. The first one is that although data and IP can be used to track the device that creates the content, it does not mean the owner of that device created the content. Second, forensic examination of social media content is time-consuming and expensive (Uncel, 2011). In *Griffin v. State*, the Maryland Court of Appeals ruled that personal information or pictures on *MySpace* are not sufficient to authenticate pages on *MySpace*. The court noted that although *MySpace* requires each user to register with a unique username and password, other individuals can post on the site. Moreover, other individuals can create a fictitious profile and post fictitious posts (*Griffin v. State*, 2011). In the previous chapters, we have seen just such behavior; cybercriminals use fictitious profiles to conduct phishing, and the police likewise use fictitious profiles to conduct undercover investigations.

The third prerequisite is overcoming a hearsay test (Hoffmeister, 2014). If a person makes a statement in the court that is made by another person out of court, the statement will be hearsay and, therefore not admissible (Johnson, 2023). In fact, quite often, social media messages and social media posts are hearsay. For example, "I saw he posted on *Facebook* that he would bomb the school." The statement is generally hearsay because the declarant did not actually see the accused make that post. Instead, what she/he saw was the post. However, courts have generally allowed social media posts and messages to be admissible by adopting exceptions to the hearsay rule. For example, a social media post will not be hearsay if it is a party's post offered against that party. The logic behind this is that a cross-examination can occur to ensure the credibility of the evidence (Johnson, 2023). For instance, in the previous example, the defendant who posted a bomb threat on *Facebook* is in the courtroom, and he/she can testify if the *Facebook* post is true. There are other exceptions for admitting hearsay social media evidence, such as *present sense impression* (a statement describing an event is made immediately after the declarant sees it) and *excited utterance* (a statement describing a startling event is made when the declarant is still under the influence of the event) (Hoffmeister, 2014; also see Kilies & Martin, 2020).

The fourth prerequisite is concordance with the best evidence rule (Hoffmeister, 2014). The best evidence rule requires parties to provide original documents (e.g., writing, recording, or photograph) if they want these documents to be admissible in the court. Sometimes, it is difficult for social media evidence to meet this rule. For example, in *Edwards v. Junior State of America Foundation* (2021), the plaintiff claimed that another student had sent racist and homophobic *Facebook* messages to him. The plaintiff provided a picture of part of a screen that contained these messages. The Junior State of America Foundation (JSA) asked the plaintiff to provide an actual screenshot of the messages or native *Facebook* message files, along with all conversations between the plaintiff and the accused on *Messenger*. The plaintiff could not provide them as he had deleted these messages. The judge ruled that the plaintiff had failed to authenticate the messages, hence that evidence could not be admitted into evidence. In another case, *United States v. Avenatti* (2021), the defendant sought to suppress the evidence of screenshots of his *WhatsApp* messages because the government did not acquire the original, electronically stored versions. The judge ruled that if properly authenticated (e.g., having a witness), screenshots could be admissible.

The last prerequisite is character evidence (Hoffmeister, 2014). It is a type of evidence that proves a person behaves in accordance with his or her predisposition. Character evidence is generally not admissible (Sevier, 2019), particularly when the prosecution in a criminal case uses it as circumstantial evidence. For example, even if a person's pictures on *Instagram* make him look like a gangster, it does not prove that this person is a gangster. Defenders of the banning of character evidence claim that without other empirical proof, jurors would overvalue character evidence (Sevier, 2019). Moreover, social media drives individuals to polarize extremes (Hopp et al., 2020; Lim & Bentley, 2022), but extreme postings do not mean the social media posters are prone to behave accordingly. Thus, for instance, if a person displays himself as a strict vegetarian on social media and claims he hates people who eat meat, it does not automatically prove that this person murdered another person because he/she eats meat. Clearly, individuals may behave quite differently online than in their daily lives. In fact, many people are highly talkative and prone to excess on social media but are shy and retiring persons in their daily lives.

Interestingly, a 2019 study involving over 1,200 participants revealed that jurors may not overly weigh character evidence as much as we once believed (Sevier, 2019). Acting in the role of jurors, study participants showed themselves to be rather competent in carefully evaluating character evidence along with other evidence pertinent to criminal case adjudication (Sevier, 2019). Most importantly, the study found that the inclusion of character evidence increased the study subjects' perception of procedural fairness at trial (Sevier, 2019). While such evidence is generally deemed inadmissible, character evidence can be deemed admissible when the defense side uses it as circumstantial evidence in support of their defense. In addition, Federal Rules of Evidence 404 holds that character evidence "may be admissible for another purpose, such as proving motive, opportunity, intent, preparation, plan, knowledge, identity, absence of mistake, or lack of accident" under some circumstances (Hoffmeister, 2014, p. 163). Given all these considerations, admitting social media character evidence must be considered on a case-by-case basis by presiding judicial officers.

A Model of Regulating Social Media in the Courtroom

Our review of research on the use of social media in the courtroom reveals that organizational regulation of social media use by courts is necessary to balance transparency, publicity, and privacy in this digital age (Puddister & Small, 2019). As an entity, courts can use social media to (1) engage in community outreach and sustain interaction with the public; (2) disseminate timely information related to the operation of courts; (3) provide public self-services such as uploading forms; (4) facilitate internal communication; and (5) engage in the recruitment of staff (Meyer, 2014). Meanwhile, as an organization constituting a key democratic institution in U.S. communities, as we have advocated for other criminal justice organizations to routinize the use of social media in our previous chapters, we extend this recommendation to the courts as well. Accordingly, we propose the following five detailed organizational recommendations for courts wishing to take advantage of the beneficial uses of social media.

First, the court must determine if it needs a social media presence and clarify the purposes of using social media for sustaining that presence. Almost all police agencies now employ social media (Hu & Lovrich, 2020), but only a certain proportion of courts have created social media pages (NCSC, 2023). In the preceding chapter, we argued that the prevalence of social media among police agencies is an unavoidable phenomenon because social media helps the police build transparency, legitimacy, and public trust in the police, conditions which are of utmost importance in modern policing. Compared to police agencies, the general public has far fewer opportunities to interact with courts. Social media presents courts with an opportunity to interact with the public more often and create an image of responsible and unbiased service to society. Studies done on court use of social media indicate that some courts have started using social media because they believe it helps them communicate with the public more directly, improving the courts' reputation (Jackson & Shelly, 2015). At the same time, legal scholars have long argued that courts should maintain a certain level of detachment from the public to maintain neutrality in cases brought before them (e.g., Blackham & Williams, 2013). Consequently, courts need to be cautious about adopting social media and judicious in what they post. Once courts decide to use social media, they also need to decide the purposes of using social media and social media platforms. Different social media platforms are good at different functions. For instance, *Twitter* can be used for real-time communication (Meyer, 2014), and *YouTube* is a good tool for educating social media users in how to make use of court services (Meyer, 2014). It is almost impossible to adopt all mainstream social media platforms, but courts may simply adopt those which are most popular among their targeted population.

Second, the courts should determine who shall have access to official social media accounts and what information can be posted. Social media information should be examined to ensure it is appropriate before posting (Mattan et al., 2020). Failure to do so may lead to public criticism and thereby damage the courts' reputation (Blackham & Williams, 2013). As with police agencies, many courts today employ public information officers. In some courts, public information officers report that the use of social media has become standard practice, just like phone calls and emails (Johnston, 2017). Staff who maintain social media should realize that the job may go beyond an eight-hour workday (Jackson & Shelly, 2015). While court staff do not need to create a social media platform, social media management is time-consuming (Henderson, 2018), considering there are so many platforms from which to choose. Courts may also need to form a social media staff workgroup to construct an official procedure for posting information on social media platforms.

Third, the courts should tailor the use of social media based on public needs. Courts can have different audiences they want to target. For example, some courts may want to target primarily legal professionals (Jackson & Shelly, 2015). Some courts may focus on providing timely legal education to the public (Jackson & Shelly, 2015). Studies suggest that legal professionals largely agree that the main benefit of using social media to fulfill "open justice" is to educate the public (Flower, 2023). Courts must be open to criticism from the public (Mattan et al., 2020). Courts may also use social media to improve customer service in courts (Keyzer et al., 2013). These perspectives require courts to be flexible on what to post and on what platforms. However, open justice does not mean courts should disclose all information that the public wants to know. Once again, balancing publicity and privacy is important here, and it should be decided case by case.

Fourth, privacy and confidentiality are major concerns. Social media posts should be careful about including details of cases (Jackson & Shelly, 2015). Besides privacy and confidentiality, concerns about inaccurate and prejudicial reporting on social media should be raised (Findlay, 2015). Therefore, courts may need to rule who can live-report (e.g., live tweeting and live-blog) cases in the courtrooms. Well-trained journalists may be a good choice, although judicial officers sometimes find that their reports are different from what actually transpired in their courtrooms (Krawitz, 2013). Although we must respect all individuals' privacy and confidentiality in the courtrooms, we think at least one situation must be exposed to the public as soon as possible – misbehavior in the courtrooms performed by legal professionals, including but not limited to judges, prosecutors, and defense attorneys. Public confidence in the legal system will be greatly eroded if the public discovers egregious conduct in the courtroom (think about Judge Nalley's case in the opening story). Thus, it may be wise for courts to release this type of information by themselves. After all, who does not have a camera-equipped phone these days?

Fifth, internal policies should be drafted, formally adopted, and implemented (Jackson & Shelly, 2015). In 2010, the *Resource Packet for Developing Guidelines on Use of Social Media by Judicial Employees* was published by the Judicial Conference of the U.S. to provide some guidance on how courts regulate their employees on the use of social media. However, Janoski-Haehlen (2011) argues that the guide does not provide a full draft of a uniform policy. The guide provides some examples and leaves the decision to draft and implement court rules to individual courts (Janoski-Haehlen, 2011). While internal policies are often used to regulate court officials, courts should also draft and adopt external policies on regulating how other courtroom actors should use social media. For example, court officials should explicitly tell journalists what to do regarding their use of social media in the courtrooms (Krawitz, 2013). While in many local jurisdictions each judge is responsible for doing this, a written policy for journalists makes it easier for people reporting on trials to follow and for court officials to punish journalists who violate the policy (Krawitz, 2013). We discuss this matter in depth in the following section.

Besides these five organization recommendations, we also propose recommendations to major courtroom players. Reviewing related literature

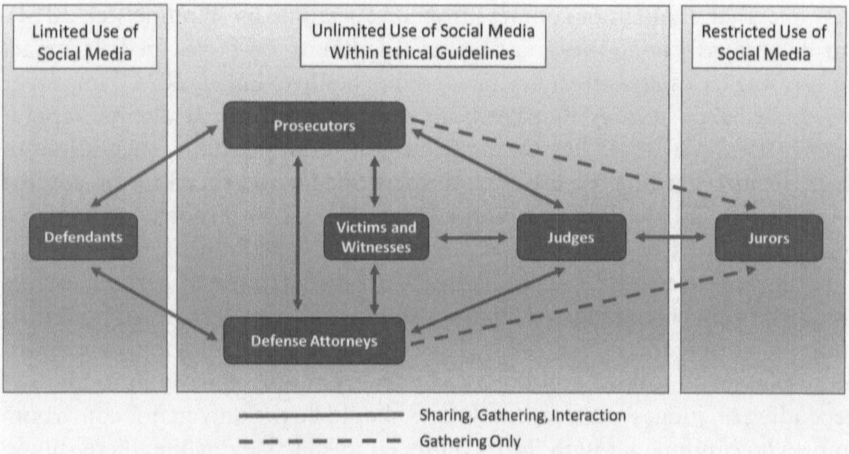

FIGURE 5.2 A model of regulating social media in the courtroom.

leads us to construct a model for regulating social media in the courtroom (Figure 5.2). In this model, we categorize the level of use of social media into three levels: (1) unlimited use of social media with ethical guidelines; (2) limited use of social media; and (3) restricted use of social media. Different courtroom players are placed in different groups. Also, we use solid lines and dotted lines to indicate whether social media communication between two players should be one-way or two-way.

Defendants should be limited regarding the use of social media. On the one hand, for the purpose of protecting victims and witnesses, defendants should not be allowed to interact with them on social media. They should not be allowed to interact with judges or jurors. On the other hand, limited use of social media protects defendants. We have noted that improper use of social media among defendants may jeopardize their privacy, incriminate themselves, create an unappealing public image, and contribute unduly to their conviction (Keyzer et al., 2013; Murphy & Fontecilla, 2012; Neubauer & Fradella, 2014). Although defendants should not be allowed to interact with victims, witnesses, or jurors on social media, they can use social media to seek exculpatory evidence. They can also use social media to maintain connections with prosecutors and defense attorneys. After all, these players are most likely to work on a plea deal that sufficiently meets the partial needs of all parties and is acceptable to the presiding judicial officer.

Prosecutors and defense attorneys should be regulated similarly regarding use of social media. They can use social media to stay connected with judges and defendants. They can contact victims and witnesses on social media with extra cautions. They both can use social media to research prospective jurors. However, they must perform these tasks under strict ethical guidelines. For example, they should not contact jurors on social media (Hoffmeister, 2014). For defense attorneys, they must be careful about their social media's impact on ongoing cases and attorney-client confidentiality (Fuller, 2022). Improper social media posts may damage both their own and their clients' reputations (McPeak, 2019). They should be careful about providing suggestions to their clients regarding the use of both social media and social media content (Hoffmeister, 2014). For prosecutors, they should be prudent in handling social media-related evidence and cases (Neubauer & Fradella, 2014).

In this proposed model of regulating social media in the courtroom, judges are at the very core. Judges often have broad authority to control how their courtrooms operate (Fuller, 2022). They should set clear rules for other courtroom players to follow, and these can vary from one courtroom to another depending on judges' preferences. Judges should be the only major courtroom actor who can interact with jurors on social media. Meanwhile, there should be some regulations constraining judges. A code of ethics must be employed to provide guidance to judges (Meyer, 2014). The public does not want to see more judges (e.g., Angela Dempsey, Eugenio Mathis, Lee Johnson, and Shirley Saffold) who behave very badly on social media (Browning, 2014). Judges face ethical issues regarding the use of social media. For example, they may face the issue of disclosure of social media friendships (Browning, 2014). Judges must conduct a case-by-case analysis of their interaction with other legal professionals (e.g., attorneys) on social media to decide whether there is a conflict of interest (Fuller, 2022). Therefore, judges may need to distinguish clearly between their personal and their professional use of social media. Maintaining separate accounts for professional and personal use may be a good choice (McPeak, 2019). However, some scholars have argued that the strict distinction between personal and professional profiles on social media is very difficult to maintain (Janoski-Haehlen, 2011). Common people already have mixed personal and professional lives on social media. They post all kinds of things related to their life, jobs, and worldviews. Why should judges be any different? Moreover, judges need ongoing in-service training on recognizing and handling social media evidence (Kessler, 2011).

Victims and witnesses, as well as other courtroom audiences such as journalists, should follow judges' and courts' regulations on the use of social media in the courtrooms. Outside the courtroom, they can use social media freely most of the time. However, they still need to follow some ethical principles and attempt to be guided by the spirit of those principles. For instance, they must ensure that unpolished victim narratives on social media adhere to the truth. They can be emotionally aggressive (Sheley, 2017) but must not be fictional. They should not release confidential information gathered in the courtrooms. They should not use social media as a weapon of false accusation. Witnesses should not use information on social media to tailor their testimony. Meanwhile, victims and witnesses must learn how to protect themselves from victim blaming, intimidation, and bullying (Keyzer et al., 2013; Klein & Yamamoto, 2020).

The only courtroom player who should be restricted from using social media is a jury. The model suggests that jurors should only be allowed to interact with judges via social media. They are not allowed to have contact with other major courtroom players, although prosecutors and defense attorneys may be allowed to scan their public social media posts. As we have discussed in the previous section, jurors' use of social media is one of the major issues in today's criminal trials. Today's jurors are contradictory. On the one hand, they are legally uninformed regarding how to remain unbiased in the presence of ubiquitous social media. Few jurors intentionally misbehave; most just do not know what they are allowed to do. For example, a study conducted in the U.K. showed that nearly one-in-four jurors admitted to being confused about what they are allowed to do online (Akhtar, 2020). On the other hand, jurors are no longer *tabula rasa* vis-à-vis social media, and they are active pursuers of information because they want to try their best to make the right decision (Akhtar, 2020). Often, this desire to "get it right" leads to using social media for more information gathering during trial. Clearly, court rules and jury instructions need to address the challenges brought on by social media (Janoski-Haehlen, 2011).

Some scholars have argued that efficacious jury instructions may be the key to reducing the likelihood of improper use of social media by jurors (e.g., Braun, 2017). Jury instructions on the use of social media should be provided as early as in *voir dire* when prospective jurors report for jury duty (Aaronson & Patterson, 2013). Jury instructions may need to focus on two types of jury misconduct: improper use of social media to conduct research and improper use of social media to communicate with others (Aaronson & Patterson, 2013). Jury instructions should include at least four aspects of expected juror compliance: (1) instructions should be written in plain language and use contemporary social media terminology; (2) instructions should illustrate examples of prohibited social media conduct; (3) instructions should explain why the use of social media needs to be restricted; and (4) instructions should describe the punishment associated with violating social media use restrictions (Aaronson & Patterson, 2013). Figure 5.3 is an example of jury instructions on the use of social media during trials proposed by Aaronson and Patterson (2013).

In addition to explicit jury instructions, courts may also require jurors to swear an oath (Bartels & Lee, 2013). Perhaps, a "juror misconduct hotline" is another good option to be considered (Bartels & Lee, 2013). Early detection of misconduct is the key, but courts must ensure the process used to detect misbehavior is accurate (Bartels & Lee, 2013). The crucial role of

- Let me remind you once again that you must decide this case based only on the evidence introduced at trial. You must not communicate or share any information with anyone about this case or disclose your thoughts about it or the individuals participating in it. This includes, but is not limited to, discussing the evidence, the lawyers, the court, or your thoughts, opinions, and reactions about any aspect of the case. In addition to not talking face to face with anyone about the case, you must not communicate information about the case by any means including texting, emailing, tweeting, or posting on social networking sites like Facebook. You also must not read or listen to any news accounts of the case. Finally, you must not conduct your own research or investigation about the case or try to get information from any source other than what you see and hear in the courtroom. This means, for example, you cannot use a dictionary or a Google search to obtain even something as simple as the definition of a word you do not understand.
- In summary, do not "Google" the parties, witnesses, issues, or counsel; do not "tweet" or text about the trial; do not text or email information on the case; do not post updates about the trial on Facebook; do not use Google Maps or other Internet sources. Even using something as seemingly innocent as "Wikipedia" to obtain information related to this case can result in serious consequences.

FIGURE 5.3 A sample of jury instructions on use of social media during trial.
Source: made from Aaronson and Patterson (2013, p. 35)

who ensures good jury instructions are provided, a thorough investigation on potential violation of regulations occurs, and a proper punishment is meted out when a juror indeed violates these rules of conduct is the judge (or his court staff) (Pollack, 2022; Robinson, 2011). Judges would be well advised to periodically send reminders to jurors about established social media use rules (Robinson, 2011) and be ready to answer jurors' questions so they will not be tempted to turn to social media for answers (Marder, 2014). All these responsibilities can be carried out via both personal interaction and the appropriate use of social media. That is why, in our model, jurors are only allowed to interact with judges on social media while engaged in jury duty. Judges also would be well advised to evaluate whether a given juror's misuse of social media is fatal to a trial and what remedies can be made to ensure a sound trial (Aaronson & Patterson, 2013). To be noted, jurors should not be completely isolated from social media. They should be allowed to use social media in matters that are not related to the trials in which they are performing their jury.

Conclusion

In this chapter, we have focused on social media's influence on criminal trials, including but not limited to social media's impact on court proceedings, jury dynamics, admission of social media evidence, and use of social media among defendants, defense attorneys, prosecutors, and judges. We reviewed and summarized both the positive and negative sides of using social media in (sometimes outside of) the courtroom which been noted in the research literature. Based on the review of empirical research and legal commentaries and important court opinions, we propose a model for regulating social media use among all major players in the courtroom to maximize the benefits of using social media and minimize the disadvantages.

6

SOCIAL MEDIA AND CORRECTIONS

Opening Story: As of March 2024, a *TikTok* account with the name "untiktolard" has more than 430,000 followers and has received 7.8 million "likes" on *TikTok*. While these are not very large numbers compared to famous celebrities or influencers active on *TikTok*, the account belongs to a convicted inmate serving time in a French prison. As of 2023, untiktolard has posted 43 *TikTok* videos about food in prison and how to make food in prison, and 20 videos about entertaining moments in prison such as dancing and responding to *TikTok* challenges. A VICE reporter interviewed the creator of this account in 2021 after untiktolard became France's most famous inmate *TikToker*. Untiktolard revealed to his interviewer that he had purchased a smartphone for €800 and accessed the Internet via 4G in his prison cell (Chedeville, 2021). He noted that he wanted outsiders to see what it was like in prison, and it turned out that many people were highly interested in this topic (Chedeville, 2021). Untiktolard also noted that he had engaged with many *TikTok* users via live streams, but the connection became rather unstable because the prison authorities had installed jammers (Chedeville, 2021). When asked what the most important thing he got out of his experience, untiktolard said:

> To be honest, it's a form of therapy. When you're in prison, you're removed from society. On *TikTok* I can get attention from people, and I receive super positive messages . . . I also know everything could come crashing down overnight. But I live every day as it comes and I stay positive.
>
> *(Chedeville, 2021)*

DOI: 10.4324/9781003360049-7

Corrections and Their Appearance on Mass Media

Untiktolard's experiences are far from unique. The public now can find many prison videos posted on social media, amateur videos putatively filmed within correctional facilities such as jails and prisons (although viewers cannot be quite sure about authenticity). As one of the three major components of the criminal justice system, corrections often include county jails, state prisons, federal prisons, private prisons, and community corrections such as probation and parole. Jails often hold quite different kinds of inmates. The most common groups are (1) people who are presumed innocent and waiting trial; (2) people who are convicted and awaiting sentencing; and (3) convicted offenders whose sentence is to be incarcerated for less than one year (Stohr & Walsh, 2019). Prisons often incarcerate inmates who are convicted of a felony and whose sentence is one year or longer. Probation allows convicted offenders to remain in the community instead of being sent to prison (Stohr & Walsh, 2019). Due to a variety of reasons (e.g., primarily overcrowding in jails and prisons), probation is widely used in the U.S. It is estimated that about 90% of convicted offenders receive some type of probation with conditions of compliance attached (Stohr & Walsh, 2019). Parole refers to the early release of inmates from prisons before they complete their entire sentences because they have been compliant during their imprisonment (Stohr & Walsh, 2019). In the U.S., the federal parole system was abolished in 1987 under the Sentencing Reform Act of 1984. As of 2018, 16 states have likewise abolished discretionary parole (Renaud, 2019). The other 34 states maintain parole boards, which have the authority to grant or withhold parole after assessing inmates' cases on a case-by-case basis.

The 2022 report can be accessed at https://bjs.ojp.gov/document/p22st.pdf (accessed on March 17, 2024).

The U.S. has the largest number of imprisoned persons in the world. Figure 6.1 shows the trend of prisoners in state and federal correctional facilities in the U.S. from 2013 to 2022. The figure shows a consistent decline in the overall prison population from 2013 (1.57 million) to 2021 (1.20 million), with a total reduction of 370,400 (23.5%). A steep drop in imprisonment occurred between 2019 (1.43 million) and 2020 (1.22 million), with an astonishing decline rate of 15%. An increase of 2% is found between 2021 and 2022, which is the first increase in nearly a decade. Besides correctional facilities run by county, state, and federal agencies, there are many private prison facilities in operation. Figure 6.2 shows the trend of prisoners housed in private prison facilities. In general, the trend mimics the trend of overall prison population – a consistent decline from 2013 to 2022, with a slight increase between 2015 and 2016. Moreover, the prison population in local jails generally declined in the period 2013 to 2021. There was a tiny

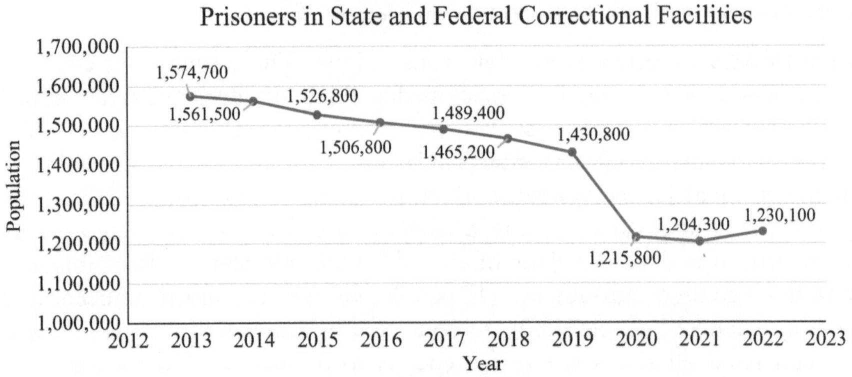

FIGURE 6.1 Prison population under the jurisdiction of state and federal correctional facilities in the U.S. from 2013 to 2022.

Data source: BJS Publication Series: Prisoners

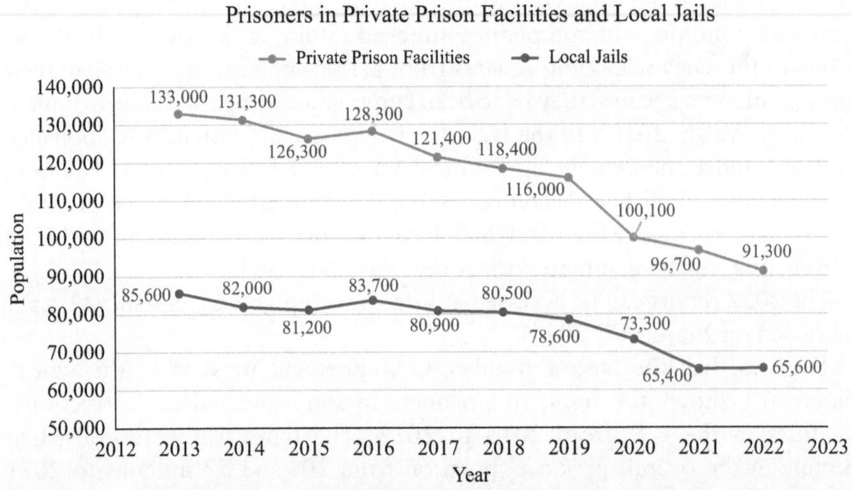

FIGURE 6.2 Prison population held in private prison facilities and local jails in the U.S. from 2013 to 2022.

Data source: BJS Publication Series: Prisoners.

increase (0.3%) between 2021 and 2022, but otherwise the overall decline is evident. The data used to generate Figures 6.1 and 6.2 are reported by the Bureau of Justice Statistics on its official website. There are three points worth noting. First, all data reported are year-end figures. As such, not all individuals who are involved in corrections are included in these data. For example, a person is not counted if he is sentenced to prison in February and released in October. It is estimated that about seven million people were sentenced to jail terms in 2022 (Sawyer & Wagner, 2024). Second, the data do not include individuals on probation, which is the major population group of convicted offenders (Stohr & Walsh, 2019). Third, although the U.S. has the largest prison population worldwide, it does not have the highest incarceration rate (per 100,000 residents). It is estimated that as of January 2024, El Salvador has the highest rate (1,086 per 100,000), followed by Cuba (794 per 100,000) and Rwanda (637 per 100,000). The U.S. ranks sixth (531 per 100,000) worldwide but first among developed countries (Statista, 2024).

The twin main goals of corrections are *fair punishment* and *community safety* (Clear et al., 2012). A detailed categorization subdivides the two main goals into four sub-goals: (1) retribution; (2) deterrence; (3) incapacitation; and (4) rehabilitation (Kifer et al., 2003). Retribution, in general, refers to punishing offenders for their offenses. Incapacitation refers to removing offenders from the community so they will not harm any members of society. Deterrence seeks to discourage offenders from committing offenses again. Furthermore, rehabilitation refers to reforming one-time offenders into law-abiding citizens (Stohr & Walsh, 2019). Before entering into the corrections system, the formal sentencing of offenders takes place (Stohr & Walsh, 2019). Typically determined in courts, sentencing is a legal process, wherein post-conviction sanctions are determined and some form of corrections is specified (Petersilia & Reitz, 2012). It should be noted that sentencing often features aspects of the same four goals noted earlier for corrections.

Compared to the police and the courts, very few citizens have *direct* knowledge or personal experience with the corrections systems described earlier (Surette, 2015a). Lacking direct experience, the mass media necessarily play a significant role in shaping the public image of corrections. However, among the three components of the criminal justice system, the area of corrections receives significantly less attention from the mass media than do the police and the courts (Surette, 2015a). In the area of crime-related news, the police take over 50% of news stories, and the courts take about 40%. Corrections take less than 10%, and most correctional news is about prison escapes, assaults in prisons, and prison riots (Surette, 2015a). Surette (2015a) opines that the low rate of correctional news reporting stems from three major factors. First, corrections-related news has a low "newsworthiness" value. The public does not care much about how inmates are doing in their jails and prisoners. News reporters tend to hold the same opinion. Second, correctional news is challenging to produce because news reporters do not have the same number of points of access for corrections as they have in the case of police or the courts. Accordingly, reporters must make an extra effort to gather correctional news. Third, reporters often lack any prior knowledge of corrections, and they do not maintain relationships with officials in corrections in the way they do with the police and the courts (Surette, 2015a).

On the corrections side, the jail and prison authorities tend to be stricter in controlling information and eschewing external scrutiny (Surette, 2015a). Because of these considerations, whatever correctional news is reported tends to come from unofficial sources, usually in the form of leaked information provided by correction officers, inmates and ex-inmates, inmates' families, researchers, criminal defense attorneys, and prisoner rights groups (Surette, 2015a).

Corrections are more often depicted in feature films, television programs, and in "infotainment" reels than in conventional print and broadcast media. These various channels have created some enduring myths about corrections – and prisons in particular. For example, prison life is universally portrayed as violent and dehumanizing (Surette, 2015a). Correctional officers are typically portrayed as villains, and prisoners are often depicted as malevolent protagonists (Surette, 2015a). Social media provides correctional agencies with an excellent tool (albeit underused thus far) for bypassing the traditional mass media and directly communicating with the public to show that prisons are not really violence-infested places. Increasingly, incarcerated social media users share their own experiences in prison on social media. Some even have access to social media when being held in prison (e.g., untiktolard in the opening story). In general, both positive and negative sides of corrections are being shared by both current inmates and ex-inmates on social media. Unfortunately, academia has not paid much attention to how social media is impacting corrections.

Corrections on Social Media

Research on corrections' use of social media remains quite insufficient compared to research on the use of social media by the police or the courts. We think there are a few reasons for this. First and foremost, use of social media is banned in most jails and prisons in the U.S. and most other countries (Schlosser & Feldman, 2022). Second, unlike the police or the courts, corrections indeed do not need to maintain ongoing contact with the public. From the public perspective, their major responsibility is to ensure that convicted criminals are safely locked up and out of sight. The public generally requires the demonstration of ongoing accountability from the police and the courts (Hu & Lovrich, 2020). Thus, they are often under the public's scrutiny. For instance, in a wrongful conviction case, the public will likely blame the police and the courts for arresting and sentencing the wrong person. The public is unlikely to blame the prison or local jail for incarceration decisions. Accordingly, compared to the police and the courts, corrections officials often are not particularly eager to establish or maintain a positive public image.

Third, the public generally does not care about what happens in corrections unless affairs are related to prison riots or seriously abusive treatment of prisoners (Surette, 2015a). There may be many social media posts related to corrections, but conventional social media platform algorithms do not circulate these posts due to the assumed lack of public interest. Fourth, although some mainstream social media platforms (e.g., *Facebook* and *Twitter*) have been active for almost two decades, research on social media and the criminal justice system remains rather scant. Within the limited research on social media available for review, overwhelming attention has been paid to the police and the courts. In the following section, we review some of the best available research done on social media and corrections.

Correctional Agencies' Use of Social Media

Like the police and the courts, corrections professionals can use social media to disseminate information to the public, gather information from the public, and interact with the public online (Hu & Lovrich, 2020). For example, during the COVID-19 pandemic many prisons used social media (e.g., *Facebook* and *Twitter*) to update the public with policy changes regarding the limitation of social contacts, COVID-19 prevention measures being adopted, and infection case identification policies being developed (Zielinski et al., 2022). A public information officer of the Johnson County (Kansas) Sheriff's Office has described well the use made of social media to disseminate COVID-19 information related to his own county jail (Erickson, 2013). Social media can be used to directly connect with the public, and social media allows the public to ask questions. Erickson (2013) argues that correctional public information officers should use multiple social media platforms (e.g., *Facebook*, *YouTube*, *Twitter*, and *Flickr*) to post content relating to the staff's (not inmates) activities so that the facility's "stakeholders" (i.e., the public) know what they have paid for. With the consent from inmates and their attorneys, they can also post conversations with inmates on social media (Erickson, 2013).

Due to the paucity of published research on correctional agencies' use of social media, we have gathered a convenience sample of state correctional facilities and have examined several of their social media uses. We picked the ten most populated states in the U.S. and visited their state corrections' websites to document their level of engagement with social media, and to see what social media platforms they were using for such engagement. Based on a 2022 report (Rozzelle, 2022), the ten states selected are California, Texas, Florida, New York, Pennsylvania, Illinois, Ohio, Georgia, North Carolina, and Michigan. Table 6.1 shows the states' estimated total population in 2022 and the social media platforms used by their respective state departments of corrections. Every single state Department of Corrections maintains a *Facebook* account. Nine out of the ten state corrections departments make ongoing use of *Twitter* accounts. Eight have *YouTube* accounts, and seven maintain *Instagram* accounts. Five of the state departments maintain a *LinkedIn* account. Both Michigan and North Carolina have *Flickr* accounts. Moreover, Georgia has a *Pinterest* account.

TABLE 6.1 State population and social media platforms used by each state Department of Corrections

State	Estimated Total Population in 2022*	Social Media Platforms**						
		Facebook	*Twitter*	*YouTube*	*Instagram*	*LinkedIn*	*Flickr*	*Pinterest*
California	39,029,342	X	X	X	X			
Texas	30,029,572	X	X	X	X			
Florida	22,244,823	X	X	X	X	X		
New York	19,677,151	X	X	X	X			
Pennsylvania	12,972,008	X	X	X				
Illinois	12,582,032	X						
Ohio	11,756,058	X	X		X	X		
Georgia	10,912,876	X	X	X		X		X
North Carolina	10,698,673	X	X	X	X	X	X	
Michigan	10,034,113	X	X	X	X	X	X	

* Estimated total population for July 1, 2022, by U.S Census Bureau
** Visited on March 25, 2024.

We discovered that state correction department social media posts are generally related to the dissemination of information, such as features on veteran correctional officers, prison programs, prison facilities, facility policies, and staff recruitment. For example, the California Department of Corrections and Rehabilitation posted the following on its *Facebook* page on March 22, 2024:

> CDCR recently became aware of a company soliciting incarcerated individuals to sign up for third party calling services. Please be advised that any third-party calling services, and or funding conduits are in violation of institutional rules and are not a part of ViaPath Technologies.

The Georgia Department of Corrections posted four recruitment videos on its *YouTube* channel over the period June 2022 to October 2022. Interestingly, these four recruitment videos are also the *only* videos posted during that five-month period.

A 2023 study examined 47 *YouTube* videos related to recruitment posted by correctional services and sheriff's offices across Canada and the U.S. The authors isolated four themes from their observations. First, most videos send out information noting that corrections is a "growth industry" (read career advancement potential) and that it provides generous paychecks and good benefits (Enkhtugs & Walby, 2023). Second, recruitment videos indicate that modern corrections programs and educational opportunities often change incarcerated people's lives in a positive direction (Enkhtugs & Walby, 2023). They portray correctional officers as being proud of their work and their contribution to public safety in their communities (Enkhtugs & Walby, 2023). Third, many recruitment videos attempt to counter popular media's stereotypical portrayal of corrections, focusing on showing a positive relationship existing between correctional officers and inmates (Enkhtugs & Walby, 2023). Additionally, many of the videos display female correctional officers, breaking the strongly engrained gender stereotype associated with corrections (Enkhtugs & Walby, 2023).

Also, we observed that the *frequency* of social media postings is relatively low among the ten state departments of corrections. Most often, they made only one social media post per day. Also noted was the fact that few in the public follow these departments' social media accounts. Table 6.2 shows the number of *Facebook* followers on *Facebook* pages maintained by these ten state departments of corrections. The Texas Department of Criminal Justice has the greatest number of Facebook followers, followed by the California Department of Corrections and Rehabilitation, the Georgia Department of Corrections, and the Illinois Department of Corrections. The North Carolina Department of Adult Correction has the least number of *Facebook* followers. As of March 2024, its *Facebook* page has only about 2,600 followers.

TABLE 6.2 Numbers of *Facebook* followers on *Facebook* pages run by state Departments of Corrections

State	*Facebook Followers**	*Follower-Population Ratio (per 10,000)*
California	58,000	14.9
Texas	120,000	39.9
Florida	31,000	13.9
New York	19,000	9.7
Pennsylvania	29,000	22.4
Illinois	41,000	32.6
Ohio	22,000	18.7
Georgia	46,000	42.2
North Carolina	2,600	2.4
Michigan	22,000	21.9

* Number of followers as of March 25, 2024.

Regarding the follower-population ratio, the Georgia Department of Corrections has the highest ratio of 42 followers per 10,000 population, followed by the Texas Department of Criminal Justice and the Illinois Department of Corrections. Since social media does not have any geographical limitations, these numbers strongly indicate that the public is not particularly interested in engaging with correctional agencies on social media. However, we need to point out that our analyses are preliminary in nature. We selected only ten state correctional agencies. It is possible that local correctional agencies may have generated more interest among the public on social media. For example, as of March 2024, the NYPD's *Facebook* page has 949,000 followers, while the New York State Police has 514,000 followers. Nevertheless, our research indicates that more research is needed in this area.

Correctional Officers' Use of Social Media

Research on correctional officers focuses on a variety of topics, such as workplace stress (e.g., Dowden & Tellier, 2004; Fusco et al., 2021; May et al., 2020), job satisfaction (e.g., Cheeseman et al., 2011; Yang et al., 2011), turnover (e.g., Griffin et al., 2014; Schaufeli & Peeters, 2000), discretionary decision-making (e.g., Haggerty & Bucerius, 2021), and job training (e.g., Burton et al., 2022; Ricciardelli & Adorjan, 2021). The features of correctional work specifically trigger correctional officers' demand for social contacts (Schaufeli & Peeters, 2000). Subjects of contact include but are not limited to prisoners, colleagues, supervisors, and family members. Social media may help them establish and maintain these social contacts. Moreover, social media may help correctional officers connect to other officers in similar roles, even if they have never met in person.

Just like police officers and court professionals, correctional officers must be quite careful about using social media, either privately or professionally. In a study based on interviews with 159 Canadian correctional officers, Adorjan and Ricciardelli (2023) explored challenges brought to the work of correctional officers by social media. First, many correctional officers do not know their own agencies' policies on the use of social media, although they all seem to have a general understanding along the lines of "you cannot post whatever you want" (Adorjan & Ricciardelli, 2023). Second, many correctional officers express serious concerns about privacy and vulnerability (Adorjan & Ricciardelli, 2023). While individuals in general have such concerns, for example, being cyberstalked and cyberbullied, correctional officers' concerns mainly come from prisoners and management. They are worried about prisoners knowing too much about their personal information and leveraging that information against them in prison (Adorjan & Ricciardelli, 2023). Many of them have a general sense that their social media posts are being monitored by management, and they need to be careful about not being investigated or disciplined (Adorjan & Ricciardelli, 2023). Meanwhile, many correctional officers are worried about being vulnerable to public scrutiny (Adorjan & Ricciardelli, 2023). The concern is understandable because abuse of power by correctional officers is not a rare occurrence; actual or perceived use of some force is an essential part of correctional work (Stohr & Walsh, 2019). The study also investigated how correctional officers typically deal with their concerns about social media. Many of them indicated that they had eliminated or reduced the use of social media, and if making use of social media, they used privacy settings to control public access to their social media profiles (Adorjan & Ricciardelli, 2023).

Correctional agencies usually develop social media policies for their correctional officers. These policies are constantly under review and revision as the prevalence and technological developments of social media unfold. In a 2011 report, Maryland's Department of Public Safety and Correctional Services (DPSCS) asked its interviewees for *Facebook* login information during job interviews (Madrigal, 2011a). DPSCS soon suspended this policy after a story on this practice went public (Madrigal, 2011a). Two months later, after DPSCS reviewed 2,689 applicants, it was reported that social media postings reviews played some role in denying seven applicants, and that one applicant was denied employment solely because of his social media content (Madrigal, 2011b). In another report, two North Carolina correctional officers came under investigation because they posted pictures related to "feeling cute" in response to a social media challenge (Simpson, 2019). One posted, "#FeelingCuteChallenge – say one wrong thing you going in cuffs" and the other one posted, "Feeling cute . . . might spray ya baby daddy" (Simpson, 2019). Both reports indicate that when correctional agencies make a policy related to their officers' use of social media, they must balance the twin goals of transparency and privacy.

Public Opinions Toward Corrections on Social Media

As we suggested in the previous chapters, social media can be used to study not only how justice agencies such as the police and the courts are doing with this "new media" but also the public opinions expressed about these agencies and criminal justice writ large. These opinions are particularly important for administrators, politicians, and policymakers to make public policy decisions in this digital age (Garth-James, 2021). Many scholars and researchers have started using social media (e.g., *Twitter*) to broadcast broadly the results of their empirical research and engage with others and agencies with a focus on the advancement of *evidence-based* policies. Meanwhile, members of the general public can also make use of social media to express their views on criminal justice-related topics, such as mass shootings, gun control, police reform, security cameras, prison reform and related topics.

In a qualitative study on about 85,000 posts related to corrections reform on *Facebook*, *Twitter*, *YouTube*, and *Reddit* during a one-year period (from February 2020 to February 2021), corrections (here refers to prisons) are mostly described as negative and bad places for inmates who indeed need "help" in the form of prison reform (Garth-James, 2021). Many active social media users want to promote prison reform, and they express what they think may be beneficial for changing current prison policies and practices. A few positive comments are related to voting rights, prison education programs, vocational training programs, individualized counseling, and religious programs (Garth-James, 2021). Language about giving offenders "a second chance" is commonly supported by social media users (Garth-James, 2021). They typically emphasize the notion that prison-based education and work programs produce positive rehabilitation results, keeping inmates from returning to prison [recidivating] (Garth-James, 2021). While most statements in these posts are moderate in tone, some posts contain radical statements such as "no prisons, defund" and "burn it all down" (for a complete table of statements, see Garth-James, 2021, p. 112). In a follow-up study, Garth-James (2022) selected 16,000 posts on *Twitter*, *YouTube*, and *Reddit* related to prison reform for analysis and reviewed survey results for 140 prison industry professionals. The findings on themes for positive reform were quite similar. Support was expressed for occupational training, access to formal education, humane treatment, and greater accountability as the essential elements of contemporary prison reform (Garth-Jame, 2022).

It may be reasonably argued that social media content should not be viewed as an entirely reliable source for analyzing public attitudes toward the police, the courts, and corrections. Some individuals with strong points of view greatly enjoy posting their opinions about the criminal justice system on social media. We believe that analyzing social media content (e.g., posts, comments, reposts, "likes," reactions, and views), despite some shortcomings, does provide a valuable view into public opinion on corrections. We further discuss the systematic use of large N data analysis of social media content in Chapter 8.

Social Media Inside the Corrections Sphere

The previous section covers how corrections, correctional officers, and researchers of corrections can use social media to fulfill their different goals. The following section discusses prisoners' rights to social media, social media use within correctional facilities, and the role of social media in the monitoring and rehabilitative guidance of the vast number of persons under monitored supervision outside correctional facilities.

Social Media Exclusion as Punishment

Despite the very large number of incarcerated persons housed in facilities in the U.S., inmate social media posts related to corrections are rarely seen. Commonly, social media is banned in prison. *Digital exclusion* is the term used to characterize denial of access by inmates to communication and information technologies while incarcerated (Wong et al., 2009).

Broadly speaking, digital exclusion can arise from a variety of sources. For example, some older people are excluded from making digital purchases and payments because they do not know how to use the apps and hardware/software interfaces involved. Others are excluded from social media because they do not care to use it. These digital exclusions, by nature, are the consequence of the fact that an individual voluntarily pursues other types of communication and information technologies (Celeste, 2021). Celeste (2021) introduces three major types of social media exclusion worthy of our attention: (1) users versus users (where users are blocked from viewing social media information posted by other users; (2) platforms versus users (where social media companies ban users because they violate policies, such as the spreading of fake news and the posting of racist comments); and (3) states versus users (where federal and state statutes prevent individuals from using social media for particular purposes deemed detrimental to public health and safety) (Celeste, 2021). In this section, we focus on the third type – social media exclusion as a formal social control.

We analyze social media exclusion from several aspects. First, does social media exclusion serve any of the four goals of corrections (i.e., retribution, deterrence, incapacitation, and rehabilitation)? One, retribution holds offenders responsible and punishes them to the same degree as the harm they cause (Stohr & Walsh, 2019). For example, capital punishment may be justified for some types of murderers. There seems to be no comparable ground for social media exclusion to be an equal punishment for an equal crime. Two, deterrence suggests that punishment will deter criminal behavior (Stohr & Walsh, 2019). Not allowing the use of social media in jails and prisons may have the same effect as strictly limited use of phone calls and supervised visits. The disconnection between inmates and the digital social world could be a factor which deters future offending. Three, incapacitation means that incarceration will remove offenders from the community so they are not able to perpetrate more harm. Social media exclusion may help achieve this goal. It may prevent offenders who use social media as a criminal tool from committing more cybercrimes. It may also prevent inmates from harassing victims, witnesses, judges, friends, and even family members. Last, rehabilitation indicates that we need to "cure" offenders so they will not recidivate (Stohr & Walsh, 2019). Clearly, the use of social media may help inmates return to society after they are released. Thus, social media exclusion may work against the accomplishment of this goal.

Second, although social media exclusion does not violate an individual's constitutional rights in most countries at this moment in history, this common practice in correctional settings raises several major knotty issues moving into the future. For example, prisoners need social support, especially elderly inmates who are more likely to enjoy family support (Stohr & Walsh, 2019). There are pay phones in jails and prisons, but they are often too expensive for inmates to use on a regular basis. There are also supervised kiosks and tablets in some prisons, allowing inmates to use them for both prison programs and the maintenance of some family connections (Kerr & Willis, 2018). Generally, these devices are not connected to the Internet, and content is monitored. Moreover, inmates are allowed to make calls only to those people approved by the correctional facility. These calls are typically relatively expensive, and they are always subject to active monitoring by correctional officers.

Despite the cost of traditional landline phones and tablets in prison, we think that social media involves more than just connecting one person with another person. Individuals use social media to contact people they know personally and to connect with online strangers, to learn about experiences and acquire new skills, to take in the daily news, to look for jobs, and even to purchase goods. A study done on 40 prisoners reveals a series of disadvantages perceived by incarcerated persons regarding prohibiting new media from being used in prisons. Prisoners feel that a lack of access to new forms of social media causes them to experience disconnection with society (Jewkes & Reisdorf, 2016). They feel they are being treated as second-class citizens in this digital age (Jewkes & Reisdorf, 2016).

Younger prisoners and older prisoners (some of whom have been incarcerated for a long time) may hold different opinions about access denial to new media. Younger prisoners tend to affirm that they miss social media (e.g., *Facebook*) a lot in prison, while older prisoners say they are worried about engaging with new media after being released (Jewkes & Reisdorf, 2016). Imagine an inmate being released after a decade of incarceration. He likely does not know how to search for a job online. He likely does not know how to use a smartphone to secure an Uber or Lyft. He likely does not know that many restaurants are now getting rid of physical menus, and he needs to scan a QR code to order. Clearly, correctional treatment and programming (e.g., education and job training) are important to fulfill the goal of rehabilitation, but prisoner reentry skills and transitional assistance are likewise a major need (Stohr & Walsh, 2019). Some practitioners and researchers argue convincingly that successful modern rehabilitation requires inmates to have a base-level knowledge of the use of information and communication technology (Taugerbeck et al., 2019). Social media awareness and skill at use are part of the base-level knowledge. Social media skill acquisition may mitigate some of the damage caused by imprisonment (Taugerbeck et al., 2019).

Another issue to be considered is that although smartphones and social media are largely officially banned in prison, they are nonetheless prevalent in many prison settings (Grommon et al., 2018; Reid & Niebuhr, 2023). In the next section, we will discuss how social media is being used behind bars in many correctional facilities. Our discussion here focuses on what would happen if inmates were permitted to use social media freely. Recall that correctional jobs are largely hidden from the public view (Stohr & Walsh, 2019). Some have argued that social media access might help expose some issues of mismanagement in corrections. For example, about 3% of inmates report in inmate surveys that they have experienced some type of sexual victimization, committed either by correction staff or by other inmates (Stohr & Walsh, 2019; Schlosser & Feldman, 2022). Social media access in jails and prisons could provide an avenue of access for the public to view the reality of correctional confinement so that issues of sexual victimization could be addressed (Schlosser & Feldman, 2022). Some correctional facilities have started using social media to display their daily work and work environment (Erickson, 2013). Inmates can also promote this goal of broadening the public's knowledge of corrections, just as the French inmate *TikToker* we mentioned in the opening story.

Allowing inmates to use social media may be beneficial in many ways, but there are numerous safety and security issues to be considered (Kerr & Willis, 2018). Correctional officers generally feel it would be a great challenge to regulate social media use among inmates. For example, social media content may trigger inmates' anger or increase their anxiety (Jewkes & Reisdorf, 2016). A study conducted on 101 African American male jail inmates found that watching videos of community-based violence posted on social media significantly increased their feelings of anger (Motley et al., 2020). Another study found that inmates can use social media to harass others (e.g., victims, family, and friends) from their cells (Jewkes & Reisdorf, 2016). Inmates may also use social media to engage in criminal activity both inside and outside of the jail/prison setting (Kerr & Willis, 2018). Clearly, regulations and policies pertaining to approved uses and ongoing monitoring are needed. A prevailing opinion on corrections reform is that corrections should work hard on incarcerating fewer low-level offenders by expanding "alternatives to incarceration" (Stohr & Walsh, 2019). Low-level offenders should be offered more chances to succeed in court-ordered treatment, rehabilitation education and training, and reentry programming. Allowing low-level offenders to have monitored access to social media with appropriate restrictions may promote this vision of corrections reform (Kerr & Willis, 2018).

While social media exclusion in prison does not violate an individual's constitutional rights, a debate is taking place within legal circles on whether the use of social media does become a constitutional right when an inmate is released from prison, whether that be on parole or upon the completion of his or her sentence (Marcum & Higgins, 2014). This issue arises for some ex-inmates who are convicted for certain types of crime (e.g., domestic violence and cybercrime). For example, an ongoing debate is whether we should restrict social media use for convicted sex offenders (Marcum & Higgins, 2014). In *Packingham v. North Carolina* (2017), the U.S. Supreme Court ruled that prohibiting registered sex offenders from using social media is an unconstitutional violation of the First Amendment. This is one of few cases heard by the U.S. Supreme Court related to social media in criminal justice and as such provides an important window into our understanding of how social media is likely to be viewed by criminal courts in the 50 U.S. states moving forward. The overwhelming majority of criminal statutes are promulgated not by the U.S. Congress but rather by state legislatures operating within a federal governmental framework wherein federal courts generally defer to states in matters of criminal law. The *Packingham* decision sets a critical foundation for criminal defense lawyers to advocate for a broad right to access to social media by their clients. Due to the overwhelming prevalence of social media, scholars have argued that "social media represent a central instrument for exercising a broad range of fundamental rights" (Celeste, 2021, p. 163). Some examples of these rights that can be achieved via social media, include communicating, publishing comments, disseminating beliefs, and organizing online protests (Celeste, 2021).

Social Media Behind Bars

Although most digital communication technologies are forbidden in prisons for inmates, the use of digital technology is nonetheless occurring with growing frequency (Reid & Niebuhr, 2023). For example, a study on contraband cell phones in U.S. prisons found that "the numbers of contraband cell phones available are at least two times larger than confiscation totals" (Grommon et al., 2018, p. 642). It is estimated that half or more inmates have had access to a contraband cell phone while incarcerated (Grommon et al., 2018). Given these findings, it is not surprising that postings by incarcerated inmates may be seen on social media.

In recent years, videos and live streams taken inside jails and prisons are not uncommon on *TikTok* and other social media platforms. Searches with keywords such as "prisontiktok," "prisontok," and "prison" yield thousands of videos on the *TikTok* platform. We used "prison" to search on *TikTok* in March 2024 and found these videos had more than 213 million views. Topics featured in the videos vary, typically depicting daily prison life, prison food, dancing in prison, and sometimes the occurrence of prison violence. Some caution is needed in appraising these postings, however. First, it is difficult to know for certain that these videos are indeed made within jails or prisons as opposed to being staged. While most videos look "pretty real," authentication is nearly impossible. Second, it may be the case that prison *TikTok* videos are biased in magnifying the dark side of jails and prisons. However, a fair number of videos display inmates expressing positive thoughts and having some degree of "fun" in prison (e.g., Schlosser & Feldman, 2022; Reid & Niebuhr, 2023). One important lesson learned from a review of these postings from the inside is that on the whole "Outsiders" (corrections reformers such as scholars and corrections professionals) care a great deal about the legal rights of the accused being observed and the prevalence of violence in prison, while Insiders (e.g., inmates and corrections staff) care more about surviving and staying positive while serving their time and carrying out their supervisory duties in prison.

Compared to traditional social media platforms (e.g., *Facebook* and *Twitter*), in recent years, *TikTok* has become the first choice among inmates wishing to engage in social media in prison. One possible explanation may be that the *TikTok* app allows users to edit their videos within the app on the phone. Untiktolard mentioned that he would just use his smartphone to film and edit prison videos without any need for a computer (Chedeville, 2021). Another possible reason may be that *TikTok* focuses on short video clips, which often last for less than 60 seconds. Short video clips tend to draw more attention than long video clips. A recent report suggests that short video clips receive 2.5 times more engagement than do long video clips (Mosby, 2024). Additionally, as major customers of *TikTok*, teenagers and young adults often prefer short videos to long videos (e.g., Almeida & Almeida, 2017; Potrel, 2022). This population also happens to be curious about novelty, such what does prisons look like? There are hundreds of *TikTok* accounts focusing on jails and prisons. Popular prison *TikTok* accounts have received millions of views. One *TikTok* account mentioned in Schlosser and Feldman's (2022) study features only six videos, but it has attracted over 190,000 followers and received a million "likes."

Inmates use *TikTok* to achieve three major goals. First, *TikTok* is used to help inmates stay connected with society and maintain some sense of cultural connection (Schlosser & Feldman, 2022). A few examples are that inmates use *TikTok* to perform "TikTok dance challenges" and "June bug challenges" (Schlosser & Feldman, 2022). Second, inmates use *TikTok* to display the everyday life of imprisonment (e.g., prison food). Furthermore, they also interact with viewers and answer their questions by continuously posting new videos in response to questions received (Schlosser & Feldman, 2022). Third, inmates use *TikTok* to raise issues concerning the correctional institution, such as why medical services and medications are lacking, why personal safety and security issues are not being addressed, and how inmates learn to cope with these ongoing problems (Schlosser & Feldman, 2022). In one study conducted on 186 prison *TikTok* videos, researchers found similar theme patterns, including types of contraband found in prisons, types of food served in prisons, positive and negative narratives regarding prison programs and practices, dance events, music performed, inside and landscape views of prison facilities, portraits of colorful inmates and some correctional officers, and commentaries on the pains of imprisonment (Reid & Niebuhr, 2023). For instance, untiktolard featured in the opening story tends to focus on both funny moments and cooking food in prison. Based on their findings drawn from the study of videos, Reid and Niebuhr (2023) also argue that inmates tend to engage with social media (i.e., *TikTok*) in a positive way most of the time. It seems that social media use can keep some inmates maintain a positive frame of mind.

Outside Jails and Prisons: Social Media in Community Corrections

Community corrections often includes probation and parole along with other diversion from incarceration programs. Convicted persons serve out their terms outside jail or prison confinement while under the supervision of probation or parole officers. Community corrections are important to adjudicated offenders in terms of successfully returning to the community and reducing recidivism. Cullen and colleagues (2017) argue that

> to reduce recidivism, it will be necessary to hold [community corrections] officials accountable for this outcome, to ensure that evidence-based supervision is practiced, to use technology to deliver treatment services, and to create information systems that can guide the development, monitoring, and evaluation of interventions.
>
> *(p. 27)*

In the U.S., although the vast majority of adjudicated offenders are under probation or parole, only a small portion of the corrections budget is typically allocated to community corrections (Drake & Russo, 2016). Given this reality, GPS-equipped smartphones, often combined with proper use of social media, may provide an effective and efficient way to help supervise un-incarcerated adjudicated offenders and provide guidance in their reentry progress.

Probation and parole officers (POs) typically focus their attention on "violations" of probation or parole conditions imposed by a criminal court. Frequently, minor violations are ignored, trust is built between the PO and offenders, and positive reinforcements are devised (Drake & Russo, 2016; Healy, 2012; Lovins et al., 2018; Worrall & Mawby, 2014). POs should be supportive and trustworthy as they enforce the conditions of release imposed by the court and ought to provide encouragement to inmates to take up a law-abiding lifestyle (Lovins et al., 2018). Non-supportive and strongly punitive relationships typically lead to high rates of recidivism (e.g., Morash et al., 2016). Social media can be used quite effectively to send messages of personal encouragement to offenders, giving them a sense of personal concern and social accomplishment (Drake & Russo, 2016). Continuous communication between probation or parole officers and the offenders they supervise is also important. In the past, officer-inmate communication may have been limited to office or field visits, phone calls, letters, and perhaps emails. Social media, viewed as a perfect tool for instant messaging, can help maintain continuous communication between offenders and POs quite conveniently.

Social media also provides inmates with real-time resources information (e.g., job leads, treatment program openings, and housing availability) (Drake & Russo, 2016). This type of information is essential in probation and parole work because treatment program slots and job opportunities help inmates stay away from incarceration (Stohr & Walsh, 2019). Inmates may also use social media to look for such information by themselves apart from the help provided by their POs. Compared to traditional communication tools, social media is a perfect tool for instantly broadcasting information to selected audiences (Hu & Lovrich, 2020). In the past, POs might have needed to call each offender and inform them of a job opportunity. With social media, officers just need to share the information on social media platforms (e.g., *Facebook* and *Twitter*) so that all offenders who may benefit from it can access the timely information.

Of course, one of the main jobs of a PO is supervising inmates to ensure they do not violate probation or parole conditions. Social media provides an important type of online surveillance. Offenders under community supervision may post pictures or videos related to weapons, contraband drugs, threats of harm or violence, and other matters constituting a violation of conditions of release (Russo, 2014). Additionally, many social media platforms allow their users to post their postings with geographical locations. Offenders may have social media posts indicating that they were somewhere where they were not supposed to be. These posts can be used as evidence of probation or parole violation (see Chapter 5 regarding social media evidence).

It should be noted, however, that not all social media pictures of drugs or weapons can be used to prove that an offender has violated their probation or parole conditions. In a Pennsylvania case *Commonwealth v. Foster* (2019), a defendant was charged with violating probation conditions because he posted pictures of guns and drugs on some of his social media accounts during his four-year probation stint. The defendant argued that he just downloaded these pictures and shared them on social media as a way of showing off to his friends. The trial court disagreed with the defendant, revoked his probation, and sentenced him to a jail term. On appeal, the Pennsylvania Supreme Court disagreed with the trial court, holding that there was not sufficient evidence establishing that the defendant actually possessed the drugs or guns shown in his social media postings. The Pennsylvania Supreme Court took note that the defendant was not seen in those pictures. Accordingly, the Commonwealth could not prove that the defendant violated probation conditions solely on the basis of these social media posts (*Commonwealth v. Foster*, 2019).

There are, of course, a few additional issues that should be addressed regarding the use of social media in community corrections. First, not all offenders are interested in using social media. It is not possible to force them to do so. Second, even if inmates are social media users, it is not guaranteed that they will read whatever probation or parole officers post on social media. Some social media users spend hours on social media; others just log in and check out their social media accounts occasionally. Third, probation and parole officers may be concerned about their personal information safety on social media (Adorjan & Ricciardelli, 2023). Many may not want to get too close to the offenders they supervise, and social media "friendship" tends to breed a certain level of interpersonal intimacy. To address such concerns, POs may establish a discrete social media account, one which is used exclusively for communicating with offenders. Meanwhile, when making use of social media as a monitoring tool (Russo, 2014), POs may require some special training regarding the authentication of social media evidence. In conclusion, probation and parole officers would be most wise to learn how to use social media as a supplement to traditional communication tools associated with their work.

Improving Use of Social Media Related to Corrections

Our review of the literature on social media and corrections suggests that, just like the police and the courts, corrections can make effective use of social media for various purposes, including providing information to the public and communicating with the public. We argue here that allowing incarcerated offenders to use social media behind bars with strict restrictions may benefit the inmates, the prison, and society alike. Accordingly, in this section, we provide several institutional suggestions for correctional facilities seeking to routinize social media use among their populations. Also, we propose a model for regulating inmates' use of social media.

Institutional Suggestions

As one of the three major components of the criminal justice system, corrections should take some major steps to adapt to social media in this digital age. Like police agencies and courts, correctional agencies should first determine what they wish to do with their social media accounts. Of course, correctional agencies can use social media to distribute information to the public, collect information from the public, and interact with the public. However, we think that two features of corrections should lead correctional agencies to devote more effort to delivering an inside view of corrections to the public. One feature is that correctional jobs are largely hidden from public view (Stohr & Walsh, 2019). The public often has little direct knowledge or experience with corrections, so the mass media unduly shape the public image of corrections (Surette, 2015a). The other is that the mass media often care rather little about corrections, so correctional agencies may need to find their own channels to communicate with the public (Surette, 2015a). Accordingly, social media can be a powerful tool for broadcasting the reality of conditions within correctional facilities to counter the myths and misconceptions about corrections. Such enhanced transparency may increase both the accountability and legitimacy of corrections. Exposing "true life" in the prison setting may help future incarcerated persons adjust their minds to prepare for their rehabilitation once in prison. It may also function as a deterrent to crime.

Second, correctional agencies should select social media platforms that can meet their needs and determine who has access to their official social media accounts. As we previously noted, correctional agencies may primarily focus on using social media to portray life behind bars for inmates and correctional officers. Given this goal of accurate portrayal, we believe a picture-focused (e.g., *Instagram*) or video-focused (e.g., *YouTube*) social media platform would be best for correctional agencies to use to achieve this goal. For instance, many correctional agencies use *YouTube* to post their recruitment videos (Enkhtugs & Walby, 2023). Of course, *Facebook* can still be a good platform for general purposes, and *Twitter* can be used to disseminate information rapidly and broadly (e.g., Erickson, 2013). In many jails and prisons, public information officers (PIOs) are the staff members who are responding to media inquiries. They are certainly the first-choice personnel for overseeing official social media accounts.

Third, correctional agencies should strive to strike a balance between publicity and privacy. Historically, corrections do not benefit sufficiently from publicity. The public acquires the false belief that prisons are violent, corrupt, desperate places from watching prison films and dramatic TV shows (Surette, 2015a). Believe it or not, social media significantly increases the publicity for corrections. It matters not whether correctional agencies wish to actively show their facilities on social media or not; many clever inmates have done this for them with the countless contraband cell phones present within correctional facilities (e.g., Grommon et al., 2018) and thousands of videos posted on social media (e.g., Schlosser & Feldman, 2022). From correctional agencies' perspective, when they decide to post their correctional officers and inmates on social media, they must be cautious about improper invasion of privacy. Obtaining consent from officers and inmates is an absolute must, as many officers and inmates do not feel comfortable having an online presence (e.g., Adorjan & Ricciardelli, 2023).

Fourth, correctional agencies should develop and adopt formal social media use policies. The National Institute of Corrections provides a manual of social media policy first drafted by the North Carolina Department of Public Safety (NCDPS) a decade ago and periodically updated. The manual provides an excellent example for correctional agencies to use as a foundation for their own policies. It emphasizes the importance of using social media to promote transparency in government and communicate with stakeholders directly (NCDPS, 2013). Most importantly, the manual contains sections on how correctional professionals should use social media. For example, social media postings should be posted in accordance with the agency's expectations and policies. Agencies should respond to appropriate comments in a timely manner. Agencies should allow the public's different opinions on their social media sites. Moreover, they should not use social media for political purposes (NCDPS, 2013). The manual also contains helpful guidelines for the regulation of personal use of social media by the agencies' employees (NCDPS, 2013).

Finally, compared to the police use of social media (Hu & Lovrich, 2020), correctional agencies will have a significantly lower number of followers on their social media platforms (Table 6.2). It is not because the public is uninterested in correction-related content. On the contrary, the success of prison *TikTok* indicates that many among the public are interested in seeing real-life behind bars conditions (e.g., Schlosser & Feldman, 2022). We think the low visibility of corrections on social media is principally due to the infrequency of postings by correctional agencies, as well as the content not being as entertaining as it is on prison *TikTok*. Therefore, we think that if correctional agencies wish to utilize social media effectively and efficiently, they should first tailor their social media posts based on public interests so they may attract more attention.

A Model for Regulating Inmates' Use of Social Media

Our previous analysis of social media exclusion in prison highlights several points. First, social media exclusion may not fulfill all the four goals of corrections (i.e., retribution, deterrence, incapacitation, and rehabilitation). Second, social media, like other information and communication technology, is important to successful contemporary rehabilitation. Inmates should at the very least be given training on use of social media before they are released. Third, even though social media is banned in prison, many ingenious inmates still find a way to possess smartphones and use them for social media dissemination. Compared to banning social media in the prison setting, we suggest that it may be a better approach to regulate inmates' use of social media with strict restrictions. As Kerr and Willis (2018) have argued, "Putting in place mechanisms to manage these security risks [caused by information and communication technology, such as social media] is far more beneficial than prohibiting access altogether" (p. 12). Accordingly, we propose a model for regulating inmates' use of social media (Figure 6.3).

The process starts with an inmate's formal application for social media. The application should be screened based on several considerations. First, the severity of the crime must be considered. Social media exclusion can be used as a tool for punishing inmates who are convicted of serious felonies such as murder, rape, and armed robbery. These inmates are often held in medium-security and high-security prisons. However, inmates held in minimum-security, low-security, and jails are often convicted of nonviolent offenses. It may not be necessary to forbid them the use social media. Second, the types of crime for which inmates have been convicted should also be considered. Although social media exclusion may not achieve the goal of retribution, some types of crime may receive retribution from social media

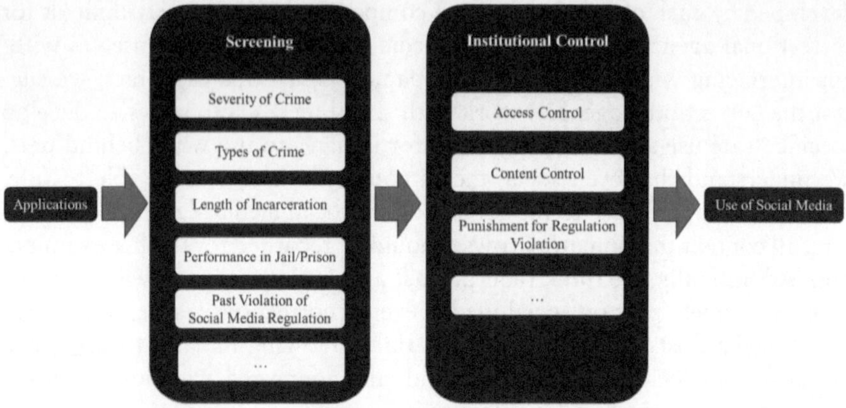

FIGURE 6.3 A model for regulating inmates' use of social media.

exclusion, such as cyberstalking and cyberbullying. It may be necessary to deny inmates who are convicted of these types of crimes the use of social media while behind bars.

The length of incarceration should be taken into serious account when screening applications. Some inmates have been incarcerated for a long time, and they should be given training in information and communication technology (including the use of social media for good purposes) before they are released on parole. Inmates' performance in jail and prison should also be considered. Granting social media access to model inmates may be used as a reward for their compliance with facility rules and regulations. Furthermore, it may be treated as a *substantial reward* for juvenile offenders as many of them make heavy use of social media (e.g., Lim et al., 2013). Moreover, past violations of social media regulation can be viewed as a red flag. Inmates may be forbidden the use of social media for a certain period if they have been shown to have misused social media in the past.

After inmates pass the screening process and are granted the use of social media, there must be institutional control with respect to several matters. The first is access control, including access to devices, the location of using social media on these devices, and the time of using social media. Devices and their systems, like the current use of phones and tablets in prison, should be customized and restricted. In medium-security and high-security prisons, inmates may be allowed to visit social media in a computer lab which is fully monitored by correctional agencies. In minimum-security and low-security prisons, inmates may be allowed to use devices in their cells. Additionally, the time of using devices should be controlled.

Correctional agencies should set strict rules regarding what social media content inmates are allowed to view. Besides using social media as a communication tool, today many people also use social media to gain a wide variety of information. The types of information are controlled by algorithms developed by each of the social media companies. It is extremely difficult for correctional agencies to filter social media information by themselves without interfacing with social media companies. Given this basic fact, we suggest the correctional agencies work with social media companies to develop specific "safe use software programs" for inmates to use while behind bars. We understand that even social media companies may not be able to fully control content feed due to the complexity of social media algorithms. Therefore, all content that inmates browse should be recorded for further examination. Additionally, we think that, at least at this time, it is not wise to allow inmates to freely post on social media, even if corrections staff reviews these social media posts before posting. We think allowing inmates to use social media to gain helpful information and stay connected with loved ones is proper, but it is risky to allow them to post anything.

It is, of course, necessary to set up rules for inmates who want to use social media and inform them of the punishment for any violation of regulations. The fundamental principle is that inmates should use social media to connect with their loved ones and advance their effective rehabilitation. The model set out here for regulating inmates' use of social media is meant to serve as a prototype. We think correctional agencies should build their own procedures and regulations with one ultimate purpose – social media exclusion should not be a stumbling block in inmates' rehabilitation and reentry.

Conclusion

In this chapter, we first noted that corrections has received significantly less attention from the mass media than the other areas of criminal justice, although there is some presence which we review in some detail. Then, we examined the literature on social media and corrections regarding three primary subjects: (1) correctional agencies' use of social media; (2) correctional officers' challenges in managing the use of social media; and (3) how social media can be employed to study public attitudes toward corrections. In examining the extant literature, we discussed prisoners' rights to social media access and social media use within correctional facilities. We show that while inmate digital devices are generally not permitted inside of correctional facilities, many social media postings have been made from within jails and prisons by inmates offering a window into jail and prison life. Also, we discussed the role of social media in the monitoring and rehabilitative guidance of the great number of persons under monitored supervision residing outside correctional facilities. Additionally, we offered our suggestions for improving corrections' use of social media and regulating inmates' use of social media to promote safe reentry into the community after serving out sentences imposed by the courts.

7

SOCIAL MEDIA AND CRIME PREVENTION

Opening Story: On February 13, 2023, police officers received a message regarding a 911 call reporting shots being fired in a student hall at 8:18 p.m. The university issued an alert at 8:31 p.m. Campus police then issued an alert of an active shooter on *Twitter* at 8:40 p.m. It later tweeted the description of the shooter at 9:56 p.m. The suspect was located, confronted by police, and shot himself to death at 11:35 p.m. The campus police updated on *Twitter* that the threat was terminated at 12:28 a.m. (Deliso, 2023). The foregoing represents a brief timeline of the 2023 Michigan State University shooting. The shooting incident led to four deaths (including the shooter) and five persons being critically injured (Sangal et al., 2023). During the tragic incident, the MSU campus police posted at least 13 *Twitter* messages within the four hours of active shooter notification, updating the public with the "Run, Hide, Fight" strategy message, background information on the subject, and police actions being taken.

The Big Question of Crime Prevention

Studies done on crime trends in the U.S. point to at least two essential facts. The *good* fact is that the overall crime rate has been falling since the 1990s. The *bad* fact is that the overall crime rate in the U.S. remains substantially higher than that in many other developed countries (Barkan & Rocque, 2021). In addition to the emotional and physical costs of crime (e.g., fear of crime, post-traumatic stress disorder, injury, and even death), the direct economic loss from crime has been estimated to be about $100 billion annually. The U.S. criminal justice system (i.e., police, courts, and corrections) require the expenditure of approximately $280 billion annually (Barkan & Rocque,

DOI: 10.4324/9781003360049-8

2021). Obviously, the impact of crime on individuals and on broader society is unquestionably enormous (Lab, 2016).

Given this large expenditure of tax dollars, a very reasonable question is *can we stop crime before it happens*? The answer is both yes and no. The "yes" answer primarily comes from criminological theories and empirical evidence. Theories such as rational choice theory, routine activity theory, crime pattern theory, and deterrence theory guide research into crime prevention. Moreover, evaluation research on crime prevention programs reflecting these approaches has documented promising results in numerous areas of public safety work.

The "no" answer primarily comes from the reasonable assumption that "outliers" will always exist in society. Some crimes of violence and property cannot be predicted, as offenders are not always rational in the conduct in which they engage. Additionally, a single or multiple crime prevention approaches do not usually cover the whole national population. For example, the Gang Resistance Education and Training (GREAT) program was designed to reduce gang involvement among teenagers (Esbensen et al., 2012). However, one evaluation of the GREAT program notes that the program does not effectively reduce violent offending (Esbensen et al., 2012). Wu and colleagues (2022) argue that this phenomenon may reflect the fact that a homogenous treatment cannot meet many differing individual needs. It follows from some GREAT program evaluations carried out with results being published in peer-reviewed journals, an effective crime prevention approach may need to be customized to specific types of settings. Since GREAT is a school-based program, it does not cover youths who drop out of school. These teenagers are often at high risk of joining gangs and engaging in serious delinquent behavior.

We believe that social media can help diminish the factors causing the "no" answer posed earlier. As we have repeatedly emphasized in previous chapters, social media can provide their users with highly customized information. Using social media to distribute timely crime prevention tips to a specific set of persons in a specific location at a specific time may be more useful/efficient and get more users' attention than relying upon face-to-face interactions between citizens and the police. For instance, if a robbery happened last night on the street near your home, you may not know about it at all – or learn about it too late to take protective actions. Social media, location-targeted services, and big data algorithms may all be used to promote public safety. You will be able to get a notification quickly that a robbery is happening or has just happened near your home. You may instantly react by staying at home and locking doors and windows. You become a beneficiary virtually immediately by virtue of timely notification. Moreover, you may benefit others by disseminating this information about a threat to public safety on your own social media accounts (e.g., retweet and share).

Besides, social media may reach the population with whom traditional/conventional crime prevention programs are unable to connect. For example, Hu and Lovrich (2020) illustrate how the police have used *Facebook* to conduct community-oriented policing with the public, particularly with underserved population such as teenagers who are at elevated risk of being both offenders and victims (Sampson & Laub, 2005). Furthermore, community-oriented policing has been viewed as an important asset for building partnerships with citizen groups and local businesses for the promotion of crime prevention (Lab, 2016). The public generally supports the practice of posting crime prevention information on social media, although the strength of this supportive disposition can be influenced by the credibility of the sources making the postings (Ismail et al., 2022). Messages from the police alone are less impactful than those reflecting a partnership with community-based groups and institutions.

Crime Prevention: Definition and Contemporary Efforts

For the average person, the idea of crime prevention is simply to reduce, if not eliminate, actual crimes. Responding to reported crimes, catching criminals, and punishing criminals all heavily rely on the core elements of the criminal justice system (i.e., police, courts, and corrections). Research has found that the public in general holds the view that the *shared* responsibility of crime prevention lies with both these formal systems and civil society more broadly (Roberts & Hastings, 2007). Unfortunately, the public is unlikely to take crime prevention actions until the risk of actual physical and emotional damage and financial loss is either immanent or actually experienced. For example, citizens frequently install cameras and alarms around their houses to prevent burglary and monitor their property only after a neighbor or they themselves have been victimized. Another example is identity theft. Even though identity theft has become one of the most common crimes perpetrated today, and many people have some fear of being victimized like many of their friends and family members (Choi et al., 2021), only a small proportion of the public makes concrete efforts to prevent it.

In this book, we embrace the straightforward definition of crime prevention proposed by Lab (2016) – namely, "crime prevention entails any action designed to reduce the actual level of crime and/or the perceived fear of crime" (p. 29). In his widely read book, Lab posits two reasons as to why his own definition differs from the traditional conception of crime prevention featuring both crime occurrence and its societal consequences. The first reason is that if crime and *fear of crime* are both addressed simultaneously, proactive actions will be more efficacious. The second reason is that we can address the consequences of victimization (and revictimization) more effectively without needing to address the complex dynamics of the many underlying types of crimes to which we are subject (Lab, 2016). Lab argues that the provision of timely supportive services to crime victims emotionally, financially, and temporally can both reduce crime revictimization and reduce fear of crime while it is at its apex. We think that Lab's definition dovetails perfectly with our conception of the utility of social media for crime prevention. On the one hand, social media-based police actions can help reduce certain crimes (e.g., online surveillance used by the police and distribution of crime prevention tips). On the other side, social media channels can help crime victims – whether they are potential, current, or repeat victims – meet their emotional needs (e.g., reducing fear of crime) by providing timely appropriate ongoing communication and engaging in supportive interactions (e.g., online support groups and #stopdomesticviolence).

In fact, we feel strongly that although social media is often viewed as a mere digital communication tool, we feel social media can prevent crime and fear of crime in ways that conventional mass media cannot. The social media crime prevention model sketched out in the next section is not built *in vacuo*. It reflects how we believe social media can be embedded more thoroughly into current conventional crime prevention efforts engaged in by law enforcement. Accordingly, a brief introduction to contemporary crime prevention approaches is appropriate at this point.

The literature on crime prevention divides contemporary crime prevention efforts into three categories. *Primary* crime prevention approaches focus on tangible physical and social environments. *Secondary* crime prevention approaches focus on individuals, families, peers, and school settings. The boundary between these groups is somewhat unclear given that they all focus on preventing crime by using aspects of informal social control. For instance, Lab (2016) places situational crime prevention under secondary prevention while Barkan and Rocque (2021) place it under primary crime prevention. *Tertiary* crime prevention refers to what the criminal justice system can do in terms of authoritative intervention. Tertiary crime prevention approaches often involve the use of varying aspects of formal social control (e.g., police presence, active police monitoring, repeat offender tracking, and "incapacitation" using jails and prisons). In this chapter, we show how social media crime prevention efforts can be embedded in nearly all crime prevention approaches noted to make them more effective.

Crime Prevention Through Environmental Design (CPTED)

CPTED refers to the core idea that physical design of a place can impact risk of crime (Casteel & Peek-Asa, 2000). The concept originally derives from Newman's (1972) concept of defensible space, the idea that various physical characteristics of a place impact the behavior of both potential victims and potential offenders. For example, appearance of orderliness of a place creates a more caring attitude among residents, leading them to maintain and improve that appearance over time. Such an appearance also sends a signal to potential offenders that this place is being taken care of, thereby generating a deterrent effect among would-be offenders.

Different researchers and practitioners have come up with differing classifications of the components of CPTED because the key concepts in CPTED have not been precisely defined (Ekblom, 2011). However, these classifications share several components in common. The first component is *active surveillance*. A space or facility can be designed so that adequate surveillance can be applied, either on site or remotely. The second component is *access control*, which refers to the ability to regulate who can access the space/facility in question. The third component is *image*. The space or facility should have the clear appearance that it is being well taken care of by people who use it. The fourth component is *activity support*, which refers to interactive activities among community members making use of a common space or facility. The fifth component is *target hardening*, which refers to the practice of making it necessary for offenders to make a serious effort to commit a crime in the space or facility. The final component is *territoriality*, which is a sense of collective ownership of a space or facility (see Lab, 2016, pp. 56–62; also see Barkan & Rocque, 2021). Classic examples of CPTED planning include the use of ample lighting, closed-circuit television (CCTV), multiple locks, alarms, monitored entrance and exit, and the holding of periodic safety drills involving users of the space or facility.

The systematic evaluation of CPTED projects is often difficult due to the complexity of the CPTED process. Cozens and Love (2015) argue that individual CPTED projects typically suffer from research quality issues because so many factors need to be considered. Also, each CPTED project is unique, resulting in limited generalizability (Cozens & Love, 2015). Despite these difficulties in assessing outcomes for entire projects, it may be possible to evaluate CPTED projects effectively "piece-by-piece." Lab (2016) summarizes some empirical evidence on CPTED process outcomes in his book. Lighting, alarms, and informal surveillance (i.e., natural surveillance) would seem to be effective in reducing burglary, for example. Lighting and informal surveillance may reduce theft. Furthermore, external landscape and internal ambient lighting, closed circuit TV deployment, and ongoing informal surveillance have all been shown to reduce fear of crime (Lab, 2016).

In today's digital society, both physical places and online places witness serious crime occurrence. Cybercrime, for example, takes place on the World Wide Web facilitated by the Internet and its related communication technology (Maras, 2017). Many heretofore face-to-face crimes now have their cyber version (e.g., stalking and cyberstalking, trespass and cybertrespass, and theft and cybertheft). Will CPTED work on preventing some of these crimes? This would depend on whether offenders need a physical place to exchange a good or service for funds.

For example, today many websites (e.g., Craigslist) and even some social media platforms (e.g., *Facebook Marketplace*) provide peer-to-peer (P2P) commerce opportunities for buying and selling items. One person advertises an item on *Facebook Marketplace*, and another person will meet him or her face to face to complete the merchandise transaction (Vasquez et al., 2020). This situation may allow an offender (buyer or seller) to target a suitable victim (seller or buyer) and conduct a legal robbery. Some scholars define this type of crime as "appointment robbery" (Vasquez et al., 2020). A qualitative study conducted on 12 active appointment robbers revealed that access control, activity support, surveillance, and territoriality indeed deter their decision to commit robbery (Vasquez et al., 2020). Meanwhile, some of CPTED's concepts (e.g., target hardening) are still useful even if they are not applied to physical locations. We will discuss this notion in detail in the next section.

Situational Crime Prevention

Some scholars consider CPTED as an antecedent of situational crime prevention (Barkan & Rocque, 2021) since they both involve crime opportunities and assume that potential offenders will make rational decisions. The original situational crime prevention model focuses on three major *efforts* (i.e., increasing watchfulness effort, increasing risk of detection, and reducing rewards of crime commission) and 12 related *techniques*. Later, Clarke (1995) modified and expanded upon the model with four major groups (i.e., increasing perceived effort, increasing perceived risks, reducing anticipated rewards, and *removing excuses*) and 16 related techniques. The situational crime prevention model in widest use today has five major groups (i.e., increasing effort, increasing risk, reducing rewards, removing excuses, and reducing provocations) and 25 related techniques (Cornish & Clarke, 2003). Table 7.1 provides a detailed description of these 25 techniques.

Regarding the effectiveness of situational crime prevention, Shariati and Guerette (2017) point out that systematic evaluation studies generally indicate that situational crime prevention offers an effective approach to reducing crime. They reach this conclusion based on a few comprehensive evaluation studies carried out on some major situational crime prevention initiatives (e.g., Bowers & Guerette, 2014; Eck & Guerette, 2012; Welsh & Farrington, 1999). In terms of places, situational crime prevention works best in recreational places, followed by retail, transportation, residential, and public passageways. Regarding preventive actions taken, CCTV, ample lighting, access control, place management, and street redesign each show high potential for crime prevention (Shariati & Guerette, 2017; also see Eck & Guerette, 2012). Despite these promising findings, Shariati and Guerette (2017) point out that it is challenging indeed to evaluate situational crime prevention interventions considering that it is an ongoing, customized, and location-based approach. Given these factors, generalizability is quite

TABLE 7.1 Situational crime prevention 25 techniques. (Also see Barkan & Rocque, 2021, p. 148; Lab, 2016, pp. 225–226)

Increase Effort	*Increase Risk*	*Reduce Rewards*	*Reduce Provocations*	*Remove Excuses*
Harden targets • Locks	Extend guardianship • Walk in groups, not alone	Hide targets • Scrub outside house	Reduce stresses • Quick lines for business	Set rules • Record agreements
Control access • Pass cards	Improve natural surveillance • Street lighting	Remove targets • Park in garage	Reduce disputes • Crowd control in games	Post instructions • No loitering signs
Screen exits • Tickets for exit	Improve formal surveillance • Alarms in the house	Mark property • Name tags on luggage	Reduce emotional arousal • Avoid violent media	Activate conscience • Speed limit signs
Deflect offenders • Disperse pubs	Use place managers • CCTV cameras	Disrupt markets • Sell licenses	Control peer influences • G.R.E.A.T. program	Assist compliance • Public dumpsters
Control crime tools • Gun trigger locks	Reduce anonymity • Check IDs in bars	Deny benefits • Speed bumps	Discourage imitation • Clean graffiti	Control substances • Limit alcohol sales

limited, and crime displacement must be considered when evaluating the use of situational crime prevention.

Neighborhood Crime Prevention

Like CPTED, neighborhood crime prevention is carried out primarily in residential locations where homes and apartments are the venues of interest. Neighborhood crime prevention places primary emphasis on residents' behaviors. Building social cohesion and encouraging citizen participation in safety planning serve to create an active guardianship mentality which can deter potential offenders (Lab, 2016). A variety of neighborhood crime prevention approaches are present in the crime prevention literature. For example, neighborhood watch may be the most widely adopted neighborhood crime prevention approach. The core idea of neighborhood watch is to disseminate self-protective knowledge with the neighborhood and help neighbors to become better acquainted with each other. "Outsiders" will be more easily identified, and perhaps more quickly scrutinized when they enter the neighborhood. Meanwhile, residents work with their local police agency to proactively identify crime-related issues in the neighborhood. Along with a more active neighborhood watch approach, "citizen patrols" are often adopted in communities engaged in neighborhood crime prevention (e.g., Hino, 2018; Kim, 2013). Voluntary (and sometimes paid) individuals patrol the neighborhood either on foot or in vehicles. Interestingly, daily activities such as walking, jogging, and greeting school buses may also function as crime prevention patrols in the neighborhoods (Hino, 2018).

Neighborhood watch has been widely used worldwide as a community crime prevention effort. There are many reasonable explanations for why neighborhood watch can reduce crime. For example, neighborhood watch typically raises the visibility of crime prevention efforts within the community (signage is often displayed indicating "this neighborhood is under surveillance"). It can reduce opportunities for crime because knowledge of suspicious activities is disseminated and conveyed to the police. It may help the police solve crime by providing timely information for police investigations (Wood & Thompson, 2021). Despite these positive attributes, neighborhood watch programs have been the target of several criticisms. A significant concern raised is that it often is used with elderly persons residing in virtually crime-free communities (Kelly & Finlayson, 2015). Another concern is that, in general, neighborhood crime prevention requires periodic face-to-face meetings, get-togethers which may be very difficult to sustain in many places (e.g., COVID; see Hu & Lovrich, 2022). Younger persons, in particular, are inclined to prefer social media contact to face-to-face encounters.

Does neighborhood crime prevention work? Lab (2016, p. 113) opines that sound evidence is available indicating that neighborhood watch programs have a positive impact on burglary, theft, and robbery. Community anti-drug abuse programs likewise seem to impact drug abuse and violence favorably in the communities where they are implemented. The authors of a systematic review and meta-analysis of 18 studies on neighborhood crime prevention conclude that neighborhood watch effectively reduces crime (Bennett et al., 2006). Regarding its impact on fear of crime, Lab (2016) opines that both neighborhood watch and citizen patrols seem to reduce fear of crime in most settings. However, some studies have found that neighborhood watch does not reduce crime or fear of crime in all cases. Some studies report that neighborhood watch had only a modest effect on reducing crime (e.g., Bennett et al., 2008). Some scholars have reported that neighborhood watch actually *increased* fear of crime because it made residents more aware of local crime (e.g., Wood & Thompson, 2021; Zhao et al., 2002).

Although neighborhood crime prevention programs are typically run and managed by local community members and volunteers, local police often participate as active partners. Many scholars have argued that neighborhood crime prevention involving the police positively impact police legitimacy, enhance public confidence in the ability of police to combat crime, and improve police responsiveness (Kelly & Finlayson, 2015; Ren et al., 2005). Even if a neighborhood crime prevention program does not appreciably reduce crime, it still has the potential to benefit the neighborhood in multiple ways promotive of public safety.

Addressing Crime Displacement

CPTED, situational crime prevention, and neighborhood crime prevention encounter a common troublesome question: do these programs reduce crime overall or simply move crime around to other less well-protected areas (e.g., Weisburd et al., 2006)? In the crime prevention literature, *crime displacement* refers not only to the geographical movement of crime but also to other forms of "crime migration" (Lab, 2016). Six distinct types of crime displacement have been identified in the research literature, five of which are proposed by Reppetto (1976) and one which comes from the work of Barr and Pease (1990). The first type is *territorial displacement*. This happens when crime moves from one place to another because some crime prevention activities occur in the first place.

The second type is *temporal displacement*. This occurs when offenders choose to commit crime at a different time when "defenses are lax" or guardians are not present. The third type is *tactical displacement*, which refers to offenders changing the methods of committing crime. The fourth type is *target displacement*. This is where offenders pick a different victim in the same area because the original victim targeted is well protected. The fifth type is *functional displacement*. This refers to the situation in which offenders stop committing one type of crime and move to the commission of a different type of crime. The last type is *perpetrator displacement*, referring to the situation in which one offender of limited ability is replaced by another more capable or audacious offender (see also Lab, 2016, p. 117).

Studies have found some evidence of crime displacement following on the heels of geographically targeted crime prevention efforts. For example, when a neighborhood watch program works well in one community, it often pushes crimes to a nearby community (Kelly & Finlayson, 2015). That said, crime prevention may also bring about a welcomed diffusion of benefits. Diffusion of benefits simply means that crime prevention may benefit places and individuals other than those targeted (Lab, 2016). The question then becomes, "can diffusion of benefits overcome crime displacement?" One of the most comprehensive examinations ever carried out on crime displacement and diffusion of benefits was conducted by Guerette and Bowers (2009). They conducted a systematic review of situational crime prevention programs. In total, they derive 574 observations from 102 evaluation studies done on situational crime prevention efforts. All six types of displacement were found to have taken place, and each displacement had its related diffusion of benefits (for more details, see Guerette & Bowers, 2009, Table 7.1). About 26% of observations show displacement, and 27% show diffusion. Guerette and Bowers (2009) further examined 19 observations from 13 studies that allow them to compare displacement and diffusion, concluding that even though displacement does occur, it tends to be less harmful than the benefits gained by diffusion.

However, the occurrence of crime displacement and diffusions of benefits may vary based on crime types and the size of locations. For example, in a 2014 systematic review of quasi-experimental studies on crime control interventions in large-scale geographic areas, Telep and his colleagues discover that diffusion of benefits is more likely to occur than crime displacement based on narrative results. However, their meta-analysis finds no significant evidence on either crime displacement or diffusion of benefits when crime control interventions do reduce crimes significantly (Telep et al., 2014). A study on examining terrorism intervention discovers more support for diffusion of benefits than displacement (Hsu et al., 2018).

Developmental Crime Prevention

Developmental crime prevention comes from the idea that criminal behavior results from early learning and adverse childhood experiences (Homel, 2013). If we can deal with these risk factors, we can reduce an affected person's likelihood of adopting a criminal lifestyle as an adult. Risk factors often come from different levels, such as psychological (e.g., aggressiveness and impulsivity), family (e.g., poor parental supervision, abuse, and parental criminality), peers (e.g., delinquent peers and gang membership), school experience (e.g., academic failure and dropping out), and community conditions (e.g., economic poverty, crimes, and rampant gang activity) (Farrington, 2007; also see Lab, 2016). To be noted, some inherent demographic factors (e.g., gender, age, and race) are proven to be risk factors as well; however, we do not develop crime prevention programs around these immutable factors.

Many crime prevention programs are developed based on this developmental perspective. Featured programs focusing on youth are the Promoting Alternative Thinking Strategies (PATHS) program and the FRIENDS program (feelings, relax and feel good, I can do it, explore solutions, now reward yourself, do it every day, stay calm). The PATHS program is often taught in elementary schools and is intended to treat kids' emotional and behavioral issues and improve their problem-solving skills (Domitrovich et al., 2007). Similarly, the FRIENDS program focuses on self-confidence, emotional resilience, and problem-solving among middle school populations (Shortt et al., 2001). Evaluations of both programs often report positive results, such as improved problem-solving ability, increased self-esteem, reduced anxiety, and reduced aggression (e.g., Domitrovich et al., 2007; Fisak et al.,2023; Greenberg et al., 1995; Kam et al., 2003; Shek et al., 2010; Shortt et al., 2001). Some examples of programs designed to deal with risk factors in families and schools are the Early Infancy Project, the Syracuse Family Development Research program, the Positive Parenting program (Triple P), the Nurse-Family Partnership (NFP) program, the Perry Preschool program, the Juvenile Mentoring program (JUMP), and the Incredible Years program (Lab, 2016; Barkan & Rocque, 2021). Most evaluation studies on these programs have documented positive results (e.g., Miller, 2015; Piquero et al., 2009; Tolan et al., 2014).

Partnership With the Criminal Justice System

Previous crime prevention efforts focus on preventing a crime from happening. This section discusses how our criminal justice system could help handle potential offenders and keep them from committing crimes again. Currently, the partnership phenomenon primarily focuses on active collaboration between the police and community (Lab, 2016). We have mentioned community-oriented policing (COP) and E-COP in the chapter on social media and the police (Chapter 4). The impact of E-COP on crime remains largely unknown, but many studies have evaluated whether COP can reduce crime occurrence and fear of crime. A good number of systematic studies have found that COP does indeed reduce crime. For instance, Connell and colleagues (2008) report that COP did reduce violent and property crime. On the contrary, some other studies indicate that COP had little or no effect on reducing crime (e.g., Gill et al., 2014; MacDonald, 2002; Mastrofski, 2006;

Weisburd & Eck, 2004). In a 2013 study, Sozer and Merlo (2013) reported that a problem-solving partnership had a troublesome positive relationship to crime rates. Hu and Lovrich (2020) explain this phenomenon by arguing that COP does not aim at crime reduction directly. Rather, COP focuses on the improvement of police-public relations and residents' quality of life. Hot spots policing may be more promising in terms of reducing crimes. A meta-analysis conducted by Braga and his colleagues in 2014 indicated that hot spots policing leads to a small but noteworthy crime reduction as an overall impact.

Lab (2016) mentions several other crime prevention partnerships in his book. For example, civil abatement uses administrative laws and codes to change community-degrading behavior at specific geographic locations. Injunctions and court orders can be used to restrict the behavior of individuals and compel municipal authorities to act (Lab, 2016). Some programs, such as Oakland's Specialized Multi-Agency Response Teams (SMART) and San Diego's Drug Abatement Response Team (DART), have shown that treatment areas have fewer crimes and drug abuse issues compared to control areas (Lab, 2016).

Lab (2016, p. 260) summarizes eight key features of successful crime prevention partnerships: (1) strong leaders and managers; (2) agreement on problems and interventions; (3) qualified staff; (4) sufficient research on the problems; (5) grassroots support; (6) adequate funding and resources; (7) good oversight of project implementation; and (8) effective evaluation research on outcomes. As we will demonstrate in the next section, social media can help with some of these features of successful police/public partnerships. For example, social media can provide online surveys to carry out research on local problems. Broadcasting crime prevention efforts and posting successful stories on social media can help gain public support. Social media may also provide a convenient, inexpensive, and ongoing group message exchange channel that helps communications flow among police and community-based leaders, managers, and staff.

Another noteworthy partnership deserving mention is the sex offender registry program. All 50 states and D.C. have sex offender registry programs, and most information on sex offenders is open to the public (visit https://www.nsopw.gov/ for more information). The public once had only limited access to this information on official websites. Now, ordinary citizens can also download a variety of phone applications that contain official information and simply use their smartphones to check on areas of interest. According to most state and federal legislation, sex offenders must be registered on sex offender registry programs after a conviction (or pleading guilty) to sex offenses. The logic behind the program is that if people know there is a sex offender near their homes or workplaces, they can take extra precautions – especially for their children. Sex offenders are widely believed to have a high recidivism rate, so the registry program is intended to deter them from committing new sex offenses.

However, this popular notion pertaining to the high likelihood of reoffending does not receive empirical support (e.g., Hanson et al., 2003). This widely held belief overlooks four basic facts. First, empirical studies have not confirmed that sex offender registry programs reduce sex crimes; findings on this question are mixed at best (e.g., Prescott & Rockoff, 2011; Vásquez et al., 2008; Zevitz, 2006). A 2023 meta-analysis on nearly 480,000 formerly incarcerated individuals reveals that the presence of sex offender registry program does not materially impact recidivism of either sexual or non-sex offenses (Mitchell & Zgoba, 2023). Second, a quite small percentage of sex offenders do in fact have an elevated recidivism rate, and they will re-commit sex offenses regardless of whether they are registered or not registered. Third, many sex offenders have not committed serious sex offenses, yet they will all be registered regardless of the seriousness of their offenses. It makes sense to put strict restrictions on dangerous sex offenders, but for many one-time offenders the stigmatization can be the cause of new life adjustment problems. And fourth, few people actually access sex offender registry information (Kernsmith et al., 2009). And even after viewing the registry for their neighborhood, many people still believe no active sex offenders live in their community (Kernsmith et al., 2009).

Despite these facts, the public generally supports the sex offender registry program. The public fears sex offenses and sex offenders, and that fear leads to strong support of the sex offender registry system nationwide (Kernsmith et al., 2009). The program is viewed as a crime prevention tool rather than as an ongoing punishment for onetime offenders. Persons thusly labeled (and their families) have reported being unduly harmed due to the program, citing such things as mental health issues, loss of employment, loss of housing, endurance of verbal and physical assaults, and even being murdered (Clarke, 2017; Levenson, 2018; Levenson & Tewksbury, 2009; Tewksbury, 2005; Tolson & Klein, 2015).

A Model of Conducting Crime Prevention Through Social Media

Our model of using social media in crime prevention draws heavily from Bowers and Johnson's (2013) framework for using mass media in crime prevention and situational crime prevention (Clarke, 1995). Bowers and Johnson (2013) propose a thoughtful theoretical model of how mass media can help prevent crimes (Figure 7.1). The core of mass media crime prevention activities is the use of *targeted publicity* (Bowers & Johnson, 2013; see also Lab, 2016). Bowers and Johnson (2013) propose that four core purposes can be achieved by using targeted publicity in crime-fighting: (1) increasing the actual risk of detection to offenders; (2) increasing the perceived risk of

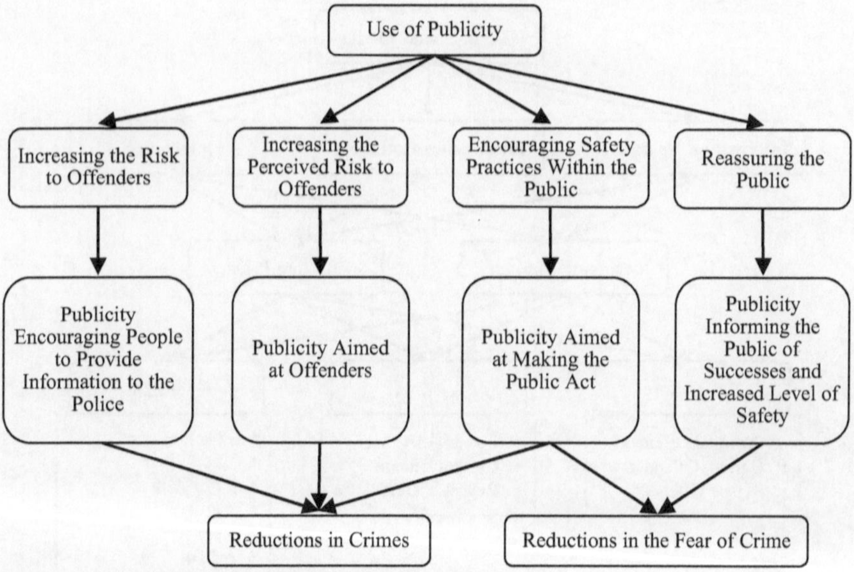

FIGURE 7.1 Use of publicity in crime prevention proposed by Bowers and Johnson (2013), also see Lab (2016) on page 144.

detection to offenders; (3) encouraging safety practices within the public; and, (4) providing diffuse reassurance to the general citizenry.

Enlightened by this useful framework, we propose an advanced model of using social media in crime prevention (Figure 7.2). The new model is also informed by routine activity theory (Cohen & Felson, 1979), which holds that a crime is more likely to happen if there is a motivated offender, a suitable target, and a lack of guardianship taking place at the same place at the same time over time.

We construct this model using three fundamental assumptions. First, social media is widely considered to be just one aspect of mass media, even though it has the added powerful features of timely distribution, broad dissemination, and real-time interaction. Accordingly, as Bowers and Johnson (2013) aver, the use of publicity may achieve the four core purposes of crimes fighting and fear of crime reduction; these same four purposes apply to social media in the same way they apply to mass media. Unfortunately, the many evaluations done of mass media's crime prevention efforts (e.g., the McGruff crime prevention campaign, the D.A.R.E. program, local crime newsletters, and publicized law enforcement information lines) suggest either mixed or minimally positive results (Lab, 2016). Despite this evidence of weak effect, Lab (2016) argues that smaller-scale and highly targeted publicity efforts may be quite effective forms of crime prevention. We believe that adroit use of

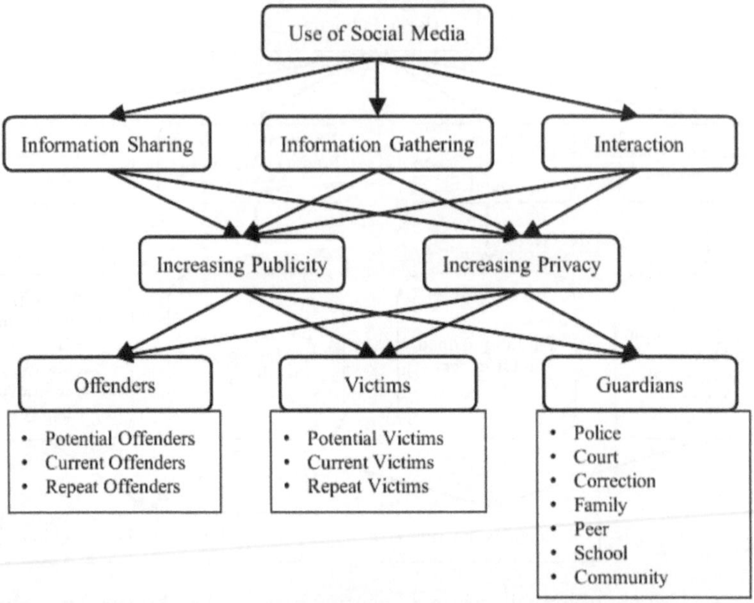

FIGURE 7.2 Social media crime prevention model.

social media can help achieve this more targeted and more efficacious type of crime prevention effort.

Second, we assume our model and other crime prevention approaches are functional on rational individuals and organizations. Rational choice theory in criminology generally suggests that most criminal offenses are committed when the rewards of the crime materially outweigh the punishment for the crime (Paternoster et al., 2017). We expand on this idea that all parties related to crime prevention must be rationally calculative for a particular crime prevention effort to be effective. From a routine activity theory perspective (Cohen & Felson, 1979), for example, offenders must be deterred by the likelihood of detection and subsequent punishment. Prospective victims must actively participate in crime prevention activities. And guardians, including official guardians (e.g., police, courts, and corrections) and informal guardians (e.g., family members, close friends, and communities), must fulfill guardianship responsibilities. Of course, even the most well-conceived crime prevention program may not work since not all parties calculate risks in a rational way.

Third, the primary product that a person acquires from using social media is relevant and timely information. Social media does not shape an individual's behavior directly; indeed, it alters an individual's thinking such that certain behaviors (i.e., crime preventive actions) may occur accordingly.

Additionally, social media does not provide any tangible entity to individuals. For example, it does not provide you with locks, security cameras, or even more police officers to protect you and your property. All you get is information, which you use to adjust your behavior – such as installing more effective locks and adding security cameras in your immediate whereabouts. As a communication tool in extremely broad use, social media can be a supplement to contemporary (or future) crime prevention approaches.

The three main functions of social media, as we discussed in the previous chapters, are to disseminate information, to help gather crime-related information, and to promote interaction among users. These functions all help achieve the four purposes of which Bowers and Johnson's (2013) write. Potential and repeat victims can use social media to acquire crime prevention advice to reduce their likelihood of being victimized. Current victims, such as individuals in an active shooter situation, can use social media to get precious timely updates about the situation and take preventive actions accordingly. Meanwhile, potential and repeat offenders may be deterred when crime prevention activities are circulated on social media in their area of operation. Current offenders may be apprehended when the public provides sound clues to the police via social media. Regarding guardianship, law enforcement agencies have used social media to locate wanted persons and provide crime prevention tips (Hu et al., 2018). Other formal and informal social organizations can also use social media to disseminate useful crime prevention information. Social media provides a two-way avenue for community engagement between citizens and public safety organizations, a collaborative engagement which carries a great potential to increase effective collective action in places where face-to-face communication is achieved only with great expenditure of staff time and police agency resources (see Smith, 2020 for crime prevention in rural communities).

The main feature of our model is that we recognize that social media not only achieves the goal of broadened publicity, but it also provides a chance to preserve personal privacy. Such privacy helps create individualized/customized crime prevention advice, which may be more effective than a global publicity blast (Wu et al., 2022). Contemporary social media platforms all embed privacy control options, which permit users to determine if certain information (e.g., personal traits, pictures, videos) are to be public or private. Using these controls more broadly may help reduce the likelihood of cyberstalking. The dissemination of such information among the public can be an effective avenue of crime prevention, especially among youth.

In addition, private interaction on social media allows victims to communicate with each other safely and to gain the benefit of sound advice and interpersonal support. For example, victims of domestic violence and date rape are unlikely to call the police due to personal privacy concerns and/or fear of reprisal (Felson et al., 2002). Male victims of domestic violence have even a lower reporting rate in major part because they do not believe the police will do anything to address the issue (Drijber et al., 2013). Social media may provide these victims with an anonymous channel of getting needed forms of support. For instance, some research has found that a number of victims of domestic violence have used *Reddit* to share their victimization experiences and get help from each other (Schrading et al., 2015; Sivagurunathan et al., 2021). *Facebook* maintains many community pages regarding domestic violence (e.g., Stop Domestic Violence). Social media can also promote private communications among victims and between victims and crime victim support organizations – community-based and criminal justice system-based alike. For example, the National Domestic Violence Hotline has its own *Facebook* page, and, as of February 2023, the organization has more than a hundred thousand followers.

Unfortunately, offenders can also get the same information as victims from social media. In other words, criminals use social media too! Taking advantage of social media, offenders often are able to locate suitable targets and pick a criminal opportunity when capable guardians are absent. For instance, a newspaper reporter notes that a Houston gang often uses social media searches to locate burglary targets who keep valuable artwork in their homes (or offices) and conducts burglaries when these owners are away from home, on vacation, or otherwise not providing guardianship (Almasy, 2019). Offenders also use social media to conduct identity theft, cyberstalking, cyber-casing, and phishing (e.g., Soomro & Hussain, 2019; for more social media and crime, see Chapter 3). Offenders can also get to know about crime prevention efforts through social media and respond accordingly, such as avoiding areas that have high-intensity crime prevention programs in operation.

Interestingly, Smith and colleagues (2002) use the term "anticipatory benefit" to describe the phenomenon whereby the success of crime prevention efforts often occurs *before* crime prevention actions are implemented. They selected 52 crime prevention evaluation reports and found that 22 demonstrated anticipatory benefit outcomes (Smith et al., 2002). Lab (2016) attributes anticipatory benefit outcomes to publicity, indicating that mass media help spread crime prevention initiatives so that offenders, victims, and others know about the initiatives and take public safety coproduction actions in anticipation of better conditions in the future. Many studies have reported that local police agencies often publicize their crime prevention activities on social media. For example, on July 4, 2014, the Houston Police Department announced that "additional officers will be deployed at high-risk locations around the Houston area to conduct DWI enforcement efforts" on its *Facebook* page (Hu & Lovrich, 2020, p. 82).

In conclusion, the purpose of building this police media outreach model is not to suggest what a social media crime prevention initiative should look like. Instead, we hope researchers, law enforcement practitioners, engaged citizen groups, and public policymakers can better understand the mechanisms by which social media may be used to enhance crime prevention, and why social media is different from traditional mass media in this regard.

Contemporary Social Media Efforts in Crime Prevention

A broad definition of social media covers websites and applications (predominately phone apps) that allow users to create and share information online. One significant change in social media in the past decade is that using social media on smartphones has become extremely convenient. While back in the early days of the digital age, social media had to be accessed by desktop or laptop, today the majority of people choose to use their phones and tablets for visiting social media sites. A survey conducted in 2019 found that Internet-enabled mobile phones (basically smartphones) accounted for 79% of social media site visits in the U.S. (Dixon, 2022). Similarly, in the U.K., adults spend four hours on average per day on their smartphones (Anderez et al., 2021). Additionally, mobile social media is widely accepted among teenagers worldwide, and this trend toward early acquisition of mobile phone use appears to be continuing (Dixon, 2022). With a broad definition of social media that covers both websites and phone apps, there are a variety of choices for social media crime prevention initiatives. Two major types of initiatives tend to predominate: (1) those are initiatives of general use, such as *Facebook* and *Twitter* and (2) those which are explicitly created to promote crime prevention (e.g., CityCop, Citizen, CrimePush, see Estellés-Arolas, 2022, p. 699, for more apps).

Online Neighborhood Watch Groups

Neighborhood watch was discussed in the previous section, and several limitations of the approach have been noted. Failure to engage the targeted population, scant implementation in high-crime communities, and limited engagement between the public and the police have been noted in prior studies. Scholars have suggested that enhanced use of social media to conduct neighborhood watch might address these limitations (Kelly & Finlayson, 2015). A successful neighborhood watch program relies upon ongoing collaboration among different parties (i.e., the local community, block watch volunteers, and the police). Social media provides an excellent channel of ongoing communication to achieve neighborhood watch goals. Additionally, the use of social media would seem to be very cost-effective as social media adoption and digital communication technology advance (Meijer, 2014).

Reynald (2019) points out that offline citizen patrol and neighborhood watch can be accompanied by online counterparts. Such online neighborhood watch groups in general can be separated into two principal types: (1) those that use functions within traditional social media (e.g., *Facebook*, *Twitter*, and *Instagram*) and (2) those that use social communication apps (e.g., *WhatsApp*, *Telegram*, and *Discord*). Using social media to carry out online neighborhood watch is rather commonplace today. A study conducted in The Netherlands reports that between 2015 and 2019, more than 7,200 *WhatsApp* neighborhood crime prevention groups were registered, many of which were initiated by citizen groups (Pridmore et al., 2019). Group members report what they see and hear in the community, share crime-related information and statistics, and communicate nonurgent matters with the police. The police actively participate in some of these groups (Pridmore et al., 2019). In a case study, police officers reported use of chats in the groups to collect information about auto thefts and other property crimes (van Steden & Mehlbaum, 2022).

Wood and Thompson (2021) develop a theory of the mechanisms at play in local social media-facilitated neighborhood watch, focusing on two features: *swarm intelligence* and *stigmergy*. Swarm intelligence refers to the action of individuals getting together to deal with a problem that cannot be solved by a single person. Stigmergy refers to the idea that in some situations one action will stimulate further actions (Wood & Thompson, 2021). After analyzing the Springsclare Crime prevention *Facebook* group, Wood and Thompson (2021) argue that *Facebook* community crime prevention groups can achieve the goal of putting "many eyes on the street" and promoting more crime prevention activities on the part of potential crime victims. The following posting illustrates how this *Facebook* group operates: "Just patrolled surrounding areas, nothing suspicious. Feel free to patrol your surrounding area and upload a screenshot so everyone knows when and where you patrolled" (Wood & Thompson, 2021, p. 424).

Some positive findings have been reported in the research literature regarding online neighborhood watch groups. One study reported that neighborhood burglaries experienced a 40% decrease after *WhatsApp* neighborhood crime prevention groups were initiated in Tilburg, The Netherlands (Pridmore et al., 2019). Another study suggests that the initiation of online neighborhood watch groups may attract more people to crime prevention activities. A study in Malaysia reported that crime prevention groups on *Facebook* attracted the attention of citizens and got them to participate in crime prevention by "lowering the barriers to engagement" (Tim et al., 2017). These groups gave the police an opportunity to inquire into unreported crimes (Tim et al., 2017). Neighborhood crime prevention groups can generate a sense of belonging in a community (Dixon, 2018), enhancing social cohesion and facilitating collective action in service to public safety (Pattavina et al., 2006), sometimes forming a virtuous cycle of activity elevating the quality of life in a local neighborhood.

Online neighborhood watch groups can be highly effective, but they too have limitations. First, not all local community members are willing to join these groups. One study reported that residents who are most likely to participate in online crime prevention groups are the ones who have already participated in other community activities and believe that effective prevention approaches can make a neighborhood safer (Schreurs et al., 2020). Although it is quite easy to join and use these groups, community members may still have social and privacy concerns. Some local communities suffer from long-standing enmities between and among community members, making it difficult to gain a genuine cross-section of the community for active involvement. Thus, online neighborhood watch groups may face the same issues as traditional neighborhood watch – namely, how to attract people and then keep them actively engaged. Second, research reveals that residents are more likely to feel safe in the neighborhood if they believe that local online neighborhood prevention groups can be effectively maintained over time. However, one noteworthy finding is that participants in these programs feel less safe if they are active participants as they come to witness suspicious behaviors and learn of lax guardianship norms on the part of some neighbors (Pridmore et al., 2019).

Unfortunately, the fund of evaluation research carried out on online neighborhood watch groups remains scant. There is not yet clear evidence that these groups can prevent crime in a wide array of contextual settings. Some scholars have pointed out that although it appears to be inexpensive to use social media platforms to conduct neighborhood watch, some noteworthy social and moral costs must also be considered along with the potential benefits of crime reduction (van Steden & Mehlbaum, 2022). For example, vigilantism, discrimination, and unwarranted exclusion of strangers may occur once online neighborhood watch programs are established. Moreover, these groups require participants to gather and post information. Most often, a rather small number of program participants contribute most of the information, a fact which may create undesirable biases and even alienate some neighbors (Reynald, 2019). On a related matter, it may be rather difficult to attest to the accuracy of the information collected and posted.

Crime Prevention Apps

With the advancement of digital technology, many individuals – especially young people – tend to deal with most of their business on smartphones. As noted previously, many people prefer to access social media on their phones via phone apps. This section reviews how phone apps can and do contribute materially to crime prevention. Examples of popular IOS apps with high ratings are US Department of Justice NSOPW App (4.6 stars with 1.6k ratings), Citizen: Local Safety Alerts (4.7 stars with 401k ratings), and Offender

Locator Lite (4.5 stars with 21k ratings) (visited in March 2024). To be noted, the crime prevention apps discussed in this section do not include social media apps with an intended primary goal of facilitating social communication (e.g., *Facebook*, *Twitter*, and *WhatsApp*). We focus on those apps that are mainly designed for crime prevention.

In a 2022 study, reviewing over 60 peer-reviewed studies on crime prevention apps, Wood and colleagues (2022) categorize current crime prevention apps into six major types: *self-surveillance*, *decision aid*, *child-tracking*, *education*, *crime-mapping*, and *crime reporting*. Self-surveillance apps allow users to share their locations with friends and family members and send alerts to them (and the police) whenever their users feel unsafe or are under duress. Interestingly, most of these apps target the safety of women (Wood et al., 2022; also see Maxwell et al., 2020). A case study on domestic violence suggests that such an app (TecSOS) reduces the risk of repeat victimization, increases victim protection, helps police apprehend offenders, and strengthens the evidence required for effective prosecution (Natarajan, 2016). Other studies have found that such apps may increase users' feelings of safety and well-being (McCarthy et al., 2016; Potter et al., 2020). However, an evaluation of an app aiming to reduce sexual victimization (Co6) found that the app is not used very frequently when made available, arguing that this app may not meet the needs of college women in the real world interacting with a range of men in school settings and in party situations (Blayney et al., 2018).

Decision aid apps primarily focus on intimate partner violence (IPV) by providing constantly available information on resources, risk assessment questionnaires, and interactive visual aids (Wood et al., 2022). Based on focus group interviews, Tarzia and colleagues (2017) reported that users of this app favor such safety tools because they can always access information on their phones and do not need to worry about being judged when they try to get some help. Unlike decision aid apps, which customize information based on each user's particular safety needs, educational apps provide users with general crime prevention ideas and tips (Wood et al., 2022). A study conducted on primary school children found that a sexual abuse prevention mobile app, which provides general education on sexual abuse, can materially enhance kids' awareness of sexual abuse and increase their skills to avoid being the victims of sexual abuse (Moon et al., 2017).

Crime-mapping apps provide crime-related information based on users' locations (Wood et al., 2022). In combination with crime-reporting apps, these phone apps can show users crimes reported to the police in surrounding areas in *real time*. Wood and colleagues (2022) review several studies on crime-mapping and crime-reporting apps. Overall, these studies suggest that these particular phone apps can make users feel safer when in public places (Weiss, 2016). Users also report that they are prepared to help other users if they receive a call for help (Ceccato, 2019). Sadly, as is the case with decision aid apps and education apps, many studies on crime-mapping and crime-reporting apps focus exclusively on users' feelings and personal experiences. A lack of genuine evaluation of their crime prevention efficacy remains an unfortunate shortcoming of existing research in this area.

Child-tracking apps typically use GPS to geo-track other vulnerable individuals, specifically children and elderly family members (Wood et al., 2022). Logically, parents should feel relieved if they are able to know where their children are at any given time. However, some research suggests that these apps may create "a new anxiety about the need to know exactly where one's family members are at all times" (Hasinoff, 2017). These apps may also lead parents to develop overreliance on technology, which can be both distractive and reduce the amount of face-to-face interaction taking place between parents and their children (Gabriels, 2016). Meanwhile, being monitored 24/7 may raise the issue of the children's privacy, autonomy, and timely acquisition of confidence and self-reliance (Gabriels, 2016; Simpson, 2014). Moreover, as is the case with previous crime prevention apps, evaluation research on child-tracking apps is lacking vis-à-vis the efficacy of the apps in the reduction of child victimization.

Social Media Crime Prevention Efforts Used by the Police

In the previous two sections, social media efforts in crime prevention are primarily initiated by members of the public, with a certain level of police participation. This section discusses how the police proactively use social media to perform crime prevention efforts. As we noted in Chapter 4, police social media pages feature a variety of themes (i.e., crimes and criminals, tips, police-public relations, agency personnel, and links to other social media; see Hu et al., 2018; also see Lieberman et al., 2013). The most common activity for police use of social media to promote crime prevention is to post crime prevention tips.

Hu and Lovrich (2020) analyzed 7,744 police *Facebook* posts collected from 15 U.S. police departments during a one-year period. Among them, 292 posts are related to crime prevention tips. In general, these tips can be categorized into four groups based on different primary purposes. The first such purpose is to educate the public on how to conduct crime prevention activities. For example, the Dallas Police Department (December 17, 2013) posted some shopping safety tips as follows: "Keep your purse close to your body. Avoid talking on cell phones as you walk through malls, parking lots . . . Carry only the credit cards you need and avoid carrying large amount of cash" (Hu & Lovrich, 2020, p. 81). The second such purpose is to teach the public what to do if they are victimized. For example, in the same post, the Dallas Police Department also writes, "Don't resist if someone tries to take any of your belongings. Don't chase someone who robs you . . . Instead, call

911" (Hu & Lovrich, 2020, p. 81). The *Twitter* alerts from the Michigan State University Campus Police during an active shooter event portrayed in the opening story are also an excellent example of how law enforcement can effectively utilize social media to disseminate crime prevention information and timely public safety directives.

The third purpose is to illustrate the consequences of committing a crime, anticipating a possible deterrence effect to occur. For example, the Boston Police Department often labels this type of posting as "Know the Law." Here is an example of stopping for a school bus discharging its students. "Did you know failing to stop for a school bus with flashing red lights can result in a $250 fine?" (Hu & Lovrich, 2020, p. 82). The final such purpose is to openly broadcast police crime prevention activities to the public so that the desired "anticipatory benefit" may occur (Smith et al., 2002, see previous section in this chapter). Hu and Lovrich (2020) report that DWI checkpoints have a very high frequency of police use in crime prevention-related posts on police social media pages. To be noted, these four separate purposes can be intermixed and placed in one social media post, potentially resulting in a mutually reinforcing effect.

The variety of crime types featured on police social media crime prevention tips indicates that, compared to traditional crime prevention initiates which often focus on one or several types of crime (e.g., theft, robbery, and burglary), law enforcement agencies can post crime prevention tips on all kinds of crimes on social media (Surette, 2015a), including largely invisible offenses such as white-collar crime and identity theft (Hu & Lovrich, 2020). Regarding the message delivery format of these crime prevention tips, in addition to narrative scripts, the police can also post pictures and video clips on social media. They can either work in concert with local media outlets and media firms to produce crime prevention videos (see Hu & Lovrich, 2020; Las Vegas Metropolitan Police Department works with FOX-5vegas to produce "Behind the Badge," p. 81) or make videos on their own. In fact, many police agencies across the U.S. have their own YouTube channels and post a variety of video clips (Hu et al., 2020).

In addition to social media websites, the police may participate in citizen-initiated crime prevention groups on phone apps. Pridmore and colleagues (2019) report that while it is not commonplace, many police officers do actively participate in some WhatsApp Neighborhood Crime Prevention groups and act as direct participants, project advisors, or external connections. These officers tend to argue that joining these groups can be considered an aspect of the implementation of community policing (Pridmore et al., 2019), which is an important tool for building and maintaining a healthy police-public relationship in modern policing. Additionally, at least in The Netherlands where Pridmore and his colleagues conducted the research, community policing also focuses on core police goals such as criminal investigation. Community policing-engaged officers typically use the information acquired in WhatsApp Neighborhood Crime Prevention groups to investigate auto theft and other property crimes (van Steden & Mehlbaum, 2022).

Issues and Barriers to Using Social Media in Crime Prevention

Using social media in crime prevention certainly raises some potential issues. The very first issue is *digital vigilantism*, which refers to "a process where citizens are collectively offended by other citizen activity, and respond through coordinated retaliation on digital media, including mobile devices and social media platforms" (Trottier, 2017, p. 56). Dunsby and Howes (2019) argue that *Facebook* has become one of the most common avenues for digital vigilantism by naming and shaming. Social media makes it possible for citizens to be informants and would-be detectives as they are able to spread information online, gather information, and "analyze" the information shared on social media. However, the information shared on social media is often inaccurate, and the analysis of information posted is not always sufficient. The consequence is that innocent people can be unfairly targeted and accused of wrongdoing (Booth, 2013).

Moreover, even if the target of naming and shaming is an actual offender, naming and shaming often make policing more difficult (Trottier, 2017). For instance, Smith (2020) points out that naming and shaming sex offenders may expose them to possible vigilante attacks, may increase their likelihood of reoffending, and make them go underground, making it difficult for the police to conduct post-release surveillance. Sadly, a study on 122 *Facebook* users revealed that more than one-in-four users (27%) of respondents believe the naming and shaming of sex offenders is justified as an appropriate means for fostering community awareness. Additionally, although many of the respondents think that naming and shaming is appropriate after the person is convicted of a prior offense, 15% think naming and shaming is appropriate regardless of conviction status due to the severity of the crime (Dunsby & Howes, 2019).

Naming and shaming phenomenon do not apply to individuals exclusively. Wood and colleagues (2022) point out that crime prevention apps, such as active crime mapping and crime reporting, may profile racial and socioeconomic groups related to locations. They used two apps as examples. On an app called "SketchFacotor," users can report sketchy behavior and sketchy areas to alert other users so that they can avoid harassment. An app named GhettoTracker allows users to rate the safety of a location to help them avoid dangerous areas (Wood et al., 2022). Both apps were quickly taken down by their creators soon after they were labeled as being racist (Wood et al., 2022).

Citizens, who are empowered by information – whether verified or fraudulent – can lead them to cause harmful results if they act irresponsibly

(Pridmore et al., 2019). At a time when modern policing relies heavily on citizens' participation (Hu & Lovrich, 2020), perhaps there should still be a boundary between what the police should do and what citizens should do. Participatory policing refers to the fact that citizens are actively assisting the police by monitoring, reporting, and sharing information (Larsson, 2017). It is a reasonably positive concept until social media gives citizens power to behave like the police (e.g., conducting surveillance and investigation online). Mols and Pridmore (2019) point out that citizen-initiated participatory policing "default to lateral surveillance, ethnic profiling, risky vigilantism, and distrust towards neighbors and strangers" (p. 272). Newspaper reports have documented many incidents wherein citizens attempt to carry out justice as they see it. A 2013 report, for example, describes how vigilante pedophile hunters use social media to lure in suspected pedophiles. It turns out that most people who get baited are innocent, but they may face threats to their lives because their suspect actions are recorded and spread on social media (Booth, 2013).

Legal issues, particularly related to right to privacy, often occur in the activities of social media crime prevention groups. Some research has found that most groups focus more on reporting crimes than preventing crimes (Walby & Joshua, 2021a). When they report, details are provided such as suspect's picture, name, other identifications, and alleged crime. Oftentimes, the information collected is not examined thoroughly. Unwanted consequences may occur if the wrong information is distributed (see the vigilante pedophile hunters' case, Booth, 2013). In contrast, when the police conduct crime prevention, their work is often aimed at crime control on a jurisdiction-wide scale. On social media, this means that the police not only distribute crime prevention tips but also actively search for criminal behavior/evidence which can lead to arrest (Kelly, 2012). Fourth Amendment issues arise as to what information posted on social media the police can use without a judicially ordered search warrant demonstrating sufficient probable cause to investigate. Correll (2022) argues that if the information can be seen on *Facebook* by other users, that information should not enjoy the Fourth Amendment protection. Criminal defense lawyers and public defenders argue, in opposition, that a case-by-case approach should be used to decide admissibility of social media evidence in criminal cases in U.S. trial courts. The National Association of Criminal Defense Lawyers provides *amicus* assistance on the federal and state level in those cases that present issues of importance to criminal defendants, criminal defense lawyers, and the criminal justice system as a whole.

The feature of social media whereby it does not have a physical geographical boundary represents a kind of double-edged sword. On the one hand, users on social media can acquire all kinds of crime prevention techniques and select the ones that meet their needs. On the other hand, users may be overwhelmed by information on crime that does not even happen in their communities, new information which can cause unwarranted fear (Walby & Joshua, 2021a). Moreover, it is difficult to be certain that crime-related information is accurate, particularly on social media crime prevention groups and crime reporting and mapping apps if the police do not run these groups and monitor those apps.

For citizen-initiated social media crime prevention groups, capable and responsible group moderators become the key to successful operation. Some moderators are self-appointed, and some are already leaders in their local communities. A case study on three Chicago communities indicates that participants hold a more positive attitude toward group moderators whom they know personally and who have already been leaders in their communities (Erete et al., 2014). However, it is not easy to be an effective moderator. They spend lots of time and energy on facilitating these groups without compensation. Moderators, for example, must deal with irrelevant content often sent by group members (Pridmore et al., 2019). In addition, participants in app groups (e.g., WhatsApp Neighborhood Crime Prevention) quite frequently discuss nonurgent/non-crime-related issues, greatly annoying other participants (van Steden & Mehlbaum, 2022).

In general, police are in favor of using social media in crime prevention (Peters & Ojedokun, 2019). Some academics have urged the police to be more active on social media (Hu & Lovrich, 2020; Hu et al., 2018; Kelly & Finlayson, 2015). Others have urged the police to routinize their use of social media instead of treating it as a dispensable add-on to their public safety promotion activities (Hu & Lovrich, 2020). However, even if the police try very hard, the results may not be uniformly favorable. For example, a 2017 study on Chicago residents reported that people from high-crime neighborhoods and people with a low level of trust in police are less likely to agree that the police should use social media on crime prevention (Israni et al., 2017). On the positive side, most participants in the 2017 study believed that social media can promote crime prevention by facilitating citizen-citizen communication (Israni et al., 2017). Meanwhile, the police may try to consider using a variety of social media platforms and apps in the hopes that one or more of them fit their circumstance and those of neighborhood residents.

In sum, although we have reviewed a good number of systematic evaluation studies on social media and crime prevention, clearly more studies are sorely needed. Although evaluation program studies need to be carefully planned and implemented, the good news with respect to the evaluation of social media initiatives to conduct crime prevention is that such programs are typically far less expensive than traditional crime prevention programs which place an emphasis on face-to-face interactions between citizens and police personnel. Social media efforts such as online neighborhood watch groups, crime prevention apps, and police use of social media to distribute crime prevention tips represent relatively low cost and low workforce utilization investments. This is because many social media platforms (e.g., *Facebook* and *WhatsApp*) have already built the technical foundation for large-scale application to public safety promotion purposes (Hu & Lovrich, 2020). Additionally, using social media to conduct evaluations, such as citizen surveys, is also effective and efficient for researchers seeking to determine the efficacy of social media-based crime prevention programs.

Conclusion

Many empirical studies have reported that social media platforms can be used effectively to broadcast crime prevention tips to citizens and local businesses. A fair number of pioneering police agencies did this type of activity early on, and many others have been quick to follow their example. To expand our knowledge about such proactive crime prevention actions, in this chapter we reviewed the definition of crime prevention, and we explicated several contemporary crime prevention approaches. We developed a social media crime prevention model to explain why social media may serve to substantially enhance the efficacy of these crime prevention approaches. We also reviewed three specific types of social media efforts made in the arena of crime prevention: (1) online neighborhood watch groups; (2) crime prevention apps; and (3) social media crime prevention efforts employed by law enforcement agencies. We argue that in addition to having police make use of social media in crime prevention, citizens can also use social media to carry out crime prevention activities.

Some noteworthy issues and barriers to using social media in crime prevention are also discussed in considerable detail, including the too-frequent misuses of social media in the crime prevention arena such as the naming and shaming of sex offenders. Also discussed is the question of police use of social media-based evidence in criminal arrests and prosecutions, noting that the right to privacy and Fourth Amendment protections can collide with social media-based crime prevention efforts in such a way that legal scholars characterize the situation as "the brave new world of online social networking," wherein the advancements in digital technology have raised new questions about what aspects of our social networking are open to police surveillance and what aspects are protected by privacy and Fourth Amendment rights established in U.S. law and jurisprudence (Petrashek, 2010).

8

THE FUTURE OF SOCIAL MEDIA, CRIMINOLOGY, AND THE CRIMINAL JUSTICE SYSTEM

Opening Story: It is not a secret that the police have started using social media to monitor and collect social media posts. In a 2021 newspaper report, the Los Angeles Police Department (LAPD) worked with a private company to monitor and collect millions of tweets, thousands of which are related to racial justice protests (Levin & Bhuiyan, 2021). Although there is no official record showing what the LAPD did with the data and derivative analyses, it was reported that the agency might use these data for public safety and strategic communications, such as adroitly addressing any "negative narratives" with counternarratives informed by their analysis (Levin & Bhuiyan, 2021). In another news report, the University of California, Davis (UC Davis) is reported to be monitoring students' social media posts (Gray, 2022). UC Davis Police Department, a campus police agency, claimed that they used social media monitoring software and AI algorithms to detect students who were at risk of harming themselves or others (Gray, 2022). According to the report, some students exhibited concerns as the campus police's action was viewed by them as an invasion of privacy, but the police insisted that they did this monitoring to keep UC Davis students safe (Gray, 2022).

Rethinking Social Media

This book seeks to document the impact of social media on criminology and the criminal justice system up to now and speculate on its likely impact out into the future. While neither we nor other scientists can predict exactly what social media will become in the next decades, we are all certain that social media will continue evolving into an ever more important aspect of daily life. An increasing proportion of the population has incorporated social media

DOI: 10.4324/9781003360049-9

into their daily life, one in which the carrying of a cell phone is essential to one's life. The non-stop, ongoing evolution of social media will doubtless bring new challenges to society and the criminal justice system. Several features of how social media may evolve can be predicted with some confidence.

First, there will be a consistent increase in the number of social media users in the future despite a massive number of users who have already used a variety of social media platforms. For example, *YouTube* has about 2.5 billion monthly users, and *Instagram* has about two billion worldwide (Statista, 2023d). Meanwhile, social media users seem to choose different social media platforms based on their generation, which is closely linked to their exposure to modern information and communication technologies (e.g., Briggs, 2022). For example, nowadays, teenagers are more likely to use *YouTube*, *TikTok*, *Snapchat*, and *Instagram* as their primary social media platforms rather than either *Facebook* or *Twitter* (Vogels et al., 2022). In addition, there will be an increasing number of social media users using social media platforms for more than just virtual communication and recreation. They will use social media to gain social capital and build friendships, acquire public affairs news, gain knowledge and skills shared by others, purchase goods and services, and even conceptualize and then conduct social movements (e.g., Fox & Diehm, 2017).

This trend of broadening uses pushes social media companies to develop and integrate ever more functions and technologies into their original products to attract more new users and retain old users. For example, *Facebook* now has regular videos, Reels (short videos), live streams, and an active marketplace. To keep users active on social media, social media companies will continue to develop powerful new AI algorithms. These algorithms will allow users to view more personalized content in which they are interested. The more time users spend on social media means the more advertisements they will see and the more valuable advertising space will become for social media firms to market (Muha, 2022). These customized advertisements, empowered by AI algorithms, will more likely trigger social media users' decision-making on their online and in-store purchases.

This all seems to be a good business model for social media companies. However, having people spend an increasing amount of time on social media platforms will lead to some major societal consequences in the future. Although large social media platforms will continue to be the first choices for many social media users, an increasing number of users will use social media as a tool for information gathering rather than just sharing thoughts and information with social media friends. The feature of social media that its content is user-generated makes social media platforms a perfect place to acquire knowledge and skills and acquire capital by selling user-generated content. In a 2022 study, over 95% of teens in the survey reported using *YouTube*, and most of them watched *YouTube* videos instead of making them for posting (Vogels et al., 2022). That means an increasing number of social media users may use social media as an alternative to Internet-based television. This trend makes large social media platforms "less social" in some respects (Chen, 2023). Patterns of social interaction on social media may switch to become more about interaction among smaller groups on large social media platforms (e.g., *Facebook Groups*) or greater use of smaller social media platforms designed to meet users' special interests (Bajarin, 2023).

The allure of "easy-to-make-money on social media" has, and will continue to, significantly impact the general population, especially the young generation in the coming decade. In a 2019 news report, a survey of 3,000 kids aged between 8 and 12 in the U.S., the U.K., and China discovered that nearly 33% said that they wanted to become a "YouTuber/Influencer" when they grew up (Taylor, 2019). In this report, *YouTube* was the top career aspiration for kids from the U.S. and the U.K. and the fifth for kids from China (Taylor, 2019). In contrast, the report also showed the results of a 2017 survey on 1,000 U.S. kids under 12. Most of those kids wanted to become doctors when they grew up, followed by a vet and engineer (Taylor, 2019). MrBeast, who is the most-subscribed individual and second most-subscribed channel on *YouTube* (as of 2023), has warned teenagers who want to be an influencer that "for every person like me that makes it, thousands don't" (Pringle, 2024). Some social science researchers have started researching social media influencers in some depth. Despite their lavish lifestyles and noteworthy contributions to commercial marketing, many are suffering from the anxiety of constantly searching for followers and attracting likes, giving up their personal privacy, and being forced to comply with the demands of advertisers and promoters to produce new content (Hudders & Lou, 2023). Meanwhile, some influencers feel guilt knowing that they may "harm followers' physical health and psychological well-being by flaunting idealized images, glamorous lifestyles, and unhealthy food choices" (Hudders & Lou, 2023, p. 151).

While social media influencers can strongly influence innocent young children (De Veirman et al., 2019), adults are not immune to such powerful emotive effects either. The #metoo and #BlackLivesMatter movements have shown that major social movements can start with online communities, then transfer to the physical world in a matter of weeks. There will be likely to be more online social movements spawned on social media. Asking people to go out on the street and participate in social movements is a big task, indeed. However, many individuals do not mind just posting a few terms (e.g., #metoo) on their social media accounts to show their support or opposition to a budding movement (Rhode, 2019). Some policymakers and policy researchers have been aware of the importance of online activism (e.g., online protests) in making policies (e.g., Breindl, 2010; Ceron & Negri, 2016; Hong & Kim, 2021). Interestingly, one study found that whether respondents believe that social media could influence policymaking is not a significant predictor of their participation in social media activism (Hong & Kim, 2021). Rather, their participation is significantly related to a strong motivation for sharing and expressing their opinions (Hong & Kim, 2021).

Additionally, more advanced technologies such as virtual reality (VR) and augmented reality (AR) will allow social media users to interact with both reality and virtual environments simultaneously. The emergence of social media has vastly expanded the geographical boundaries once associated with physical locations (Hu & Lovrich, 2020). The prevalence of VR, AR, and other wearable technologies will break the boundary between virtual environments and the real world. It may be possible, in the near future, for the public to observe police behavior on live streaming when wearing VR glasses to virtually accompany patrol officers, just as they did in ride-along programs in the past. Meanwhile, the development of AI can now produce realistic and imaginative scenes just from text instructions (e.g., *Sora* created by OpenAI). It may be used in a good way, such as creating a hostage situation to train law enforcement officers. Sadly, it may also be used in a malevolent way, such as creating a fake police brutality video and spreading it widely on social media.

Finally, more troublesome issues will likely emerge along with the evolution of social media, especially when other AI technologies are combined with social media. Some issues are related to social media and other information and communication technologies themselves, such as privacy and security, malware sharing, and large-scale hacking. For example, in March 2024, it was reported that data of about 73 million current and former AT&T customers was leaked to the dark web (Diaz & Shields, 2024). The data included customers' names, addresses, email addresses, social security numbers, dates of birth, and phone numbers (Diaz & Shields, 2024).

Some troublesome issues are related to how individuals and organizations use social media, such as for the dissemination of misinformation and false information, cyberharassment and cyberbullying, partisan polarization and promotion of extremism, and social media addiction. DeepFake generation methods, which use machine learning and AI algorithms to replace one person's appearance and likeness, are being developed faster than reliable DeepFake detection methods (Juefei-Xu et al., 2022). One day you will watch a video on *Facebook* about a speech given by President Joe Biden. You may need to consider whether it really comes from President Biden himself or is instead a product of a DeepFake producer being paid by political groups seeking to harm the standing of President Biden. Additionally, some issues are related to how society and governmental agencies respond to the rapid evolution of social media, such as the passage of legislation and development of administrative regulations over live-stream sex chat rooms, to what extent the police can monitor users' social media activities, and how any social media evidence gathered in a civil or criminal case should be properly authenticated. We will discuss these issues in further depth in the next section.

Rethinking Criminology and the Criminal Justice System in a Digital Age

Technology issues will not attract the justice system's attention unless they impact a large population whose patterns of use raise concerns about the work police, courts, and corrections professionals must accomplish. After being developed for almost two decades, social media clearly has attracted the attention of the criminal justice discipline and criminal justice professionals. Social media has made media content creation and distribution more decentralized, leading to powerful social effects (Surette, 2015a). Meanwhile, the non-stop evolution of social media will doubtless bring new challenges to society and the criminal justice system. In the following section, we list a few things that are happening or will likely happen along with the further evolution of social media.

Imitation and Polarization

Traditional mass media may not be completely responsible for producing "copycat" crimes (Surette, 2015a). The main argument is that motivated offenders get criminal instructional models from traditional mass media instead of acquiring "criminal motives." Social media, in contrast, may stimulate criminal motives. For example, individuals are more likely to share extreme opinions and feelings (positive or negative) on social media (Conway, 2020). Social media not only allows them to share such opinions and feelings but also helps connect them with others who share the same opinions and feelings. Although many social media platforms have algorithms for detecting and deleting extreme posts such as racist and hateful posts, most often such public posts do see the light of day. Private messages and groups are often ignored by social media platforms due to a respect for personal privacy. Such postings can generate an "echoing effect," which can polarize a person viewing the post, possibly pushing him or her to become more extremist. It has been reported that both *Facebook* and *Discord* were sued by victims' families involved in the 2022 Buffalo NY shooting because they believed that these social media platforms helped fuel the shooter with fallacious but evocative conspiracy theories (Thompson, 2023).

Perhaps, Payton Gendron, the perpetrator of the 2022 Buffalo shooting, had a propensity toward racism, and social media just pushed him to the extreme of the commission of a hate crime. In his online diary, Gendron wrote, "If I could go back maybe I'd tell myself to get the fuck off 4chan . . . and get an actual life" (Frosch et al., 2022). Based on his diary, social media did not bring him to enjoy more social interaction. Indeed, he spent years being online *alone* (Frosch et al., 2022).

A further related question is raised as to whether social media cultivates/produces criminal behavior. While social influence theory (Kelman, 1958) and social learning theory (Skinner, 1965) may theoretically predict such cultivation, there is no solid evidence at this time. However, some studies may provide some "soft" forms of evidence. For example, a study on young adults and their drinking culture suggests that social media is heavily integrated into drinking culture (Lyons et al., 2014). Uploading and sharing pictures of drinking on *Facebook* is how some young adults create their identities (Lyons et al., 2014). For many young adults, continuing to participate in drinking practices and events and sharing them on social media is important for identity formation (Lyons et al., 2014). Another study on performance crime indicates that social media may make performance crime much more prevalent (Surette, 2015b). We have introduced in a prior chapter the case of an offender having beheaded his father and displaying the head on *YouTube* (Chapter 3) (Goldman, 2024).

We do not, of course, predict with confidence that imitation and polarization caused by social media will bring about more crimes in the coming decade. However, the evidence we have reviewed in this book sets a good foundation for offering such a dire speculation. More and more crimes may shift from the physical world to an online environment (e.g., stalking and cyberstalking, harassment and cyberharassment, and bullying and cyberbullying). Meanwhile, imitation and polarization make it easier to foster hate crimes, which are often performed in a more horrific way such as mass shootings (e.g., the 2022 Buffalo shooting) and public event bombings (e.g., the 2013 Boston Marathon bombing).

Online Surveillance

One or two homogeneous social media posts will not lead to imitation or polarization, but dozens may do the trick. And dozens of postings per day for an extended period certainly increases the likelihood. The repeated appearance of homogeneous posts is mainly due to social media algorithms (Sunstein, 2017). If you are still wondering whether you have been monitored on social media platforms, you are being extremely naïve. Here, we do not mean that the government or law enforcement monitors your social media posts 24/7. Rather, you are being watched by social media companies on an ongoing basis. More precisely, you are being systematically monitored by social media algorithms. Have you ever wondered why the stories and information you see on your *Facebook* differ from what your parents, partners, siblings, or friends may see? Nowadays, when many people use social media primarily to gather information, social media companies ensure that social media algorithms will try their very best to keep you logged on to their platforms (Hu & Lovrich, 2020). Meanwhile, algorithms try to make you see the ads that you may be most interested in seeing (Muha, 2022).

It is almost unavoidable to keep seeing homogeneous posts (or ads) on social media because social media companies' revenue relies on them (Muha,

2022). These social media algorithms are also considered to be responsible for social media addiction (e.g., Cheng et al., 2021; Masoed et al., 2021; Zakon, 2020). Besides algorithms that focus on feeding social media users with homogeneous content, some algorithms are used to control social media content so it does not go against the companies' policies. For example, many social media platforms (e.g., *Facebook* and *Instagram*) do not allow nudity or sexually explicit content (i.e., adult content). Once detected by algorithms, offending posts with adult content will be deleted automatically. However, there are some approaches for tricking the algorithms. For example, according to *Instagram* policy, breastfeeding photos and videos are allowed (*Instagram*, 2024). It is reported that many *OnlyFans* stars make use of baby dolls to pretend to be breastfeeding so they can bypass *Instagram*'s nudity restrictions (Best, 2024). The motive is simple – advertising their *OnlyFans* accounts (Best, 2024). These algorithms also help remove violent social media content. However, they cannot guarantee complete success in their filtering. For example, in the beheading case, the bloody video stayed on *YouTube* for hours before it was removed (Goldman, 2024). Algorithms could not detect it because the type of incident was extremely rare, so the AI had not yet "learned" it (Goldman, 2024).

Besides social media companies, criminal justice agencies, particularly law enforcement agencies, now use software to monitor social media content. Most often, police agencies do not have the technical knowledge to conduct social media surveillance on their own. Typically, they often work with private companies which conduct the monitoring and sell their results (e.g., Levin & Bhuiyan, 2021). The police generally monitor public social media posts of suspected offenders, a type of investigative activity which does not require a search warrant (Murphy & Fontecilla, 2012). Undercover social media surveillance (i.e., creating a fake profile to friend people so the police can gain access to their private content) is currently allowed under some circumstances, but the practice remains debatable due to the danger of entrapment (Murphy & Fontecilla, 2012). It is reasonable to predict that the police will continue to use this practice in the future. They will also work with private companies to develop more effective and efficient algorithms to detect potential threats. However, the police must be very cautious about doing so. One study indicates that some police agencies are interested in social media posts featuring gang signs (Fallik et al., 2020). However, only focusing on gang signs (e.g., graffiti and tattoos) without further examination may lead to the overidentification of gang members (Hu & Dittmann, 2019), which may do harm to police legitimacy.

While the justice system may monitor individuals' behavior on social media, the public can also utilize social media to monitor the justice system. Criminal justice agencies and professionals nowadays have encountered situations where the public discovers the negative side of the criminal justice system and exposes it on social media, such as the *Plain View Project* on racist police officers (Epstein, 2019) and misbehaving judges (e.g., Castaneda, 2016). It is reasonable to believe that justice agencies will encounter similar situations more often in the future as the number of social media users keeps increasing and their channels of dissemination proliferate (Hu & Lovrich, 2020).

Privacy and Other Legal Issues

Both public surveillance of the justice system and the justice system's surveillance of the public will confront the issue of privacy rights. The rapid development of modern technology constantly strikes up against the legal system in this regard. Legislation *always* lags far behind the emergence of modern technology. Sometimes, this is not completely due to the technology itself but the difficulty of balancing individual privacy and the justice system's interests. Take the DNA technology as an example.

For decades, DNA technology has played a significant role in criminal investigation, conviction, and even exoneration (Hu et al., 2017). In the U.S., all 50 states now have post-conviction DNA statutes, laws which allow justice agencies to collect DNA samples from convicted offenders. However, only about 30 states have pre-conviction DNA statutes, which allow the police to collect DNA samples from an arrestee (Hu et al., 2017). The police are also limited to the use of pre-conviction DNA samples. From the justice system's interest, the police can certainly use these samples for matching DNA samples in unsolved cases, just like it has been done with fingerprints for decades. However, from an individual privacy perspective, as Justice Scalia argued in the dissenting opinion in *Maryland v. King* (2013), "identifying an individual that is not the crime for which he or she was originally arrested for is considered a suspicion-less search, which is forbidden by the Fourth Amendment" (Hu et al., 2017, p. 28). Despite the dissenting opinion, in *Maryland v. King* (2013) the U.S. Supreme Court ruled that collecting DNA samples from arrestees is constitutional.

Following this logic, social media has brought novel issues related to privacy and the justice system's interests, and it will bring more such issues as it keeps evolving. In the previous section, we point out that social media can be a powerful surveillance tool for both sides: the justice system (primarily the police) can use social media to conduct online surveillance, and the public can use social media to supervise the justice system (primarily the police). However, many questions remain unanswered as this type of surveillance continues to evolve. For example, in most jurisdictions police activities are allowed to be filmed during traffic stops. Under what circumstances should we allow the videos to be uploaded to social media platforms, such as *YouTube*, for public scrutiny? Is it only when the police officer *actually* misbehaved? Or is it when the driver *felt* that the officer misbehaved? Regarding public safety, how closely should we allow the police to monitor our social media posts?

On August 28, 2023, a professor at the University of North Carolina Chapel Hill was shot and killed by a graduate student. While the student's *Twitter* account is no longer accessible, screenshots published by newspapers indicate that the student might have suffered from bullying for a long time leading up to his crime. On August 18, 2022, the student posted, "Just have a talk with my PI and get his promise. He should have more experience to handle with these girls and tattletales." On October 31, 2022, the student posted,

> Both the group of people to say I am lazy and that to prove me working hard instead of telling me that are trying to consume my privacy. I judge their motivation is only to tell my PI then control me by taletelling.

On June 12, 2023, the student posted, "When this kind of girl shows her 'best' to beg others to 'help' me, all people then look down on me. Kind of angelic bitch" (Aoraha, 2023; Sharp, 2023). After the student was arrested, two separate mental evaluations indicated that the student was likely to suffer from schizophrenia (Schoenbaum, 2023).

When the 2023 UNC-Chapel Hill shooting appeared on social media, the public started discussing whether the police could possibly stop such a tragedy before it happened. Specifically, the student is a Chinese student. In Xiaohongshu (a Chinese version of *Instagram* that has millions of users), after seeing the student's tweets, users commented as to why there was no early detection of the student's victimization by the bullying or mental health issue when his tweets "clearly" indicated that a problem existed. The same type of discussion has occurred frequently in recent years. The gunman who conducted the Uvalde school shooting in 2022, which killed 19 children and two teachers, posted three messages on *Facebook* before the shooting (Fieldstadt & Stelloh, 2022). The first one said he was going to shoot his grandmother. The second one said he had shot his grandmother. And the third one, posted about 15 minutes before the school shooting, said he was going to shoot up an elementary school (Albert, 2022). When *Facebook* argued that these messages were private text messages sent by the shooter to a girl in Germany, the public still questioned if they could be detected by the company (Fieldstadt & Stelloh, 2022). Meanwhile, the German girl in Frankfurt was found guilty of failing to report these planned crimes (Lang, 2022).

The German girl was found guilty mainly due to her reply of "cool" after seeing the shooter's messages of intent to killer (Lang, 2022). However, will the burden of reporting a planned crime be too much to place on the shoulders of an ordinary person who just met the shooter online for less than a month prior? The shooter was also believed to have posted pictures of "my guns" on *Instagram* four days before the massive shooting (*The Guardian*, 2022). Should *Instagram* also be responsible for not detecting the danger of these pictures? In another report, victims' relatives of the 2022 Buffalo shooting, which killed ten African Americans, sued social media companies like *Facebook* and *Discord* for fueling the shooter's ire with the delivery of conspiracy theories online (Thompson, 2023). *Twitch* was also sued because it was the social media platform that the shooter used to livestream his shooting (Thompson, 2023). All these legal issues and challenges will be brought to the criminal justice system in the near future to be adjudicated and ultimately resolved by the courts and to provide legal guidelines for criminal justice system actors.

Dealing With Massive Data

From traditional policymaking to evidence-based policymaking, acquiring and analyzing timely and accurate data has always been at the core of the work of criminologists and criminal justice scholars and practitioners. Data are being gathered and analyzed throughout all steps of conducting evidence-based policymaking, including during program assessments, budget development meetings, implementation oversight hearings, outcome monitoring, and targeted evaluation studies (Fedorowicz & Aron, 2021). Researchers and practitioners often complain about how difficult it is to gather data to support their research and policies. Social media now provides an alternative way to gather valuable data compared to traditional social science methods, such as surveys, field observations, focus group sessions, and personal interviews.

Social media has come to play a significant role in the daily lives of ever more number of people in all walks of life and at all stages of life – in youth, during productive years, and in retirement. Many people are now making use of social media to read the news, receive continuing education, enjoy video and musical entertainment, look for jobs, build social connections, gather timely knowledge, and shop for goods and services in this now very digital world. Meanwhile, many people contribute to the world of social media by posting their daily activities and opinions, sharing their knowledge and skills, and echoing others' emotions and perspectives. These activities produce a tremendous amount of retrievable digital data (Statista, 2023a). Although not all such data are public, at least some of it is publicly accessible. The data available for CJC researchers and criminal justice agencies to use is both of great potential value and of high quality. However, most CJC researchers and practitioners are facing many practical and some legal issues related to the analysis of big data. For instance, (1) How do we gather and store the mountain of social media data in a cost-effective way? (2) How can social media data be analyzed and "mined" for useful information for crime control and crime prevention? In other words, while we may have come to understand that social media can provide much fruitful data of practical value to scholars and practitioners alike, we do not quite yet know how best to utilize it.

A related issue with dealing with massive amounts of data by criminal justice agencies and CJC researchers is that we must understand it is important to be able to adapt to the rapid evolution of social media. Agencies and researchers have started using and analyzing data from social media platforms such as *Facebook*, *Twitter*, and *YouTube* (e.g., Fortin et al., 2023; Hu & Lovrich, 2020; Silva et al., 2016; Williams et al., 2017). A number of law enforcement agencies have started monitoring public posts on *Facebook* and *Twitter* (e.g., Gray, 2022; Levin & Bhuiyan, 2021). However, will *Facebook* and *Twitter* continue to be the major social media platforms in common use in the next decade? For Generation Z, the most popular platforms today are *Snapchat*, *Instagram*, and *TikTok* (Statista, 2023v). Unfortunately, these platforms are not commonly adopted by criminal justice agencies and are seldom studied by criminal justice researchers and criminologists.

Additionally, brainy criminals may not choose to use social media publicly. They often may intentionally use private groups (or similar functions) on large social media platforms. For example, it is reported that criminals frequently make use of *Telegram* channels to recruit "walkers" (who are physically shown in the bank) for committing bank fraud (Javers & Tortorelli, 2023). One report states that the largest such channel has as many as 20,000 members (Javers & Tortorelli, 2023). Here come the questions facing criminal justice researchers and practitioners: How should the police deal with these 20,000 channel members even if they decide to target the channel? Should prosecutors prosecute all these channel members? A more fundamental question is whether these people should be considered criminals just because they are in the channel suspected of organizing criminal activity.

Researching Social Media and Criminal Justice in the Next Decade

In this section, we briefly summarize what we know now in terms of researching social media and criminal justice. All detailed observations can be traced back to the previous seven chapters of this book. Then, we move on to propose the areas where we should move forward, focusing on social media *data collection*, social media *data analysis*, and the emphasis on the *impact* of social media in criminal justice research.

Where Are We Now?

While there is an increasing amount of research on social media and criminal justice, we think that we are still at the initial stage of making a good foundation for showing how social media heavily influences criminology and the criminal justice system. In criminology, researchers have paid attention to how conventional crime is enhanced by social media and how cybercrime is often conducted on social media (e.g., Chan et al., 2019; Maras, 2017; Silva et al., 2016; Yar, 2012; Yardley, 2017). Most studies are more descriptive than analytical and do not use social media as a major independent variable (e.g., Gainsbury et al., 2016; Whittaker & Kowalski, 2015). Meanwhile, the use of social media is often roughly measured instead of going into pertinent details. While there is a good amount of research on social media and human behavior in psychology (e.g., Andrews et al., 2020; Azucar et al., 2018; Seidman, 2013), incorporating social media variables into research on criminological theories is seldom seen, despite some variables used in criminological theories are likely mightily influenced by the use of social media, such as self-control (e.g., Du et al., 2018), strains (e.g., Wolfers & Utz, 2022), and delinquent online peers (e.g., Miller & Morris, 2016).

In policing research, current research heavily focuses on two aspects. The first is how the police can use social media to fight crime (e.g., Fallik et al., 2020; Fortin et al., 2023; Schneider & Trottier, 2012). The second aspect is how the police can use social media to communicate with the public (e.g., Dai et al., 2017; Hu & Lovrich, 2020; Lieberman et al., 2013). These studies are, once again, primarily descriptive rather than analytical. However, because the police use of social media research is the most frequently investigated in social media and the criminal justice system, the existing research findings can give us a good idea of how the police can improve their use of social media for both crime-fighting and police-public communication purposes. Meanwhile, a few studies have explored how the public reacts to police use of social media (e.g., Cartwright & Shaw, 2020; Hu et al., 2020; Jeanis et al., 2021). The findings of these studies, in general, can support suggestions given to improve police use of social media.

In court research, most studies are conducted by legal researchers on the topics of social media use in the courtrooms and the effective use of social media evidence in criminal trials (e.g., Hoffmeister, 2014; Jackson & Shelly, 2015; McPeak, 2019). Among them, significant attention is given to the use of social media among jury members (e.g., Hoffmeister, 2014; Marder, 2014; Murphy & Fontecilla, 2012; Pollack, 2022). A few studies have explored what courts post on social media (e.g., Banks, 2022; Mattan et al., 2020; Ure, 2019). As the judicial branch of the criminal justice system, social media is primarily concerned with its impact on judicial independence and impartiality in trials.

In corrections research, social media has not been adequately studied. A limited number of studies have been conducted on how correctional agencies use social media and how correctional officers make use of social media (e.g., Adorjan & Ricciardelli, 2023; Erickson, 2013; Zielinski et al., 2022).

Some studies have discussed the prisoner's legal rights to social media (e.g., Celeste, 2021; Jewkes & Reisdorf, 2016) and analyzed social media content posted by jail and prison inmates (e.g., Schlosser & Feldman, 2022; Reid & Niebuhr, 2023). Currently (as of 2023), the general research topic is still whether inmates should have the right to social media in prison and the consequences of its presence on rehabilitation and facility safety and security issues.

In victimization and crime prevention research, a few studies have explored how social media can be used to conduct crime prevention efforts by both individuals and law enforcement agencies (e.g., Kelly & Finlayson, 2015; Reynald, 2019; Wood & Thompson, 2021; Wood et al., 2022). For example, social media platforms can be used as online neighborhood watch groups. The police can broadcast crime prevention tips on social media (e.g., Hu et al., 2018). However, the current studies on these topics are primarily descriptive. Unlike traditional crime prevention strategies that have received much evaluation, few studies have examined the effectiveness and efficiency of social media crime prevention efforts (e.g., Blayney et al., 2018; Pridmore et al., 2019).

The brief review of research on social media and criminal justice in this section and the detailed review by previous chapters indicate that at this moment (as of 2023) the overwhelming majority of research on social media and criminal justice is more descriptive than analytical. While it is important and necessary to start researching a new topic with descriptive methods, we think it is time to start more in-depth research on how social media impacts criminology and the criminal justice system.

Where Should We Move Forward?

Research on social media and criminal justice has used traditional social science research methods related to data collection (e.g., observations, surveys, focus groups, and experiments) and data analysis (e.g., qualitative analysis, quantitative analysis, and mixed-method analysis) (e.g., Hu & Lovrich, 2020). Since social media is one of the modern information and communication technologies, it is important to include methods enhanced with recent developments in computer science. In data collection, for example, data available on social media is literally countless. Most of the time, when social media data are available to the public, the process of getting approval from the institutional review board (IRB) is simplified and quick. Meanwhile, there are plenty of approaches to collecting social media data available to social scientists.

For example, *web crawling* is often used to download web pages. A web crawler is "a system for the bulk downloading of web pages" (Olston & Najork, 2010, p. 1). Imagine you go to a website and save all the content on the website to your personal computer. Then you click a link on the website, and it takes you to another web page. You also save all the content on the second web page to your computer. By repeatedly doing so, you will gain an extensive database. Web crawlers will automatically perform this "search and download" work for you, so you will not need to do this tedious work (Hu & Lovrich, 2020). In fact, the most popular search engine, *Google*, mainly uses web crawling as its first step to show you the search results you are looking for when making a request. In this step, crawlers will download texts, images, and videos from the web pages they locate. Then *Google* analyzes these texts, images, and videos, and stores the information in an extensive database called "*Google* Index." When a user types in keywords in a *Google* search, *Google* uses the keywords to match whatever it has in the "*Google* Index" and returns the results to the requester (*Google*, 2024). Of course, this is an oversimplified interpretation of how a *Google* search works.

Web crawling can help researchers gather great volumes of data regarding research on topics related to social media and criminal justice. For example, Hu and Lovrich (2020) pointed out that they were able to use web crawlers to download all the comments on a police agency's *Facebook* posts and analyze what public attitudes toward the police agency look like in those posts. In fact, there are many tools available for CJC researchers to use in terms of collecting and downloading massive social media data without knowing specific computer science techniques.

For example, *Facepager* (https://github.com/strohne/Facepager) is a tool for fetching public data from *Facebook*, *Twitter*, and *YouTube* based on APIs (i.e., application programming interfaces) (Jünger & Keyling, 2019). Social media APIs allow social media platforms to integrate with third-party apps and tools. They help share the data on social media platforms with third-party developers without going to the actual social media accounts. For example, with *Facebook* APIs, *Facepager* can download posts and images, comments and reactions to these posts and images, and the number of "likes" from many *Facebook* accounts (Jünger & Keyling, 2019). APIs are controlled by social media companies. Sometimes, companies close some APIs due to security and privacy issues (Fung, 2019; Willingham, 2023). *Facepager* has been used a number of times in social science research. For example, Henisa and Wilantika (2021) used *Facepager* to collect data and analyze citizen engagements on government agencies' social media accounts. Steiner (2020) used *Facepager* to collect data and conduct a content analysis of political *Facebook* posts.

Facepager is just one of the user-friendly software packages that can help CJC researchers conduct research on social media and criminal justice. Perhaps, it is better for CJC researchers to work with professionals and researchers in Computer Science in terms of large data collection and analysis. In their book on researching social media and the police in the future, Hu and Lovrich (2020) emphasize the importance of machine learning and AI approaches in terms of analyzing large social media data. In recent years, traditional social science data analysis approaches such as regressions and p-values have been questioned by statisticians and mathematicians, particularly on their capability of *making predictions* (e.g., Amrhein et al., 2019; Berk, 2012; Shmueli, 2010). Recently (as of 2023), there has been an increasing number of CJC researchers using machine learning and AI approaches to make predictions in CJC topics, such as recidivism (e.g., Berk, 2017; Kovalchuk et al., 2023; Neuilly et al., 2011; Travaini et al., 2022; Wang et al., 2023), court decisions (e.g., Berk et al., 2016), justice policy interventions (e.g., Manning et al., 2018), forensic science (e.g., Carriquiry et al., 2019), public attitudes toward the police (e.g., Hu et al., 2021b), identity theft victimization (e.g., Hu et al., 2022), and legal studies (e.g., Bell et al., 2021).

It should be noted, however, that machine learning and AI approaches are not perfect. For example, when these approaches are good at making predictions, it is often difficult to interpret a single independent variable (also called a feature in computer science) and its directional impact on a dependent variable (i.e., positive or negative) (e.g., Hu et al., 2021a, 2022). Therefore, we think that CJC researchers should work with Computer Science researchers and professionals to research topics related to social media and criminal justice via both conventional social statistical techniques and modern computer science techniques for better *interpretation* and more accurate *prediction.*

Besides methodological approaches to researching social media and criminal justice, research topics and themes are also important. A literature review on research papers about social media published between 1997 and 2017 may shed some light on what we should research in the next decade. The review notes that there are a variety of research themes related to social media, including but not limited to user behavior on social media, organizational purposes of using social media, social media as a marketing medium, risks associated with social media, benefits of using social media, the use of social media during crisis events, and using social media in political campaigns and public administration practice (Kapoor et al., 2018). Borrowing these themes, as well as the content we reviewed in the previous chapters, we summarize a few promising future research topics as follows.

In criminology, future research should primarily focus on how social media impacts an individual's behavior and mindset, leading to either criminal or law-abiding behavior. The young generation is growing up with social media, and the youth are deeply embedded within social media. The impact of social media on the contemporary youth will be more significant than that of traditional mass media, such as movies and TV shows. Moreover, many traditional mass media companies have started to transition to incorporating social media into their strategic plan of providing content and marketing.

For example, you can read news on your phone using the *Facebook* app and make comments directly related to the news reported on *Facebook*. Others can also make comments, and they can reply to your comments. On a related matter, the instant social interaction provided by social media changes how individuals view friendship. We all agree that delinquent peers are one of the most significant predictors of an individual's delinquency (e.g., Wu et al., 2023). It is about time to consider online delinquent peers. Additionally, in Chapter 1, we introduced individual and organizational theories used to interpret individual and organizational social media behavior. In Chapter 3, we introduced contemporary criminological theories and how social media might be incorporated into them. Future studies may find a way to merge these two types of theories together to understand more fully how social media impacts criminal or law-abiding behavior performed by individuals and organizations.

In the police area, which has been the most frequently researched topic in social media and criminal justice, we should continue researching how police agencies can use social media to establish and maintain a good relationship with the public. Advanced technology in social media may need to be included in this line of research. For example, many police agencies now have ride-along and citizen-police academy programs. Ride-along programs allow citizens to accompany patrol officers to gain insights into the police's daily activities. Historically, ride-alongs have been considered to entail a level of danger because citizens must sit in patrol cars when officers are engaged in enforcement work. With virtual reality (VR) technology, citizens can just wear a headset or goggles, stay at home, and virtually accompany patrol officers as they carry out their duties. The same applies to citizen-police academy sessions. Additionally, researchers should explore how the police can use a mass of social media data to conduct some law enforcement duties. Social media monitoring is what the police are doing now, and they will continue doing it. However, the scope and depth of social media monitoring remain lacking. Moreover, the legitimacy of doing so is often related to court decisions in the area of reasonable expectation to privacy. The Fourth Amendment to the U.S. Constitution tells us that we have the right to be free from warrantless police searches in areas in which we have a "reasonable expectation of privacy." This refers to certain areas, or aspects of one's personal life, in which a reasonable person would expect privacy. Specifically, the Fourth Amendment refers to our "persons, houses, papers and effects" as areas that should not be searched without a warrant. How precisely this constitutional right is to apply to social media will be a matter of repeated litigation as new forms of social media and new methods of digital information recovery become available.

In the courts area, VR can also be used in the courtrooms to make public trials "more public." Most importantly, courts must continue exploring several critical issues caused by social media, such as how to criminalize improper behavior on social media, balancing privacy and publicity in trials, balancing the First Amendment and social media monitoring, balancing the Fourth Amendment and social media searches, and balancing open justice and judicial independence. For example, judges and legislatures will continue facing issues on how social media evidence is legally collected and then authenticated. They will continue facing issues when their administrative rules and existing legislation contradict public opinions on social media. With the development of AI technology, courts will soon find that it will be more difficult to authenticate pictures and videos on social media because algorithms (e.g., *Sora*) can generate entirely fictional but "very real" pictures and videos. Moreover, the jury's use of social media is going to be a critical issue for the right to trial by an impartial jury of one's peers. Unfortunately, these knotty issues will not be easy to solve, and repeated adjudications are likely as new developments in digital storage, retrieval, and analysis come into being.

In the corrections area, researchers should continue researching social media and corrections because, as we mentioned, this is the most under-investigated component of the criminal justice system. Two particular areas are well worth exploring. The first area is how we can allow inmates to keep their *digital social identity* when they are incarcerated. Finding an approach to allowing (and teaching) inmates to use social media for good purposes (with strict restrictions) may be essential for successful reentry. The second area is how to use social media for achieving better community corrections outcomes. We know we can use social media to disseminate helpful, timely information to offender on probation or on parole. We also know we can make use of social media (especially the GPS tracking feature of cell phones) to detect their probation or parole violations. However, the research on these topics is woefully insufficient at this time.

In the victimization and crime prevention area, there is no doubt that social media produces more ways of committing traditional street crimes and cybercrimes. Crime control and prevention researchers and policymakers may need to test and adjust current theories and policies with the adroit inclusion of a social media component. For example, from a gang prevention perspective, physically removing gang appearance near schools may not be too difficult (e.g., Wu et al., 2022). However, how can we prevent teenagers from accessing gang-related information on social media? Of course, social media companies may take down social media accounts owned by gangs. However, they may be unable to detect or remove gang-related information communicated in private messages. While social media may create more issues of concern in victimization and crime prevention, social media may also provide additional solutions to conduct crime prevention, such as sharing crime prevention tips on social media and providing crime victims with targeted timely information.

In conclusion, CJC researchers, policymakers, legal professionals, and justice system administrators can continue doing what they are doing now but with an understanding that social media is significantly different from traditional mass media. Social media must be considered whenever it is possible to be included in CJC research, in public safety policies, and in federal and state legislation. When enhanced with modern AI technology, social media will continue to have profound impacts on most subjects involved with Criminal Justice and Criminology.

Conclusion

In this final chapter we have addressed three major questions: (1) how social media will evolve in the near future; (2) how the evolution of social media may continue to impact criminology and the criminal justice system; and (3) how we should continue researching topics related to social media and criminal justice in the future. We argue that studying social media effects on criminal justice will be an important – perhaps critical – component of research in criminology and in the criminal justice discipline.

Researchers in colleges and universities and research centers and contemplative practitioners in our major law enforcement agencies around the country will need to learn how to analyze "big data" (e.g., the massive digital archives of social media content, video footage, and audio records from evermore ubiquitous cameras) in our criminal justice research. The ongoing systematic study of social media in criminal justice will become an absolutely indispensable core element of criminological and criminal justice system research in the coming decade and beyond. Maximizing the benefits of social media and minimizing the societal costs coming along with benefits will be a task that the criminal justice global community of scholars cannot ignore. The practitioner community will need to be informed by this scholarship as its carries out its duty in an increasingly digital modern society.

BIBLIOGRAPHY

Aaronson, D. E., & Patterson, S. M. (2013). Modernizing jury instructions in the age of social media. *Criminal Justice, 27*(4), 26–35.

Abbass, Z., Ali, Z., Ali, M., Akbar, B., & Saleem, A. (2020). A framework to predict social crime through Twitter tweets by using machine learning. In *2020 IEEE 14th international conference on semantic computing (ICSC)*, San Diego, CA (pp. 363–368).

ABC News. (2015). "Cybervandalism": ISIS supporters hijack US military social media accounts. *ABC News*. Retrieved March 9, 2024, from https://abcnews.go.com/International/us-military-twitter-account-apparently-hijacked-isis-supporters/story?id=28170963

ABC News. (2016). Video shows Maryland judge ordering deputy to stun defendant. *ABC News*. Retrieved November 2, 2023, from https://abcnews.go.com/US/video-shows-maryland-judge-ordering-deputy-stun-defendant/story?id=38129308

Abeling-Judge, D. (2021). Social bonding experiences facilitating desistance in adolescence. *Crime & Delinquency, 67*(2), 287–315.

Abrah, P. B. (2019). Labeling theory and life stories of juvenile delinquents transitioning into adulthood. *International Journal of Offender Therapy and Comparative Criminology, 63*(2), 179–197.

Adachi, P. J., & Willoughby, T. (2011). The effect of violent video games on aggression: Is it more than just the violence? *Aggression and Violent Behavior, 16*(1), 55–62.

Adler, P. S., & Kwon, S. W. (2002). Social capital: Prospects for a new concept. *Academy of Management Review, 27*(1), 17–40.

Adorjan, M., & Ricciardelli, R. (2021). Smartphone and social media addiction: Exploring the perceptions and experiences of Canadian teenagers. *Canadian Review of Sociology, 58*(1), 45–64.

Adorjan, M., & Ricciardelli, R. (2023). Correctional officers and social media: Policies, challenges, and vulnerabilities. *Social Media + Society, 9*(3), 20563051231193739.

Agnew, R. (1992). Foundation for a general strain theory of crime and delinquency. *Criminology, 30*(1), 47–88.

Agnew, R. (2005). *Why do criminals offend? A general theory of crime and delinquency*. Roxbury Publishing Co.

Agnew, R. (2013). When criminal coping is likely: An extension of general strain theory. *Deviant Behavior, 34*(8), 653–670.

Agnew, R. (2017). Building on the foundation of general strain theory: Specifying the types of strain most likely to lead to crime and delinquency. In S. Henry (Ed.), *Recent developments in criminological theory* (pp. 311–354). Routledge.

Agnew, R., & White, H. R. (1992). An empirical test of general strain theory. *Criminology, 30*(4), 475–500.

Aichner, T., Grünfelder, M., Maurer, O., & Jegeni, D. (2021). Twenty-five years of social media: A review of social media applications and definitions from 1994 to 2019. *Cyberpsychology, Behavior, and Social Networking, 24*(4), 215–222.

Aizenkot, D., & Kashy-Rosenbaum, G. (2021). Cyberbullying victimization in WhatsApp classmate groups among Israeli elementary, middle, and high school students. *Journal of Interpersonal Violence, 36*(15–16), NP8498–NP8519.

Ajzen, I., & Fishbein, M. (1980). *Understanding attitudes and predicting social behavior*. Prentice-Hall.

Akbari, A., & Gabdulhakov, R. (2019). Platform surveillance and resistance in Iran and Russia: The case of Telegram. *Surveillance & Society, 17*(1–2), 223–231.

Akers, R. L., & Jennings, W. G. (2016). Social learning theory. In A. R. Piquero (Ed.), *The handbook of criminological theory* (pp. 230–240). John Wiley & Sons, Inc.

Akers, R. L., & Jensen, G. F. (2017). The empirical status of social learning theory of crime and deviance: The past, present, and future. In F. Cullen, J. Wright, & K. Blevins (Eds.), *Taking stock: The status of criminological theory* (pp. 37–76). Routledge.

Akers, R. L., & Silverman, A. L. (2014). Toward a social learning model of violence and terrorism. In M. Zahn, H. Brownstein, & S. Jackson (Eds.), *Violence: From theory to research* (pp. 27–44). Routledge.

Akhtar, Z. (2020). Social media access, jury restraint, and the right to a fair trial. *Journal of Media Law & Ethics, 8*(2), 4–20.

Al Boni, M., & Gerber, M. S. (2016). Predicting crime with routine activity patterns inferred from social media. In *2016 IEEE international conference on systems, man, and cybernetics* (SMC) (pp. 001233–001238). Institute of Electrical and Electronic Engineers.

Albert, V. (2022). Texas elementary school gunman posted messages about attack right before shooting, governor said. *CBS News*. Retrieved April 2, 2024, from https://www.cbsnews.com/live-updates/texas-school-shooting-uvalde-facebook-messages/

Aleroud, A., & Zhou, L. (2017). Phishing environments, techniques, and countermeasures: A survey. *Computers & Security, 68*, 160–196.

Allahverdi, F. Z. (2022). The relationship between the items of the social media disorder scale and perceived social media addiction. *Current Psychology, 41*(10), 7200–7207.

Almasy, S. (2019). Houston burglary gang used social media to find houses with high-end art to steal, police say. *CNN*. Retrieved January 16, 2024, from https://www.cnn.com/2019/07/24/us/houston-burglary-gang-social-media-stakeouts/index.html

Almeida, C., & Almeida, P. (2017). Preferences of teenagers about online video: How to incorporate educational informal videos in their daily consumption routines. In *INTED2017 proceedings* (pp. 1526–1532). IATED.

American Psychological Association (APA). (2018). *APA dictionary of psychology*. Retrieved January 5, 2024, from https://dictionary.apa.org/personality

Amoruso, M., Anello, D., Auletta, V., Cerulli, R., Ferraioli, D., & Raiconi, A. (2020). Contrasting the spread of misinformation in online social networks. *Journal of Artificial Intelligence Research, 69*, 847–879.

Amrhein, V., Greenland, S., & McShane, B. (2019). Retire statistical significance. *Nature, 567*, 305–307.

Anderez, D. O., Kanjo, E., Amnwar, A., Johnson, S., & Lucy, D. (2021). The rise of technology in crime prevention: Opportunities, challenges, and practitioners' perspectives. arXiv preprint arXiv:2102.04204. https://doi.org/10.48550/arXiv.2102.04204

Anderson, C. A., Sakamoto, A., Gentile, D. A., Ihori, N., Shibuya, A., Yukawa, S., Naito, M., & Kobayashi, K. (2008). Longitudinal effects of violent video games on aggression in Japan and the United States. *Pediatrics, 122*(5), e1067–e1072.

Anderson, J., & Duerr, B. (2022). In a storm of lies and half-truths: The role of media professionals in spreading and combatting misinformation about the International Criminal Court. *Journal of International Criminal Justice, 20*(1), 191–201.

Anderson, M., & Toor, S. (2018). How social media users have discussed sexual harassment since #MeToo went viral. *Pew Research Center*. Retrieved October 1, 2023, from https://www.pewresearch.org/short-reads/2018/10/11/how-social-media-users-have-discussed-sexual-harassment-since-metoo-went-viral/

Anderson, P. R., & Newman, D. J. (1998). *Introduction to criminal justice* (6th ed.). McGraw-Hill.

Andrews, N. P., Yogeeswaran, K., Wang, M. J., Nash, K., Hawi, D. R., & Sibley, C. G. (2020). Is social media use changing who we are? Examining the bidirectional relationship between personality and social media use. *Cyberpsychology, Behavior, and Social Networking, 23*(11), 752–760.

Antonaccio, O., & Tittle, C. R. (2008). Morality, self-control, and crime. *Criminology, 46*(2), 479–510.

Antony, M. G., & Thomas, R. J. (2010). 'This is citizen journalism at its finest': YouTube and the public sphere in the Oscar Grant shooting incident. *New Media & Society, 12*(8), 1280–1296.

Anwar, N. (2019). Forensic authentication of WhatsApp messenger using the information retrieval approach. *International Journal of Cyber-Security and Digital Forensics, 8*(3), 206–213.

Aoraha, C. (2023). Tailei Qi's rambling social media posts calling out bullies and 'tattle tale' girls as he's arrested over University of North Carolina shooting that left a faculty member dead. *Dailymail*. Retrieved April 2, 2024, from https://www.dailymail.co.uk/news/article-12455587/Wuhan-student-UNC-shooting-arrested.html

Armstrong, T. A., Boisvert, D. L., Wells, J., Lewis, R. H., Cooke, E. M., Woeckener, M., & Harper, J. M. (2022). Testosterone, cortisol, and criminal behavior in men and women. *Hormones and Behavior, 146*, 105260.

Arntfield, M. (2015). Toward a cybervictimology: Cyberbullying, routine activities theory, and the anti-sociality of social media. *Canadian Journal of Communication, 40*(3), 371–388.

Aurrekoetxea-Casaus, M. (2020). San fermines# la manada case: An exploratory analysis of social support for victims of sexual violence on Twitter. *Computers in Human Behavior, 108*, 106299.

Azucar, D., Marengo, D., & Settanni, M. (2018). Predicting the big 5 personality traits from digital footprints on social media: A meta-analysis. *Personality and Individual Differences, 124*, 150–159.

Babko-Malaya, O., Cathey, R., Hinton, S., Maimon, D., & Gladkova, T. (2017). Detection of hacking behaviors and communication patterns on social media. In *2017 IEEE international conference on big data (big data)* (pp. 4636–4641). Institute of Electrical and Electronic Engineers.

Bachman, R., & Schutt, R. K. (2013). *The practice of research in criminology and criminal justice* (5th ed.). SAGE Publications, Inc.

Back, S., Soor, S., & LaPrade, J. (2018). Juvenile hackers: An empirical test of self-control theory and social bonding theory. *International Journal of Cybersecurity Intelligence & Cybercrime, 1*(1), 40–55.

Bain, A., Robinson, B. K., & Conser, J. (2014). Perceptions of policing: Improving communication in local communities. *International Journal of Police Science & Management, 16*(4), 267–276.

Bajarin, T. (2023). The future of social media will be special interest focused. *Forbes*. Retrieved October 2, 2023, from https://www.forbes.com/sites/timbajarin/2023/04/27/the-future-of-social-media-will-be-special-interest-focused/?sh=43d5ddff595b

Bakken, S. A., & Harder, S. K. (2023). From dealing to influencing: Online marketing of cannabis on Instagram. *Crime, Media, Culture, 19*(1), 135–157.

Ballard, M. M., & Rodriguez, N. (2023). Police department websites and digital language accessibility: A platform for achieving effective communication between limited English proficient communities and the police. *Policing and Society, 33*(2), 129–149.

Banks, I. (2022). Facilitating# dialogue or# buildingsupport? An exploration of the International Criminal Court's use of 280 characters. *Journal of International Criminal Justice, 20*(1), 55–80.

Baran, S. J., & Davis, D. K. (2015). *Mass communication theory: Foundations, ferment, and future* (7th ed.). Cengage Learning.

Barcelos, R. H., Dantas, D. C., & Sénécal, S. (2018). Watch your tone: How a brand's tone of voice on social media influences consumer responses. *Journal of Interactive Marketing, 41*(1), 60–80.

Barkan, S. E., & Rocque, M. (2021). *Crime prevention: Programs, policies, and practices*. SAGE Publications, Inc.

Barnes, J. C., Boutwell, B. B., & Beaver, K. M. (2016). Contemporary biosocial criminology: A systematic review of the literature, 2000–2012. In A. R. Piquero (Ed.), *The handbook of criminological theory* (pp. 75–99). John Wiley & Sons, Inc.

Baron, S. W. (2003). Self-control, social consequences, and criminal behavior: Street youth and the general theory of crime. *Journal of Research in Crime and Delinquency, 40*(4), 403–425.

Barr, R., & Pease, K. (1990). Crime placement, displacement, and deflection. *Crime and Justice, 12*, 277–318.

Barrett, J. (2011). Open justice or open season: Developments in judicial engagement with new media. *Queensland University of Technology Law & Justice Journal, 11*, 1–30.

Bartels, L., & Lee, J. (2013). Jurors using social media in our courts: Challenges and responses. *Journal of Judicial Administration, 23*, 35–57.

Basto-Pereira, M., & Farrington, D. P. (2022). Developmental predictors of offending and persistence in crime: A systematic review of meta-analyses. *Aggression and Violent Behavior, 65*, 101761.

Bekkers, L. M., Moneva, A., & Leukfeldt, E. R. (2022). Understanding cybercrime involvement: A quasi-experiment on engagement with money mule recruitment ads on Instagram. *Journal of Experimental Criminology, 18*(2), 1–20.

Bell, K., Hong, J., McKeown, N., & Voss, C. (2021). The recon approach: A new direction for machine learning in criminal law. *Berkeley Technology Law Journal, 36*, 821–860.

Bellair, P. (2017). Social disorganization theory. In *Oxford research encyclopedia of criminology and criminal justice*. https://doi.org/10.1093/acrefore/9780190264079.013.253

Bendler, J., Brandt, T., Wagner, S., & Neumann, D. (2014). *Investigating crime-to-twitter relationships in urban environments-facilitating a virtual neighborhood watch*. Proceedings of the European Conference on Information Systems (ECIS) 2014, Tel Aviv. https://aisel.aisnet.org/ecis2014/proceedings/track11/10/

Bennett, T., Holloway, K., & Farrington, D. P. (2006). Does neighborhood watch reduce crime? A systematic review and meta-analysis. *Journal of Experimental Criminology, 2*, 437–458.

Bennett, T., Holloway, K., & Farrington, D. P. (2008). The effectiveness of neighborhood watch. *Campbell Systematic Reviews, 4*(1), 1–46.

Berk, R. (2012). *Criminal justice forecasts of risk: A machine learning approach*. Springer Science & Business Media.

Berk, R. (2017). An impact assessment of machine learning risk forecasts on parole board decisions and recidivism. *Journal of Experimental Criminology, 13*(2), 193–216.

Berk, R., & MacDonald, J. (2010). Policing the homeless: An evaluation of efforts to reduce homeless-related crime. *Criminology & Public Policy, 9*(4), 813–840.

Berk, R. A., Sorenson, S. B., & Barnes, G. (2016). Forecasting domestic violence: A machine learning approach to help inform arraignment decisions. *Journal of Empirical Legal Studies, 13*(1), 94–115.

Bernburg, J. G. (2019). Labeling theory. In M. Krohn, N. Hendrix, G. Hall, & A. Lizotte (Eds.), *Handbook of crime and deviance* (2nd ed., pp. 179–196). Springer Nature.

Bernburg, J. G., & Krohn, M. D. (2003). Labeling, life chances, and adult crime: The direct and indirect effects of official intervention in adolescence on crime in early adulthood. *Criminology, 41*(4), 1287–1318.

Bernburg, J. G., Krohn, M. D., & Rivera, C. J. (2006). Official labeling, criminal embeddedness, and subsequent delinquency: A longitudinal test of labeling theory. *Journal of Research in Crime and Delinquency, 43*(1), 67–88.

Bertot, J. C., Jaeger, P. T., & Hansen, D. (2012). The impact of polices on government social media usage: Issues, challenges, and recommendations. *Government Information Quarterly, 29*(1), 30–40.

Besemer, S., Farrington, D. P., & Bijleveld, C. C. (2017). Labeling and intergenerational transmission of crime: The interaction between criminal justice intervention and a convicted parent. *PLoS One, 12*(3), e0172419.

Beshears, M. L. (2017). Effectiveness of police social media use. *American Journal of Criminal Justice, 42*, 489–501.

Best, S. (2024). OnlyFans stars are shamelessly bypassing Instagram's nudity restrictions by pretending to breastfeed baby dolls. *Daily Mail*. Retrieved April 9, 2024, from https://www.dailymail.co.uk/sciencetech/article-13145103/OnlyFans-stars-shamelessly-bypassing-Instagrams-nudity-restrictions-pretending-breastfeed-baby-dolls-furious-viewers-claim-making-complete-mockery-mothers.html

Blackham, A., & Williams, G. (2013). Australian courts and social media. *Alternative Law Journal, 38*(3), 170–175.

Blankers, M., Van der Gouwe, D., Stegemann, L., & Smit-Rigter, L. (2021). Changes in online psychoactive substance trade via Telegram during the COVID-19 pandemic. *European Addiction Research, 27*(6), 469–474.

Blayney, J. A., Jenzer, T., Read, J. P., Livingston, J. A., & Testa, M. (2018). Enlisting friends to reduce sexual victimization risk: There's an app for that . . . but nobody uses it. *Journal of American College Health, 66*(8), 767–773.

Boateng, F. D. (2018). Crime reporting behavior: Do attitudes toward the police matter? *Journal of Interpersonal Violence, 33*(18), 2891–2916.

Boda, Z., & Szabo, G. (2011). The media and attitudes towards crime and the justice system: A qualitative approach. *European Journal of Criminology, 8*(4), 329–342.

Bode, L., Vraga, E. K., & Tully, M. (2020). Do the right thing: Tone may not affect correction of misinformation on social media. *Harvard Kennedy School Misinformation Review, 1*(4), 1–12.

Boisvert, D., Wells, J., Armstrong, T., Lewis, R. H., Woeckener, M., & Nobles, M. R. (2020). Low resting heart rate and stalking perpetration. *Journal of Interpersonal Violence, 35*(11–12), 2271–2296.

Booth, R. (2013). Vigilante pedophile hunters ruining lives with internet stings. *The Guardian*. Retrieved March 2, 2023, from https://www.theguardian.com/uk-news/2013/oct/25/vigilante-paedophile-hunters-online-police

Bosland, J. J., & Townend, J. (2018). Open justice, transparency, and the media: Representing the public interest in the physical and virtual courtroom. *Communications Law, 23*(4), 183–202.

Bossler, A. M., & Holt, T. J. (2009). On-line activities, guardianship, and malware infection: An examination of routine activities theory. *International Journal of Cyber Criminology, 3*(1), 400–420.

Bowers, K. J., & Guerette, R. T. (2014). Effectiveness of situational crime prevention. In A. A. Braga & D. L. Weisburd (Eds.), *Encyclopedia of criminology and criminal justice* (pp. 1318–1329). Springer.

Bowers, K. J., & Johnson, S. (2013). Using publicity for preventive purposes. In N. Tilley (Ed.), *Handbook of crime prevention and community safety* (pp. 355–380). Willan.

Braga, A. A., Papachristos, A. V., & Hureau, D. M. (2014). The effects of hot spots policing on crime: An updated systematic review and meta-analysis. *Justice Quarterly, 31*(4), 633–663.

Braga, A. A., & Weisburd, D. L. (2012). The effects of focused deterrence strategies on crime: A systematic review and meta-analysis of the empirical evidence. *Journal of Research in Crime and Delinquency, 49*(3), 323–358.

Braga, A. A., Welsh, B. C., & Schnell, C. (2015). Can policing disorder reduce crime? A systematic review and meta-analysis. *Journal of Research in Crime and Delinquency, 52*(4), 567–588.

Brainard, L. A., & Derrick-Mills, T. (2011). Electronic commons, community policing, and communication: Online police-citizen discussion groups in Washington, DC. *Administrative Theory & Praxis, 33*(3), 383–410.

Brainard, L. A., & Edlins, M. (2015). Top 10 US municipal police departments and their social media usage. *The American Review of Public Administration, 45*(6), 728–745.

Brauer, J. R. (2009). Testing social learning theory using reinforcement's residue: A multilevel analysis of self-reported theft and marijuana use in the national youth survey. *Criminology, 47*(3), 929–970.

Braun, K. (2017). Yesterday is history, tomorrow is a mystery: The fate of the Australian jury system in the age of social media dependency. *The University of New South Wales Law Journal, 40*(4), 1634–1662.

Breindl, Y. (2010). Internet-based protest in European policymaking: The case of digital activism. *International Journal of E-Politics (IJEP), 1*(1), 57–72.

Briggs, E. (2022). Gen Z is extremely online. *Morning Consult*. Retrieved September 25, 2023, from https://pro.morningconsult.com/instant-intel/gen-z-social-media-usage

Broidy, L. M. (2001). A test of general strain theory. *Criminology, 39*(1), 9–36.

Broidy, L. M., & Agnew, R. (1997). Gender and crime: A general strain theory perspective. *Journal of Research in Crime and Delinquency, 34*(3), 275–306.

Brown, G. R. (2016). The blue line on thin ice: Police use of force modifications in the era of cameraphones and YouTube. *British Journal of Criminology, 56*(2), 293–312.

Browning, J. G. (2014). Why can't we be friends? Judges' use of social media. *University of Miami Law Review, 68*(2), 487–533.

Brunner, H. G., Nelen, M., Breakefield, X. O., Ropers, H. H., & Van Oost, B. A. (1993). Abnormal behavior associated with a point mutation in the structural gene for monoamine oxidase A. *Science, 262*(5133), 578–580.

Bruns, A., Burgess, J., Crawford, K., & Shaw, F. (2012). *Crisis communication on Twitter in the 2011 South East Queensland floods*. ARC Centre of Excellence for Creative Industries and Innovation. Retrieved October 24, 2023, from https://apo.org.au/sites/default/files/resource-files/2012-01/apo-nid27948.pdf

Buchanan, M., Castro, E. D., Kushner, M., & Krohn, M. D. (2020). It's f**ing chaos: COVID-19's impact on juvenile delinquency and juvenile justice. *American Journal of Criminal Justice, 45*(4), 578–600.

Buil-Gil, D., Miró-Llinares, F., Moneva, A., Kemp, S., & Díaz-Castaño, N. (2021). Cybercrime and shifts in opportunities during COVID-19: A preliminary analysis in the UK. *European Societies, 23*(Suppl. 1), S47–S59.

Bullock, K. (2018). (Re) presenting 'order' online: The construction of police presentational strategies on social media. *Policing and Society, 28*(3), 345–359.

Bullock, K., Harkness, A., Mellberg, J., & Christmas, H. (2023). Police engagement with rural communities on Facebook. *Policing: A Journal of Policy and Practice*. Online First. https://doi.org/10.1093/police/paad067

Burgoon, J. K. (1978). A communication model of personal space violations: Explication and an initial test. *Human Communication Research, 4*(2), 129–142.

Burgoon, J. K., & Hale, J. L. (1988). Nonverbal expectancy violations: Model elaboration and application to immediacy behaviors. *Communications Monographs, 55*(1), 58–79.

Burke, M. (2024). Taylor Swift's name not searchable on X days after sexually explicit deepfakes go viral. *NBC News*. Retrieved March 6, 2024, from https://www.nbcnews.com/news/us-news/taylor-swifts-name-not-searchable-x-days-sexually-explicit-deepfakes-g-rcna136017

Burke Winkelman, S., Oomen-Early, J., Walker, A. D., Chu, L., & Yick-Flanagan, A. (2015). Exploring cyber harassment among women who use social media. *Universal Journal of Public Health, 3*(5), 194–201.

Burkhardt, J., & Lenhard, W. (2022). A meta-analysis on the longitudinal, age-dependent effects of violent video games on aggression. *Media Psychology, 25*(3), 499–512.

Burruss, G. W., & Giblin, M. J. (2014). Modeling isomorphism on policing innovation: The role of institutional pressures in adopting community-oriented policing. *Crime and Delinquency, 60*(3), 331–355.

Burt, C. H., & Simons, R. L. (2013). Self-control, thrill seeking, and crime: Motivation matters. *Criminal Justice and Behavior, 40*(11), 1326–1348.

Burton, A. L., Jonson, C. L., Barnes, J. C., Miller, W. T., & Burton Jr, V. S. (2022). Training as an opportunity for change: A pretest–posttest study of pre-service correctional officer orientations. *Journal of Experimental Criminology*, 1–23. Online First. https://doi.org/10.1007/s11292-022-09544-8

Bushman, B. J., & Gibson, B. (2011). Violent video games cause an increase in aggression long after the game has been turned off. *Social Psychological and Personality Science, 2*(1), 29–32.

Cacioppo, J. T., & Petty, R. E. (1982). The need for cognition. *Journal of Personality and Social Psychology, 42*(1), 116–131.

Callanan, V. J. (2012). Media consumption, perceptions of crime risk and fear of crime: Examining race/ethnic differences. *Sociological Perspectives, 55*(1), 93–115.

Cammaerts, B. (2015). Social media and activism. In R. Mansell & P. Hwa (Eds.), *The international encyclopedia of digital communication and society (The Wiley Blackwell-ICA International Encyclopedias of Communication series)* (pp. 1027–1034). Wiley-Blackwell.

Canevez, R. N., Karabelnik, M., & Winter, J. S. (2022). Police brutality and racial justice narratives through multi-narrative framing: Reporting and commenting on the George Floyd murder on YouTube. *Journalism & Mass Communication Quarterly, 99*(3), 696–717.

Carlyle, K. E., Guidry, J. P., & Burton, C. (2021). Recipes for prevention: An analysis of intimate partner violence messages on Pinterest. *Journal of Interpersonal Violence, 36*(11–12), NP6106–NP6123.

Carr, C. T., & Hayes, R. A. (2015). Social media: Defining, developing, and divining. *Atlantic Journal of Communication, 23*(1), 46–65.

Carrier, J., Bennell, C., Semple, T., & Jenkins, B. (2021). Online Canadian police recruitment videos: Do they focus on factors that potential employees consider when making career decisions? *Police Practice and Research, 22*(6), 1585–1602.

Carriquiry, A., Hofmann, H., Tai, X., & VanderPlas, S. (2019). Machine learning in forensic applications. *Significance, 16*, 29–35.

Cartwright, A., & Shaw, C. (2020). Evidence based social media use: An exploratory UK investigation into residents' perceptions of police Facebook use. *Safer Communities, 19*(2), 61–71.

Castaneda, R. (2016). Former Md. judge sentenced for ordering electrical shock for defendant. *The Washington Post*. Retrieved November 2, 2023, from https://www.washingtonpost.com/local/public-safety/former-md-judge-sentenced-for-ordering-electrical-shock-for-defendant/2016/03/31/56e31728-f752-11e5-a3ce-f06b5ba21f33_story.html

Casteel, C., & Peek-Asa, C. (2000). Effectiveness of crime prevention through environmental design (CPTED) in reducing robberies. *American Journal of Preventive Medicine, 18*(4), 99–115.

CBS. (2017). 80-year-old judge becomes unlikely internet star. *CBS News*. Retrieved December 20, 2023, from https://www.cbsnews.com/news/frank-caprio-80-year-old-judge-becomes-internet-star-providence/

Ceccato, V. (2019). Eyes and apps on the streets: From surveillance to sousveillance using smartphones. *Criminal Justice Review, 44*(1), 25–41.

Ceccato, V., Solymosi, R., & Müller, O. (2021). The use of Twitter by police officers in urban and rural contexts in Sweden. *International Criminal Justice Review, 31*(4), 456–476.

Celeste, E. (2021). Digital punishment: Social media exclusion and the constitutionalizing role of national courts. *International Review of Law, Computers & Technology, 35*(2), 162–184.

Cerdá, M., Tracy, M., Messner, S. F., Vlahov, D., Tardiff, K., & Galea, S. (2009). Misdemeanor policing, physical disorder, and gun-related homicide: A spatial analytic test of "broken-windows" theory. *Epidemiology*, 533–541.

Ceron, A., & Negri, F. (2016). The "social side" of public policy: Monitoring online public opinion and its mobilization during the policy cycle. *Policy & Internet, 8*(2), 131–147.

Chadee, D., & Ditton, J. (2005). Fear of crime and the media: Assessing the lack of relationship. *Crime, Media, Culture, 1*(3), 322–332.

Chai, S., & Kim, M. (2010). What makes bloggers share knowledge? An investigation on the role of trust. *International Journal of Information Management, 30*(5), 408–415.

Chan, J. B. (2001). The technological game: How information technology is transforming police practice. *Criminal Justice, 1*(2), 139–159.

Chan, J. B., Mojumder, P., & Ghose, A. (2019). The digital Sin City: An empirical study of Craigslist's impact on prostitution trends. *Information Systems Research, 30*(1), 219–238.

Chappell, A. T., Monk-Turner, E., & Payne, B. K. (2011). Broken windows or window breakers: The influence of physical and social disorder on quality of life. *Justice Quarterly, 28*(3), 522–540.

Chapple, M. (2019). Taking social security numbers public could fix our data breach crisis. *CNN Business Perspectives*. Retrieved March 8, 2024, from https://www.cnn.com/2019/06/05/perspectives/labcorp-quest-diagnostics-data-breach-social-security-numbers/index.html

Charis, E. K., & Ronald, W. (2017). New directions in social disorganization theory. In S. Henry (Ed.), *Recent developments in criminological theory* (pp. 265–294). Routledge.

Charnley, H., & Nkhoma, P. (2020). Moving beyond contemporary discourses: Children, prostitution, modern slavery, and human trafficking. *Critical and Radical Social Work, 8*(2), 205–221.

Chauhan, A., & Hughes, A. L. (2015). *Facebook and Twitter adoption by Hurricane Sandy-affected police and fire departments.* ISCRAM. Retrieved October 24, 2023, from http://citeseerx.ist.psu.edu/viewdoc/download?doi=10.1.1.1090.6697&rep=rep1&type=pdf

Chedeville, L. (2021). I'm France's biggest inmate *TikToker. VICE.* Retrieved March 16, 2024, from https://www.vice.com/en/article/z3xgya/im-frances-biggest-inmate-tiktoker

Cheeseman, K. A., Kim, B., Lambert, E. G., & Hogan, N. L. (2011). Correctional officer perceptions of inmates and overall job satisfaction. *Journal of Crime and Justice, 34*(2), 81–102.

Chen, B. X. (2023). The future of social media is a lot less social. *The New York Times.* Retrieved December 30, 2023, from https://www.nytimes.com/2023/04/19/technology/personaltech/tiktok-twitter-facebook-social.html

Cheng, C., Lau, Y. C., Chan, L., & Luk, J. W. (2021). Prevalence of social media addiction across 32 nations: Meta-analysis with subgroup analysis of classification schemes and cultural values. *Addictive Behaviors, 117*, 106845.

Cheng, T. (2021). Social media, socialization, and pursuing legitimation of police violence. *Criminology, 59*(3), 391–418.

Cheung, C. M., & Lee, M. K. (2010). A theoretical model of intentional social action in online social networks. *Decision Support Systems, 49*(1), 24–30.

Chiricos, T., Eschholz, S., & Gertz, M. (1997). Crime, news, and fear of crime: Toward an identification of audience effects. *Social Problems, 44*(3), 342–357.

Cho, S. Y., Dreher, A., & Neumayer, E. (2013). Does legalized prostitution increase human trafficking? *World Development, 41*, 67–82.

Choi, J., Kruis, N. E., & Choo, K. S. (2021). Explaining fear of identity theft victimization using a routine activity approach. *Journal of Contemporary Criminal Justice, 37*(3), 406–426.

Choi, K. S. (2008). Computer crime victimization and integrated theory: An empirical assessment. *International Journal of Cyber Criminology, 2*(1), 308–333.

Choi, K. S., & Lee, J. R. (2017). Theoretical analysis of cyber-interpersonal violence victimization and offending using cyber-routine activities theory. *Computers in Human Behavior, 73*, 394–402.

Chon, M. G., & Park, H. (2020). Social media activism in the digital age: Testing an integrative model of activism on contentious issues. *Journalism & Mass Communication Quarterly, 97*(1), 72–97.

Clarke, M. (2017). Vigilantes assault, rob and murder registered sex offenders. *Prison Legal News.* Retrieved October 10, 2023, from https://www.prisonlegalnews.org/news/2017/may/5/vigilantes-assault-rob-and-murder-registered-sex-offenders/

Clarke, R. V. (1995). Situational crime prevention. *Crime and Justice, 19*, 91–150.

Clarke, R. V., & Cornish, D. B. (2001). Rational choice. In R. Paternoster & R. Bachman (Eds.), *Explaining criminals and crime: Essays in contemporary criminological theory* (pp. 23–42). Roxbury Publishing Company.

Clear, T. R., Reisig, M. D., Turpin-Petrosino, C., & Cole, G. F. (2012). *American corrections in brief.* Wadsworth Cengage Learning.

Cochran, J. K., Maskaly, J., Jones, S., & Sellers, C. S. (2017). Using structural equations to model Akers' social learning theory with data on intimate partner violence. *Crime & Delinquency, 63*(1), 39–60.

Cohen, L. E., & Felson, M. (1979). Social change and crime rate trends: A routine activity approach. *American Sociological Review, 44*(4): 588–608.

Collins, R. (2007). Strolling while poor: How broken-windows policing created a new crime in Baltimore. *Georgetown Journal on Poverty Law & Policy, 14*(3), 419–439.

Commonwealth v. Foster, 214 A.3d 1240 (Pa. 2019).

Connell, N. M., Miggans, K., & McGloin, J. M. (2008). Can a community policing initiative reduce serious crime? *Police Quarterly, 11*(2), 127–150.

Conway, M. (2020). Routing the extreme right: Challenges for social media platforms. *The RUSI Journal, 165*(1), 108–113.

Cooke, E. M., Armstrong, T., Boisvert, D., Wells, J., Lewis, R. H., Hughes-Stamm, S., & Gangitano, D. (2018). The relationship between the MAOA-uVNTR polymorphism, delinquent peer affiliation, and antisocial behavior with a consideration of sex differences. *Psychiatric Quarterly, 89*, 841–853.

Cooper, B. P. (2014). Judges and social media: Disclosure as disinfectant. *SMU Science and Technology Law Review, 17*(4), 521–539.

Cordner, G., & Perkins, E. B. (2013). *E-cop: Using the web to enhance community-oriented policing*. Office of Community Oriented Policing Services, US Department of Justice. Retrieved October 17, 2023, from https://cops.usdoj.gov/RIC/Publications/cops-w0706-pub.pdf

Cornish, D. B., & Clarke, R. V. (2003). Opportunities, precipitators, and criminal decisions: A reply to Wortley's critique of situational crime prevention. *Crime Prevention Studies, 16*, 41–96.

Cornish, D. B., & Clarke, R. V. (Eds.). (2014). *The reasoning criminal: Rational choice perspectives on offending*. Transaction Publishers.

Correa, T., Hinsley, A. W., & de Zuniga, H. G. (2010). Who interacts on the web? The intersection of users' personality and social media use. *Computers in Human Behavior, 26*(2), 247–253.

Correll, C. M. (2022). Facebook, crime prevention, and the scope of the private search post-Carpenter. *Georgia Law Review, 56*(2), 787–818.

Cowley, S. (2019). Equifax to pay at least $650 million in largest-ever data breach settlement. *The New York Times Business*. Retrieved March 8, 2024, from https://www.nytimes.com/2019/07/22/business/equifax-settlement.html

Cox, S. M., McCamey, W. P., & Scaramella, G. L. (2013). *Introduction to policing* (2nd ed.). SAGE Publication, Inc.

Cozens, P., & Love, T. (2015). A review and current status of crime prevention through environmental design (CPTED). *Journal of Planning Literature, 30*(4), 393–412.

Crank, J. P. (1994). Watchman and community: Myth and institutionalization in policing. *Law & Society Review, 28*(2), 325–352.

Crank, J. P. (2015). *Understanding police culture* (2nd ed.). Routledge.

Crockett, M. J., Clark, L., Lieberman, M. D., Tabibnia, G., & Robbins, T. W. (2010). Impulsive choice and altruistic punishment are correlated and increase in tandem with serotonin depletion. *Emotion, 10*(6), 855–862.

Crump, J. (2011). What are the police doing on Twitter? Social media, the police, and the public. *Policy & Internet, 3*(4), 1–27.

Culatta, E., Clay-Warner, J., Boyle, K. M., & Oshri, A. (2020). Sexual revictimization: A routine activity theory explanation. *Journal of Interpersonal Violence, 35*(15–16), 2800–2824.

Cullen, F. T., Jonson, C. L., & Mears, D. P. (2017). Reinventing community corrections. *Crime and Justice, 46*(1), 27–93.

Cvetojevic, S., & Hochmair, H. H. (2018). Analyzing the spread of tweets in response to Paris attacks. *Computers, Environment and Urban Systems, 71*, 14–26.

Dai, M., He, W., Tian, X., Giraldi, A., & Gu, F. (2017). Working with communities on social media: Varieties in the use of Facebook and Twitter by local police. *Online Information Review, 41*(6), 782–796.

Dai, M., & Hu, X. (2021). Exploring the duration of police–citizen encounters. *Policing: A Journal of Policy and Practice, 15*(2), 1129–1143.

Dai, M., Hu, X., & Gu, F. (2020). Citizen characteristics, neighborhood conditions, and prior contacts with the police: A comparative study of public satisfaction with the police. *Canadian Journal of Criminology and Criminal Justice, 62*(4), 77–101.

Dai, M., Hu, X., & Time, V. (2019). Understanding public satisfaction with the police: Military background and interactions between higher education and prior contact with the police. *Policing: An International Journal, 42*(4), 571–584.

Davies, H. (2023). Telegram vs WhatsApp: Which messaging app should you use? *Trusted Reviews*. Retrieved October 4, 2023, from https://www.trustedreviews.com/versus/telegram-vs-whatsapp-4294342

Davis, F. D. (1989). Perceived usefulness, perceived ease of use, and user acceptance of information technology. *MIS Quarterly, 13*(3), 319–340.

Day, J. J., & Carelli, R. M. (2007). The nucleus accumbens and Pavlovian reward learning. *The Neuroscientist, 13*(2), 148–159.

De Veirman, M., Hudders, L., & Nelson, M. R. (2019). What is influencer marketing and how does it target children? A review and direction for future research. *Frontiers in Psychology, 10*, 498106.

De Wit, J., Van der Kraan, A., & Theeuwes, J. (2020). Live streams on twitch help viewers cope with difficult periods in life. *Frontiers in Psychology, 11*, 586975.

Dean, K. (2000). The epidemic of cyberstalking. *WIRED*. Retrieved January 15, 2024, from https://www.wired.com/2000/05/the-epidemic-of-cyberstalking/

Dekker, R., Van den Brink, P., & Meijer, A. (2020). Social media adoption in the police: Barriers and strategies. *Government Information Quarterly, 37*(2), 101441.

Del Vicario, M., Bessi, A., Zollo, F., Petroni, F., Scala, A., Caldarelli, G., Stanley, E., & Quattrociocchi, W. (2016). The spreading of misinformation online. *Proceedings of the National Academy of Sciences, 113*(3), 554–559.

Delcea, C., & Enache, A. (2021). Personality traits as predictors of crime. *Romanian Journal of Legal Medicine*, 2, 227–231.

Deliso, M. (2023). How Michigan State University shooting unfolded: Timeline. *abcNews*. Retrieved February 24, 2023, from https://abcnews.go.com/US/timeline-michigan-state-university-shooting-unfolded/story?id=97194142

Denef, S., Bayerl, P. S., & Kaptein, N. A. (2013). Social media and the police: Tweeting practices of British police forces during the August 2011 riots. In *Proceedings of the SIGCHI conference on human factors in computing systems*, Paris, France (pp. 3471–3480).

Dewald, S. (2023). Detectives and technological frames: Integrating technology and social media into everyday work. *Policing and Society, 33*(1), 111–128.

Dewan, S. (2019). When police officers vent on Facebook. *New York Times*. Retrieved January 26, 2024, from https://www.nytimes.com/2019/06/03/us/politics/police-officers-facebook.html

Diamond, S. S., & Rose, M. R. (2018). The contemporary American jury. *Annual Review of Law and Social Science, 14*, 239–258.

Diaz, A., & Shields, T. (2024). AT&T says data from 73 million accounts leaked on dark web. *Bloomberg*. Retrieved April 8, 2024, from https://www.bloomberg.com/news/articles/2024-03-30/at-t-says-data-from-73-million-accounts-leaked-on-dark-web?utm_source=website&utm_medium=share&utm_campaign=copy

Dixon, N. (2018). Stranger-ness and belonging in a neighborhood WhatsApp group. *Open Cultural Studies, 1*(1), 493–503.

Dixon, S. (2022). Mobile social media usage in the United States – statistics & facts. *Statista*. Retrieved March 2, 2023, from https://www.statista.com/topics/4689/mobile-social-media-usage-in-the-united-states/#topicOverview

Doe v. Prosecutor, Marion County Indiana, 705 F.3d 694 (7th Cir. 2013).

Dogan, H., Norman, H., Alrobai, A., Jiang, N., Nordin, N., & Adnan, A. (2019). A web-based intervention for social media addiction disorder management in higher education: Quantitative survey study. *Journal of Medical Internet Research, 21*(10), e14834.

Domahidi, E. (2018). The associations between online media use and users' perceived social resources: A meta-analysis. *Journal of Computer-Mediated Communication, 23*(4), 181–200.

Domitrovich, C. E., Cortes, R. C., & Greenberg, M. T. (2007). Improving young children's social and emotional competence: A randomized trial of the preschool "PATHS" curriculum. *The Journal of Primary Prevention, 28*, 67–91.

Dong, B., & Wu, X. (2022). Reaching and engaging people: Analyzing tweeting practices of large US police departments pre-and post-the killing of George Floyd. *PLoS One, 17*(7), e0269288.

Donohue, G. A., Tichenor, P. J., & Olien, C. N. (1973). Mass media functions, knowledge, and social control. *Journalism Quarterly, 50*(4), 652–659.

Doswell, W. M., Braxter, B. J., Cha, E., & Kim, K. H. (2011). Testing the theory of reasoned action in explaining sexual behavior among African American young teen girls. *Journal of Pediatric Nursing, 26*(6), e45–e54.

Dowden, C., & Tellier, C. (2004). Predicting work-related stress in correctional officers: A meta-analysis. *Journal of Criminal Justice, 32*(1), 31–47.

Dowler, K. (2003). Media consumption and public attitudes toward crime and justice: The relationship between fear of crime, punitive attitudes, and perceived police effectiveness. *Journal of Criminal Justice and Popular Culture, 10*(2), 109–126.

Dowsett, A., & Jackson, M. (2019). The effect of violence and competition within video games on aggression. *Computers in Human Behavior, 99*, 22–27.

Drake, G., & Russo, J. (2016). The smartphone as a community corrections tool. *Journal of Offender Monitoring, 29*(1), 5–8.

Drawve, G., Thomas, S. A., & Walker, J. T. (2014). The likelihood of arrest: A routine activity theory approach. *American Journal of Criminal Justice, 39*, 450–470.

Drijber, B. C., Reijnders, U. J., & Ceelen, M. (2013). Male victims of domestic violence. *Journal of Family Violence, 28*, 173–178.

Du, J., Van Koningsbruggen, G. M., & Kerkhof, P. (2018). A brief measure of social media self-control failure. *Computers in Human Behavior, 84*, 68–75.

Duhart, S. E., & Smith, J. (2021). Virtual court proceedings in North Carolina. *UNC Criminal Justice Innovation Lab.* Retrieved November 7, 2023, from https://cjil.sog.unc.edu/wp-content/uploads/sites/19452/2021/03/Virtual-Courts-Findings-Report-FINAL-3.15.2021docx.pdf

Dunsby, R. M., & Howes, L. M. (2019). The NEW adventures of the digital vigilante! Facebook users' views on online naming and shaming. *Australian & New Zealand Journal of Criminology, 52*(1), 41–59.

Durkin, K. F., Wolfe, T. W., & Clark, G. (1999). Social bond theory and binge drinking among college students: A multivariate analysis. *College Student Journal, 33*, 450–462.

Eck, J. E., & Guerette, R. T. (2012). "Own the place, own the crime" prevention: How evidence about place-based crime shifts the burden of prevention. In R. Loeber & B. Welsh (Eds.), *The future of criminology* (pp. 166–177). Oxford University Press.

Edwards v. Junior State of America Foundation, (No. 4:19-CV-140-SDJ) (E.D. Tex. Apr. 23, 2021).

Ekblom, P. (2011). Deconstructing CPTED . . . and reconstructing it for practice, knowledge management and research. *European Journal on Criminal Policy and Research, 17*, 7–28.

Ellis, J. R. (2023). Social media, police excessive force and the limits of outrage: Evaluating models of police scandal. *Criminology & Criminal Justice, 23*(1), 117–134.

Elonis v. United States, 575 U.S. 723 (2015).

Elphick, C., Philpot, R., Zhang, M., Stuart, A., Walkington, Z., Frumkin, L. A., Pike, G., Gardner, K., Lacey, M., Levine, M., Price, B., Bandara, A., & Nuseibeh, B. (2021). Building trust in digital policing: A scoping review of community policing apps. *Police Practice and Research, 22*(5), 1469–1491.

Enkhtugs, B., & Walby, K. (2023). Fantastical authenticity in correctional officer recruitment videos. *Corrections: Policy, Practice and Research*, 1–22. Online First. https://doi.org/10.1080/23774657.2023.2209748

Epstein, K. (2019). Racist posts from police officers' social media accounts trigger a wave of investigations. *The Washington Post*. Retrieved September 13, 2023, from https://www.washingtonpost.com/nation/2019/06/04/racist-posts-police-officers-social-media-accounts-trigger-wave-investigations/

Eraslan, L., & Kukuoglu, A. (2019). Social relations in virtual world and social media aggression. *World Journal on Educational Technology: Current Issues, 11*(2), 1–11.

Erete, S. L., Miller, R., & Lewis, D. A. (2014, February). Differences in technology use to support community crime prevention. In *Proceedings of the companion publication of the 17th ACM conference on computer supported cooperative work & social computing*, Baltimore, MD (pp. 153–156).

Erickson, T. (2013). Johnson County Sheriff: The social media experiment. *American Jails, 27*(3), 51–53.

Errol, Z., Madsen, J. B., & Moslehi, S. (2021). Social disorganization theory and crime in the advanced countries: Two centuries of evidence. *Journal of Economic Behavior & Organization, 191*, 519–537.

Esbensen, F. A., Peterson, D., Taylor, T. J., & Osgood, W. (2012). Results from a multi-site study of the G.R.E.A.T. program. *Justice Quarterly, 29*(1), 125–151.

Estellés-Arolas, E. (2022). Using crowdsourcing for a safer society: When the crowd rules. *European Journal of Criminology, 19*(4), 692–711.

Eysenck, S. B. (1981). Impulsiveness and antisocial behavior in children. *Current Psychology, 1*, 31–37.

Fallik, S. W., Deuchar, R., Crichlow, V. J., & Hodges, H. (2020). Policing through social media: A qualitative exploration. *International Journal of Police Science & Management*, 22(2), 208–218.

Farley, M. (2009). Theory versus reality: Commentary on four articles about trafficking for prostitution. In *Women's studies international forum* (Vol. 32, No. 4, pp. 311–315). Elsevier Science.

Farmer, A. K., & Copenhaver, A. (2022). Policing in a pandemic: How law enforcement communicates with the public. *Policing: An International Journal, 45*(1), 124–138.

Farrington, D. P. (2003). Developmental and life-course criminology: Key theoretical and empirical issues-the 2002 Sutherland Award address. *Criminology, 41*(2), 221–225.

Farrington, D. P. (2007). Childhood risk factors and risk-focused prevention. In M. Maguire, R. Morgan, & R. Reiner (Eds.), *The oxford handbook of criminology* (4th ed., pp. 602–640). Oxford University Press.

Fedorowicz, M., & Aron, L. Y. (2021). Improving evidence-based policymaking: A review. *Urban Institute*. https://www.urban.org/sites/default/files/publication/104159/improving-evidence-based-policymaking-a-review_0.pdf

Felson, M., & Cohen, L. E. (1980). Human ecology and crime: A routine activity approach. *Human Ecology, 8*, 389–406.

Felson, R. B., & Lane, K. J. (2009). Social learning, sexual and physical abuse, and adult crime. *Aggressive Behavior: Official Journal of the International Society for Research on Aggression, 35*(6), 489–501.

Felson, R. B., Messner, S. F., Hoskin, A. W., & Deane, G. (2002). Reasons for reporting and not reporting domestic violence to the police. *Criminology, 40*(3), 617–648.

Fenn, R. (2022). This isn't a reality show: How social media livestreams of high-profile criminal trials may violate one's right to a fair trial. *St. John's Law Review, 96*(3), 789–814.

Ferguson, C. J., Rueda, S. M., Cruz, A. M., Ferguson, D. E., Fritz, S., & Smith, S. M. (2008). Violent video games and aggression: Causal relationship or byproduct of family violence and intrinsic violence motivation? *Criminal Justice and Behavior, 35*(3), 311–332.

Ferguson, L., & Soave, V. (2021). #'Missing to# found: Exploring police Twitter use for missing persons investigations. *Police Practice and Research, 22*(1), 869–885.

Fielder, S. (2023). Trial by media: Where fact & fiction co-exist in high-profile cases. Lincoln *Memorial University Law Review, 10*(2), 81–111.

Fieldstadt, E., & Stelloh, T. (2022). Texas gunman warned of Uvalde school shooting in private Facebook message. *NBC News*. Retrieved April 2, 2024, from https://www.nbcnews.com/news/us-news/texas-elementary-school-shooting-victims-one-classroom-official-says-rcna30456

Findlay, L. (2015). Courting social media in Australia's criminal courtrooms: The continuing tension between promoting open justice and protecting procedural integrity. *Current Issues in Criminal Justice, 27*(2), 237–245.

Fingas, J. (2023). Twitter Blue users can now post tweets with up to 4,000 characters. *Engadget*. Retrieved October 4, 2023, from https://www.engadget.com/twitter-blue-4000-characters-tweets-205319437.html

Fisak, B., Griffin, K., Nelson, C., Gallegos-Guajardo, J., & Davila, S. (2023). The effectiveness of the FRIENDS programs for children and adolescents: A meta-analytic review. *Mental Health & Prevention*. Online First. https://doi.org/10.1016/j.mhp.2023.200271

Flower, L. (2023). Live blogs can't handle the truth? A contemporary cross-cultural consideration of transparency and procedural justice. *Oñati Socio-Legal Series, 13*(5), 1690–1710.

Flower, L., & Ahlefeldt, M. S. (2021). The criminal trial as a live event: Exploring how and why live blogs change the professional practices of judges, defense lawyers and prosecutors. *Media, Culture & Society, 43*(8), 1480–1496.

Fortin, F., Kentzinger, C., Delle Donne, J., & Chopin, J. (2023). From the virtual frontlines: Law enforcement's experience with social media in policing activities. *Journal of Crime and Justice*, 1–16. Online First. https://doi.org/10.1080/0735648X.2023.2211558

Fowler, B. M. (2017). Stealing thunder and filling the silence: Twitter as a primary channel of police crisis communication. *Public Relations Review, 43*(4), 718–728.

Fox, K. A., & Diehm, J. (2017). # MeToo's global moment: The anatomy of a viral campaign. *CNN*. Retrieved October 1, 2023, from https://www.cnn.com/2017/11/09/world/metoo-hashtag-global-movement/index.html

Fox, K. A., Nobles, M. R., & Akers, R. L. (2011). Is stalking a learned phenomenon? An empirical test of social learning theory. *Journal of Criminal Justice, 39*(1), 39–47.

France, L. R., & Verdier, C. (2016). Kardashian heist: Police say social media made her a target. *CNN*. Retrieved March 6, 2024, from https://www.cnn.com/2016/10/04/entertainment/kim-kardashian-police-social-media/index.html

Frosch, D., McWhirter, C., Vielkind, J., & Wells, G. (2022). Buffalo shooter's 673-page diary reveals descent into racist extremism. *The Wall Street Journal*. Retrieved April 9, 2024, from https://www.wsj.com/articles/buffalo-shooting-supermarket-673-page-diary-reveals-suspects-descent-into-racist-extremism-11652814938

Frye, J. (2018). From politics to policy: Turning the corner on sexual harassment. *The Center for American Progress*. Retrieved September 13, 2023, from https://www.americanprogress.org/article/politics-policy-turning-corner-sexual-harassment/

Fuller, P. B. (2022). Social media use in courtrooms. In D. R. Stewart (Ed.), *Social media and the law* (pp. 170–192). Routledge.
Fung, B. (2019). Facebook says 100 app developers could have improperly accessed user data for months. *CNN*. Retrieved April 3, 2024, from https://www.cnn.com/2019/11/05/tech/facebook-apps-user-data/index.html
Fusco, N., Ricciardelli, R., Jamshidi, L., Carleton, R. N., Barnim, N., Hilton, Z., & Groll, D. (2021). When our work hits home: Trauma and mental disorders in correctional officers and other correctional workers. *Frontiers in Psychiatry, 11*, 493391.
Gabriels, K. (2016). 'I keep a close watch on this child of mine': A moral critique of other-tracking apps. *Ethics and Information Technology, 18*(3), 175–184.
Gainsbury, S. M., King, D. L., Hing, N., & Delfabbro, P. (2015). Social media marketing and gambling: An interview study of gambling operators in Australia. *International Gambling Studies, 15*(3), 377–393.
Gainsbury, S. M., King, D. L., Russell, A. M., Delfabbro, P., Derevensky, J., & Hing, N. (2016). Exposure to and engagement with gambling marketing in social media: Reported impacts on moderate-risk and problem gamblers. *Psychology of Addictive Behaviors, 30*(2), 270.
Garett, R., Lord, L. R., & Young, S. D. (2016). Associations between social media and cyberbullying: A review of the literature. *mHealth, 2*(12), 1–7.
Garth-James, K. (2021). A proposal for studying social media sentiments about corrections in the United States. *World Journal of Social Sciences and Humanities, 7*(3), 106–116.
Garth-James, K. (2022). Ethical considerations and reimaging state corrections: Education and work partnerships for offenders return to home and community. *International Journal on Social and Education Sciences, 4*(1), 1–16.
Gau, J. M. (2015). Procedural justice, police legitimacy, and legal cynicism: A test for mediation effects. *Police Practice and Research, 16*(5), 402–415.
Gau, J. M., Corsaro, N., & Brunson, R. K. (2014). Revisiting broken windows theory: A test of the mediation impact of social mechanisms on the disorder–fear relationship. *Journal of Criminal Justice, 42*(6), 579–588.
Gayadeen, S. M., & Phillips, S. W. (2014). The innovation of community policing and the COPS office: Does diffusion of innovation theory hold in a manipulated environment? *International Journal of Police Science and Management, 16*(3), 228–242.
Gerber, M. S. (2014). Predicting crime using Twitter and kernel density estimation. *Decision Support Systems, 61*, 115–125.
Gerbner, G., Gross, L., Morgan, M., & Signorielli, N. (1994). Growing up with television: The cultivation perspective. In J. Bryant & D. Zillmann (Eds.), *LEA's communication series. Media effects: Advances in theory and research* (pp. 17–41). Lawrence Erlbaum Associates, Inc.
Ghazali, S., & Ghani, N. M. (2018). Perception of female students towards social media-related crimes. *Pertanika Journal of Social Sciences & Humanities, 26*(2), 769–786.
Gibson, K. (2024). Fake and graphic images of Taylor Swift started with AI challenge. *CBS News*. Retrieved March 6, 2024, from https://www.cbsnews.com/news/taylor-swift-artificial-intellignence-ai-4chan/
Gilbert, B. (2019). The 10 most-viewed fake-news stories on Facebook in 2019 were just revealed in a new report. *Business Insider*. Retrieved December 29, 2023, from https://www.businessinsider.com/most-viewed-fake-news-stories-shared-on-facebook-2019-2019-11
Gill, C., Weisburd, D., Telep, C., Vitter, Z., & Bennett, T. (2014). Community-oriented policing to reduce crime, disorder and fear and increase satisfaction and legitimacy

among citizens: A systematic review. *Journal of Experimental Criminology, 10*(4), 399–428.
Giumetti, G. W., & Kowalski, R. M. (2022). Cyberbullying via social media and well-being. *Current Opinion in Psychology, 45*, 101314.
Glancy, D. J. (1979). Invention of the right to privacy. *Arizona Law Review, 21*(1), 1–39.
Golbeck, J., Robles, C., & Turner, K. (2011). Predicting personality with social media. In *CHI'11 extended abstracts on human factors in computing systems*, Vancouver, BC, Canada (pp. 253–262).
Goldman, D. (2024). Why was a revolting YouTube video of a purported decapitated head left online for hours? *CNN*. Retrieved March 1, 2024, from https://www.cnn.com/2024/01/31/tech/youtube-decapitation-video/index.html
Goldstein, H. (1979). Improving policing: A problem-oriented approach. *Crime and Delinquency, 25*(2), 236–258.
Golladay, K. A. (2017). Reporting behaviors of identity theft victims: An empirical test of Black's theory of law. *Journal of Financial Crime, 24*(1), 101–117.
Goodman, M. D. (2013). Shame, angry judges, and the social media effect. *Catholic University Law Review, 63*, 589–623.
Google. (2024). In-depth guide to how Google search works. *Google for Developers*. Retrieved April 3, 2024, from https://developers.google.com/search/docs/fundamentals/how-search-works#:~:text=Googlebot%20uses%20an%20algorithmic%20process,fast%20to%20avoid%20overloading%20it
Gordon, F. (2019). Preserving lifelong anonymity orders into adulthood: New challenges for the courts in the age of social media. *Journal of Social Welfare and Family Law, 41*(4), 491–494.
Gordon, S. A., & Fernandez, N. (2023). What is Telegram and why should I use it? *Android Authority*. Retrieved October 4, 2023, from https://www.androidauthority.com/what-is-telegram-messenger-979357/
Gottfredson, M. (2017). Self-control theory and crime. In *Oxford research encyclopedia of criminology and criminal justice*. Retrieved February 28, 2024, from https://doi.org/10.1093/acrefore/9780190264079.013.252
Gottfredson, M., & Hirschi, T. (1990). *A general theory of crime*. Stanford University Press.
Gover, A. R., Harper, S. B., & Langton, L. (2020). Anti-Asian hate crime during the COVID-19 pandemic: Exploring the reproduction of inequality. *American Journal of Criminal Justice, 45*(4), 647–667.
Grabowski, M. (2011). Are technical difficulties at the Supreme Court causing a" disregard of duty"? *Journal of Law, Technology, & the Internet, 3*(1), 93–112.
Gramlich, J. (2023). Fewer than 1% of federal criminal defendants were acquitted in 2022. *Pew Research Center*. Retrieved August 28, 2023, from https://www.pewresearch.org/short-reads/2023/06/14/fewer-than-1-of-defendants-in-federal-criminal-cases-were-acquitted-in-2022
Gray, S. (2022). UC Davis police using software to track students' social media posts. *CBS News*. Retrieved April 4, 2024, from https://www.cbsnews.com/sacramento/news/uc-davis-uses-social-media-scanning-software-to-monitor-students-online-posts/
Graziani, T. (2018). How Douyin became China's top short-video App in 500 days. *WalkTheChat*. Retrieved September 29, 2023, from https://walkthechat.com/douyin-became-chinas-top-short-video-app-500-days/
Greenberg, M. T., Kusche, C. A., Cook, E. T., & Quamma, J. P. (1995). Promoting emotional competence in school-aged children: The effects of the PATHS curriculum. *Development and Psychopathology, 7*(1), 117–136.
Greitemeyer, T. (2018). The spreading impact of playing violent video games on aggression. *Computers in Human Behavior, 80*, 216–219.

Griffin, M. L., Hogan, N. L., & Lambert, E. G. (2014). Career stage theory and turnover intent among correctional officers. *Criminal Justice and Behavior, 41*(1), 4–19.

Griffin v. State, 419 Md. 343, 19 A.3d 415 (Md. 2011).

Griffiths, M. (1999). Violent video games and aggression: A review of the literature. *Aggression and Violent Behavior, 4*(2), 203–212.

Grimmelikhuijsen, S. G., & Meijer, A. J. (2015). Does Twitter increase perceived police legitimacy? *Public Administration Review, 75*(4), 598–607.

Groff, E. R. (2007). Simulation for theory testing and experimentation: An example using routine activity theory and street robbery. *Journal of Quantitative Criminology, 23*, 75–103.

Grommon, E., Carter, J., & Scheer, C. (2018). Quantifying the size of the contraband cell phone problem: Insights from a large rural state penitentiary. *The Prison Journal, 98*(5), 630–648.

Grossman, N., & Lev-On, A. (2023). Social media jurors: Conceptualizing and analyzing online public engagement in reference to legal cases. *Crime, Law, and Social Change, 79*(3), 223–240.

Grunwald, B., Nyarko, J., & Rappaport, J. (2022). Police agencies on Facebook overreport on Black suspects. *Proceedings of the National Academy of Sciences, 119*(45), e2203089119.

Grygiel, J., & Lysak, S. (2021). Police social media and broadcast news: An investigation into the impact of police use of Facebook on journalists' gatekeeping role. *Journalism Practice, 15*(7), 994–1011.

The Guardian. (2022). Texas gunman allegedly texted German teenager plans for attack. *The Guardian*. Retrieved April 2, 2024, from https://www.theguardian.com/us-news/2022/may/26/texas-shooter-texted-german-teenager-plans

Guerette, R. T., & Bowers, K. J. (2009). Assessing the extent of crime displacement and diffusion of benefits: A review of situational crime prevention evaluations. *Criminology, 47*(4), 1331–1368.

Guitton, M. J. (2020). Cybersecurity, social engineering, artificial intelligence, technological addictions: Societal challenges for the coming decade. *Computers in Human Behavior, 107*, 106307.

Hadero, H., & Swenson, A. (2024). A beheading video was on YouTube for hours, raising questions about why it wasn't taken down sooner. *AP*. Retrieved March 1, 2024, from https://apnews.com/article/beheaded-father-pennsylvania-man-youtube-2d9231aa710324d07b1729f02b3d6a61

Hagel, J. (1999). Net gain: Expanding markets through virtual communities. *Journal of Interactive Marketing, 13*(1), 55–65.

Haggerty, K. D., & Bucerius, S. M. (2021). Picking battles: Correctional officers, rules, and discretion in prison. *Criminology, 59*(1), 137–157.

Halder, D., & Jaishankar, K. (2014). Online victimization of Andaman Jarawa Tribal women: An analysis of the 'Human Safari' YouTube videos (2012) and its effects. *British Journal of Criminology, 54*(4), 673–688.

Hand, L. C., & Ching, B. D. (2020). Maintaining neutrality: A sentiment analysis of police agency Facebook pages before and after a fatal officer-involved shooting of a citizen. *Government Information Quarterly, 37*(1), 101420.

Hanson, R. K., Morton, K. E., & Harris, A. J. (2003). Sexual offender recidivism risk: What we know and what we need to know. *Annals of the New York Academy of Sciences, 989*(1), 154–166.

Hao, J., & Dai, H. (2016). Social media content and sentiment analysis on consumer security breaches. *Journal of Financial Crime, 23*(4), 855–869.

Harcourt, B. E., & Ludwig, J. (2006). Broken windows: New evidence from New York City and a five-city social experiment. *The University of Chicago Law Review, 73*(1), 271–320.

Harrington, C. (2019). Neo-liberal subjectivity, self-branding and 'my rape story' YouTube videos. *Critical Sociology, 45*(7–8), 1181–1194.

Hasher, L., Goldstein, D., & Toppino, T. (1977). Frequency and the conference of referential validity. *Journal of Verbal Learning and Verbal Behavior, 16*(1), 107–112.

Hasinoff, A. A. (2017). Where are you? Location tracking and the promise of child safety. *Television & New Media, 18*(6), 496–512.

Hau, Y. S., & Kim, Y. G. (2011). Why would online gamers share their innovation-conducive knowledge in the online game user community? Integrating individual motivations and social capital perspectives. *Computers in Human Behavior, 27*(2), 956–970.

Hausegger, L., Hennigar, M., & Riddell, T. (2014). *Canadian courts: Law, politics, and process*. Oxford University Press.

Hawdon, J., Parti, K., & Dearden, T. E. (2020). Cybercrime in America amid COVID-19: The initial results from a natural experiment. *American Journal of Criminal Justice, 45*(4), 546–562.

Hay, C., & Meldrum, R. (2015). *Self-control and crime over the life course*. Sage Publications.

Hayes, R. M., & Levett, L. M. (2013). Community members' perceptions of the CSI effect. *American Journal of Criminal Justice, 38*(2), 216–235.

Haynes, T. (2023). Judge takes pity on young single mom who racked up multiple parking tickets while unemployed. *YourTango*. Retrieved December 27, 2023, from https://www.yourtango.com/news/judge-takes-pity-young-single-mom-who-racked-up-multiple-parking-tickets-while-unemployed

Healy, D. (2012). Advise, assist, and befriend: Can probation supervision support desistance? *Social Policy & Administration, 46*(4), 377–394.

Helfgott, J. B. (2015). Criminal behavior and the copycat effect: Literature review and theoretical framework for empirical investigation. *Aggression and Violent Behavior, 22*, 46–64.

Helfgott, J. B. (2023). *Copycat crime: How media, technology, and digital culture inspire criminal behavior and violence*. Bloomsbury Publishing Inc.

Hemmens, C., Brody, D. C., & Spohn, C. (2017). *Criminal courts: A contemporary perspective* (3rd ed.). SAGE Publications.

Henderson, A. (2017). Social media used to report crime instead of going to the police. *Fox Illinois*. Retrieved December 25, 2023, from https://foxillinois.com/news/local/social-media-used-to-report-crime-instead-of-going-to-the-police-12-08-2017

Henderson, A. (2018). The high court and the cocktail party from hell: Can social media improve community engagement with the courts? *The Responsive Judge: International Perspectives*, 121–141.

Henisa, D., & Wilantika, N. (2021). Content characteristics of government social media and the impact on citizen engagement rate. In *2021 International conference on informatics, multimedia, cyber and information system (ICIMCIS)* (pp. 349–355). IEEE.

Heverin, T., & Zach, L. (2010). Twitter for city police department information sharing. *Proceedings of the American Society for Information Science and Technology, 47*(1), 1–7.

Hews, R., & Suzor, N. (2017). 'Scum of the earth': An analysis of prejudicial twitter conversations during the Baden-Clay murder trial. *University of New South Wales Law Journal, 40*(4), 1604–1633.

Hinds, L. (2009). Public satisfaction with police: The influence of general attitudes and police-citizen encounters. *International Journal of Police Science and Management, 11*(1), 54–66.

Hino, K. (2018). Plus Bouhan: A new community-based approach to crime prevention in Japan. *International Journal of Law, Crime and Justice, 54*, 79–88.

Hirschfield, A., & Bowers, K. J. (1997). The effect of social cohesion on levels of recorded crime in disadvantaged areas. *Urban Studies, 34*(8), 1275–1295.
Hirschi, T. (1969). *The causes of delinquency*. University of California Press.
Hitz, J. (2014). Removing disfavored faces from Facebook: The freedom of speech implications of banning sex offenders from social media. *Indiana Law Journal, 89*(3), 1327–1363.
Hlavka, H. R., & Mulla, S. (2018). "That's how she talks": Animating text message evidence in the sexual assault trial. *Law & Society Review, 52*(2), 401–435.
Hoeve, M., Stams, G. J. J., Van der Put, C. E., Dubas, J. S., Van der Laan, P. H., & Gerris, J. R. (2012). A meta-analysis of attachment to parents and delinquency. *Journal of Abnormal Child Psychology, 40*, 771–785.
Hoffmann, J. P., & Dufur, M. J. (2018). Family social capital, family social bonds, and juvenile delinquency. *American Behavioral Scientist, 62*(11), 1525–1544.
Hoffmeister, T. (2014). *Social media in the courtrooms: A new era for criminal justice?* ABC-CLIO, LLC.
Hoffmeister, T., & Watts, A. C. (2018). Social media, the internet, and trial by jury. *Annual Review of Law and Social Science, 14*, 259–270.
Hollingdale, J., & Greitemeyer, T. (2014). The effect of online violent video games on levels of aggression. *PLoS One, 9*(11), e111790.
Holmgren, J. A., & Fordham, J. (2011). The CSI effect and the Canadian and the Australian jury. *Journal of Forensic Sciences, 56*(1), 63–71.
Holt, T. J., & Bossler, A. M. (2008). Examining the applicability of lifestyle-routine activities theory for cybercrime victimization. *Deviant Behavior, 30*(1), 1–25.
Homel, R. (2013). Developmental crime prevention. In N. Tilley (Ed.), *Handbook of crime prevention and community safety* (pp. 97–132). Willan.
Hong, H., & Kim, Y. (2021). What makes people engage in civic activism on social media? *Online Information Review, 45*(3), 562–576.
Hopp, T., Ferrucci, P., & Vargo, C. J. (2020). Why do people share ideologically extreme, false, and misleading content on social media? A self-report and trace data–based analysis of countermedia content dissemination on Facebook and Twitter. *Human Communication Research, 46*(4), 357–384.
Hosterman, A. R., Johnson, N. R., Stouffer, R., & Herring, S. (2018). Twitter, social support messages, and the# MeToo movement. *The Journal of Social Media in Society*, 7(2), 69–91.
Howell, K. B. (2009). Broken lives from broken windows: The hidden costs of aggressive order-maintenance policing. *New York University Review of Law & Social Change, 33*, 271–329.
Hsu, C. L., & Lin, J. C. C. (2008). Acceptance of blog usage: The roles of technology acceptance, social influence and knowledge sharing motivation. *Information & Management, 45*(1), 65–74.
Hsu, H. Y., Vásquez, B. E., & McDowall, D. (2018). A time-series analysis of terrorism: Intervention, displacement, and diffusion of benefits. *Justice Quarterly, 35*(4), 557–583.
Hu, X. (2016). *Moving toward the electronic community-oriented policing era: Content and strategies of police use of social media*. Sam Houston State University. ProQuest Central; ProQuest Dissertations & Theses Global. (1860917926).
Hu, X., Dai, M., DeValve, M. J., & Lejeune, A. (2020). Understanding public attitudes towards the police: Co-variates of satisfaction, trust, and confidence. *Canadian Journal of Criminology and Criminal Justice, 62*(1), 26–49.
Hu, X., & Dittmann, L. (2016). Nothing works or something works? Gang-crimes and interventions in the print media. *Journal of Gang Research, 23*(4), 29–50.
Hu, X., & Dittmann, L. (2019). How does print media describe gang members? Analysis of newspaper reports and policy implications. *Journal of Criminal Justice and Popular Culture, 19*(1), 19–36.

Hu, X., Dong, B., & Lovrich, N. P. (2022). "We are all in this together:" Police use of social media during the COVID-19 pandemic. *Policing: An International Journal, 45*(1), 106–123.

Hu, X., Lee, J., & Lovrich, N. P. (2023). Do commonly recommended preventive actions deter identity theft victimization? Findings from NCVS identity theft surveys. *Journal of Crime and Justice, 46*(2), 172–193.

Hu, X., & Lovrich, N. P. (2019). Social media and the police: A study of organizational characteristics associated with the use of social media. *Policing: An International Journal, 42*(4), 654–670.

Hu, X., & Lovrich, N. P. (2020). *Electronic community-oriented policing: Theories, contemporary efforts, and future directions.* Lexington Books.

Hu, X., & Lovrich, N. P. (2021). Small police agency use of social media: Positive and negative outcomes noted in a case study. *Policing: A Journal of Policy and Practice, 15*(2), 1584–1599.

Hu, X., & Lovrich, N. P. (2023). A model of police-public online communication: Learning from policing under Covid-19 pandemic conditions. In M. Deflem (Ed.), *Crime and social control in pandemic times (sociology of crime, law and deviance)* (Vol. 28, pp. 173–189). Emerald Publishing Limited.

Hu, X., Naito, M. E., & del Carmen, R. V. (2017). Pre- and post-conviction DNA laws in the United States: An analysis of model statutes. *Journal of Criminal Justice and Law, 1*(1), 25–42.

Hu, X., Rodgers, K., & Lovrich, N. P. (2018). "We are more than crime fighter:" Social media images of police departments. *Police Quarterly, 21*(4), 544–572.

Hu, X., Rodgers, K., & Lovrich, N. P. (2020). Public preferences regarding police Facebook posts: A macro-level analysis. *Police Practice and Research, 21*(3), 227–245.

Hu, X., Wu, J., DeValve, M. J., & Fisher, B. S. (2020). Exploring violent crime reporting among school-age victims: Findings from NCVS SCS 2005–2015. *Victims & Offenders, 15*(2), 141–158.

Hu, X., Zhang, X., & Lovrich, N. P. (2021a). Forecasting identity theft victims: Analyzing characteristics and preventive actions through machine learning approaches. *Victims & Offenders, 16*(4), 465494.

Hu, X., Zhang, X., & Lovrich, N. P. (2021b). Public perceptions of police behavior during traffic stops: Logistic regression and machine learning approaches compared. *Journal of Computational Social Science, 4*(1), 355–380.

Hu, X., Zhang, X., & Lovrich, N. P. (2022). Forecasting identity theft victims: Analyzing characteristics and preventive actions through machine learning approaches. In D. Rebovich & J. M. Byrne (Eds.), *The new technology of financial crime: New crime commission technology, new victims, new offenders, and new strategies for prevention and control* (pp. 183–212). Routledge.

Huang, Y., Huo, S., Yao, Y., Chao, N., Wang, Y., Grygiel, J., & Sawyer, S. (2016). Municipal police departments on Facebook: What are they posting and are people engaging? In *Proceedings of the 17th international digital government research conference on digital government research* (pp. 366–374).

Hudders, L., & Lou, C. (2023). The rosy world of influencer marketing? Its bright and dark sides, and future research recommendations. *International Journal of Advertising, 42*(1), 151–161.

Hughes, D. J., Rowe, M., Batey, M., & Lee, A. (2012). A tale of two sites: Twitter vs. Facebook and the personality predictors of social media usage. *Computers in Human Behavior, 28*(2), 561–569.

Hughes, D. M. (2000). The" Natasha" trade: The transnational shadow market of trafficking in women. *Journal of International Affairs, 53*(2), 625–651.

Huie, K., Butler, M., & Percy, A. (2023). Identifying trends and patterns in offending and victimization on Snapchat: A rapid review. *Security Journal*, 1–18.

Hutchings, A., & Hayes, H. (2009). Routine activity theory and phishing victimization: Who gets caught in the "net?" *Current Issues in Criminal Justice, 20*(3), 433–452.

Hutchinson, A. (2019). Instagram stories is now being used by 500 million people daily. *Social Media Today*. Retrieved September 29, 2023, from https://www.socialmediatoday.com/news/instagram-stories-is-now-being-used-by-500-million-people-daily/547270/

Instagram. (2024). Does Instagram allow photos of mothers breastfeeding? *Instagram Help Center*. Retrieved April 9, 2024, from https://help.instagram.com/172319602942927

Intravia, J., Jones, S., & Piquero, A. R. (2012). The roles of social bonds, personality, and perceived costs: An empirical investigation into Hirschi's "new" control theory. *International Journal of Offender Therapy and Comparative Criminology*, 56(8), 1182–1200.

Intravia, J., & Pickett, J. T. (2019). Stereotyping online? Internet news, social media, and the racial typification of crime. *Sociological Forum, 34*(3), 616–642.

Intravia, J., Wolff, K. T., Paez, R., & Gibbs, B. R. (2017). Investigating the relationship between social media consumption and fear of crime: A partial analysis of mostly young adults. *Computers in Human Behavior, 77*, 158–168.

Irshad, S., & Soomro, T. R. (2018). Identity theft and social media. *International Journal of Computer Science and Network Security, 18*(1), 43–55.

Ismail, N., Noor, S. M., Ahmad, J., & Jamri, M. H. (2022). Understanding factors influencing crime prevention information on social media. *Intellectual Discourse, 30*(2), 289–313.

Israni, A., Erete, S., & Smith, C. L. (2017). Snitches, trolls, and social norms: Unpacking perceptions of social media use for crime prevention. In *Proceedings of the 2017 ACM conference on computer supported cooperative work and social computing*, Portland, OR (pp. 1193–1209).

Jackson, M., & Shelly, M. (2015). The use of Twitter by Australian courts. *Journal of Law, Information and Science, 24*(1), 83–100.

Janoski-Haehlen, E. M. (2011). The courts are all a Twitter: The implications of social media use in the courts. *Valparaiso University Law Review, 46*, 43–68.

Javers, E., & Tortorelli, P. (2023). Criminals use Telegram to recruit 'walkers' as America's big banks see an 84% increase in check fraud. *CNBC*. Retrieved April 9, 2024, from https://www.cnbc.com/2023/02/06/criminals-use-telegram-to-recruit-walkers-as-americas-big-banks-see-an-84percent-increase-in-check-fraud.html

Jeanis, M. N. (2020). Missing persons and runaway youth: The role of social media as an alert system and crime control tool. In B. Fox, J. Reid, & A. Masys (Eds.), *Science informed policing* (pp. 181–193). Springer Nature.

Jeanis, M. N., Muniz, C. N., & Molbert, C. L. (2021). Law enforcement and social media usage: An analysis of engagement. *Policing: A Journal of Policy and Practice, 15*(1), 570–583.

Jennings, W. G., Piquero, A. R., Rocque, M., & Farrington, D. P. (2015). The effects of binge and problem drinking on problem behavior and adjustment over the life course: Findings from the Cambridge study in delinquent development. *Journal of Criminal Justice, 43*(6), 453–463.

Jewkes, Y., & Reisdorf, B. C. (2016). A brave new world: The problems and opportunities presented by new media technologies in prisons. *Criminology & Criminal Justice, 16*(5), 534–551.

Johnson, C. R. (2023). Courts are going to "love" this: An analysis of the Facebook "reactions" as hearsay. *Houston Law Review, 60*(4), 961–988.

Johnson, J., & Schell-Busey, N. (2016). Old message in a new bottle: Taking gang rivalries online through rap battle music videos on YouTube. *Journal of Qualitative Criminal Justice & Criminology, 4*(1), 42–81.

Johnston, J. (2017). Courts' use of social media: A community of practice model. *International Journal of Communication, 11*, 669–683.

Johnston, J. (2018). Three phases of courts' publicity: Reconfiguring Bentham's open justice in the twenty-first century. *International Journal of Law in Context, 14*(4), 525–538.

Jolliffe, D., & Farrington, D. P. (2004). Empathy and offending: A systematic review and meta-analysis. *Aggression and Violent Behavior, 9*(5), 441–476.

Jonathan-Zamir, T., Mastrofski, S. D., & Moyal, S. (2015). Measuring procedural justice in police-citizen encounters. *Justice Quarterly, 32*(5), 845–871.

Jones, B. (2016). Ex-police chief Oliver cannot police in Ohio. *News 5 Cleveland*. Retrieved October 31, 2023, from https://www.news5cleveland.com/news/local-news/oh-portage/former-brimfield-police-chief-david-oliver-due-in-court-on-criminal-charges

Jones, D. J. (2020). The potential impacts of pandemic policing on police legitimacy: Planning past the COVID-19 crisis. *Policing: A Journal of Policy and Practice, 14*(3), 579–586.

Judge, R. (2015). Social media: The attorney's best friend when investigating jurors. *North East Journal of Legal Studies, 33*(1), 47–71.

Juditha, C., Maryani, E., Abdullah, A. C. E. N. G., & Setiawati, R. A. H. M. I. (2022). Promotion of prostitution services on social media. *Jurnal Komunikasi Malaysian Journal of Communication, 38*(2), 1–15.

Juefei-Xu, F., Wang, R., Huang, Y., Guo, Q., Ma, L., & Liu, Y. (2022). Countering malicious deepfakes: Survey, battleground, and horizon. *International Journal of Computer Vision, 130*(7), 1678–1734.

Jungblut, M., & Jungblut, J. (2022). Spreading information or engaging the public? The German police's communication on Twitter. *Public Management Review*. Online First. https://doi.org/10.1080/14719037.2022.2142653

Jungblut, M., Kümpel, A. S., & Steer, R. (2022). Social media use of the police in crisis situations: A mixed-method study on communication practices of the German police. *New Media & Society*, 1–22. Online First. https://doi.org/10.1177/14614448221127899

Jünger, J., & Keyling, T. (2019). An application for automated data retrieval on the web. Source code and releases. *Facepager*. https://github.com/strohne/Facepager/

Kaakinen, M., Sirola, A., Savolainen, I., & Oksanen, A. (2020). Young people and gambling content in social media: An experimental insight. *Drug and Alcohol Review, 39*(2), 152–161.

Kam, C. M., Greenberg, M. T., & Walls, C. T. (2003). Examining the role of implementation quality in school-based prevention using the PATHS curriculum. *Prevention Science, 4*, 55–63.

Kantor, J., & Twohey, M. (2017). Harvey Weinstein paid off sexual harassment accusers for decades. *The New York Times*. Retrieved October 1, 2023, from https://www.nytimes.com/2017/10/05/us/harvey-weinstein-harassment-allegations.html

Kantor, J., & Twohey, M. (2022). How to measure the impact of #MeToo? *The New York Times*. Retrieved October 1, 2023, from https://www.nytimes.com/interactive/2022/10/03/us/me-too-five-years.html

Kapoor, K. K., Tamilmani, K., Rana, N. P., Patil, P., Dwivedi, Y. K., & Nerur, S. (2018). Advances in social media research: Past, present, and future. *Information Systems Frontiers, 20*, 531–558.

Katz, C. M., Maguire, E. R., & Roncek, D. W. (2002). The creation of specialized police gang units: A macro-level analysis of contingency, social threat, and resource dependency explanations. *Policing: An International Journal of Police Strategies & Management, 25*(3), 472–506.

Kaur, P., Dhir, A., Tandon, A., Alzeiby, E. A., & Abohassan, A. A. (2021). A systematic literature review on cyberstalking. An analysis of past achievements and future promises. *Technological Forecasting and Social Change, 163*, 120426.

Kay, S., Mulcahy, R., & Parkinson, J. (2020). When less is more: The impact of macro and micro social media influencers' disclosure. *Journal of Marketing Management, 36*(3–4), 248–278.

Kelling, G. L., & Coles, C. M. (1997). *Fixing broken windows: Restoring order and reducing crime in our communities*. Simon & Schuster Inc.

Kelling, G. L., & Wilson, J. Q. (1982). Broken windows. *Atlantic Monthly, 249*(3), 29–38.

Kelly, A., & Finlayson, A. (2015). Can Facebook save neighborhood watch? *The Police Journal, 88*(1), 65–77.

Kelly, H. (2012). Police embrace social media as crime-fighting tool. *CNN*. Retrieved March 3, 2023, from https://www.cnn.com/2012/08/30/tech/social-media/fighting-crime-social-media/index.html

Kelman, H. C. (1958). Compliance, identification, and internalization three processes of attitude change. *Journal of Conflict Resolution, 2*(1), 51–60.

Kernsmith, P. D., Comartin, E., Craun, S. W., & Kernsmith, R. M. (2009). The relationship between sex offender registry utilization and awareness. *Sexual Abuse, 21*(2), 181–193.

Kernsmith, P. D., Craun, S. W., & Foster, J. (2009). Public attitudes toward sexual offenders and sex offender registration. *Journal of Child Sexual Abuse, 18*(3), 290–301.

Kerr, A., & Willis, M. (2018). Prisoner use of information and communications technology. *Trends and Issues in Crime and Criminal Justice, 560*, 1–19.

Kesharwani, A. (2020). Do (how) digital natives adopt a new technology differently than digital immigrants? A longitudinal study. *Information & Management, 57*(2), 103170.

Kessler, G. C. (2011). Judges' awareness, understanding, and application of digital evidence. *Journal of Digital Forensics, Security and Law, 6*(1), 55–72.

Keyzer, P., Johnston, J., Pearson, M., Rodrick, S., & Wallace, A. (2013). The courts and social media: What do judges and court workers think? *Judicial Officers Bulletin, 25*(6), 47–51.

Ki, C. W. C., & Kim, Y. K. (2019). The mechanism by which social media influencers persuade consumers: The role of consumers' desire to mimic. *Psychology & Marketing, 36*(10), 905–922.

Kifer, M., Hemmens, C., & Stohr, M. K. (2003). The goals of corrections: Perspectives from the line. *Criminal Justice Review, 28*(1), 47–69.

Kiley, J. (2017). In a polarized era, fewer Americans hold a mix of conservative and liberal views. *Pew Research Center*. Retrieved December 25, 2023, from https://www.pewresearch.org/fact-tank/2017/10/23/in-polarized-era-fewer-americans-hold-a-mix-of-conservative-and-liberal-views/

Kilies, J., & Martin, W. (2020). The ins and outs of social media in litigation. *ALFA International*. Retrieved December 22, 2023, from https://www.hbblaw.com/wp-content/uploads/2020/09/The_Ins_and_Outs_of_Social_Media_in_Litigation.pdf

Kim, H. Y. (2013). An examination of citizen involvement in crime prevention. *Social Sciences, 2*(5), 161–167.

Kingshott, B. F. (2011). Effective police management of the media. *Criminal Justice Studies: A Critical Journal of Crime, Law, and Society, 24*(3), 241–253.

Kingston, B., Huizinga, D., & Elliott, D. S. (2009). A test of social disorganization theory in high-risk urban neighborhoods. *Youth & Society, 41*(1), 53–79.

Kircaburun, K., Jonason, P. K., & Griffiths, M. D. (2018). The Dark Tetrad traits and problematic social media use: The mediating role of cyberbullying and cyberstalking. *Personality and Individual Differences, 135*, 264–269.

Kirk, D. S., & Sampson, R. J. (2013). Juvenile arrest and collateral educational damage in the transition to adulthood. *Sociology of Education, 86*(1), 36–62.

Klein, C., & Yamamoto, S. (2020). Detecting victim blaming biases using social media. *Journal of Forensic Psychology Research and Practice, 20*(5), 436–450.

Koch, M., & Jackson, M. (2023). Pleasant Hill officer resigns after racist social media post discovered. *Fox4*. Retrieved January 26, 2024, from https://fox4kc.com/news/missouri-news/pleasant-hill-officer-fired-after-racist-social-media-post-discovered/

Kochanska, G., & Aksan, N. (2004). Conscience in childhood: Past, present, and future. *Merrill-Palmer Quarterly, 50*(3), 299–310.

Kokkinos, C. M., & Saripanidis, I. (2017). A lifestyle exposure perspective of victimization through Facebook among university students: Do individual differences matter? *Computers in Human Behavior, 74*, 235–245.

Konijn, E. A., Nije Bijvank, M., & Bushman, B. J. (2007). I wish I were a warrior: The role of wishful identification in the effects of violent video games on aggression in adolescent boys. *Developmental Psychology, 43*(4), 1038–1044.

Konkel, R. H., Ratkowski, D., & Tapp, S. N. (2019). The effects of physical, social, and housing disorder on neighborhood crime: A contemporary test of broken windows theory. *ISPRS International Journal of Geo-Information, 8*(12), 583.

Koon-Magnin, S., Bowers, D., Langhinrichsen-Rohling, J., & Arata, C. (2016). Social learning, self-control, gender, and variety of violent delinquency. *Deviant Behavior, 37*(7), 824–836.

Kounadi, O., Lampoltshammer, T. J., Groff, E., Sitko, I., & Leitner, M. (2015). Exploring Twitter to analyze the public's reaction patterns to recently reported homicides in London. *PLoS One, 10*(3), e0121848.

Kourti, A., Stavridou, A., Panagouli, E., Psaltopoulou, T., Spiliopoulou, C., Tsolia, M., Sergentanis, T., & Tsitsika, A. (2023). Domestic violence during the COVID-19 pandemic: A systematic review. *Trauma, Violence, & Abuse, 24*(2), 719–745.

Kovalchuk, O., Karpinski, M., Banakh, S., Kasianchuk, M., Shevchuk, R., & Zagorodna, N. (2023). Prediction machine learning models on propensity convicts to criminal recidivism. *Information, 14*(3), 161.

Kozinets, R. (2017). How social media fires people's passions – and builds extremist divisions. *The Conversation*. Retrieved December 25, 2023, from http://theconversation.com/how-social-media-fires-peoples-passions-and-builds-extremist-divisions-86909

Krawitz, M. (2013). Stop the presses, but not the tweets: Why Australian judicial officials should permit journalists to use social media in the courtroom. *Flinders Law Journal, 15*(1), 1–39.

Krohn, M. D., & Massey, J. L. (1980). Social control and delinquent behavior: An examination of the elements of the social bond. *The Sociological Quarterly, 21*(4), 529–544.

Kudla, D., & Parnaby, P. (2018). To serve and to tweet: An examination of police-related Twitter activity in Toronto. *Social Media + Society, 4*(3), 1–13.

Kühn, S., Kugler, D. T., Schmalen, K., Weichenberger, M., Witt, C., & Gallinat, J. (2019). Does playing violent video games cause aggression? A longitudinal intervention study. *Molecular Psychiatry, 24*(8), 1220–1234.

Kumar, P., Gruzd, A., & Mai, P. (2021). Mapping out violence against women of influence on Twitter using the cyber–lifestyle routine activity theory. *American Behavioral Scientist, 65*(5), 689–711.

Kupchik, A., & Bracy, N. L. (2009). The news media on school crime and violence: Constructing dangerousness and fueling fear. *Youth Violence and Juvenile Justice, 7*(2), 136–155.

Lab, S. P. (2016). *Crime prevention: Approaches, practices, and evaluations* (9th ed.). Routledge.

Laestadius, L. I., Guidry, J. P., Greskoviak, R., & Adams, J. (2019). Making "weedish fish": An exploratory analysis of cannabis recipes on Pinterest. *Substance Use & Misuse, 54*(13), 2191–2197.

Lang, A. (2022). Mädchen aus Frankfurt nach Chat mit Uvalde-Attentäter verurteilt. *FAZ*. Retrieved April 2, 2024, from https://www.faz.net/aktuell/rhein-main/frankfurt/usa-maedchen-aus-frankfurt-nach-chat-mit-uvalde-attentaeter-verurteilt-18412842.html

Langworthy, R. H., & Travis, L. F. (2002). *Policing in America: A balance of forces* (3rd ed.). Prentice Hall.

Larsson, S. (2017). A first line of defense? Vigilant surveillance, participatory policing, and the reporting of "suspicious" activity. *Surveillance and Society, 15*(1), 94–107.

Latané, B., Williams, K., & Harkins, S. (1979). Many hands make light the work: The causes and consequences of social loafing. *Journal of Personality and Social Psychology, 37*(6), 822.

Laub, J. H., & Sampson, R. J. (2006). *Shared beginnings, divergent lives: Delinquent boys to age 70*. Harvard University Press.

Lawrence v. Texas, 539 U.S. 558 (2003).

Le Blanc, M. (2020). On the future of the individual longitudinal age-crime curve. *Criminal Behavior and Mental Health, 30*(4), 183–195.

Lee, H. D., Kim, D., Armocida, M., & Reyns, B. W. (2023). The relationship between media engagement and procedural justice. *Deviant Behavior, 44*(12), 1735–1745.

Lee, H. W. (2017). Taking deterrence seriously: The wide-scope deterrence theory of punishment. *Criminal Justice Ethics, 36*(1), 2–24.

Lee, M., & McGovern, A. (2014). *Policing and media: Public relations, simulations, and communications*. Routledge.

Leppert, K., Saliterer, I., & Korać, S. (2022). The role of emotions for citizen engagement via social media–a study of police departments using Twitter. *Government Information Quarterly, 39*(3), 101686.

Leukfeldt, E. R. (2014). Phishing for suitable targets in the Netherlands: Routine activity theory and phishing victimization. *Cyberpsychology, Behavior, and Social Networking, 17*(8), 551–555.

Leukfeldt, E. R., & Yar, M. (2016). Applying routine activity theory to cybercrime: A theoretical and empirical analysis. *Deviant Behavior, 37*(3), 263–280.

Levenson, J. S. (2018). Sex offender management policies and evidence-based recommendations for registry reform. *Current Psychiatry Reports, 20*(21), 1–7.

Levenson, J. S., & Tewksbury, R. (2009). Collateral damage: Family members of registered sex offenders. *American Journal of Criminal Justice, 34*, 54–68.

Levin, S., & Bhuiyan, J. (2021). Revealed: LAPD used 'strategic communications' firm to track 'defund the police' online. *The Guardian*. Retrieved April 4, 2024, from https://www.theguardian.com/us-news/2021/dec/15/revealed-los-angeles-police-social-media-surveillance-technology

Li, Y., Ren, L., & Luo, F. (2016). Is bad stronger than good? The impact of police-citizen encounters on public satisfaction with police. *Policing: An International Journal of Police Strategies and Management, 39*(1), 109–126.

Lieberman, J. D., Koetzle, D., & Sakiyama, M. (2013). Police departments' use of Facebook: Patterns and policy issues. *Police Quarterly, 16*(4), 438–462.

Lilly, J. R., Cullen, F. T., & Ball, R. A. (2018). *Criminological theory: Context and consequences*. SAGE Publications.

Lim, S. L., & Bentley, P. J. (2022). Opinion amplification causes extreme polarization in social networks. *Scientific Reports, 12*(1), 18131.

Lim, S. S., Chan, Y. H., Vadrevu, S., & Basnyat, I. (2013). Managing peer relationships online: Investigating the use of Facebook by juvenile delinquents and youths-at-risk. *Computers in Human Behavior, 29*(1), 8–15.

Lind, K., Kääriäinen, J., & Kuoppamäki, S. M. (2015). From problem gambling to crime? Findings from the Finnish national police information system. *Journal of Gambling Issues, 30*, 98–123.

Lipnicky, A., Kelly, P. J., & Ramaswamy, M. (2020). Facebook as a follow-up tool for women with criminal justice histories. *International Journal of Prisoner Health, 16*(2), 117–122.

Liu, L., Preotiuc-Pietro, D., Samani, Z. R., Moghaddam, M. E., & Ungar, L. (2016). Analyzing personality through social media profile picture choice. In *Proceedings of the international AAAI conference on web and social media*, Cologne, Germany (Vol. 10, No. 1, pp. 211–220).

Livingstone, R. M. (2022). Public relations and public service: Police departments on Facebook. *Policing and Society, 32*(5), 598–610.

Loeber, R., & Le Blanc, M. (1990). Toward a developmental criminology. *Crime and Justice, 12*, 375–473.

Long, A. (2023). Waynesville Police launch new mobile app. *The Mountaineer*. Retrieved January 22, 2024, from https://www.themountaineer.com/news/waynesville-police-launch-new-mobile-app/article_2a26db4a-c9d0-11ed-bf8b-1b33a9bf4ce5.html

Longshore, D., Chang, E., Hsieh, S. C., & Messina, N. (2004). Self-control and social bonds: A combined control perspective on deviance. *Crime & Delinquency, 50*(4), 542–564.

Lopes, G., Krohn, M. D., Lizotte, A. J., Schmidt, N. M., Vásquez, B. E., & Bernburg, J. G. (2012). Labeling and cumulative disadvantage: The impact of formal police intervention on life chances and crime during emerging adulthood. *Crime & Delinquency, 58*(3), 456–488.

Loughran, T. A., Paternoster, R., Chalfin, A., & Wilson, T. (2016). Can rational choice be considered a general theory of crime? Evidence from individual-level panel data. *Criminology, 54*(1), 86–112.

Lovins, B. K., Cullen, F. T., Latessa, E. J., & Jonson, C. L. (2018). Probation officer as a coach: Building a new professional identity. *Federal Probation, 82*, 13–19.

Lu, H. O., & Hsiao, K. L. (2010). The influence of extro/introversion on the intention to pay for social networking sites. *Information & Management, 47*(3), 150–157.

Lummen, D. L. M. (2023). *Is Telegram the new darknet? A comparison of traditional and emerging digital criminal marketplaces*. University of Twente. https://purl.utwente.nl/essays/94687

Lynch, M. J., & Boggess, L. N. (2016). A radical grounding for social disorganization theory: A political economic investigation of the causes of poverty, inequality, and crime in urban areas. *Radical Criminology, 6*, 11–69.

Lyons, A., McCreanor, T., Hutton, F., Goodwin, I., Barnes, H. M., Griffin, C., Kerryellen, V., O'Carroll, A. D., Niland, P., & Samu, L. (2014). *Flaunting it on Facebook: Young adults, drinking cultures and the cult of celebrity*. Massey University School of Psychology. https://mro-ns.massey.ac.nz/bitstream/handle/10179/5187/DrinkingCulturesReportWeb.pdf?sequence=3&isAllowed=y

MacDonald, H. (2015). The new nationwide crime wave. *The Wall Street Journal*. Retrieved January 24, 2024, from https://www.wsj.com/articles/the-new-nationwide-crime-wave-1432938425

MacDonald, J. M. (2002). The effectiveness of community policing in reducing urban violence. *Crime & Delinquency, 48*(4), 592–618.

Madrigal, A. C. (2011a). Maryland agency stops asking interviewees for Facebook login. *The Atlantic*. Retrieved March 28, 2024, from https://www.theatlantic.com/technology/archive/2011/02/maryland-agency-stops-asking-interviewees-for-facebook-login/71582/

Madrigal, A. C. (2011b). Seven corrections officer candidates rejected because of social media. *The Atlantic*. Retrieved March 28, 2024, from https://www.theatlantic.com/technology/archive/2011/04/7-corrections-officer-candidates-rejected-because-of-social-media/236908/

Mahdi, A., Farah, M. F., & Ramadan, Z. (2022). What to believe, whom to blame, and when to share: Exploring the fake news experience in the marketing context. *Journal of Consumer Marketing, 39*(3), 306–316.

Maheshwari, S., & Holpuch, A. (2023). Why countries are trying to ban TikTok. *The New York Times*. Retrieved September 29, 2023, from https://www.nytimes.com/article/tiktok-ban.html

Malleson, N., & Andresen, M. A. (2015). The impact of using social media data in crime rate calculations: Shifting hot spots and changing spatial patterns. *Cartography and Geographic Information Science, 42*(2), 112–121.

Manhas, R. (2013). Responding to independent juror research in the internet age: Positive rules, negative rules, and outside mechanisms. *Michigan Law Review, 112*(5), 809–832.

Manning, M., Wong, G. T., Graham, T., Ranbaduge, T., Christen, P., Taylor, K, Wortley, R., Makkai, T., & Skorich, P. (2018). Towards a 'smart' cost–benefit tool: Using machine learning to predict the costs of criminal justice policy interventions. *Crime Science, 7*(1), 12.

Manning, P. (2013). YouTube 'drug videos' and drugs education. *Drugs: Education, Prevention and Policy, 20*(2), 120–130.

Manzoni, P., & Schwarzenegger, C. (2019). The influence of earlier parental violence on juvenile delinquency: The role of social bonds, self-control, delinquent peer association and moral values as mediators. *European Journal on Criminal Policy and Research, 25*, 225–239.

Maras, M. (2017). *Cybercriminology*. Oxford University Press.

March, L. (2023). Most popular messaging apps worldwide 2023. *Similarweb*. Retrieved October 4, 2023, from https://www.similarweb.com/blog/research/market-research/worldwide-messaging-apps/

Marcum, C. D., & Higgins, G. E. (2014). Corrections and social networking websites. In C. D. Marcum & G. E. Higgins (Eds.), *Social Networking as a criminal enterprise* (pp. 221–230). CRC Press.

Marcum, C. D., Higgins, G. E., & Ricketts, M. L. (2010). Potential factors of online victimization of youth: An examination of adolescent online behaviors utilizing routine activity theory. *Deviant Behavior, 31*(5), 381–410.

Marder, N. S. (2014). Jurors and social media: Is a fair trial still possible. *SMU Law Review, 67*(3), 617–668.

Markowitz, F. E., Bellair, P. E., Liska, A. E., & Liu, J. (2001). Extending social disorganization theory: Modeling the relationships between cohesion, disorder, and fear. *Criminology, 39*(2), 293–319.

Maryland v. King, 133 S. Ct. 1958 (2013).

Maskaly, J., & Donner, C. M. (2015). A theoretical integration of social learning theory with terror management theory: Towards an explanation of police shootings of unarmed suspects. *American Journal of Criminal Justice, 40*, 205–224.

Masoed, E. S., Omar, R., Magd, A., & Elashry, R. (2021). Social media addiction among adolescents: Its relationship to sleep quality and life satisfaction. *International Journal of Research in Paediatric Nursing, 3*(1), 69–78.

Mastrofski, S. D. (2006). Community policing: A skeptical view. In D. L. Weisburd & A. A. Braga (Eds.), *Policing innovation: Contrasting perspectives* (pp. 44–76). Cambridge University Press.

Matsueda, R. L., Kreager, D. A., & Huizinga, D. (2006). Deterring delinquents: A rational choice model of theft and violence. *American Sociological Review, 71*(1), 95–122.

Mattan, A. J., Puddister, K., & Small, T. A. (2020). Tweet justice: The Canadian court's use of social media. *American Review of Canadian Studies, 50*(2), 229–244.

Matthews, R., Lovell, K., & Sorell, M. (2021). Ghost protocol–Snapchat as a method of surveillance. *Forensic Science International: Digital Investigation, 36*, 301112.

Mawby, R. C. (2010). Police corporate communications, crime reporting and the shaping of policing news. *Police & Society, 20*(1), 124–139.

Maxwell, L., Sanders, A., Skues, J., & Wise, L. (2020). A content analysis of personal safety apps: Are they keeping us safe or making us more vulnerable? *Violence Against Women, 26*(2), 233–248.

May, D. C., Lambert, E. G., Leone, M. C., Keena, L. D., & Haynes, S. H. (2020). Stress among correctional officers: An organizational justice approach. *American Journal of Criminal Justice, 45*, 454–473.

Mayes, L. (2021). Social media and community-oriented policing: Examining the organizational image construction of municipal police on Twitter and Facebook. *Police Practice and Research, 22*(1), 903–920.

Mazerolle, L., Bennett, S., Davis, J., Sargeant, E., & Manning, M. (2013). Procedural justice and police legitimacy: A systematic review of the research evidence. *Journal of Experimental Criminology, 9*(3), 245–274.

McAdams, A. (2021). WPD stops allowing comments on its Facebook page, sparking First Amendment questions. *WECT News*. Retrieved January 20, 2024, from https://www.wect.com/2021/08/11/wpd-stops-allowing-comments-its-facebook-page-sparking-first-amendment-questions/

McCarthy, O. T., Caulfield, B., & O'Mahony, M. (2016). How transport users perceive personal safety apps. *Transportation Research Part F: Traffic Psychology and Behavior, 43*, 166–182.

McCrae, R. R., & John, O. P. (1992). An introduction to the five-factor model and its applications. *Journal of Personality, 60*(2), 175–215.

McGlynn, C., & Rackley, E. (2017). Image-based sexual abuse. *Oxford Journal of Legal Studies, 37*(3), 534–561.

McMann, T. J., Calac, A., Nali, M., Cuomo, R., Maroulis, J., & Mackey, T. K. (2022). Synthetic cannabinoids in prisons: Content analysis of TikTok. *JMIR Infodemiology, 2*(1), e37632.

McPeak, A. (2019). The internet made me do it: Reconciling social media and professional norms for lawyers, judges, and law professors. *Idaho Law Review, 55*, 205–232.

McVey, J. A. (2022). Point and shoot: Police media labor and technologies of surveillance in end of watch. *Crime, Media, Culture, 18*(3), 375–392.

Meek, N. (2022). Ex-burglars reveal how they use your social media accounts to target your home. *Yahoo News*. Retrieved January 16, 2024, from https://uk.news.yahoo.com/ex-burglars-reveal-social-media-123925605.html

Meijer, A. J. (2014). New media and the coproduction of safety: An empirical analysis of Dutch practices. *The American Review of Public Administration, 44*(1), 17–34.

Meijer, A. J., & Torenvlied, R. (2016). Social media and the new organization of government communications: An empirical analysis of Twitter usage by the Dutch police. *The American Review of Public Administration, 46*(2), 143–161.

Mergel, I. (2012). The social media innovation challenge in the public sector. *Information Polity: The International Journal of Government & Democracy in the Information Age, 17*(3–4), 281–292.

Merton, R. (1938). Social structure and anomie. *American Sociological Review, 3*(5), 672–682.

Messner, S. F., Galea, S., Tardiff, K. J., Tracy, M., Bucciarelli, A., Piper, T. M., Frye, V., & Vlahov, D. (2007). Policing, drugs, and the homicide decline in New York City in the 1990s. *Criminology, 45*(2), 385–414.

Meta. (2023). What is the metaverse? *Meta*. Retrieved October 8, 2023, from https://about.meta.com/what-is-the-metaverse/

Meyer, N. H. (2014). Social media and the courts: Innovative tools or dangerous fad? A practical guide for court administrators. *International Journal of Court Administration, 6*(1), 2–28.

Miller, B., & Morris, R. G. (2016). Virtual peer effects in social learning theory. *Crime & Delinquency, 62*(12), 1543–1569.

Miller, J. (2013). Individual offending, routine activities, and activity settings: Revisiting the routine activity theory of general deviance. *Journal of Research in Crime and Delinquency, 50*(3), 390–416.

Miller, T. R. (2015). Projected outcomes of nurse-family partnership home visitation during 1996–2013, USA. *Prevention Science, 16*(6), 765–777.

Mills, L., Truelove, V., Freeman, J., & Davey, J. (2022). Police location pages and groups on Facebook: Does knowing where the police are influence perceptions of certainty and drug driving behavior? *Safety Science, 147*, 105601.

Mingus, W., & Burchfield, K. B. (2012). From prison to integration: Applying modified labeling theory to sex offenders. *Criminal Justice Studies, 25*(1), 97–109.

Mirbabaie, M., Bunker, D., Stieglitz, S., & Deubel, A. (2020). Who sets the tone? Determining the impact of convergence behavior archetypes in social media crisis communication. *Information Systems Frontiers, 22*, 339–351.

Mishna, F., Regehr, C., Lacombe-Duncan, A., Daciuk, J., Fearing, G., & Van Wert, M. (2018). Social media, cyber-aggression, and student mental health on a university campus. *Journal of Mental Health, 27*(3), 222–229.

Mitchell, M., & Zgoba, K. M. (2023). The effectiveness of sex offender registration and notification: A meta-analysis of 25 years of findings. *Journal of Experimental Criminology, 19*, 71–96.

Mitchell, N. J. (2012). Judge 2.0: A new approach to judicial ethics in the age of social media. *Utah Law Review, 4*, 2127–2158.

Möller, I., & Krahé, B. (2009). Exposure to violent video games and aggression in German adolescents: A longitudinal analysis. *Aggressive Behavior: Official Journal of the International Society for Research on Aggression, 35*(1), 75–89.

Mols, A., & Pridmore, J. (2019). When citizens are "actually doing police work:" The blurring of boundaries in WhatsApp neighbourhood crime prevention groups in The Netherlands. *Surveillance & Society, 17*(3–4), 272–287.

Monagas, E. A., & Monagas, C. E. (2015). Prosecuting threats in the age of social media. *Northern Illinois University Law Review, 36*, 57–78.

Moody-Ramirez, M., & Cole, H. (2018). Victim blaming in Twitter users' framing of Eric Garner and Michael Brown. *Journal of Black Studies, 49*(4), 383–407.

Moon, B., Hays, K., & Blurton, D. (2009). General strain theory, key strains, and deviance. *Journal of Criminal Justice, 37*(1), 98–106.

Moon, K. J., Park, K. M., & Sung, Y. (2017). Sexual abuse prevention mobile application (SAP_MobAPP) for primary school children in Korea. *Journal of Child Sexual Abuse, 26*(5), 573–589.

Morash, M., Kashy, D. A., Smith, S. W., & Cobbina, J. E. (2016). The connection of probation/parole officer actions to women offenders' recidivism. *Criminal Justice and Behavior, 43*(4), 506–524.

Morgan, M., & Shanahan, J. (2010). The state of cultivation. *Journal of Broadcasting & Electronic Media, 54*(2), 337–355.

Mosby, A. (2024). Short form video statistics of 2024 (usage & trends). *Yaguara*. Retrieved March 29, 2024, from https://www.yaguara.co/short-form-video-statistics/

Motley, R. O., Chen, Y. C., Johnson, C., & Joe, S. (2020). Exposure to community-based violence on social media among black male emerging adults involved with the criminal justice system. *Social Work Research, 44*(2), 87–97.

Moule, R. K., Jr., Pyrooz, D. C., & Decker, S. H. (2013). From 'what the F#@% is a Facebook?' to 'who doesn't use Facebook?': The role of criminal lifestyles in the adoption and use of the internet. *Social Science Research, 42*(6), 1411–1421.

Mourtgos, S. M., & Adams, I. T. (2021). COVID-19 vaccine program eliminates law enforcement workforce infections: A Bayesian structural time series analysis. *Police Practice and Research, 22*(5), 1557–1565.

Muha, T. (2022). Social media prioritizes profit over people. *The Michigan Daily*. Retrieved December 30, 2023, from https://www.michigandaily.com/opinion/social-media-prioritizes-profit-over-people/

Müller, K., & Schwarz, C. (2021). Fanning the flames of hate: Social media and hate crime. *Journal of the European Economic Association, 19*(4), 2131–2167.

Murphy, J. P., & Fontecilla, A. (2012). Social media evidence in government investigations and criminal proceedings: A frontier of new legal issues. *Richmond Journal of Law & Technology, 19*(3), 1–30.

Murphy, K. (2009). Public satisfaction with police: The importance of procedural justice and police performance in police-citizen encounters. *The Australian and New Zealand Journal of Criminology, 42*(2), 159–178.

Murray, T. (2022). Depp v Heard: How courtroom live-streaming turned an ugly battle between exes into a circus. *Independent*. Retrieved August 30, 2023, from https://www.independent.co.uk/arts-entertainment/films/features/johnny-depp-amber-heard-trial-livestream-b2072870.html

Nagin, D. S. (2013). Deterrence in the twenty-first century. *Crime and Justice, 42*(1), 199–263.

Nance, A. R. (2015). Social media selection: How jury consultants can use social media to build a more favorable jury. *Law and Psychology Review, 39*, 267–285.

Napier, S., Teunissen, C., & Boxall, H. (2021). How do child sexual abuse live streaming offenders access victims? *Trends and Issues in Crime and Criminal Justice, 642*, 1–18.

Näsi, M., Räsänen, P., Kaakinen, M., Keipi, T., & Oksanen, A. (2017). Do routine activities help predict young adults' online harassment: A multi-nation study. *Criminology & Criminal Justice, 17*(4), 418–432.

Näsi, M., Tanskanen, M., Kivivuori, J., Haara, P., & Reunanen, E. (2021). Crime news consumption and fear of violence: The role of traditional media, social media, and alternative information sources. *Crime & Delinquency, 67*(4), 574–600.

Natarajan, M. (2016). Police response to domestic violence: A case study of TecSOS mobile phone use in the London Metropolitan Police Service. *Policing: A Journal of Policy and Practice, 10*(4), 378–390.

National Center for State Courts. (2023). Courts and social media accounts. *NCSC*. Retrieved August 24, 2023, from https://www.ncsc.org/consulting-and-research/areas-of-expertise/communications,-civics-and-disinformation/home/overview

National Policing Institute. (2020). *Police body cameras: What have we learned over ten years of deployment?* Retrieved March 8, 2024, from https://www.policinginstitute.org/publication/police-body-cameras-what-have-we-learned-over-ten-years-of-deployment

Neubauer, D. W., & Fradella, H. F. (2014). *America's courts: And the criminal justice system* (11th ed.). Wadsworth/Cengage Learning.

Neuilly, M. A., Zgoba, K. M., Tita, G. E., & Lee, S. S. (2011). Predicting recidivism in homicide offenders using classification tree analysis. *Homicide Studies, 15*(2), 154–176.

Newman, O. (1972). *Defensible space: People and design in the violent city*. Architecture Press.

Ngai, E. W. T., Tao, S. S. C., & Moon, K. K. L. (2015). Social media research: Theories, constructs, and conceptual frameworks. *International Journal of Information Management, 35*, 33–44.

Nix, J., Wolfe, S. E., & Campbell, B. A. (2018). Command-level police officers' perceptions of the "war on cops" and de-policing. *Justice Quarterly, 35*(1), 33–54.

Noheatstroke. (2024). Heatstroke deaths of children in vehicles. *Noheatstroke*. Retrieved January 15, 2024, from https://www.noheatstroke.org/

North Carolina Department of Public Safety. (2013). Social media policy. *National Institute of Corrections*. Retrieved March 27, 2024, from https://nicic.gov/weblink/north-carolina-department-public-safety-social-media-policy-2013

Nouri, S., & Kochel, T. R. (2022). Residents' perceptions of policing and safety during the COVID-19 pandemic. *Policing: An International Journal, 45*(1), 139–153.
Nowacki, J. S., & Willits, D. (2018). Adoption of body cameras by United States police agencies: An organizational analysis. *Policing & Society: An International Journal of Research and Policy, 28*(7), 841–853.
Nuzum, K. C. (2019). Letting Google into the jury room: A proposed study on the effect of abolishing the juror research admonition. *Jurimetrics, 60*, 105–123.
O'Brien, D. T., Farrell, C., & Welsh, B. C. (2019). Looking through broken windows: The impact of neighborhood disorder on aggression and fear of crime is an artifact of research design. *Annual Review of Criminology, 2*, 53–71.
O'Connor, C. D. (2017). The police on Twitter: Image management, community building, and implications for policing in Canada. *Policing and Society, 27*(8), 899–912.
O'Connor, C. D., & Zaidi, H. (2021). Communicating with purpose: Image work, social media, and policing. *The Police Journal, 94*(3), 333–352.
Oglesby-Neal, A., Tiry, E., & Kim, K. (2019). Public perceptions of police on social media. *Urban Institute, 12*, 1–12.
Oh, J., & Ki, E. J. (2019). Factors affecting social presence and word-of-mouth in corporate social responsibility communication: Tone of voice, message framing, and online medium type. *Public Relations Review, 45*(2), 319–331.
Oliver, D. A. (2013). *No mopes allowed: A small-town police chief rants and babbles about hugs and high fives, meth busts, internet celebrity, and other adventures*. Gray & Company Publishers.
Oliver, M. B. (1994). Portrayals of crime, race, and aggression in "reality-based" police shows: A content analysis. *Journal of Broadcasting & Electronic Media, 38*(2), 179–192.
Oliver, W. M. (2000). The third generation of community policing: Moving through innovation, diffusion, and institutionalization. *Police Quarterly, 3*(4), 367–388.
Oliver, W. M. (2008). *Community-oriented policing: A systemic approach to policing* (4th ed.). Prentice Hall.
Olston, C., & Najork, M. (2010). Web crawling. *Foundations and Trends in Information Retrieval, 4*(3), 175–246.
Özgüven, N., & Mucan, B. (2013). The relationship between personality traits and social media use. *Social Behavior and Personality: An International Journal, 41*(3), 517–528.
Packingham v. North Carolina, 582 U.S. 98 (2017).
Palmer, C., & Roebuck, J. (2023). Firings overturned for 5 Philly officers fired over social media posts. *The Philadelphia Inquirer*. Retrieved September 13, 2023, from https://www.police1.com/officer-misconduct-internal-affairs/articles/firings-overturned-for-5-philly-officers-fired-over-social-media-posts-qPU24S5wa3cc0eCd/
Parascandola, R. (2011). NYPD forms new social media unit to mine Facebook and Twitter for mayhem. *New York Daily News*. Retrieved November 4, 2023, from https://www.nydailynews.com/2011/08/10/nypd-forms-new-social-media-unit-to-mine-facebook-and-twitter-for-mayhem/
Patel, P., Kannoorpatti, K., Shanmugam, B., Azam, S., & Yeo, K. C. (2017). A theoretical review of social media usage by cyber-criminals. In *2017 International conference on computer communication and informatics* (ICCCI) (pp. 1–6). Institute of Electrical and Electronic Engineering.
Paternoster, R. (1987). The deterrent effect of the perceived certainty and severity of punishment: A review of the evidence and issues. *Justice Quarterly, 4*(2), 173–217.
Paternoster, R. (2010). How much do we really know about criminal deterrence? *Journal of Criminal Law and Criminology, 100*(3), 765–824.
Paternoster, R., & Iovanni, L. (1989). The labeling perspective and delinquency: An elaboration of the theory and an assessment of the evidence. *Justice Quarterly, 6*(3), 359–394.

Paternoster, R., Jaynes, C. M., & Wilson, T. (2017). Rational choice theory and interest in the "fortune of others." *Journal of Research in Crime and Delinquency, 54*(6), 847–868.

Paternoster, R., & Mazerolle, P. (1994). General strain theory and delinquency: A replication and extension. *Journal of Research in Crime and Delinquency, 31*(3), 235–263.

Pattavina, A., Byrne, J. M., & Garcia, L. (2006). An examination of citizen involvement in crime prevention in high-risk versus low-to moderate-risk neighborhoods. *Crime & Delinquency, 52*(2), 203–231.

Pegoraro, R. (2022). What is 5G, and does it actually make a difference? *The New York Times*. Retrieved October 8, 2023, from https://www.nytimes.com/wirecutter/guides/what-is-5g/

Pérez, D. M., Jennings, W. G., & Gover, A. R. (2008). Specifying general strain theory: An ethnically relevant approach. *Deviant Behavior, 29*(6), 544–578.

Peters, S. E., & Ojedokun, U. A. (2019). Social media utilization for policing and crime prevention in Lagos, Nigeria. *Journal of Social, Behavioral, and Health Sciences, 13*(1), 166–181.

Petersilia, J., & Reitz, K. R. (2012). Introduction sentencing and corrections: Overlapping and inseparable subjects. In J. Petersilia & K. R. Reitz (Eds.), *The Oxford handbook of sentencing and corrections* (pp. 3–20). Oxford University Press.

Petrashek, N. (2010). The fourth amendment and the brave new world of online social networking. *Marquette Law Review, 93*(4), 1494–1528.

Petty, R. E., & Cacioppo, J. T. (1986). The elaboration likelihood model of persuasion. In *Communication and persuasion* (pp. 1–24). Springer.

Phorn, B. (2018). Economist who won Nobel Prize thought early morning call was a telemarketer, let it go to voicemail – twice! *ABC News*. Retrieved December 30, 2023, from https://abcnews.go.com/US/economist-won-nobel-prize-thought-early-morning-call/story?id=58358633

Piquero, A. R., Farrington, D. P., Welsh, B. C., Tremblay, R., & Jennings, W. G. (2009). Effects of early family/parent training programs on antisocial behavior and delinquency. *Journal of Experimental Criminology, 5*, 83–120.

Piquero, A. R., Jennings, W. G., Farrington, D. P., Diamond, B., & Gonzalez, J. M. R. (2016). A meta-analysis update on the effectiveness of early self-control improvement programs to improve self-control and reduce delinquency. *Journal of Experimental Criminology, 12*, 249–264.

Piquero, A. R., Riddell, J. R., Bishopp, S. A., Narvey, C., Reid, J. A., & Piquero, N. L. (2020). Staying home, staying safe? A short-term analysis of COVID-19 on Dallas domestic violence. *American Journal of Criminal Justice, 45*(4), 601–635.

Piquero, N., & Sealock, M. D. (2010). Race, crime, and general strain theory. *Youth Violence and Juvenile Justice, 8*(3), 170–186.

Pollack, A. (2022). Failing to "follow" the Sixth Amendment threat posed by juror social media access. *Maryland Law Review Online, 81*, 46–70.

Pollock, J. M. (2019). *Ethical dilemmas and decisions in criminal justice* (9th ed.). Cengage Learning.

Popp, A. M., & Peguero, A. A. (2012). Social bonds and the role of school-based victimization. *Journal of Interpersonal Violence, 27*(17), 3366–3388.

Potrel, V. (2022). Five insights into the popularity of short-form video content. *Forbes*. Retrieved March 29, 2024, from https://www.forbes.com/sites/forbescommunicationscouncil/2022/09/06/five-insights-into-the-popularity-of-short-form-video-content/

Potter, S. J., Moschella, E. A., Smith, D., & Draper, N. (2020). Exploring the usage of a violence prevention and response app among community college students. *Health Education & Behavior, 47*(1s), 44S–53S.

Powell, A., Overington, C., & Hamilton, G. (2018). Following# JillMeagher: Collective meaning-making in response to crime events via social media. *Crime, Media, Culture, 14*(3), 409–428.

Prabowo, T. L., & Rusfian, E. Z. (2019). Efforts to build the legitimacy and reputation of institutions through social media (study of Instagram police public relations division). *International Journal of Scientific and Technology Research, 8*(9), 1331–1338.

Pratt, T. C. (2008). Rational choice theory, crime control policy, and criminological relevance. *Criminology and Public Policy, 7*(1), 43–52.

Pratt, T. C., Cullen, F. T., Blevins, K. R., Daigle, L. E., & Madensen, T. D. (2017). The empirical status of deterrence theory: A meta-analysis. In F. Cullen, J. Wright, & K. Blevins (Eds.), *Taking stock: The status of criminological theory* (pp. 367–395). Routledge.

Pratt, T. C., Cullen, F. T., Sellers, C. S., Thomas Winfree Jr, L., Madensen, T. D., Daigle, L. E., Fearn, N. E., & Gau, J. M. (2010). The empirical status of social learning theory: A meta-analysis. *Justice Quarterly, 27*(6), 765–802.

Pratt, T. C., Holtfreter, K., & Reisig, M. D. (2010). Routine online activity and internet fraud targeting: Extending the generality of routine activity theory. *Journal of Research in Crime and Delinquency, 47*(3), 267–296.

Pratt, T. C., Turanovic, J. J., Fox, K. A., & Wright, K. A. (2014). Self-control and victimization: A meta-analysis. *Criminology, 52*(1), 87–116.

Prescott, J. J., & Rockoff, J. E. (2011). Do sex offender registration and notification laws affect criminal behavior? *The Journal of Law and Economics, 54*(1), 161–206.

President's Task Force on 21st Century Policing. (2015). *Final report of the president's task force on 21st century policing*. Office of Community Oriented Policing Services. Retrieved October 24, 2023, from https://cops.usdoj.gov/pdf/taskforce/taskforce_finalreport.pdf

Prichard, J., Watters, P., Krone, T., Spiranovic, C., & Cockburn, H. (2015). Social media sentiment analysis: A new empirical tool for assessing public opinion on crime? *Current Issues in Criminal Justice, 27*(2), 217–236.

Pridmore, J., Mols, A., Wang, Y., & Holleman, F. (2019). Keeping an eye on the neighbors: Police, citizens, and communication within mobile neighborhood crime prevention groups. *The Police Journal, 92*(2), 97–120.

Prieto Curiel, R., Cresci, S., Muntean, C. I., & Bishop, S. R. (2020). Crime and its fear in social media. *Palgrave Communications, 6*(1), 1–12.

Pringle, E. (2024). MrBeast says it's 'painful' watching wannabe YouTube influencers quit school and jobs for a pipe dream: 'For every person like me that makes it, thousands don't.' *Fortune*. Retrieved April 5, 2024, from https://fortune.com/2024/03/15/youtube-biggest-star-mrbeast-jimmy-donaldson-painful-watch-would-be-influencers-quit-school-jobs-pipe-dream/

Procter, R., Crump, J., Karstedt, S., Voss, A., & Cantijoch, M. (2013). Reading the riots: What were the police doing on Twitter? *Policing and Society, 23*(4), 413–436.

Puddister, K., & Small, T. A. (2019). Navigating the principle of open court in the digital age: The more things change, the more they stay the same. *Canadian Public Administration, 62*(2), 202–224.

Pusch, N., & Holtfreter, K. (2021). Sex-based differences in criminal victimization of adolescents: A meta-analysis. *Journal of Youth and Adolescence, 50*, 4–28.

Ralph, L., Jones, M., Rowe, M., & Millie, A. (2022). Maintaining police-citizen relations on social media during the COVID-19 pandemic. *Policing and Society, 32*(6), 764–777.

Randa, R., & Reyns, B. W. (2020). The physical and emotional toll of identity theft victimization: A situational and demographic analysis of the national crime victimization survey. *Deviant Behavior, 41*(10), 1290–1304.

Razalan, A. (2022). Beyond words: Threat messages of Filipinos in Facebook messenger. *Psychology and Education: A Multidisciplinary Journal, 6*(6), 558–565.

Reed, B. (2021). Judges weigh social media posts in criminal sentences for U.S. Capitol attack. *The Guardian*. Retrieved November 8, 2023, from https://www.theguardian.com/us-news/2021/dec/13/judges-weigh-social-media-posts-criminal-sentences-us-capitol-attack

Reid, K., & Niebuhr, D. (2023). "Prison TikTok:" Incarcerated life shared on social media. *Journal of Qualitative Criminal Justice and Criminology, 12*(2), 158–177.

Relia, K., Li, Z., Cook, S. H., & Chunara, R. (2019). Race, ethnicity and national origin-based discrimination in social media and hate crimes across 100 US cities. In *Proceedings of the international AAAI conference on web and social media*, Münich, Germany (Vol. 13, pp. 417–427).

Ren, L., Cao, L., Lovrich, N., & Gaffney, M. (2005). Linking confidence in the police with the performance of the police: Community policing can make a difference. *Journal of Criminal Justice, 33*(1), 55–66.

Ren, L., Zhao, J. S., & He, N. P. (2019). Broken windows theory and citizen engagement in crime prevention. *Justice Quarterly, 36*(1), 1–30.

Renaud, J. (2019). Grading the parole release systems of all 50 states. *Prison Policy Initiative*. Retrieved March 14, 2024, from https://www.prisonpolicy.org/reports/grading_parole.html

Reppetto, T. A. (1976). Crime prevention and the displacement phenomenon. *Crime & Delinquency, 22*(2), 166–177.

Restivo, E., & Lanier, M. M. (2015). Measuring the contextual effects and mitigating factors of labeling theory. *Justice Quarterly, 32*(1), 116–141.

Revier, K. (2021). The 'worst of the worst': Punitive justice frames in criminal sentencing clips on YouTube. *Contemporary Justice Review, 24*(4), 436–456.

Revital, S., & Haviv, N. (2023). Juvenile delinquency and COVID-19: The effect of social distancing restrictions on juvenile crime rates in Israel. *Journal of Experimental Criminology, 19*, 785–808.

Reynald, D. M. (2019). Guardianship in the digital age. *Criminal Justice Review, 44*(1), 11–24.

Reyns, B. W., Henson, B., & Fisher, B. S. (2011). Being pursued online: Applying cyberlifestyle–routine activities theory to cyberstalking victimization. *Criminal Justice and Behavior, 38*(11), 1149–1169.

Reznik, M. (2012). Identity theft on social networking sites: Developing issues of internet impersonation. *Touro Law Review, 29*(2), 455–484.

Rhode, D. L. (2019). #Metoo: Why now? What next? *Duke Law Journal, 69*(2), 377–428.

Ricciardelli, R., & Adorjan, M. (2021). Correctional officer training: Opportunities and challenges of the AMStregnth program in Canada. *Journal of Forensic Psychology Research and Practice, 21*(1), 40–60.

Richmond, T. (2023). Explainer: University of Wisconsin latest to ban TikTok. *AP*. Retrieved September 29, 2023, from https://apnews.com/article/technology-politics-united-states-government-china-privacy-26b0ee0d4c8421fa7f58b06f76651dc1

Ridings, C. M., Gefen, D., & Arinze, B. (2002). Some antecedents and effects of trust in virtual communities. *The Journal of Strategic Information Systems, 11*(3–4), 271–295.

Rɪos, V., & Ferguson, C. J. (2020). News media coverage of crime and violent drug crime: A case for cause or catalyst? *Justice Quarterly, 37*(6), 1012–1039.

Robbers, M. L. (2008). Blinded by science: The social construction of reality in forensic television shows and its effect on criminal jury trials. *Criminal Justice Policy Review, 19*(1), 84–102.

Roberts, B. W., Lejuez, C., Krueger, R. F., Richards, J. M., & Hill, P. L. (2014). What is conscientiousness and how can it be assessed? *Developmental Psychology, 50*(5), 1315–1330.

Roberts, J. V., & Hastings, R. (2007). Public opinion and crime prevention: A review of international findings. *IPC Review, 1*(1), 193–218.

Robinson, E. P. (2011). Jury instructions for the modern age: 50-state survey of jury instructions on internet and social media. *Reynolds Courts & Media Law Journal, 1*(3), 307–422.

Rocque, M., Bierie, D. M., Posick, C., & MacKenzie, D. L. (2013). Unraveling change: Social bonds and recidivism among released offenders. *Victims & Offenders, 8*(2), 209–230.

Roesner, F., Gill, B. T., & Kohno, T. (2014). Sex, lies, or kittens? Investigating the use of Snapchat's self-destructing messages. In N. Christin & R. Safavi-Naini (Eds.), *Financial cryptography and data security. FC 2014. Lecture notes in computer science* (Vol. 8437). Springer.

Rogers, E. M. (2003). *Diffusion of innovations*. Simon & Schuster, Inc.

Rolando, S., Arrighetti, G., Fornero, E., Farucci, O., & Beccaria, F. (2023). Telegram as a space for peer-led harm reduction communities and netreach interventions. *Contemporary Drug Problems, 50*(2), 190–201.

Romer, D., Jamieson, K. H., & Aday, S. (2003). Television news and the cultivation of fear of crime. *Journal of Communication, 53*(1), 88–104.

Rosen, P. A., & Kluemper, D. H. (2008). The impact of the big five personality traits on the acceptance of social networking website. *AMCIS 2008 Proceedings, 274*, 1–10.

Rosenfeld, R. (2015). Was there a "Ferguson effect" on crime in St. Louis? *The Sentencing Project*. Retrieved January 24, 2024, from https://www.sentencingproject.org/wp-content/uploads/2015/09/Ferguson-Effect.pdf

Rosenfeld, R., Fornango, R., & Rengifo, A. F. (2007). The impact of order-maintenance policing on New York City homicide and robbery rates: 1988–2001. *Criminology, 45*(2), 355–384.

Rowan, M. (2017). The illusion of broken windows theory: An ethnographic engagement with the theory that was not there. *William & Mary Policy Review, 9*, 1–49.

Rozzelle, J. (2022). These are the 10 most populated states in the U.S. *US News*. Retrieved March 25, 2024, from https://www.usnews.com/news/best-states/slideshows/most-populated-states-in-the-us

Ruddell, R., & Jones, N. (2013). Social media and policing: Matching the message to the audience. *Safer Communities, 12*(2), 64–71.

Russo, J. (2014). The use of social media in community corrections: An APAA issue paper. *Perspectives, 38*(4), 22–26.

Sachdeva, N., & Kumaraguru, P. (2017). Call for service: Characterizing and modeling police response to serviceable requests on Facebook. In *Proceedings of the 2017 ACM conference on computer supported cooperative work and social computing*, Portland, OR (pp. 336–352).

Salahdine, F., & Kaabouch, N. (2019). Social engineering attacks: A survey. *Future Internet, 11*(4), 89.

Salter, M. (2016). *Crime, justice, and social media*. Routledge.

Sampson, R. J. (2004). Neighbourhood and community. *New Economy, 11*(2), 106–113.

Sampson, R. J., & Groves, W. B. (1989). Community structure and crime: Testing social-disorganization theory. *American Journal of Sociology, 94*, 774–802.

Sampson, R. J., & Laub, J. H. (2005). A life-course view of the development of crime. *The Annals of the American Academy of Political and Social Science, 602*(1), 12–45.

Sampson, R. J., & Laub, J. H. (2017). A life-course view of the development of crime. In P. Mazerolle (Ed.), *Developmental and life-course criminological theories* (pp. 329–362). Routledge.

Sangal, A., Vogt, A., Vales, L., Hammond, E., Powell, T. B., & Vera, A. (2023). Michigan state university shooting leaves 3 dead, 5 injured. *CNN*. Retrieved February 24, 2023, from https://www.cnn.com/us/live-news/michigan-state-university-shooting-updates-2-14-23/index.html

Sawyer, W., & Wagner, P. (2023). Mass incarceration: The whole pie 2023. *Prison Policy Initiative*. Retrieved December 28, 2023, from https://www.prisonpolicy.org/reports/pie2023.html

Sawyer, W., & Wagner, P. (2024). Mass incarceration: The whole pie 2024. *Prison Policy Initiative*. Retrieved March 17, 2024, from https://www.prisonpolicy.org/reports/pie2024.html

Scarduzio, J. A., Malvini Redden, S., Fletcher, J., & Wilson, K. (2019). "There is a fine line between one's personal life and professional one": Handling employee sexual harassment on Facebook from the victim's perspective. *Qualitative Research Reports in Communication, 20*(1), 42–49.

Scharrer, E. (2012). More than "just the facts?" Portrayals of masculinity in police and detective programs over time. *The Howard Journal of Communications, 23*(1), 88–109.

Schaufeli, W. B., & Peeters, M. C. (2000). Job stress and burnout among correctional officers: A literature review. *International Journal of Stress Management, 7*(1), 19–48.

Schenwar, M., Macare, J., & Price, A. (2016). *Who do you serve, who do you protect? Police violence and resistance in the United States*. Haymarket Books.

Schlosser, J. A., & Feldman, L. R. (2022). Doing time online: Prison TikTok as social reclamation. *Incarceration, 3*(2), 1–17.

Schnebly, S. M. (2008). The influence of community-oriented policing on crime-reporting behavior. *Justice Quarterly, 25*(2), 223–251.

Schneider, C. J. (2016a). *Policing and social media: Social control in an era of new media*. Lexington Books.

Schneider, C. J. (2016b). Police presentational strategies on Twitter in Canada. *Policing and Society, 26*(2), 129–147.

Schneider, C. J. (2017). Body worn cameras and police image work: News media coverage of the Rialto Police Department's body worn camera experiment. *Crime, Media, Culture, 14*(3), 449–466.

Schneider, C. J. (2018). An exploratory study of public perceptions of police conduct depicted in body worn camera footage on YouTube. *Annual Review of Interdisciplinary Justice Research, 7*, 118–148.

Schneider, C. J., & Trottier, D. (2012). The 2011 Vancouver riot and the role of Facebook in crowd-sourced policing. BC studies: *The British Columbian Quarterly, 175*, 57–72.

Schoenbaum, H. (2023). University of North Carolina shooting suspect found unfit for trial, sent to mental health facility. *Associated Press*. Retrieved April 2, 2024, from https://apnews.com/article/university-of-north-carolina-shooting-suspect-33de740be6908ae40efd0712e0710cc3

Schoepfer, A., & Piquero, A. R. (2006). Self-control, moral beliefs, and criminal activity. *Deviant Behavior, 27*(1), 51–71.

Schrading, N., Alm, C. O., Ptucha, R., & Homan, C. (2015). An analysis of domestic abuse discourse on reddit. In *Proceedings of the 2015 conference on empirical methods in natural language processing*, Lisbon, Portugal (pp. 2577–2583).

Schreck, C. J. (1999). Criminal victimization and low self-control: An extension and test of a general theory of crime. *Justice Quarterly, 16*(3), 633–654.

Schreurs, W., Franjkić, N., Kerstholt, J. H., De Vries, P. W., & Giebels, E. (2020). Why do citizens become a member of an online neighborhood watch? A case study in The Netherlands. *Police Practice and Research, 21*(6), 687–701.

Scigliano, E. (2021). Zoom court is changing how justice is served. *The Atlantic*. Retrieved November 7, 2023, from https://www.theatlantic.com/magazine/archive/2021/05/can-justice-be-served-on-zoom/618392/

Seidman, G. (2013). Self-presentation and belonging on Facebook: How personality influences social media use and motivations. *Personality and Individual Differences, 54*(3), 402–407.

Semenzin, S., & Bainotti, L. (2020). The use of Telegram for non-consensual dissemination of intimate images: Gendered affordances and the construction of masculinities. *Social Media + Society, 6*(4), 1–12.

Sever, B., Elg, E., & Ellis, S. (2021). Law enforcement and the depiction of minorities and women on social media: A review of municipal police department Facebook pictures. *Race and Justice, 11*(2), 127–159.

Sevier, J. (2019). Legitimizing character evidence. *Emory Law Journal, 68*(3), 441–508.

Shahria, M. M., Uddin, M. N., & Ahmed, M. (2020). Social media security: Identity theft prevention. *International Journal of Innovative Science and Research Technology, 5*(8), 1656–1662.

Shami, S., & Ashfaq, A. (2018). Strategic political communication, public relations, reputation management and relationship cultivation through social media. *Journal of the Research Society of Pakistan, 55*(2), 139–154.

Shariati, A., & Guerette, R. T. (2017). Situational crime prevention. In B. Teasdale & M. Bradley (Eds.), *Preventing crime and violence: Advances in prevention science* (pp. 261–268). Springer.

Sharp, R. (2023). UNC shooting suspect's social media complaints about murdered faculty member revealed. *Independent*. Retrieved April 2, 2024, from https://www.the-independent.com/news/world/americas/crime/unc-shooter-tailei-qi-twitter-posts-b2401256.html

Shaw, C. R., & McKay, H. D. (1942). *Juvenile delinquency and urban areas*. University of Chicago Press.

Shejuti, K. K. (2023). Role of social media on deviance and crime: A study on content creators of TikTok. *American Journal of Multidisciplinary Research and Innovation, 2*(2), 130–137.

Shek, D. T. L., Ng, C. S. M., & Tsui, P. F. (2010). Qualitative evaluation of the Project P.A.T.H.S.: Findings based on focus groups. *International Journal on Disability and Human Development, 9*(4), 307–313.

Sheley, E. L. (2017). Victim impact statements and expressive punishment in the age of social media. *Wake Forest Law Review, 52*, 157–192.

Shiue, Y. C., Chiu, C. M., & Chang, C. C. (2010). Exploring and mitigating social loafing in online communities. *Computers in Human Behavior, 26*(4), 768–777.

Shmueli, G. (2010). To explain or to predict? *Statistical Science, 25*(3), 289–310.

Shortt, A. L., Barrett, P. M., & Fox, T. L. (2001). Evaluating the FRIENDS program: A cognitive-behavioral group treatment for anxious children and their parents. *Journal of Clinical Child Psychology, 30*(4), 525–535.

Shrum, L. J. (2009). Media consumption and perceptions of social reality: Effects and underlying processes. In *Media effects* (pp. 66–89). Routledge.

Shulman, E. P., Steinberg, L. D., & Piquero, A. R. (2013). The age-crime curve in adolescence and early adulthood is not due to age differences in economic status. *Journal of Youth and Adolescence, 42*(6), 848–860.

Siegel, L. J., & Worrall, J. L. (2016). *Introduction to criminal justice* (15th ed.). Cengage Learning.

Silva, L., Mondal, M., Correa, D., Benevenuto, F., & Weber, I. (2016). Analyzing the targets of hate in online social media. *Proceedings of the International AAAI Conference on Web and Social Media, 10*(1), 687–690.

Similarweb. (2023). Top websites ranking: Most visited websites in August 2023. *Similarweb*. Retrieved September 27, 2023, from https://www.similarweb.com/top-websites/

Simpler, M. F., III. (2012). The unjust web we weave: The evolution of social media and its psychological impact on juror impartiality and fair trials. *Law & Psychology Review, 36*, 275–296.

Simpson, B. (2014). Tracking children, constructing fear: GPS and the manufacture of family safety. *Information & Communications Technology Law, 23*(3), 273–285.

Simpson, T. (2019). North Carolina prison guards under investigation after 'feeling cute' social media challenge. *6ABC*. Retrieved March 28, 2024, from https://6abc.com/prison-guards-social-media-challenge-violence-raleigh-police/5278070/

Sivagurunathan, M., Walton, D. M., Packham, T., Booth, R., & MacDermid, J. (2021). "Punched in the balls:" Male intimate partner violence disclosures and replies on Reddit. *American Journal of Men's Health, 15*(4), 1–14.

Sjöberg, J., Cassinger, C., & Rampazzo Gambarato, R. (2023). Communicating a sense of safety: The public experience of Swedish Police Instagram communication. *Journal of Communication Management,* 1–19. Online First. https://doi.org/10.1108/JCOM-03-2023-0033

Skinner, B. F. (1965). *Science and human behavior*. Simon & Schuster Inc.

Skogan, W. G. (2008). Broken windows: Why-and how-we should take them seriously. *Criminology and Public Policy, 7*(2), 195–202.

Skogan, W. G., & Hartnett, S. M. (2005). The diffusion of information technology in policing. *Police Practice and Research, 6*(5), 401–417.

Small, T. A., & Puddister, K. (2020). Play-by-play justice: Tweeting criminal trials in the digital age. *Canadian Journal of Law and Society, 35*(1), 1–22.

Smith, A. (2023). 23 Essential Twitter statistics to guide your strategy in 2023. *Sprout Social*. Retrieved October 4, 2023, from https://sproutsocial.com/insights/twitter-statistics/

Smith, M. J., Clarke, R. V., & Pease, K. (2002). Anticipatory benefits in crime prevention. *Crime Prevention Studies, 13*, 71–88.

Smith, N. (2020). Social media, rural communities, and crime prevention. In A. Harkness (Ed.), *Rural crime prevention: Theory, tactics and techniques* (pp. 73–83). Routledge.

Smith, S., Gomez Auyong, Z. E., & Ferguson, C. (2019). Social learning, social disorganization, and psychological risk factors for criminal gangs in a British youth context. *Deviant Behavior, 40*(6), 722–731.

Smylie, C., Duxbury, L., & Bennell, C. (2023). Community policing during the pandemic. *Police Practice and Research*, 1–14. Online First. https://doi.org/10.1080/15614263.2023.2222869

Sobkin, V. S., & Fedotova, A. V. (2021). Adolescents on social media: Aggression and cyberbullying. *Psychology in Russia, 14*(4), 186–201.

Soh, P. C. H., Chew, K. W., Koay, K. Y., & Ang, P. H. (2018). Parents vs peers' influence on teenagers' Internet addiction and risky online activities. *Telematics and Informatics, 35*(1), 225–236.

Soomro, T. R., & Hussain, M. (2019). Social media-related cybercrimes and techniques for their prevention. *Applied Computer Systems, 24*(1), 9–17.

Sozer, M. A., & Merlo, A. V. (2013). The impact of community policing on crime raters: Does the effect of community policing differ in large and small law enforcement agencies? *Police Practice & Research, 14*(6), 506–521.

Sparrow, M. K., Moore, M. H., & Kennedy, D. M. (1992). *Beyond 911: A new era for policing*. Basic Books Inc.

Spizman, R. J., & Miller, M. K. (2013). Plugged-in policing: Student perceptions of law enforcement's use of social media. *Applied Psychology in Criminal Justice, 9*(2), 100–123.
St Eve, A. J., Burns, C. P., & Zuckerman, M. A. (2014). More from the #jury box: The latest on juries and social media. *Duke Law & Technology Review, 1*, 64–91.
State v. Corwin, 295 S.W.3d 572 (Mo. Ct. App. 2009).
Statista. (2022). Distribution of TikTok users in the United States in 2022, by age group. *Statista*. Retrieved September 29, 2023, from https://www.statista.com/statistics/1095186/tiktok-us-users-age/
Statista. (2023a). Volume of data/information created, captured, copied, and consumed worldwide from 2010 to 2020, with forecasts from 2021 to 2025. *Statista*. Retrieved October 25, 2023, from https://www.statista.com/statistics/871513/worldwide-data-created/
Statista. (2023b). Number of social media users worldwide from 2017 to 2027. *Statista*. Retrieved August 26, 2023, from https://www.statista.com/statistics/278414/number-of-worldwide-social-network-users/
Statista. (2023c). Daily time spent on social networking by internet users worldwide from 2012 to 2023. *Statista*. Retrieved August 26, 2023, from https://www.statista.com/statistics/433871/daily-social-media-usage-worldwide/
Statista. (2023d). Most popular social networks worldwide as of January 2023, ranked by number of monthly active users. *Statista*. Retrieved August 26, 2023, from https://www.statista.com/statistics/272014/global-social-networks-ranked-by-number-of-users/
Statista. (2023e). Number of monthly active Facebook users worldwide as of 2nd quarter 2023. *Statista*. Retrieved September 27, 2023, from https://www.statista.com/statistics/264810/number-of-monthly-active-facebook-users-worldwide/
Statista. (2023f). Share of Facebook users in the United States as of August 2023, by age group. *Statista*. Retrieved September 27, 2023, from https://www.statista.com/statistics/187549/facebook-distribution-of-users-age-group-usa/
Statista. (2023g). YouTube: Statistics & facts. *Statista*. Retrieved September 27, 2023, from https://www.statista.com/topics/2019/youtube/#topicOverview
Statista. (2023h). Worldwide visits to YouTube.com from June to November 2022, by device. *Statista*. Retrieved September 27, 2023, from https://www.statista.com/statistics/1256720/youtubecom-monthly-visits-by-device/
Statista. (2023i). WhatsApp: Statistics & facts. *Statista*. Retrieved September 27, 2023, from https://www.statista.com/topics/2018/whatsapp/#topicOverview
Statista. (2023j). Share of adults in the United States who have a WhatsApp account as of May 2022, by age group. *Statista*. Retrieved September 27, 2023, from https://www.statista.com/statistics/814649/whatsapp-users-in-the-united-states-by-age/
Statista. (2023k). Distribution of Instagram users worldwide as of January 2023, by age group. *Statista*. Retrieved September 29, 2023, from https://www.statista.com/statistics/325587/instagram-global-age-group/
Statista. (2023l). Countries with the largest TikTok audience as of July 2023. *Statista*. Retrieved September 29, 2023, from https://www.statista.com/statistics/1299807/number-of-monthly-unique-tiktok-users/
Statista. (2023m). Distribution of TikTok creators worldwide as of September 2022, by age group. *Statista*. Retrieved September 29, 2023, from https://www.statista.com/statistics/1257721/tiktok-creators-by-age-worldwide/
Statista. (2023n). Share of Facebook Messenger users in the United States as of August 2023, by age group. *Statista*. Retrieved October 4, 2023, from https://www.statista.com/statistics/951142/facebook-messenger-user-share-in-usa-age/
Statista. (2023o). Most popular channel categories on Telegram in 2023. *Statista*. Retrieved October 4, 2023, from https://www.statista.com/statistics/1252771/leading-telegram-channels-by-category/

Statista. (2023p). Share of Gen Z users in the United States using Instagram, Snapchat, and TikTok weekly from 2019 to 2021. *Statista.* Retrieved October 4, 2023, from https://www.statista.com/statistics/1278136/instagram-snapchat-tiktok-weekly-usage/

Statista. (2023q). Distribution of Snapchat users worldwide as of January 2023, by age and gender. *Statista.* Retrieved October 4, 2023, from https://www.statista.com/statistics/933948/snapchat-global-user-age-distribution/

Statista. (2023r). Leading countries based on number of X (formerly Twitter) users as of January 2023. *Statista.* Retrieved October 4, 2023, from https://www.statista.com/statistics/242606/number-of-active-twitter-users-in-selected-countries/

Statista. (2023s). Number of monetizable daily active X (formerly Twitter) users (mDAU) in the United States from 1st quarter 2017 to 2nd quarter 2022. *Statista.* Retrieved October 4, 2023, from https://www.statista.com/statistics/970911/monetizable-daily-active-twitter-users-in-the-united-states/

Statista. (2023t). Number of monetizable daily active X (formerly Twitter) users (mDAU) worldwide from 1st quarter 2017 to 2nd quarter 2022. *Statista.* Retrieved October 4, 2023, from https://www.statista.com/statistics/970920/monetizable-daily-active-twitter-users-worldwide/

Statista. (2023u). Distribution of Pinterest users worldwide as of January 2023, by gender. *Statista.* Retrieved October 4, 2023, from https://www.statista.com/statistics/248168/gender-distribution-of-pinterest-users/

Statista. (2023v). Number of generation Z users in the United States on selected social media platforms from 2020 to 2025. *Statista.* Retrieved October 4, 2023, from https://www.statista.com/statistics/1276021/instagram-snapchat-tiktok-gen-z-users/

Statista. (2023w). Number of internet and social media users worldwide as of October 2023. *Statista.* Retrieved October 31, 2023, from https://www.statista.com/statistics/617136/digital-population-worldwide/

Statista. (2024). Countries with the largest number of prisoners per 100,000 of the national population, as of January 2024. *Statista.* Retrieved March 17, 2024, from https://www.statista.com/statistics/262962/countries-with-the-most-prisoners-per-100-000-inhabitants/

Steck, E., & Kaczynski, A. (2021). Marjorie Taylor Greene removes social media posts amid scrutiny of past controversial comments. *CNN.* Retrieved November 7, 2023, from https://www.cnn.com/2021/01/28/politics/kfile-marjorie-taylor-greene-removes-social-media-posts/index.html

Steele, J. L., & Blau, N. (2023). An analysis of police department crisis communication via social media. *Police Quarterly*, 1–25. Online First. https://doi.org/10.1177/10986111221150505

Steenbeek, W., & Hipp, J. R. (2011). A longitudinal test of social disorganization theory: Feedback effects among cohesion, social control, and disorder. *Criminology, 49*(3), 833–871.

Steinberg, S. B. (2016). # Advocacy: Social media activism's power to transform law. *Kentucky Law Journal, 105*(3), 413–452.

Steiner, M. (2020). Soft presentation of hard news? A content analysis of political Facebook posts. *Media and Communication, 8*(3), 244–257.

Stevens, F., Nurse, J. R., & Arief, B. (2021). Cyber stalking, cyber harassment, and adult mental health: A systematic review. *Cyberpsychology, Behavior, and Social Networking, 24*(6), 367–376.

Steyn, P., Salehi-Sangari, E., Pitt, L., Parent, M., & Berthon, P. (2010). The social media release as a public relations tool: Intentions to use among B2B bloggers. *Public Relations Review, 36*(1), 87–89.

Stickle, B. F., Hicks, M., Hutchinson, Z., & Stickle, A. (2020). Porch pirates: Examining unattended package theft through crime script analysis. *Criminal Justice Studies, 33*(2), 79–95.

Stickle, B. F., Kulig, T. C., Creel, S., Meyer, K. N., Maynard, B., & Jeanes, G. C. (2022). Human trafficking awareness and reporting: Insights from Tennessee police websites and Twitter. *Policing: An International Journal, 45*(6), 1051–1063.

Stohr, M. K., & Walsh, A. (2019). *Corrections: The essentials* (3rd ed.). Sage Publications.

Sultana, S., Deb, M., Bhattacharjee, A., Hasan, S., Alam, S. R., Chakraborty, T., Roy, P., Ahmed, S. F., Moitra, A., Amin, M. A., Islam, A. K. M. N., & Ahmed, S. I. (2021). "Unmochon:" A tool to combat online sexual harassment over Facebook Messenger. In *Proceedings of the 2021 CHI conference on human factors in computing systems*, Yokohama, Japan (pp. 1–18).

Sunardi, H., & Ardiningtias, S. R. (2022). A comparative analysis of digital forensic investigation tools on Facebook Messenger applications. *Journal of Cyber Security and Mobility, 11*(5), 655–672.

Sunstein, C. R. (2017). *#Republic: Divided democracy in the age of social media.* Princeton University Press.

Surette, R. (2013). Cause or catalyst: The interaction of real world and media crime models. *American Journal of Criminal Justice, 38*, 392–409.

Surette, R. (2014). Estimating the prevalence of copycat crime: A research note. *Criminal Justice Policy Review, 25*(6), 703–718.

Surette, R. (2015a). *Media, crime, and criminal justice: Images, realities, and policies* (5th ed.). Cengage Learning.

Surette, R. (2015b). Performance crime and justice. *Current Issues in Criminal Justice, 27*(2), 195–216.

Surette, R. (2016). Measuring copycat crime. *Crime, Media, Culture, 12*(1), 37–64.

Sutherland, E. H., Cressey, D. R., & Luckenbill, D. F. (1992). *Principles of criminology* (11th ed.). General Hall Inc.

Sutton, R. (2015). The dangers of de-policing – will cops just stand down? *New York Post.* Retrieved January 24, 2024, from https://nypost.com/2015/05/05/the-dangers-of-de-policing-will-cops-just-stand-down/

Swanson, J. (2016). Sexual liberation or violence against women? The debate on the legalization of prostitution and the relationship to human trafficking. *New Criminal Law Review, 19*(4), 592–639.

Tappan, P. (1947). Who is the criminal? *American Sociological Review, 12*, 96–112.

Tarzia, L., Iyer, D., Thrower, E., & Hegarty, K. (2017). "Technology doesn't judge you": Young Australian women's views on using the internet and smartphones to address intimate partner violence. *Journal of Technology in Human Services, 35*(3), 199–218.

Taugerbeck, S., Ahmadi, M., Schorch, M., Unbehaun, D., Aal, K., & Wulf, V. (2019). Digital participation in prison: A public discourse analysis of the use of ICT by inmates. *Proceedings of the ACM on Human-Computer Interaction, 3*(GROUP), 1–26.

Taylor, C. (2019). Kids now dream of being professional YouTubers rather than astronauts, study finds. *CNBC.* Retrieved April 5, 2024, from https://www.cnbc.com/2019/07/19/more-children-dream-of-being-youtubers-than-astronauts-lego-says.html

Taylor, R. (2018). *Breaking away from broken windows: Baltimore neighborhoods and the nationwide fight against crime, grime, fear, and decline.* Routledge.

Tehrani, H. D., & Yamini, S. (2020). Parenting practices, self-control, and anti-social behaviors: Meta-analytic structural equation modeling. *Journal of Criminal Justice, 68*, 101687.

Telep, C. W., Weisburd, D., Gill, C. E., Vitter, Z., & Teichman, D. (2014). Displacement of crime and diffusion of crime control benefits in large-scale geographic areas: A systematic review. *Journal of Experimental Criminology, 10*, 515–548.

Terburg, D., Morgan, B., & Van Honk, J. (2009). The testosterone–cortisol ratio: A hormonal marker for proneness to social aggression. *International Journal of Law and Psychiatry, 32*(4), 216–223.

Tessler, H., Choi, M., & Kao, G. (2020). The anxiety of being Asian American: Hate crimes and negative biases during the COVID-19 pandemic. *American Journal of Criminal Justice, 45*(4), 636–646.

Tewksbury, R. (2005). Collateral consequences of sex offender registration. *Journal of Contemporary Criminal Justice, 21*(1), 67–81.

Thomas, A. L., Hatten, D. N., & Connealy, N. T. (2022). Does police use of twitter align with and enhance community policing objectives? An analysis of the New York City Police Department's Twitter activity. *Police Quarterly, 25*(4), 443–469.

Thomas, C. W. (1998). Maintaining and restoring public trust in government agencies and their employees. *Administration & Society, 30*(2), 166–193.

Thomas, K. J., Baumer, E. P., & Loughran, T. A. (2022). Structural predictors of choice: Testing a multilevel rational choice theory of crime. *Criminology, 60*(4), 606–636.

Thompson, C. (2023). Lawsuit by Buffalo supermarket shooting victims pins blame on Facebook, Amazon, and other tech giants. *Associated Press*. Retrieved April 2, 2024, from https://apnews.com/article/tops-supermarket-mass-shooting-meta-gendron-buffalo-cbb53152b949e9b05a4f023ae252a5d2

Tillery, A. B. (2019). What kind of movement is black lives matter? The view from Twitter. *Journal of Race, Ethnicity, and Politics, 4*(2), 297–323.

Tim, Y., Pan, S. L., Bahri, S., & Fauzi, A. (2017). Digitally enabled crime-fighting communities: Harnessing the boundary spanning competence of social media for civic engagement. *Information & Management, 54*(2), 177–188.

Tippett, E. C. (2018). The legal implications of the metoo movement. *Minnesota Law Review, 103*, 229–302.

Tipples, J. (2008). Negative emotionality influences the effects of emotion on time perception. *Emotion, 8*(1), 127.

Todd, S. (2017). Tokyo's adorable police mascot Pipo-kun is basically cuteness, weaponized. *Quartz*. Retrieved December 25, 2023, from https://qz.com/1164167/tokyos-adorable-police-mascot-pipo-kun-is-basically-cuteness-weaponized/

Tolan, P. H., Henry, D. B., Schoeny, M. S., Lovegrove, P., & Nichols, E. (2014). Mentoring programs to affect delinquency and associated outcomes of youth at risk: A comprehensive meta-analytic review. *Journal of Experimental Criminology, 10*, 179–206.

Tolson, D., & Klein, J. (2015). Registration, residency restrictions, and community notification: A social capital perspective on the isolation of registered sex offenders in our communities. *Journal of Human Behavior in the Social Environment, 25*(5), 375–390.

Tomkovicz, J. J. (2011). *Constitutional exclusion: The rules, rights, and remedies that strike the balance between freedom and order*. Oxford University Press.

Tompros, L. W., Crudo, R. A., Pfeiffer, A., & Boghossian, R. (2017). The constitutionality of criminalizing false speech made on social networking sites in a post-Alvarez, social media-obsessed world. *Harvard Journal of Law & Technology, 31*(1), 65–109.

Travaini, G. V., Pacchioni, F., Bellumore, S., Bosia, M., & De Micco, F. (2022). Machine learning and criminal justice: A systematic review of advanced methodology for recidivism risk prediction. *International Journal of Environmental Research and Public Health, 19*(17), 10594.

Trisnasenjaya, H., & Riadi, I. (2019). Forensic analysis of Android-based WhatsApp messenger against fraud crime using the National Institute of Standard and Technology Framework. *International Journal of Cyber-Security and Digital Forensics, 8*(1), 89–98.

Trivedi-Bateman, N., & Crook, E. L. (2022). The optimal application of empathy interventions to reduce antisocial behavior and crime: A review of the literature. *Psychology, Crime & Law, 28*(8), 796–819.

Trottier, D. (2017). Digital vigilantism as weaponization of visibility. *Philosophy & Technology, 30*, 55–72.

Tubridy, K. (2020). Facebook and a fair trial: Caution, challenge, and contradiction. *Law, Technology and Humans, 2*(1), 135–151.

Twitter. (2023). *X help center*. Retrieved January 26, 2024, from https://help.twitter.com/en/using-x/x-premium

Uebelacker, S., & Quiel, S. (2014). The social engineering personality framework. In *2014 Workshop on socio-technical aspects in security and trust* (pp. 24–30). Institute of Electrical and Electronics Engineering.

Uhl, C. A., Rhyner, K. J., Terrance, C. A., & Lugo, N. R. (2018). An examination of nonconsensual pornography websites. *Feminism & Psychology, 28*(1), 50–68.

Uncel, M. (2011). Facebook is now friends with the court: Current federal rules and social media evidence. *Jurimetrics, 52*(1), 43–70.

Uniform Crime Reporting. (2019). *Clearances*. Retrieved February 28, 2024, from https://ucr.fbi.gov/crime-in-the-u.s/2019/crime-in-the-u.s.-2019/topic-pages/clearances

United States v. Avenatti, (S1) 19 Cr. 373 (PGG) (S.D.N.Y. Jul. 6, 2021).

Ure, M. (2019). Social media use in justice administration: Disintermediation, conversation, and collaboration. *Global Media Journal, 17*(32), 1–11.

Vaccari, C., & Chadwick, A. (2020). Deepfakes and disinformation: Exploring the impact of synthetic political video on deception, uncertainty, and trust in news. *Social Media + Society, 6*(1), 1–13.

Vakhitova, Z. I., Alston-Knox, C. L., Reynald, D. M., Townsley, M. K., & Webster, J. L. (2019). Lifestyles and routine activities: Do they enable different types of cyber abuse? *Computers in Human Behavior, 101*, 225–237.

Van de Velde, B., Meijer, A., & Homburg, V. (2015). Police message diffusion on Twitter: Analyzing the reach of social media communications. *Behavior & Information Technology, 34*(1), 4–16.

Van den Hoven, P. (2015). The judge on Facebook; neglecting a persistent ritual? *International Journal for Court Administration, 7*(1), 18–26.

Van Laer, T. (2014). The means to justify the end: Combating cyber harassment in social media. *Journal of Business Ethics, 123*(1), 85–98.

Van Steden, R., & Mehlbaum, S. (2022). Do-it-yourself surveillance: The practices and effects of WhatsApp neighborhood crime prevention groups. *Crime, Media, Culture, 18*(4), 543–560.

Van Wilsem, J. (2011). Worlds tied together? Online and non-domestic routine activities and their impact on digital and traditional threat victimization. *European Journal of Criminology, 8*(2), 115–127.

Vasquez, A. G., Rodriguez, A., Suh, J., & Martinez-Cosio, M. (2020). Appointment robbery: Do crime prevention through environmental design strategies work? Voices from the street. *American Journal of Qualitative Research, 4*(1), 16–37.

Vásquez, B. E., Maddan, S., & Walker, J. T. (2008). The influence of sex offender registration and notification laws in the United States: A time-series analysis. *Crime & Delinquency, 54*(2), 175–192.

Vazsonyi, A. T., Mikuška, J., & Kelley, E. L. (2017). It's time: A meta-analysis on the self-control-deviance link. *Journal of Criminal Justice, 48*, 48–63.

Verplanken, B. (1993). Need for cognition and external information search: Responses to time pressure during decision-making. *Journal of Research in Personality, 27*(3), 238–252.

Vițelar, A. (2019). Like me: Generation Z and the use of social media for personal branding. *Management Dynamics in the Knowledge Economy, 7*(2), 257–268.

Vitis, L., & Gilmour, F. (2017). Dick pics on blast: A woman's resistance to online sexual harassment using humor, art, and Instagram. *Crime, Media, Culture, 13*(3), 335–355.

Vogels, E. A., Gelles-Watnick, R., & Massarat, N. (2022). Teens, social media, and technology 2022. *Pew Research Center*. Retrieved September 25, 2023, from https://www.pewresearch.org/internet/2022/08/10/teens-social-media-and-technology-2022/

Vomfell, L., Härdle, W. K., & Lessmann, S. (2018). Improving crime count forecasts using Twitter and taxi data. *Decision Support Systems, 113*, 73–85.

Walby, K., & Gumieny, C. (2020). Public police's philanthropy and Twitter communications in Canada. *Policing: An International Journal, 43*(5), 755–768.

Walby, K., & Joshua, C. (2021a). Community crime prevention and crime watch groups as online private policing. *Safer Communities, 20*(4), 237–250.

Walby, K., & Joshua, C. (2021b). Framing fantasies: Public police recruiting videos and representations of women. *Current Issues in Criminal Justice, 33*(2), 151–169.

Walby, K., & Wilkinson, B. (2023). The visual politics of public police Instagram use in Canada. *New Media & Society, 25*(5), 898–920.

Walker, S., & Katz, C. (2018). *The police in America: An introduction* (9th ed.). McGraw-Hill Education.

Walker, S., & Katz, C. (2022). *The police in America: An introduction* (10th ed.). McGraw Hill LLC.

Walkington, Z., Pike, G., Strathie, A., Havard, C., Harrison, V., & Ness, H. (2019). Entitlement to tell on police Facebook sites. *Cyberpsychology, Behavior, and Social Networking, 22*(5), 355–357.

Walkington, Z., Pike, G., Strathie, A., Havard, C., Ness, H., & Harrison, V. (2018). Are you talking to me? How identity is constructed on police-owned Facebook sites. *Narrative Inquiry, 28*(2), 280–300.

Walsh, A. (2012). *Criminology: The essentials*. SAGE Publications.

Walsh, A., & Hemmens, C. (2020). *Law, justice, and society* (5th ed.). Oxford University Press.

Walsh, A., & Jorgensen, C. (2020). *Criminology: The essentials* (4th ed.). Sage Publications.

Walsh, J. P., & O'Connor, C. (2019). Social media and policing: A review of recent research. *Sociology Ccompass, 13*(1), e12648.

Walters, G. D. (1990). *The criminal lifestyle: Patterns of serious criminal conduct*. SAGE Publications.

Walters, G. D. (2018). Personality and crime: Mediating the agreeableness–offending and conscientiousness–offending relationships with proactive and reactive criminal thinking. *Personality and Individual Differences, 129*, 166–170.

Walther, S., & McCoy, A. (2021). US extremism on Telegram. *Perspectives on Terrorism, 15*(2), 100–124.

Wang, C., Han, B., Patel, B., & Rudin, C. (2023). In pursuit of interpretable, fair, and accurate machine learning for criminal recidivism prediction. *Journal of Quantitative Criminology, 39*(2), 519–581.

Wang, X., Gerber, M. S., & Brown, D. E. (2012). Automatic crime prediction using events extracted from twitter posts. In *International conference on social computing, behavioral-cultural modeling, and prediction* (pp. 231–238). Springer.

Warner, B. D. (2003). The role of attenuated culture in social disorganization theory. *Criminology, 41*(1), 73–98.

Watt, B., Howells, K., & Delfabbro, P. (2004). Juvenile recidivism: Criminal propensity, social control, and social learning theories. *Psychiatry, Psychology and Law, 11*(1), 141–153.

Webb, T. (1997). Community policing online. *FBI Law Enforcement Bulletin, 66*(4), 6–10.

Wei, L. (2009). Filter blogs vs. personal journals: Understanding the knowledge production gap on the Internet. *Journal of Computer-Mediated Communication, 14*(3), 532–558.

Weimann, G., & Masri, N. (2023). Research note: Spreading hate on TikTok. *Studies in Conflict & Terrorism, 46*(5), 752–765.

Weisburd, D. L., & Eck, J. E. (2004). What can police do to reduce crime, disorder, and fear? *Annals of the American Academy of Political and Social Science, 593*, 42–65.

Weisburd, D. L., Hinkle, J. C., Famega, C., & Ready, J. (2011). The possible "backfire" effects of hot spots policing: An experimental assessment of impacts on legitimacy, fear, and collective efficacy. *Journal of Experimental Criminology, 7*, 297–320.

Weisburd, D. L., Wyckoff, L. A., Ready, J., Eck, J. E., Hinkle, J. C., & Gajewski, F. (2006). Does crime just move around the corner? A controlled study of spatial displacement and diffusion of crime control benefits. *Criminology, 44*(3), 549–592.

Weiss, M. (2016). An analysis of anti-gender-based street harassment mobile applications. *Intersect: The Stanford Journal of Science, Technology, and Society, 9*(3), 1–8.

Wellman, B., Salaff, J., Dimitrova, D., Garton, L., Gulia, M., & Haythornthwaite, C. (1996). Computer networks as social networks: Collaborative work, telework, and virtual community. *Annual Review of Sociology, 22*(1), 213–238.

Welsh, B. C., Braga, A. A., & Bruinsma, G. J. (2015). Reimagining broken windows: From theory to policy. *Journal of Research in Crime and Delinquency, 52*(4), 447–463.

Welsh, B. C., & Farrington, D. P. (1999). Value for money? A review of the costs and benefits of situational crime prevention. *British Journal of Criminology, 39*(3), 345–368.

West, R., & Turner, L. (2013). *Introducing communication theory: Analysis and application* (5th ed.). McGraw-Hill Education.

White, M. D., & Fradella, H. F. (2020). Policing a pandemic: Stay-at-home orders and what they mean for the police. *American Journal of Criminal Justice, 45*(4), 702–717.

White-Gosselin, C.-É., & Poulin, F. (2024). Associations between young adults' social media addiction, relationship quality with parents, and internalizing problems: A path analysis model. *Canadian Journal of Behavioral Science, 56*(1), 61–69.

Whittaker, E., & Kowalski, R. M. (2015). Cyberbullying via social media. *Journal of School Violence, 14*(1), 11–29.

Wikström, P. O. H., & Svensson, R. (2010). When does self-control matter? The interaction between morality and self-control in crime causation. *European Journal of Criminology, 7*(5), 395–410.

Wikström, P. O. H., & Treiber, K. (2007). The role of self-control in crime causation: Beyond Gottfredson and Hirschi's general theory of crime. *European Journal of Criminology, 4*(2), 237–264.

Wilford, M. M., Shestak, A., & Wells, G. L. (2019). Plea bargaining. In N. Brewer & A. B. Douglass (Eds.), *Psychological science and the law* (pp. 266–292). The Guilford Press.

Williams, M. L. (2016). Guardians upon high: An application of routine activities theory to online identity theft in Europe at the country and individual level. *British Journal of Criminology, 56*(1), 21–48.

Williams, M. L., Burnap, P., & Sloan, L. (2017). Crime sensing with big data: The affordances and limitations of using open-source communications to estimate crime patterns. *British Journal of Criminology, 57*(2), 320–340.

Willingham, A. J. (2023). Why Twitter users are upset about the platform's latest change. *CNN*. Retrieved April 3, 2024, from https://www.cnn.com/2023/02/03/tech/twitter-api-what-is-pricing-change-cec/index.html

Wilson, J. Q., & Kelling, G. L. (1982, March). Broken windows: The police and neighborhood safety. *Atlantic Monthly*, 29–38. Retrieved October 24, 2023, from http://www.manhattan-institute.org/pdf/_atlantic_monthly-broken_windows.pdf

Winter, T., Antonshchuk, V., Smith, P., & Radnofsky, C. (2024). Pennsylvania man arrested after allegedly killing his father and displaying his decapitated head on YouTube. *NBC News*. Retrieved March 1, 2024, from https://www.nbcnews.com/news/us-news/pa-man-arrested-decapitating-father-youtube-video-rcna136509

Winton, R. (2021). 9 Oakland police officers disciplined over racist, sexist social media posts. *Los Angeles Times*. Retrieved January 26, 2024, from https://www.latimes.com/california/story/2021-09-20/9-oakland-police-officers-disciplined-over-social-media-posts

Wolfe, S. E., & Nix, J. (2016). The alleged "Ferguson effect" and police willingness to engage in community partnership. *Law and Human Behavior, 40*(1), 1–10.

Wolfers, L. N., & Utz, S. (2022). Social media use, stress, and coping. *Current Opinion in Psychology, 45*, 101305.

Wong, Y. C., Law, C. K., Fung, J. Y. C., & Lam, J. C. Y. (2009). Perpetuating old exclusions and producing new ones: Digital exclusion in an information society. *Journal of Technology in Human Services, 27*(1), 57–78.

Wood, M. A. (2020). Policing's 'meme strategy': Understanding the rise of police social media engagement work. *Current Issues in Criminal Justice, 32*(1), 40–58.

Wood, M. A., & McGovern, A. (2021). Memetic copaganda: Understanding the humorous turn in police image work. *Crime, Media, Culture, 17*(3), 305–326.

Wood, M. A., Richards, I., Iliadis, M., & McDermott, M. (2019). Digital public criminology in Australia and New Zealand: Results from a mixed methods study of criminologists' use of social media. *International Journal for Crime, Justice, and Social Democracy, 8*(4), 1–17.

Wood, M. A., Ross, S., & Johns, D. (2022). Primary crime prevention apps: A typology and scoping review. *Trauma, Violence, & Abuse, 23*(4), 1093–1110.

Wood, M. A., & Thompson, C. (2021). Crime prevention, swarm intelligence and stigmergy: Understanding the mechanisms of social media-facilitated community crime prevention. *The British Journal of Criminology, 61*(2), 414–433.

Worrall, A., & Mawby, R. C. (2014). Probation worker cultures and relationships with offenders. *Probation Journal, 61*(4), 346–357.

Wright, B. R. E., Caspi, A., Moffitt, T. E., & Silva, P. A. (1999). Low self-control, social bonds, and crime: Social causation, social selection, or both? *Criminology, 37*(3), 479–514.

Wu, J., Hu, X., & Conklin, M. (2023). The relationship between victimization and vaping: Results from monitoring the future. *International Journal of Law, Crime and Justice, 74*, 100613.

Wu, J., Hu, X., & Orrick, E. A. (2022). The relationship between motivations for joining gangs and violent offending: A preliminary test on self-determination theory. *Victims & Offenders, 17*(3), 335–349.

Xu, Y., Fiedler, M. L., & Flaming, K. H. (2005). Discovering the impact of community policing: The broken windows thesis, collective efficacy, and citizens' judgment. *Journal of Research in Crime and Delinquency, 42*(2), 147–186.

Yang, D., Heaney, T., Tonon, A., Wang, L., & Cudré-Mauroux, P. (2018). CrimeTelescope: Crime hotspot prediction based on urban and social media data fusion. *World Wide Web, 21*, 1323–1347.

Yang, S. B., Brown, G. C., & Moon, B. (2011). Factors leading to corrections officers' job satisfaction. *Public Personnel Management, 40*(4), 359–369.

Yar, M. (2012). Crime, media, and the will-to-representation: Reconsidering relationships in the new media age. *Crime, Media, Culture, 8*(3), 245–260.

Yardley, E. (2017). *Social media homicide confessions: Stories of killers and their victims*. Policy Press.

Yardley, E., & Wilson, D. (2015). Making sense of 'Facebook Murder'? Social networking sites and contemporary homicide. *The Howard Journal of Criminal Justice, 54*(2), 109–134.

Yayman, E., & Bilgin, O. (2020). Relationship between social media addiction, game addiction and family functions. *International Journal of Evaluation and Research in Education, 9*(4), 979–986.

Zakon, A. (2020). Optimized for addiction: Extending product liability concepts to defectively designed social media algorithms and overcoming the communications decency act. *Wisconsin Law Review, 5*, 1107–1146.

Zavattaro, S. M., French, P. E., & Mohanty, S. D. (2015). A sentiment analysis of US local government tweets: The connection between tone and citizen involvement. *Government Information Quarterly, 32*(3), 333–341.

Zevitz, R. G. (2006). Sex offender community notification: Its role in recidivism and offender reintegration. *Criminal Justice Studies, 19*(2), 193–208.

Zhang, S., Leidner, D., Cao, X., & Liu, N. (2022). Workplace cyberbullying: A criminological and routine activity perspective. *Journal of Information Technology, 37*(1), 51–79.

Zhao, J. S., Gibson, C., Lovrich, N., & Gaffney, M. (2002). Participation in community crime prevention: Are volunteers more or less fearful of crime than other citizens? *Journal of Crime and Justice, 25*(1), 41–61.

Zhao, J. S., Lovrich, N. P., & Thurman, Q. (1999). The status of community policing in American cities: Facilitators and impediments revisited. *Policing: An International Journal of Police Strategies and Management,* 22(1), 74–92.

Zhong, B., Hardin, M., & Sun, T. (2011). Less effortful thinking leads to more social networking? The associations between the use of social network sites and personality traits. *Computers in Human Behavior, 27*(3), 1265–1271.

Zielinski, M. J., Cowell, M., Bull, C. E., Veluvolu, M., Behne, M. F., Nowotny, K., & Brinkley-Rubinstein, L. (2022). Policy and public communication methods among US state prisons during the first year of the COVID-19 pandemic. *Health & Justice, 10*(27), 1–13.

Zimmer, F., Scheibe, K., & Stock, W. G. (2018). A model for information behavior research on social live streaming services (SLSSs). In *Social computing and social media. technologies and analytics: 10th International conference, SCSM 2018, held as part of HCI international 2018, Las Vegas, NV, USA, July 15–20, 2018, proceedings, part II* (Vol. 10, pp. 429–448). Springer International Publishing.

Zuckerman, M. (1990). The psychophysiology of sensation seeking. *Journal of Personality, 58*(1), 313–345.

INDEX